*Bram Stoker*

# BRAM STOKER

## A BIOGRAPHY OF
## THE AUTHOR OF *DRACULA*

*Barbara Belford*

*Alfred A. Knopf*

*New York*

1996

*This Is a Borzoi Book*
*Published by Alfred A. Knopf, Inc.*

Copyright © 1996 by Barbara Belford

All rights reserved under International and Pan-American Copyright
Conventions. Published in the United States by Alfred A. Knopf, Inc.,
New York, and simultaneously in Canada by Random House of Canada
Limited, Toronto. Distributed by Random House, Inc., New York.

Library of Congress Cataloging-in-Publication Data

Belford, Barbara.
Bram Stoker : a biography of the author of *Dracula* / Barbara Belford.
p.  cm.
Includes bibliographic references (p.    ) and index.
ISBN 0-679-41832-6
1. Stoker, Bram, 1847–1912—Biography. 2. Novelists, English—
19th century—Biography. 3. Theatrical managers—Great Britain—Biography.
4. Theatres—England—London—History—19th century. 5. Dracula, Count
(Fictitious character). 6. Horror tales—Authorship. 7. Vampires in literature.
I. Title.
PR 6037.T617Z57    1996
823' .8-DC20
[B]                                                                         96-4632
                                                                              CIP

Manufactured in the United States of America
First Edition

*To Bill Kutik*

# Contents

# Introduction

"I only slept a few hours when I went to bed,
and feeling that I could not sleep any more,
got up. I had hung my shaving glass by the
window, and was just beginning to shave:
Suddenly I felt a hand on my shoulder, and
heard the Count's voice saying to me 'Good
morning.' I started, for it amazed me that I
had not seen him, since the reflection of the
glass covered the whole room behind
me . . . but there was no sign of a man in it,
except myself."
                    —Jonathan Harker's journal

The unseen face in the mirror reflects the soul. Therein is revealed
the darker aspects, the hidden sins, the haunting shock of self-
recognition. For the world one wears a mask; for the truth one looks
in the mirror. Isolated in an impenetrable castle, Jonathan Harker
confronts his doubleness, his other self.

Double meanings and double identities activated *Dracula* as they did
the life of its author. Nearly a decade before Bram Stoker's classic
horror story was published in 1897, a London artist preserved another doppelgänger motif: Stoker's love-hate relationship with the
celebrated Victorian actor Henry Irving, the Laurence Olivier of his

day, whom Stoker served as business manager, social secretary, and loyal friend.

An obsessive intimacy informs the drawing, no larger than a calling card: Stoker hovers to the right while Irving—impeccable in formal evening dress—straightens his tie in a triptych mirror. The artist has crosshatched Stoker into the background, diminished his presence. There but not there, Stoker is now the unseen face in the mirror, the soulless invisible man, kin to the eternal outsider: the vampire.


*Dracula* will be one hundred years old in 1997. Had Stoker achieved the physical immortality of his creation, the now-150-year-old writer would be amazed that his novel has been translated into forty-four languages; that Count Dracula, the most filmed character in history after Sherlock Holmes, has usurped the red devil with pitchfork and pointed tail as the preferred icon of evil; that members of "fang" clubs subscribe to newsletters extolling vampires and even, in the age of AIDS, self-styled vampires drink blood, but from monogamous donors.

Mostly, he would be shocked to read about himself. Calumnies have been spawned to justify the premise that no genial Irishman could have written such a perversely sexual novel. In biography and fiction, Stoker variously has been given a frigid wife, a penchant for prostitutes (particularly during their menstrual period), a sexually transmitted disease, and inherited insanity.

Starting in the 1970s, the *Dracula* exegetes squeezed out every Freudian, religious, political, and occult meaning from the novel, leaving behind innuendo and misinformation about the life of this most elusive of authors. There were no Stokerian scholars to rise up and protest, to challenge undocumented facts. It appeared that horror devotees warmed to *Dracula*'s author having a perverse nature. There had to be some unsavory explanation of why, out of an oeuvre of eighteen books, only *Dracula* succeeds as literature—in fact, is a masterpiece.


To find a usable past, biographers peel off layers of the ego in search of a universal truth about their subjects, being careful not to expose what may be only a terrible emptiness. So amorphous was Stoker's protective tissue that stripping led to nothingness. The center did not hold; it simply evaporated. Stoker was really a *matryoshki,* one of those red-and-yellow-lacquered Russian nesting dolls, identical as to costume and expression, made in diminishing sizes, one inside the other, growing backwards to infancy. The smallest *matryoshki* is the invalid child, unable to walk for seven years, who will never put a name to a defining illness.

"Childhood builds its own shrines; and these live untarnished and unimpaired to the end," Stoker wrote in *The Man,* his eighth novel. In his early works, childhood fantasies—chivalric themes of brave men rescuing good women—abound, but there are yawning gaps between child and man, the most obvious of all liminal zones. In many ways the man remained the child, always wanting—but unable—to cast a permanent reflection. Freudians would blame a weak ego or an infantile superego, or that convenient complex from *Oedipus Rex.* I, however, believe that Stoker desperately wanted to grow up, to be a separate person, but stronger forces controlled his destiny. Above all there was Henry Irving.

Stoker was not an obliging person to think about for five years. He frustrated intimate probing; his reticence was monumental. At times he fascinated and irritated me. He did not keep a personal diary but a "jotting diary," focusing almost exclusively on Henry Irving's achievements. Stoker loved codes and puzzles. Even the characters in *Dracula* conceal their thoughts by keeping journals in shorthand. In response to the question "Who are you?" I imagine him saying, "I am who you want me to be."

In Victorian memoirs Stoker enters and exits quickly, leaving a whiff of lofty manners and an aftertaste of no identity. He was the Anglo-Irish outsider, a dreamy romantic who attained a level of personal friendship with the English establishment but is remembered only as Henry Irving's factotum—crosshatched into the background. He yearned for recognition as a writer but in his lifetime remained a mediocrity, an uninstructive state for anyone. He did, however, embody an eternal theme: failure in the pursuit of dreams. He never considered leaving a paper trail for biographers. Why would anyone want to write his biography? Indeed, no one gave much thought to the author of *Dracula* until some two decades after his death, and then only because the film industry put their imprimatur on vampire films.

Stoker divided the world into good women and brave men, but such pastoral thoughts were archaic as the nineteenth century lurched to a close. Even as he sought in his novels to preserve the old order of chivalry, women clamored not for deliverance but for sexual freedom. Written during the demise of decadence and the birth of psychoanalysis, *Dracula* celebrates Stoker's final quest to safeguard embattled Victorian values from modernism, to preserve the romance of the family.

"It is bad women who seem to know men best, and to be able to influence them most," a character argues in *The Man*. "*They* can turn and twist and mold them as they choose. And *they* never hesitate to speak their own wishes; to ask for what they want. There are no tragedies, of the negative kind, in *their* lives. Why should good women leave power to such as they? Why should good women's lives be wrecked for a convention?" Why, indeed!

When historian Bram Dijkstra called *Dracula* "a central document in the late nineteenth-century war on women," he isolated only one aspect of Stoker's sexual treatise, which is riddled—albeit subliminally—with primal scenes and fears about homosexuality and the feminization of desire. Or, as author David Skal puts it, Stoker's novel is an attempt to rescue "an embattled male's deepest sense of himself as a male."

In 1897 critics filtered out erotic messages: *Dracula* was a ripping good, blood-curdling novel, perfect reading on the train for a paralyzed century. The same year Ibsen's *Ghosts,* with its unabashed depiction of the effects of hereditary venereal disease, shocked theatregoers. Ibsen was pilloried for daring to be explicit about sexual relationships in contemporary society, while Stoker blithely commands Dracula to force his way into bedrooms—even vamping Mina while her husband sleeps by her side.

Confronted by Stoker's ordinariness, baffled by his inarticulate gloom, and bewildered by his motivations for writing a novel dense with sexual innuendo, some critics claim he did not realize the import of what he was writing: it was all an unconscious dream. But they are in error. Stoker was an intelligent and insightful man, and his position at the Lyceum Theatre placed him at the social nexus of Victorian society. He was many things, but naïve was not one of them; he was fully aware of the subtexts in his horror tale.

There are too many symbolic lines, lines such as: "Van Helsing went about his work systematically. Holding his candle so that he could read the coffin plates, and so holding it that the sperm dropped in white patches which congealed as they touched the metal, he made assurance of Lucy's coffin. Another search in his bag, and he took out a turnscrew." But Stoker chose to mask the erotic in the supernatural, to use a narrative structure told through letters, recordings, journals, and other documents. By eliminating the author's voice, he distanced himself from the unspeakable.

Earlier biographies—Harry Ludlam's *A Biography of Dracula: The Life Story of Bram Stoker,* published in 1962, followed thirteen years later by Daniel Farson's *The Man Who Wrote Dracula*—lacked source notes and adequate documentation. Ludlam relied on family documents and the memory of Stoker's son, Noel. Farson added his own brand of sensationalism. Both ignored unpublished archival material, available in Britain and the United States, which is quoted for the first time in this biography. Bram Stoker's granddaughter Ann Stoker and great-grandson Noël Dobbs graciously made the family papers available to me, and I read through the material—mostly genealogical history—previously consulted by Ludlam and Farson. Since the time of their research, autographed letters from Oscar Wilde, W. S. Gilbert, and others had been sold to libraries, where I located and verified them.

At the Leeds University Library, I consulted the Brotherton Collection of some five thousand letters written to Stoker in his position as acting manager of the Lyceum. Happily, there were a few clues hidden among the letters not beginning: "May I have two box seats . . ." and "Please ask Mr. Irving if he will preside. . . ."

At Stratford-upon-Avon's library, adjacent to Shakespeare's birthplace, I examined the Bram Stoker Collection. Dedicated to Henry Irving, it apparently contains every scrap of paper Stoker did not throw away: menus, invitations, seating plans—even notations on the gummed flaps of envelopes. It was fascinating. But I was not writing a biography of Irving. I noticed there were several uncatalogued boxes and inquired if they might contain something about Stoker. They did! Expectantly I opened a box of yellowing newspaper articles and was surprised to discover that Stoker had subscribed to a personal clipping service. Here was an ego after all. I read reports of speeches given and parties attended (with his name underlined). Seeking diaries to guide me through his private life, I had unearthed a public life. Another box held musty photographs, including one of him walking away from the Theatre Royal in Bradford the morning after Henry Irving's death. This lonely scene will, for me, forever symbolize Stoker's life.

As can be seen in manuscripts at libraries in Dublin, New York, Philadelphia, and Washington, Stoker was a hasty writer who deplored self-editing, preferring the cut-and-paste journalistic style. The Folger Shakespeare Library in Washington, D.C., retains the holograph manuscript of *Reminiscences of Henry Irving.* Stoker put more of himself into this memoir than was published, and this excised material quoted here for the first time now adds to a greater understanding of his life. When it came to *Dracula,* however, his pen relaxed. Dates on the *Dracula Notes* at the Rosenbach Museum & Library in Philadelphia certify a six-year devotion to plotting and writing this vampire tale; the typescript manuscript authenticates last-minute changes in the title and ending. This was the only novel he took within himself.

As Stoker's life took shape for me, there were many unanswered questions, all dovetailing into Stoker's relationship with Irving. I asked myself: If Irving had not existed for Stoker, would *Dracula* have been stillborn? And most importantly, I asked myself: Why struggle through a definitive Stoker biography when he so obscured his tracks? My first biography was of Violet Hunt, a Kensington hostess, novelist, and self-proclaimed wife of Ford Madox Hueffer (later Ford). Violet brought Stoker into her literary circle after they first met in Whitby in 1890, the year Stoker began his notes for the novel he originally called *The Dead Un-Dead.* The chapter needed an ending.

The Bram Stoker I eventually came to call my friend was witty but sad, rigid but responsible, immature but loving. He took many secrets with him, but he left us *Dracula,* and an important message: unspeakable things can happen to ordinary people. And a warning: those who allow themselves to be subsumed by a master are intellectually diminished. Like his vampire count, Stoker desperately wanted to connect, to be part of a family, to have his achievements recognized. In *Dracula,* he wrote of a changing world he feared; he died with a sense of failure and regret. His novel achieved prominence long before its author.

It took until 1983 for *Dracula* to earn recognition in the Classics series published by Oxford University Press. It took a decade more for Stoker to be included in the revered *Dictionary of National Biography,* the scholarly enterprise that the original editor—Virginia Woolf's father, Leslie Stephen—set in motion in 1882. At his death in 1912 Stoker was not deemed worthy of inclusion in that decade's supplement. Since then letters supporting his candidacy, as well as others, accumulated in filing cabinets. In 1993 a special supplement, appropriately called *Missing Persons,* was devoted to 1,086 individuals—selected from 100,000 names—unjustly absent from previous editions.

As *Dracula's* publishing centennial approaches, Bram Stoker deserves a new version of his life. Biographical facts previously exaggerated or misconstrued need correcting, Stoker's role in molding the modern theatre needs recording, and the link between the author's life and his fiction can now be documented. Stoker is no longer among the missing.

*Bram Stoker*

# *Prologue*

On a rainy December evening in 1876, Henry Irving invited the theatre critic of Dublin's *Evening Mail* to dine with him in his suite at the Shelbourne Hotel, overlooking St. Stephen's Green. Over breakfast that morning, Irving had read Bram Stoker's review of his *Hamlet* at the Theatre Royal and asked to meet the young man. The Shelbourne then—as now—was Dublin's premier hotel, a dowager empress affording the amenities guests had come to expect from the grand hotels of London and Paris. In the lobby there was the cool, musty smell of polished brass and the warm, sweet scent of oiled wood. Stoker knew the hotel from his student days at nearby Trinity College, when awards ceremonies were held in its banquet halls, shimmering with gold and crystal.

Now that Irving was celebrated in London, he was able to turn his back on the shabby, stale rooms of his provincial touring days. Stoker, who had seen the actor only through the illusion of makeup and gaslight, was greeted by a lanky figure with the outward appearance of a benevolent, bespectacled country parson; few knew that Irving was extremely shortsighted and found his way about the stage by instinct.

Irving lacked formal education and had an unacceptable West Country accent from Cornwall, where he spent his youth. He was often nervous when thrust into groups, always fearful of making a gaffe; but in conversation with one other person, his power flowed unrestrained. After a welcoming glass of champagne, Irving compli-

mented Stoker on his review, particularly his comments on the nuances of Hamlet's parting speech to Ophelia. "To give strong
grounds for belief, where the instinct can judge more truly than the
intellect," Stoker had written, "is the perfection of suggestive acting." With this insight, Stoker revealed to Irving his understanding
of the actor's interpretation of the moody Dane. Irving had "unearthed the great, deep underlying idea of Hamlet as a mystic."

Stoker was flattered. He had fallen under Irving's spell a decade
earlier, when he first saw him as Captain Absolute in *The Rivals;*
now the actor had made the leap from the provinces to the London
stage. As Irving paced back and forth in sequences of three steps, ges-
ticulating and blowing swirls of musky cigar smoke up and around
the frescoed ceiling, he told Stoker his dream: he wanted to make acting as honorable as law or medicine—and he wanted his own
theatre.

Stoker later learned that Irving had an almost mystical regard for
the number three. If a role called for an object or person to be
touched, he would tap three times; when moving toward another
actor on stage, he advanced three measured steps. This evening as he
thrice-paced, as the decanter emptied and the cigars turned to ash,
the thirty-eight-year-old actor warmed to the husky, russet-haired
Irishman who looked quizzical at the right moments and kept up
with his host's hedonistic consumption of port and tobacco. The
hours passed swiftly. It was a perfect evening, and for the first of many
evenings to come, actor and acolyte talked until daybreak. When
Stoker stumbled out of the Shelbourne into the dawn drizzle, daz-
zled by Irving's hypnotic intensity, he wondered what the encounter
had meant.

Any understanding of Bram Stoker's life and the reason he wrote
*Dracula* begins with this first meeting. Stoker did not know it then,
but he had been chosen; later he would be tested. Loyal, clever, but
incapable of intrigue, Stoker was perfectly cast to serve Irving's extravagant ambitions. Years later, after Irving's death, Stoker emotionally recalled of these hours how his "host's heart was from the
beginning something toward me, as mine had been toward him,"

how Irving sought "to prove himself again to his new, sympathetic and understanding friend," how the evening marked the beginning of a friendship that "only terminated with Irving's life—if indeed friendship, like any other form of love, can ever terminate."

Even more prophetic than the camaraderie forged that wet and chilly December evening was something Stoker would never admit: on that night he met Count Dracula. Irving as Dracula would grow into the evil paternal role, the most felicitous ever written for him. Already imprinted on Stoker's imagination were the other leading parts, the doubles of his life. The good-father figure, Abraham Van Helsing, repository of worldly wisdom, doctor, barrister, and psychic detective, was appropriately named after Stoker's father and himself. The twenty-nine-year-old was still cultivating his alter ego, Jonathan Harker, the passionless solicitor who heroically achieves manhood when he slits Dracula's throat with a great Kukri knife. Stoker and his mother, Charlotte, inform the brave and loyal Mina; while the frivolous and fragile Lucy, yearning to marry all her suitors, echoes Stoker's socially ambitious fiancée, Florence Balcombe.

Stoker projected himself into all of Dracula's major characters. It is his most autobiographical novel. By 1890, according to his notes, he was primed to throw his fictional family into a Freudian vortex, bristling with repression and apprehension of homosexuality, devouring women, and rejecting mothers. One modern critic called it "a kind of incestuous, necrophilious, oral-anal-sadistic all-in-all wrestling match." Stoker's most revealing scene, from a biographical point of view, depicts Harker in a dreamlike state, anticipating the kisses of three vampire women:

> All three had brilliant white teeth, that shone like pearls against the ruby of their voluptuous lips. There was something about them that made me uneasy, some longing and at the same time some deadly fear. I felt in my heart a wicked, burning desire that they would kiss me with those red lips. . . . They whispered together, and then they all three laughed—such a silvery, musical laugh, but as hard as though the sound never could have come through the softness of human lips. It was like the intolerable, tingling sweetness of water-glasses when played on by a cunning hand. The fair girl shook her head coquettishly, and the other two urged her on. One said:

HENRY IRVING at thirty-eight, in 1876, when he first met Bram Stoker following Irving's triumphant performance as Hamlet at Dublin's Theatre Royal

"Go on! You are first, and we shall follow; yours is the right to begin." The other added:—

"He is young and strong, there are kisses for us all." I lay quiet looking out under my eyelashes in an agony of delightful anticipation. The fair girl advanced and bent over me till I could feel the movement of her breath upon me. Sweet it was in one sense, honey-sweet, and sent the same tingling through the nerves as her voice, but with a bitter underlying the sweet, a bitter offensiveness, as one smells in blood.

Suddenly Count Dracula appears, and the sexual tension changes. At the moment when Harker awaits the vampiric kiss, Dracula bellows: "This man belongs to me!" The vampire threat, with Dracula's hovering interest in Harker, is postponed. Still, the fear remains that Dracula will seduce, penetrate (with his phallic-shaped canine teeth), and drain another male. (In the vampire world gender roles are confusing: Dracula penetrates, but he—not the woman—receives the vital fluid, blood/semen.)

Nowhere in the novel is Irving's mesmeric control of Stoker more manifest. This scene not only titillates, with its potential for homoerotic union, but arouses as Harker discovers hidden wells of sexuality and acts out the worst nightmare—and the dearest fantasy—of Victorian men: union with a pure girl transformed into a sexually aggressive woman.

In this sensual setting Stoker has the vampire wives/daughters usurp the male prerogative of initiating sex, shattering the myth that only fallen women can experience ecstasy. Harker is passive, like a sleeping woman, immobilized by the dual thrills of "wicked burning desire" and "deadly fear." He describes the breath of the first vampire as "honey-sweet . . . but with a bitter underlying the sweet, a bitter offensiveness, as one smells in blood," expressing what would be taboo in any Victorian novel: attraction to the vagina and fear of its menstrual blood.

The staking of Lucy, which marks the novel's real—and the woman's only—climax, violates another taboo, for it so obviously depicts passionate intercourse ending in orgasm. Women readers must have gasped. Yet, throughout *Dracula,* there is no real sex; there is no lovemaking. James Twitchell has called the plotting "sex without genitalia, sex without confusion, sex without responsibility, sex without guilt, sex without love—better yet, sex without mention."

Stoker's genius was to develop a coded eroticism, shroud it in the preternatural, and then shrug off responsibility by obliterating the author's voice. In this scene, Lucy's fiancé, the shallow aristocrat Lord Godalming, delivers her from evil by acting out the wedding-night deflowering:

> Arthur took the stake and the hammer, and when once his mind was set on action his hands never trembled nor even quivered. Van Helsing opened his missal and began to read, and Quincey and I followed as well as we could. Arthur placed the point over the heart, and as I looked I could see its dint in the white flesh. Then he struck with all his might. The Thing in the coffin writhed; and a hideous, blood-curdling screech came from the opened red lips. The body shook and quivered and twisted in wild contortions; the sharp white teeth champed together till the lips were cut, and the mouth was smeared with a crimson foam. But Arthur never faltered. He looked like a figure of Thor as his untrembling arm rose and fell, driving deeper and deeper the mercy-bearing stake, whilst the blood from the pierced heart welled and spurted up around it. His face was set, and high duty seemed to shine through it; the sight of it gave us courage, so that our voices seemed to ring through the little vault. And then the writhing and quivering of the body became less, and the teeth ceased to champ, and the face to quiver. Finally it lay still. The terrible task was over.

The final primal scene takes place in the Harkers' bedroom. While Jonathan sleeps, "his face flushed and breathing heavily as if in a stupor," Dracula seduces his wife—a threesome *in flagrante delicto*—and introduces a new vampiric position, which Dr. Seward describes as resembling "a child forcing a kitten's nose into a saucer of milk to compel it to drink." Mina recalls the scene:

> He placed his reeking lips upon my throat. . . . I felt my strength fading away, and I was in a half swoon. . . . He pulled open his shirt, and with his long sharp nails opened a vein in his breast. When the blood

began to spurt out, he took my hands in one of his, holding them
tight and with the other seized my neck and pressed my mouth to
the wound, so that I must either suffocate or swallow some of the—
"Oh, my God! my God! what have I done?"

With its symbolic readings of blood/milk/semen, this scene con-
fuses Dracula's identity, leaving the reader to wonder who is doing
what to whom. This is the Count's last great moment when all his
seductive powers are indisputable, memorable, and terrifying. The
fascination and horror of Dracula, for males, was as a humiliator of
men. The vampire debases their women. In this scene a husband
sleeps while his wife is forced into fellatio, magnifying the threat to
Harker's masculinity.

Beyond a veritable sexual lexicon of Victorian taboos (seduction,
rape, gang rape, group sex, necrophilia, pedophilia, incest, adultery,
oral sex, menstruation, venereal disease, and voyeurism), there are obvious political, religious, and occult leitmotifs, ranging from the
emergence of the New Woman to the polarization of East and West
to an allegory on the tarot.

Autobiographically, *Dracula* marks an unburdening of Stoker's
rescue fantasies, which were bred in childhood and auditioned in his
early romantic novels. In the search for love and harmony, the nine
main characters reflect not only Stoker's life and times, but his secret
thoughts: a coded Victorian diary. Like an eternal volcano, this masterpiece periodically spews up molten fragments of itself for new
generations to poke and probe. It now becomes not Bram Stoker's
*Dracula* but *Dracula*'s Bram Stoker.

THE CASTLE OF THE KING, an illustration by the Rev. William Fitzgerald for *Under the Sunset*. In this collection of fairy tales, Stoker describes how the castle's "gateway with its cavernous recesses and its beetling towers took shape as a skull" (*Under the Sunset,* 1960, Borgo Press edition, p. 156).

# 1

## *Dublin Dreams*

(1847–1878)

*Chapter 1*

# THE DREAMER

"There are bad dreams for those who sleep
unwisely."
— Dracula to Jonathan Harker

That childhood fantasies bred adult nightmares is clear from Bram Stoker's fiction and from what is known of his early years in Clontarf, a coastal town three miles north of Dublin. His bedroom, on the third floor of a modest Georgian terrace house, overlooked Dublin Bay, and there he watched the stormy high tides licking the roadway and the summery clouds enclosing the harbor. He glimpsed contours of the wind-driven clipper ships departing with grain for Liverpool, to return with coal; and the storm-swatted rumrunners seeking shelter. In the distance was the North Wall docking slip, from which thousands sailed, fleeing the Irish famine of the 1840s. The sounds of the Dublin-to-Drogheda train rumbling over the viaduct marked the hours; the whispering wind and water countenanced sleep. The view was everything—a secret world—for a sickly child.

And Stoker's childhood was marred by illness. While his older brother and sister ran about the house or played games in the sprawling, leafy park outside his window, he remained in bed or was carried from room to room by his mother. That he did not walk until he was seven, yet left behind only one mention of this time, points to a secretive nature indeed. "In my babyhood I used, I understand, to be often at the point of death," he wrote in his *Reminiscences of Henry Irving*. "Certainly till I was about seven years old I never knew what it was to stand upright. I was naturally thoughtful and the leisure of long illness gave opportunity for many thoughts which were fruitful according to their kind in later years."

A master of understatement when it came to his personal life, Stoker philosophically dismissed this trauma when it was surely a primal turning point, forever marking his destiny. Denied the pivotal rites of passage from infant to child, Stoker never crawled on the floor to reach a toy; never pulled himself up a chair leg, or toddled unsteadily toward his mother's outstretched hands. Instead, he sensed the anxiety in her voice when the doctor came to examine him. Was his malady one of the mysterious fevers that swept through Ireland after the famine? (In *Dracula,* the symptoms of Lucy's vampire attack go undiagnosed for a major part of the novel.)

Stoker dispersed memories as selfishly as an old crone ladling soup. In his book on Irving, he speaks of his illness but deleted from the manuscript such telling details as: "When the nursery bell rang at night my mother would run to the room expecting to find me dying. All my early recollection is of being carried in people's arms and of being laid down somewhere or other on a bed or a sofa if within the house, on a rug or amid cushions on the grass if the weather was fine." He feared death or abandonment; rescue fantasies thread through his novels and are at the heart of *Dracula*. By the age of two he would have understood the power of the nursery bell, the power he had to turn a frantic mother into a loving one, relieved and happy to find her son alive. Stoker commanded his mother's attention, demanding his rights as a helpless infant, for three years, until Tom was born, then two years later Richard, who was followed by Margaret and finally George, in 1855.

Throughout his life Stoker was closest to Thornley, who was two when Bram was placed in his old bassinet, and to George, whose birth coincided with Bram's first steps. Stoker's realization that his mother was indeed a sexual being who belonged to his father finds an outlet in his fiction when he intermingles Oedipal conflicts with sibling rivalry, patricide, and infanticide. In *Dracula* female vampires reverse the maternal role by eating rather than nourishing babies, and five "brothers" harbor sexual desires for Mina, the mother figure, banding together to destroy Dracula, the potent father figure.

Carried outdoors and nestled in a cushion on the lawn, Stoker inhaled the aromatic soul of nature. "If I lie on the grass," he recalled in another deleted segment of *Reminiscences,* "those days come back to me with never-ending freshness. I look among the stalks or blades of the grass and wonder where the sound comes from—that gentle hum of nature which never ceases, for ears that can hear. I wonder what is below the red-brown uneven earth which seems so level at a little distance but is in reality so rugged. Then come the wisdoms of those half-forgotten thoughts which are the rudiments of philosophy."

The hothouse atmosphere of invalid life was fecund indeed. Stoker's interest in the theatre, in the gothic tradition, in the preternatural, can be traced back to these early years. Here was the genesis of his fascination with storms, shipwrecks, and sea rescues, with pirate coves, buried treasure, and the unknown. And always the sea, particularly the angry sea. In his imagination Stoker envisioned mist-clouded sails protecting cargoes of gold and silver, jewels and coins. He conjured up scenes of vast caves filled with whiskey brought in by the smugglers who stealthily oared in and out of the hidden coves around Clontarf. His solitude ordained his intelligence; the confines of his room furnished his mind.

His first short story, "The Crystal Cup," published when he was twenty-four, provides a look at his room with a view. He makes special note of the blue water and the soft, lapping sound, how the sunlight stroked the waves "ever-smiling, ever-glancing, ever-sunny." Kneeling on the window seat, he looked as far out to sea as his vision extended; he wrapped himself in daydreams, distractedly gazing at the shelves filled with old books and his "first rude efforts in art." He amused himself with ciphers. In *The Mystery of the Sea* he notes that his interest in secret writing started when he "had been an invalid for a considerable period" and had taken from the family library *Mercury: or the Secret and Swift Messenger* by Bishop Wilkins, which explains how ambassadors, spies, and secret agents corresponded.

BRAM STOKER at the age of seven,
in his first photograph

When Stoker was about seven, he posed for his first formal photograph, dressed in an oversize, ribbon-trimmed jacket, probably handed down from his older brother. A sweet face looks forlornly at the photographer—a gaze attributable more to the cheerless sitter's having to keep still long enough for the image to register on the sensitized glass plate than to a boy's entry into the fearful world of growing up. In subsequent photographs, there is always a faraway look in Stoker's steely gray eyes, as if the shutter froze him in a dream birth, a secret memory. Dourness characterizes his portraits because his small almond-shaped eyes were not in proportion to his wide forehead and oval face. Fascinated with the study of physiognomy, he found the large bump over his eyebrows an embarrassment; in fact, he thought himself ugly. But he liked his unusual gray eyes. Many of his fictional characters—women and men—are given "glorious grey eyes," or Henry Irving's aquiline nose.

As a child, Stoker's happiest times were the evenings. His mother sat by his bed and told him the myths of Ireland; his father embellished the military exploits of ancestors or, if fresh from the Theatre Royal, Dublin's major venue for touring actors, applauded the brilliance—or criticized the ineptitude—of the latest *Hamlet*. During these invalid years Stoker learned much from the skillful art of Irish storytelling. His constant companions were Thornley, who shared his room, bringing him the outside world in rocks and insects, and his sister Matilda, with whom he drew trees and animals. He was often alone, but never lonely. His mother doted on him; his father cared with a paternal intensity appropriate to the era, popping his head into the nursery to inquire, "How's my little man today?"

Abraham (later Bram) Stoker, the third of seven children, was born on November 8, 1847, at 15 Marino Crescent—then as now called The Crescent—in Clontarf, famed in Irish history as the site where King Brian Boru broke the power of the invading Danes in 1014. Held by his twenty-nine-year-old mother, Charlotte, he was christened Abraham after his father, a civil servant, on December 30 in the local Protestant church. At that time Old Testament biblical names were common, and Abraham most likely came from a Dutch ancestor. Proud of his northern European heritage, Stoker names the "good father" figure of *Dracula,* Dr. Abraham Van Helsing, after himself and his father, and has the psychic detective reside in Amsterdam; Mina is short for Wilhelmina, a traditional Dutch name.

If Stoker had been Catholic and "at the point of death," as he said, he would have been rushed to the baptismal font to avoid limbo, a state of nothingness to which those who die unbaptized are consigned, forever barred from heaven. Not recognizing limbo, the Church of Ireland states only that baptism should not be delayed, without good reason, beyond the fifth week after birth. Stoker's baptism occurred later than seven weeks, an indication of his frail health.

The year of his birth was not an auspicious time for Ireland; it was one of the nightmare years. Throughout the forties crops had failed, and the summer of 1846 brought the great potato blight. The writer Anthony Trollope recalled how the disease "fell upon the potato gardens like a dark mantle; before the end of September, entire fields were black, and the air was infected with the unwholesome odour of the blight; before the end of October it was known that the whole food of the country was gone."

Out of a population of some 8 million, 5½ million were dependent on agriculture. There were riots, looting, marches; landlords evicted tenants too weak to tend their crops; overcrowded poorhouses locked out the homeless, and starving families roamed the countryside. More than 1½ million people died from starvation and disease, and an equal number emigrated. The government's benign—

and malign—neglect during the famine years (1845–9) stirred Irish nationalism. Middle-class families with guaranteed wages like the Stokers had food on the table, but no one was completely insulated from the horrors seen and told, such as starving dogs eating babies.

The Stokers, who had been living in Dublin, fled the festering city for Clontarf, attracted by the salubrious air of the seaside bathing site. It remained a quiet place until horse-drawn trams arrived in 1870, making the north coast accessible to summer visitors. Over the years, The Crescent has changed little, and its mythology lives still in the local pubs. In 1792, the story goes, a builder by the name of Charles Ffolliott bought land in front of the mansion of Lord Charlemont, a wealthy landholder, and started building houses. The lord looked out his sitting-room window, saw that his view of Dublin Bay would be blocked, and promptly charged the builder excessive tolls on the materials taken through his turnpike gate. Ffolliott retaliated by bringing his materials in by barge. As an added indignity, he built the houses in a semicircle, totally blocking the lordly view. Ever since, The Crescent has been known as Spite Row.

Clontarf, like other jagged coastal areas, was a favorite haven for robbers, brigands, thieves, and smugglers. At the end of the eighteenth century outlaws were hanged from the Ballybough Bridge gallows and left to rot for days as an object lesson. Nearby was a plot of ground reserved for burying suicides, who, as late as the 1850s, were interred in the time-honored fashion: staked to prevent their unhappy spirits from wandering. Also to be feared was the phantom horseman: the ghost of Frederick "Buck" Jones, a legendary local magistrate, gambler, and theatre operator. It was a terrifying cast of characters to inhabit a young boy's dreams and reveries.

While tales of ghosts, decomposing corpses, and staked bodies captivated young Bram, it was the homegrown stories he most enjoyed. His mother told him how she survived the cholera epidemic of 1832 in Sligo, her birthplace; of how she heard the banshee cry when her mother died; of how some during the famine drank blood extracted from the veins of cattle, including the family cow. Stoker enjoyed the Sligo stories so much that he later asked her to write them down; the images of this plague spreading across the countryside inspired "The Invisible Giant," published in 1881 in *Under the Sunset.*

Throughout his illness Stoker was cared for by an uncle, who was associated with Dublin's Fever Hospital and House of Recovery. Like other doctors of the time, William Stoker practiced bleeding, either with leeches or by opening the temporal artery. In a paper published in 1829 on the origin, prevention, and cure of organic diseases, he announced that he "seldom hesitated to take blood freely in the sequel of measles." Doubtless measles ran its course through Bram's household, and Uncle William would have bled him and his brothers and sisters by attaching leeches to the skin.*

"The blood is the life," says Renfield as he savors eating each new species—also true when blood transfusions are used to keep Lucy alive after Dracula has drained her to the point of death. Stoker's detailed description of this procedure in the novel may have roots in personal experience. Certainly by the time his youngest brother, George, was born, Stoker would have been aware of the cries of childbirth emanating from his parents' room on the floor below, and perhaps seen the blood that accompanies an afterbirth. To a child given to fantasy, these experiences may have stimulated some of the shuddering images in *Dracula* and *The Lair of the White Worm,* Stoker's last novel.

It is curious that Stoker never defines his illness. Surely he knew what was wrong; he was too inquisitive a man not to ask what and why. Later in life, he would have consulted his three physician brothers, particularly Thornley. Was he really bedridden all that time? Or was being an invalid a romantic fantasy fed by Byronic poetry? With Stoker one never knows. He did leave one hint in *The Man,* where his alter ego, Harold, suffers a recurrence of rheumatic fever after a harrowing swim to save a child's life. (Stoker himself would risk his

---

* As a medical reformer, William Stoker was concerned with containing typhus and other contagious diseases. In an 1815 pamphlet, he advocated a ban on the sale of whiskey. It was, he allowed, "the cheapest expedient for blunting suffering," but the poor could not continue to "pass their lives between alternative intemperance and famine." Whiskey was a national evil, a blight on the Irish character, he continued. One wonders what the state of modern Irish literature would be today had this proposal taken root.

life to save a suicidal man.) Still, the seven years when he claims to have been near death remain a mystery period; no satisfactory answer was passed down to his granddaughter Ann. Whatever the infirmity, Stoker overcame it. "This early weakness passed away," he wrote, "and I grew into a strong boy and in time enlarged to the biggest member of my family."*

Bram Stoker's ancestors had lived in Ireland since the seventeenth century. They were soldiers, farmers, tailors, shoemakers, and gold-smiths, eventually distinguishing themselves as physicians and med-ical researchers. His great-grandfather Richard was a quartermaster of the Old Green Horse Dragoons, who arrived in Ireland around 1690 from Morpeth in Northumberland with William III of Orange. Richard's only son, William, a maker of stays for ladies' underwear, married Frances Smyth, an orphan, and opened a tailor's shop on St. Andrew's Street in Dublin.

In later years William Stoker was an ordinance clerk, starting a family tradition of civil service. His son Abraham, the youngest of six children, was born in 1799, two years before the Act of Union, which established the United Kingdom and marked the beginning of Dublin's decline. Once political power and influence moved to Westminster, many of Dublin's aristocrats and gentry followed, to be largely replaced by a professional class of barristers and bureaucrats who worked at Dublin Castle, the seat of the viceregal court. Three generations of Stokers would be minor bureaucrats there, regulating the life of the Protestant Ascendancy, the ruling Irish class.

Abraham followed his father to Dublin Castle to be a clerk at six-

---

* Rheumatic fever, an inflammation of the joints that occurs chiefly in children or young adults, is painful at times but not continuous. It is possible that Stoker, reluctant to share his mother, might have been a bit of a malingerer, keeping the security of his pillow longer than necessary. Generally the onset is later in childhood, with the joint pains disappearing, but the disease often affects the heart, which would have militated against Stoker's later success as a college athlete. The other probability is that the long bed rest had more to do with the treatments of the 1850s than the disease itself. Other possibilities include tuber-culosis, a nonparalytic type of polio, and asthma. Asthma could have been real or psycho-somatic; in any case it would have been treated with bed rest to avoid attacks. Asthma can suddenly disappear and never again impede strenuous activity.

teen. Plodding work filled the years, and at forty-five he settled into comfortable bachelorhood. All that changed during a vacation at Coleraine, where he met the vivacious Charlotte Matilda Blake Thornley, twenty years his junior. Ambitious, headstrong, and intellectually tough, she overpowered the withdrawn middle-aged man, and the two wed in 1844, living first in Harcourt Street, Dublin, before moving the following year to The Crescent.

Charlotte provided the flamboyant genes. On her father's side, the Thornleys traced their ancestors back to 1584, with branches in Cheshire and Derbyshire, England. The Irish Thornleys left Derbyshire for Ballyshannon in County Donegal in the 1780s, where they were born, married, and died until the mid-nineteenth century. Mostly yeomen, a title given to those who farmed their own land, they eventually represented the trades of the time: weavers, wheelwrights, tailors, shoemakers, masons, and hatters. The men served in the army, a few marrying heiresses and increasing their acreage.

Charlotte's maternal ancestors, the Blakes, made military and medical marriages in Galway, but the heroes and rogues stand out. In 1305 Richard Blake was sheriff of Connaught, a family entitlement that continued to 1654, when Galway surrendered to Cromwell. Thirty-seven Blakes were sheriffs, and eighteen were mayors of Galway. With sheriffs in the family for three centuries, young Bram was weaned on rough-and-tumble tales. The most fascinating was that of great-granduncle George Blake, hanged in 1798 for rebellion. Uncle George had joined the French army and landed in Sligo during the battle of Ballenamunch—the wrong place at the wrong time. Uncle Richard was a famous duelist, whose hints of daring exist only in a steel-pen entry on a genealogical chart: "therein hangs another story very amusing."

The two sides were united in 1817, when Capt. Thomas Thornley of the 43rd Light Infantry married Matilda Blake, one of twelve children. Thornley served in France like so many Irish boys (the wars against Napoleon had given Dublin importance as a recruiting center), enlisting when he was seventeen. On his return to Ireland, he joined the Royal Irish Constabulary, eventually dying from injuries received in the line of duty. Born in Sligo in 1818, Charlotte, the first of Thomas and Matilda's children, was followed by two brothers. She

was fourteen when she lived through the cholera epidemic that dec-
imated the West Country population.

Tell me about the sickness, Bram would ask. It was one way to
keep his mother's attention. "It was said to have come from the
East," she began, "rising out of the Yellow Sea, growing nearer and
nearer until it was in Ireland!" She told him how after the death of
"Mrs. Feeny, a very fat woman who was a music teacher, and was
buried an hour after, men looked at each other and whispered *cholera,*
but the whisper next day deepened to a roar, and in many houses lay
one, nay two or three *dead*. One house would be attacked and the
next spared. There was no telling who would go next, and when one
said 'good-bye' to a friend, he said it as if forever."

She told ghastly stories of premature burials. The terrified Sligo
townspeople pushed stricken travelers into pits and buried them
alive. The clergy fled, doctors died, and drunken prostitutes cared for
the dying when the last nurse collapsed. "Day after day and night
after night," she recalled, a priest sat "with a horsewhip to prevent
those wretches dragging the patients down the stairs by the legs with
their heads dashing on the stone steps, before they were dead." And
she told poignant stories. A husband carried his wife to the hospital
on his back, a red handkerchief wound tightly around her waist to
stop the pain. When he returned that evening, he was told she was in
the house of the dead, a makeshift barn where hundreds of bodies
were thrown one on top of the other. He rushed there, searched fran-
tically, and in the dimness glimpsed the red cloth. He carried his wife
home, where she lived many more years. "By twos and threes our
dead neighbours were carried away," his mother imprinted on
Bram's memory, until two-thirds of the population were buried. The
Blakes survived, and through this tale Stoker learned to celebrate
death and life.


Abraham Stoker drudged away in the parliamentary section at
Dublin Castle, helping to govern an Ireland that bound the Catholic
majority to a largely feudal and barbaric landowning system, enrich-
ing the Anglo-Irish landlords whose main talents were shooting birds
and hunting foxes. The only thing this class shared and suffered with

the Irish peasant—and could not avoid in their country houses—was the damp weather. Charlotte Stoker improved her position when she married into the civil service, a better life than her mother's as a military wife. The Stokers were Protestant and attended the Church of Ireland regularly; their politics were conservative and Tory. Abraham Stoker served under four monarchs—George III, George IV, William IV, and Victoria—and lived through a turbulent period in Irish history: Catholic emancipation, the Reform Act, the Tithe War, and Protestant Repeal.

Intelligent, hardworking, and literate, Stoker's parents provided a comfortable but hardly indulgent life. They had domestic help and money for books to add to the library, the family's one luxury. Charlotte bore seven children in ten years. Unremittingly ambitious for her five sons, she vowed they would go to Dublin's acclaimed Trinity College with the sons of the aristocracy. More reticent than his resourceful wife, Abraham preferred reading before a blazing fire, and occasionally treated himself to pit seats at the Theatre Royal. A man capable of moments of joy but not happiness, he was a worrier—and with cause. Fifty-five when his last son was born, he realized that his civil service ambitions were behind him; ahead were debts and death.

Still, it was prestigious to be of the Protestant bourgeoisie, and the Stokers used their Dublin Castle connections to further their sons' careers and gain introductions to the right literary and intellectual circles. But they were never "castle society"—the people who received invitations to the endless round of receptions, balls, and levees; who sent their sons to Oxford or Cambridge and used the annual viceregal ball as a matrimonial market for their daughters, even during the famine years. Grand as the name sounds, Dublin Castle, a grouping of fine period buildings around a courtyard, is a castle in name only. It was built in 1224 as a hilltop fortification and was once a jail and then a courthouse, undergoing many additions and modifications before Stoker's grandfather arrived to sit on a clerk's high stool.

The Irish novelist George Moore, destined to have much to say about Bram's brother Thornley, wrote a withering description of the castle's authority, doubtless colored by his inability to gain social acceptance: "The city sleeps; wharves, walls, and bridges are veiled and have disappeared in the fog that has crept up from the sea; the shame-less squalor of the outlying streets is enwrapped in the grey mist, but over them and dark against the sky the Castle still stretches out its arms as if for some monstrous embrace." Moore describes a menac-ing castle not unlike the one in *Under the Sunset* and *Dracula*—a cas-tle with hidden passions.

For twenty years Abraham Stoker was an invisible cipher in the parliamentary branch. He walked the three miles to and from work, arrived on time, and did his work quietly and efficiently. In 1853 he hardened his resolve and requested a promotion, stressing the years of responsible and diligent service. Promotion to senior clerk resulted, reinforcing his ego; but as he later warned Bram, the home civil ser-vice was not a place for financial or professional advancement. Abra-ham and Charlotte pursued separate interests. If there were family problems—drinking, fighting, or infidelity—Stoker never revealed it in his novels, where men mostly pursue or rescue women, with the ending a wedding; thus he avoided any analysis of happy or unhappy unions. When Jonathan marries Mina, he is conveniently semico-matose in a convent hospital.

Dublin was still provincial, a bit eccentric, reluctantly yawning from languor to vitality. While other Victorian cities were experiencing rapid manufacturing growth and increasing population, Dublin was undergoing industrial decline and demographic stagnation. As a re-sult, the city escaped a nineteenth-century building frenzy, and its Georgian buildings emerged tattered but intact, an example of the survival of the past at the expense of the present—the very essence of vampirism.

Unlike Irish writers before and after him, Stoker drew no inspi-ration from the city's social ills, even at a time when most Dubliners lived in the worst slums in Europe, humbled by poverty and disease. He preferred Ireland's superstitions, its bucolic mysteries. On outings from Clontarf, he walked with his father around the Georgian squares, taking the air in St. Stephen's Green, whose gardens glistened with perpetual mist. Any outdoor excursion delighted him, and a special treat was hiring a brougham for a Sunday ride to the country. Stoker would covet the city's sagacious literary heritage. There was Jonathan Swift, dean of Dublin's St. Patrick's Cathedral, who wrote his vitriolic satire *Gulliver's Travels* (to "vex the world rather than divert it"), and Sheridan Le Fanu, whose vampire tale, *Carmilla,* influenced *Dracula.* And the Anglo-Irish literary legacy was to be enhanced further when Wilde, Shaw, and Yeats were born between 1854 and 1865.

The seven young Stokers received their early education from their mother, who was well read for an untutored Sligo girl. Doubtless, as was customary, the local minister was invited to dinner to contribute some ethical tutorials over the stew and potatoes. Fascinated with other cultures, Charlotte read the Abbé Évariste Huc's works on China and Richard Francis Burton's African adventures. She also took an interest in the places where the Irish emigrated: Canada, Australia, and America. A middle-class reformer, Charlotte took what action she could to help Ireland overthrow its feudal past.

A stay-at-home, Abraham focused on his family, concentrating on future success for his sons, although his vision was limited to the domestic civil service and the acceptable professions of medicine and the law. He did hear younger colleagues at Dublin Castle talking about the opportunities for advancement in India. British rule, firmly established throughout most of the subcontinent by 1818, was further enriched when Queen Victoria added—not without controversy— Empress of India to her regal titles, and celebrated by wearing on New Year's Day 1877 masses of jewels given to her by Indian princes and maharajahs, including the Star of India.

Compared with Ireland, the far-flung Indian Empire was an exotic posting, offering adventure and prestige. Richard would choose the Indian Medical Service; Tom chose the foreign service, retiring after twenty-five years as secretary to the Governor of the North West Provinces. From an early age, Thornley and George had been interested in following in their uncle William's distinguished footsteps. That pleased Charlotte immensely: she would have three physicians in the family. Bram, it seemed, was left to indulge disparate interests, allowed to be the creative, free spirit of the family. After all, he had seven years to retrieve.

His sisters, Matilda (a year older) and Margaret (seven years younger), were given music and art lessons, learned lace making, and spoke Italian and French. Although dowryless, they were ladies of Victorian refinement. One family anecdote attributes to Charlotte a quote that she didn't care "tuppence" for her daughters' advancement. This remark, coming from a feminist advocate well before the suffrage movement, makes sense in terms of the only prescribed option for women of this class and time: a good marriage. What could women's liberation do for a young, middle-class Irish woman?

Charlotte worried about the outcasts of society. In the wake of famine and massive emigration, Ireland began to comprehend its vast social problems, and in a tide of self-examination, special-interest

CHARLOTTE STOKER, in her mid-thirties, had borne seven children and was a social crusader.

groups debated and evaluated issues advocating reform. Charlotte Stoker, who never forgot the plight of the poor in her native Sligo, was swept into this activism, her restless nature needing an outlet. Twenty years younger than her husband, she had been a nurturer for eighteen years. When George, the youngest, turned eight, his forty-five-year-old mother stepped into the spotlight, advocating women's rights for the poor, volunteering at the workhouses, and speaking at the Statistical and Social Inquiry Society of Ireland.

On a May evening in 1863, she supported establishing state schools for the deaf and dumb. An interested listener was Dr. William Wilde, father of then nine-year-old Oscar and a prominent eye and ear specialist, who had gathered the first statistics on the incidence of deafness in Ireland. Charlotte made an impressive showing, delivering a well-researched and confident speech. She told the audience that schools for the deaf and dumb were available in France, Prussia, and the United States but not in Great Britain. "England is known to provide so freely for the education of the poor of every other class without distinction of creed," she declared. "Why should the deaf and dumb be the exception? Why should not a privilege be granted to those speechless poor which is so liberally bestowed on all others?"

At the workhouses, the last refuges for the destitute without funds to emigrate, Charlotte listened to the complaints of women who wanted to be more than servants in the poorest households. In her next appearance before the Society, she urged that the basic skills of cooking and farmwork be taught so that women could emigrate to Canada, New Zealand, and Australia. "Any measure calculated to encourage virtue and subdue vice must be the wisest and best policy of a nation," she said. "In new countries there is a dignity in labour, and a self-supporting woman is alike respected and respectable. Why should the door of hope be closed on those poor women, and why refuse them the means of attaining that independence in other countries which they are debarred from in this?" She had these speeches privately printed and distributed, her staunch voice preserved. Rhetoric never overshadowed facts; her prose was dispassionate and her sincerity never in doubt.

Charlotte enjoyed the attention that advocacy work afforded. She assisted the disenfranchised and left her husband to shoulder the loans that allowed their five sons to walk through the gates of Trinity. A photograph taken when she was thirty-four shows a determined-looking woman with the traditional Irish bonnet framing a round, quizzical face lighted by a suggestion of a smile. Independent, decisive, and intimidating, Stoker's mother was ahead of her time. Often intrigued by viragoesque older women and heroic father figures, Stoker, even more than wanting to be admired, liked admiring. He was his father's son: efficient, unappreciated, unsure of himself. But his mother haunts his writing.

*Chapter 2*

# TRINITY MAN

"He is a young man, full of energy and talent in
his own way, and of a very faithful disposition.
He is discreet and silent."
— Mr. Hawkins describing Harker

S toker left the security of his bedroom, his view, and his protective parents at the age of twelve to spend four years at the Rev.
William Woods's school in Dublin's Rutland (now Parnell)
Square. The Stokers cultivated no academic allegiances: Thornley
studied at Wymondham Grammar, and George and Tom at Rath-
mines. The Reverend Woods, said to be a patient man, was headmas-
ter of a small prep school, a wise choice for a boy who five years earlier
had only begun to move his legs and walk. During these years Stoker
tested himself in athletics, turning himself into an endurance walker.
Perhaps he feared the return of the childhood weakness if he did not
keep moving. He recalls these times in *The Mystery of the Sea:* "At
school I was, though secretly ambitious, dull as to results."

When he matriculated at Trinity in 1863, the college in the center of Dublin founded in 1591 by Queen Elizabeth I was still a decade
away from accepting Catholics. As his mother had wished, Stoker and
his brothers joined the ranks of the educated Protestant ascendancy.
James Joyce, not a Trinity man himself (he went with the Catholics
to University College), called the institution a "dull stone set in the
ring of the city's ignorance." That was never Stoker's view. Despite

a reserved manner, he made a place for himself in college activities. Tall and ruggedly handsome, with ginger-colored hair and an enthusiasm to belong, he was soon known around the green as a "clubbable man." At college, "my big body and athletic powers," he said, "gave me a certain position in which I had to overcome my natural shyness."

The illness that had spurred his imagination had also nurtured his growth: he was six foot two and weighed 175 pounds. Stoker took to the playing fields with abandon. He made the rugby team, was an oarsman, and excelled in long-distance walking events. As University Athlete in 1867, he won awards for weight lifting and the five- and seven-mile walks. The only tournament event he failed to master was hand-over-hand rope climbing. He savored his strength. Throughout his life, walking was a narcotic, with a daily brisk pace necessary for his well-being and self-image. A fearless swimmer and risk taker, he was known to dive into huge waves on shallow shores, swimming way beyond immediate rescue. Reveling in the actions of strong, brave men, Stoker created in *Dracula* a determined group who pool their intelligence and energy—and their blood—to conquer evil, rescue the good woman, and make the British empire safe for the family.

In his novels Stoker earnestly recycled the theme of brave men rescuing good women, with an occasionally brave woman rescuing a brave man. His Victorian code was for brave men to serve good women—good women like Mina, not the sexually mischievous Lucys of the world. Once, after a stormy Atlantic crossing, he noted that in such situations "the only real comfort a poor woman can have is to hold on to a man. I happen to be a big one, and therefore of extra desirability in such cases of stress"—a thought echoed in *Dracula* when Lucy's suitors give their blood to save her life. "A brave man's blood is the best thing on this earth when a woman is in trouble," Van Helsing tells the American character, Quincey P. Morris. "You're a man, and no mistake."

As a student, Stoker was clever and did passable work, but his temperament was not in tune with intellectual investigation, knowing everything, seeing everything; perhaps this is why Van Helsing embodies such cerebral values. Stoker greedily read what he enjoyed, particularly the Romantic poetry of Byron, Keats, and Shelley; in some ways he was self-educated. He avoided long hours swotting—as students called intense study—in Trinity's baronial Long Room Library. Extracurricular activities came first. If not competing at a sporting event or attending a meeting, he spent evenings with friends in the local pubs drinking black-and-tans and animatedly talking about literature and Irish politics. His brother Thornley took education more seriously, and it was a disappointment to Stoker's parents that Bram never qualified for a scholarship.

But Stoker was invited to join The Phil and The Hist, Trinity's most prestigious student organizations. At the Philosophical Society, which attracted faculty, students, and intellectuals, including the ubiquitous Sir William Wilde, Stoker moved from secretary to president of the ninety-eighth session in 1867. From his first paper, appropriately called "Sensationalism in Fiction and Society," he went on to discuss *King Lear,* Shakespeare's fools, Keats, Shelley, and votes for women.

The Historical Society was the parliamentary debating group founded by statesman Edmund Burke in 1770. As a junior sophister, Stoker discovered a talent to persuade; and spurred on by a commanding voice, neglected courses to prepare arguments and rise in a society that has ruffled the ruling elite for more than two centuries. Silenced for acerbic political views in 1815, The Hist was revived five years later outside the Trinity gates, with meetings held in hotels such as Radley's in Dame Street or Morrison's at the corner of Dawson. In the 1830s intense debates on Irish affairs, the emergence of Catholic power, the triumph of Whiggish reform, and the suppression of the Orange Order combined to frighten Irish Tories into a reconsideration of their place in Ireland. Little had changed by Stoker's time.

At The Hist, Stoker advanced from the library committee to librarian to recording secretary; in 1872 he was elected auditor, a position equivalent to the presidency of The Union at Oxford or Cambridge. To these honors he added a silver medal in history and composition. He spoke successfully in support of voting by ballot, government support for secular education, and the proposition that nineteenth-century novels were more immoral than their predecessors. If the same question were framed today about *Dracula,* arguably the most sexually charged literary myth of the twentieth century, one wonders whether Stoker would be on the side of morality or immorality.

What Stoker enjoyed most about debating was the exhilaration of performance, being outside himself, holding an argument with energy and wit. He developed the ability to speak quickly and decisively, and mastered the split-second timing needed to frustrate threatening questions. He learned to command the stage; his ambition at this time was to be an actor. Debates were entertainment. Waiting for any noise opportunity, the student audience applauded, stamped, cheered, and hissed. Afterward, exhausted winners and losers carried their points to the nearest pub, where arguments continued until the closing bell. Stoker was always a night person; he enjoyed nothing better than seeing in the dawn, as long as there was endlessly biting talk to keep him awake and alert.

The annual meeting of The Hist (then as now) was a prominent event. Distinguished alumni came to orate and to taunt. Speaking on "The Necessity for Political Honesty" at the opening of the thirtieth session on November 13, 1872, Stoker pleaded for openness between nations in a shrinking world, a topic still unresolved. A reporter from *The Daily Express* introduced Stoker as one "whose pedestrian feats have rendered him familiar to all those even imperfectly acquainted with the history of athletics in our University." Stoker began his talk by praising the origins of The Hist, which he pointed out was founded to supplement the teachings of the college until literature and history were introduced into the curriculum. Then oratory took over. The new subjects "arose from the slow-grown want in the University of a political training school"—a change, he happily noted (to applause), that the college had allowed.

Political initiation at a young age was important. "Let it not pass from us by the slow decay of indifference or the rapid blight of opposition," Stoker thundered. "We are young enough to hope—we are old enough to act—and in hope and action lies the future of ourselves, our country and our race." "Hear! Hear!" exploded the undergraduate contingent, followed by vigorous applause. Then the spirited part of the program began, when others took the floor to challenge Stoker's premises. Was honesty a quality applicable to politics? one speaker asked, to accompanying laughter.

The Right Honorable J. T. Ball, M.P., observed that a debating society was indispensable to Ireland. "Its government, its law, and its teaching in all its churches was conducted through the medium of spoken thought," he said. But Stoker had championed debates on modern politics, and Ball had "great doubts as to the wisdom of young men, before their opinions were matured, being enlisted in adverse ranks on political subjects." The young intellects of Ireland, he added, should be trained with debates on the past, not the present and future. "Hear! Hear!" responded the older alumni. It was left to the Rev. George Chadwick to praise Stoker. "The best of all good things that awaited the Auditor," he said, "was the feeling of a good conscience, which would lead him afterwards to fulfill in his own life the principles he had so worthily asserted in his paper."

University life encouraged personal achievement and fortified Stoker's self-esteem. He did not have rooms in college, but there were many sofas available to him after a late night in the pubs. When he returned to The Crescent, though, he was disturbed by his parents' talk of money, even the outlay of the few shillings paid for servants. Once a familial time of sharing, suppers became dreary with plans for leaving Ireland, tense with talk of emigration.

Burdened with debts, bored with departmental politics, and bereft of ambition, Abraham Stoker retired in 1865 at the required age of sixty-five. It had taken him more than fifty years to attain the rank of first-class clerk, which entitled him to a full salary of £650. A sad humility permeated his letter of resignation: "At the close of service . . . I can with truth say that I am not conscious of ever having unduly neglected my duties . . . but being at all times unwilling to speak in my own behalf, and preferring to be judged by the opinion of others, I beg to submit for your consideration copies of testimonials received on the occasion of my promotion to my present position." Perhaps it was protocol to be obsequious, or perhaps it was a patriarchal trait. Stoker inherited the same compliant attitude: he pandered to Henry Irving and neglected to assert himself.

Abraham's retirement was not to be a time of comfortable contemplation on The Crescent. He did not regret his debts; over the years he had borrowed for school tuition, and his sons had brought achievement and pride to the family. Thornley had completed Trinity and was on his way to becoming a prominent surgeon. Richard was in India with the medical service. Bram took a leave of absence in 1866 to work for a year at Dublin Castle as a clerk in the Registrar of Petty Sessions; he graduated in 1871 with a degree in science and stayed on for a master's. George was into his medical apprenticeship, and Tom was still at Trinity.

Using a £1,000 life insurance policy with the London Assurance Company as collateral, Abraham secured a final loan for £300 in 1872. He paid off previous obligations and saved what remained to live abroad with Matilda and Margaret. A pension could be stretched in France and Switzerland, where room and board were five francs a day. For months number 15 was in disarray as Charlotte packed and secured the family papers in a steamer trunk to be stored at 43 Harcourt Street, where Bram was to live with Thornley. She welcomed the upheaval, anticipating the cultural advantages available for her daughters. Abraham viewed the move in terms of financial expediency; a nomadic life was not suited to his quiet nature, and his health was frail.

Before departing, he had his photograph taken. It shows a proud paradigm of rectitude and responsibility, a father worthy of sermonizing to Bram that "every night since having a family, he had prayed that he might be able to rear them in honesty and uprightness." That he had done. Only Bram, now twenty-four, was reluctant to grow up: he yearned to be the eternal student, to keep his room with a view, his daydreams, and his college friends. For him, the dismantling of his birthplace was more than a dislocation; it was a turning point, even a rejection: he was abandoned by the womanly comforters of his youth. The departure date was changed time and again. Finally, in the summer of 1872, the five brothers stood on the quay and waved goodbye to their parents and sisters, who crossed the Irish Sea not as

ABRAHAM STOKER in
1865 at age sixty-five, retiring
after more than fifty years as a
civil servant at Dublin Castle

immigrants—like the multitudes before them—but as expatriates. The sadness was the same.

Beyond commendable virtues, Abraham Stoker had imbued his son Bram with a love of the theatre, which was cultivated at school. Since its founding, Trinity College had provided a sizable and partisan section of the Dublin audience; young men of literary appreciation made it a point to attend the theatre during their student days. In 1637, the only theatre outside London was Dublin's Werbaugh Street Theatre, later replaced by the renowned Smock Alley, whose acting company thrived for more than a century.

It can be said that Irish drama began with William Phillips's *St. Stephen's Green* in 1700, and the era of notable Irish dramatists followed with productions of the still stage-worthy *The Way of the World* and *The Beaux' Stratagem,* respectively by William Congreve and George Farquhar (both Trinity men). In 1734, with the opening of the Aungier Street Theatre and the rebuilding of Smock Alley,

Dublin had two theatres to parallel London's Drury Lane and Covent Garden; all four competed with very similar repertoires. Dubliner Richard Steele is credited with replacing the outmoded moralistic comedy with the so-called "sentimental" comedy, as exemplified by *The Conscious Lovers;* the style matured in Richard Brinsley Sheridan's *The Rivals,* which introduced Mrs. Malaprop (who gave the dictionary *malapropism*), and Oliver Goldsmith's *She Stoops to Conquer,* a revival favorite.

When the Irish Parliament was abolished in 1801, theatres that once catered to aristocrats recruited the middle and working classes by offering melodrama, spectacle, Italian and German operas, as well as Shakespeare, Sheridan, and Goldsmith. Dependent on London touring companies, Dublin benefited by having all the English and international stars perform at either the Theatre Royal on Poolbeg Street, the premier theatre, or at the Queen's in Great Brunswick (now Pearse) Street. Popular entertainment was booked into the Tivoli, La Scala, Gaiety, or Palace. (Only the Gaiety in South King Street, built in 1871 with Burmese teak and Russian oak, survives.)

One evening before the family left Ireland, Stoker escorted his father to the Royal to see Barry Sullivan play the villainous Sir Giles Overreach in *A New Way to Pay Old Debts.* An acknowledged international star who had toured America and spent three years at the Theatre Royal in Melbourne as actor-manager, Sullivan returned to Dublin in the 1870s to great triumph, performing every season thereafter. Earlier Abraham Stoker had seen the estimable Edmund Kean in the same part and considered no actor his equal. Father and son sat in the third row of the pit, and when Sullivan ended the play in a greed-driven acting frenzy, fulfilling any spectator's demand for high melodrama, Abraham told Bram: "He's as good as the best of them!" Sullivan was among the last of the rhetorical, hyperbolic old-school actors; his *Macbeth* remained Stoker's model until Irving's performance in 1888. Shaw praised Sullivan's resonant voice and a stage walk of grace and dignity, recalling with pleasure how he came before the curtain to apologize for a bad show.*

---

* Another Irish actor who drew father and son to the pit was Tyrone Power, great-grandfather of the eponymous Hollywood actor and of the theatre director Tyrone Guthrie.

Afterward, Stoker and his father critiqued the performance, debating the finer points of acting and staging. To Stoker, an actor's life was an extraordinary masquerade where you could be a soldier or a King; the theatre was passion without commitment, and he was in the pit whenever he could afford a two-shilling seat. Shaw, a bored real estate clerk collecting rents in a Dublin slum and dreaming of a life elsewhere, had kindred feelings. Nine years younger than Stoker, he lived on the same Harcourt Street block and stood in the same queues for pit seats, but the two never met until London. To Shaw, the characters on the Royal stage were "mysteriously thrilling people, secretly known to you in dreams of your childhood, [who] enact a life in which terrors are as fascinating as delights; so that ghosts and death, agony and sin, became, like love and victory, phases of an unaccountable ecstasy."

Doubtless many melodramatic characters strutted across the stage of Stoker's dreams, but none more compelling than Henry Irving, whom he saw for the first time as Captain Absolute in *The Rivals* on August 28, 1867, at the Royal. Irving was twenty-nine, a touring player from the provinces, notably Edinburgh, and was appearing in Dublin with the St. James's Company, where he had once been stage manager. Irving had embraced acting as an antidote to a lonely and restrictive youth; he devoted himself to the stage from the age of twelve and conquered a disabling stammer. For the role of Romeo at age eighteen, John Henry Brodribb from Somerset shed his clunky name to become Henry Irving, in honor of Washington Irving, author of *The Sketch Book*. (In future caricatures he even resembled Ichabod Crane.)

That evening Irving became the dashing soldier of Stoker's youthful dreams, a gallant man whose code of honor was to answer insolence with the point of a sword. Irving specialized in villains and was known for his makeup wizardry. But in a scant four years he would be Britain's leading actor, sighed over by infatuated Victorian schoolgirls who pasted his picture under their desktops.

Irving introduced Stoker to a new school of romantic acting. His technique broke with the effect-snatching expedients of a Charles Kean (Edmund's son) or a Barry Sullivan, exponents of a school dependent on flamboyant gestures, movements, and phrasings. Audiences expected roles to have a consistency; each season's *Hamlet* played the same. Irving, however, had the power to make the on-looker a part of the character, to share in the suffering, to make audiences think and feel, not just react. After the first act, Stoker recognized the importance of this interior expression on the future of drama.

Irving's performance had bite and ridicule—a new interpretation of a familiar role. Stoker recalled the scene where Mrs. Malaprop asks Absolute to read his own intercepted letter to Lydia Languish, in which he refers to the old lady as "the old weather-beaten she-dragon." Irving went back and forth to the offensive words, losing his place in the letter and going back to find it, using action rather than speech for effect—"a triumph of well-bred insolence." Thereafter Irving was stamped on Stoker's mind as "a patrician figure as real as the persons of one's dreams, and endowed with the same poetic grace."

The following morning Stoker searched the newspapers for a review to justify his high opinion of Irving's performance, and was disappointed to find no mention of it. More than a week later *The Irish Times* described Irving as a "painstaking and respectable artist." This offhand dismissal annoyed Stoker, but he was too preoccupied with becoming an actor himself to take action. He made the audition rounds, earning a few minor parts and even a line or two in reviews.

One critic said his performance as David in *The Rivals* elicited frequent rounds of applause and that he "somewhat improved the part by making the faithful servant an Irishman." At the University Boat Club Dramatic Society he read the prologue for the farce *The Turkish Bath,* and he played Ram Rusti in the burlesque *The Happy Man* at the Dublin University Dramatic Society. He was Charles I, which pleased his mother, who wrote from Switzerland, "I am glad to hear you have some amusement with your hard work. I am sure you made a fine Charles & looked right Royal."

Stoker was an instinctive fan, collecting idols in his youth like stones along the shore. Thomas Carlyle's *On Heroes, Hero-Worship* (1841) had impressed his generation ("Great Men, taken up in any way, are profitable company"), and Stoker more than most was overwhelmed by men of influence. But it was a mark of continuing immaturity that he never tempered the intensity of the emotional loyalties he felt for such men. He had a succession of ardent, if platonic, male friendships, enjoying what Kipling called the austere love that springs up between men.

In 1868 Dante Gabriel Rossetti brought out a volume of selected *Poems of Walt Whitman,* often labeled unexpurgated, for Rossetti had omitted those verses from *Leaves of Grass* that might offend "modern squeamishness," including the "Children of Adam" and "Calamus" poems, and even "Song of Myself." This so-called censored version and the American edition of 1860 found admiring readers at Trinity, where Whitman's "barbaric yawp" reverberated through dining halls, clubs, and pubs. Debate raged over the American poet's unorthodox themes of love and friendship, his descriptions of "fervid comradeship," "adhesive love," and "robust love." Whitman's poetry awakened the autoerotic in many male readers and frequently was read as a universal clarion call to homosexuality.

In fact, the images were often equated with democracy, as in these lines from "For You O Democracy," one of the cluster of forty-five poems that became "Calamus":*

> Come, I will make the continent indissoluble,
> I will make the most splendid race the sun ever shone upon,
> I will make divine magnetic lands,
> > With the love of comrades,
> > With the life-long love of comrades.

The sense of comradeship that bound together the debaters in The Hist and the speakers in The Phil and the quintet of vampire

---

* Critics today see Whitman as a prophet of gay liberation, a tormented homosexual who sublimated his feelings against a fabrication of womanizing and hid behind unproven claims of fathering six children. Whatever the truth, it should be remembered that in Stoker's time, the concept of sexual identity had not been developed; the word *homosexual* was not used in English until 1892, the year of Whitman's death.

hunters in *Dracula* appealed immensely to Stoker, who was inex-
orably drawn into a group of Whitman supporters led by Edward
Dowden, his English professor and a respected Shakespearian scholar
with liberal views. Dowden was not only a professor but a mentor,
the first since the Rev. William Woods. Dowden's enthusiasm for
Whitman aroused Stoker's veneration; Whitman's celebration of
friendships between men sustained Stoker's ideal of male bonding,
the indestructibility of comradeship.

On May 4, 1871, Dowden—whom Whitman characterized as
being of the English spiritual elite, someone who understood the
language of international democracy—defended Whitman at The
Phil in a paper later published in the *Westminster Review* after being
rejected by four outraged British journals. Stoker was there to open
the debate. Dowden told students that Whitman was the poet of
democracy, who had stimulated his intellect and his "whole moral
nature." The poet "never degenerated into anything lewd," Dowden
maintained, but cautioned that he knew "no writer of eminence
who had not done injury." To many young university men in the audience, the verses, specifically the "Calamus" group, were love
poems, and what they wanted to hear about was the comradeship, the
doctrine of manly love—feelings they perhaps had secretly felt or
known but dared not mention.

Stoker yearned to communicate with Whitman, but his fear of
offending (like his father's) made him procrastinate. Finally, on the
evening of February 18, 1872, he took up his pen and in a late-night
frenzy wrote nearly two thousand words to the fifty-three-year-old
poet. It was a momentous unburdening. The letter, the only extant
document from Stoker's youthful days, reeked of adoration and insecurity. "Put it [the letter] in the fire if you like," he challenged Whitman, "but if you do you will miss the pleasure of this next sentence,
which ought to be that you have conquered an unworthy impulse."

Referring to the chant from "For You O Democracy," Stoker
said he wanted to call Whitman comrade and talk to him "as men
who are not poets do not often talk. . . . You are a true man, and I
would like to be one myself, and so I would be towards you as a
brother and as a pupil to his master. . . . You have shaken off the
shackles and your wings are free. I have the shackles on my shoulders

EDWARD DOWDEN,
Stoker's mentor and Trinity
College professor, who rallied
students in support of Walt
Whitman's poetry

still—but I have no wings. . . . I am writing to you because you are different from other men. If you were the same as the mass I would not write at all. As it is I must either call you Walt Whitman or not call you at all—and I have chosen the latter course." Stoker never discarded hero worship; he was rooted in that youthful state when a favorite teacher's aura provokes restless longings not yet understood. What—if anything—should be surmised by Stoker's choice of words in thanking Whitman for the love and sympathy given him "in common with my kind"?

Letters from young men stirred by his poetry delighted Whitman, and Stoker was a memorable correspondent. He told Whitman how he had overheard two students reading aloud from *Leaves of Grass* and laughing at some passages. "They chose only those passages which are most foreign to British ears, and made fun of them," he wrote. "Something struck me that I had judged you hastily. I took home the volume and read it far into the night. Since then I have to thank you for many happy hours, for I have read your poems with my door locked late at night, and I have read them on the seashore where I could look all round me and see no more sign of human life than the ships out at sea: and here I often found myself waking up from a reverie with the book lying open before me."*

Be assured, he told Whitman, that "a man of less than half your own age, reared a conservative in a conservative country, and who has always heard your name cried down by the great mass of people who mention it, here felt his heart leap towards you across the Atlantic and his soul swelling at the words or rather the thoughts." Whitman had awakened Stoker's curiosity about the wonders and differences of America.

Stoker noted he was twenty-four years old and an athletic champion who had won about a dozen cups. "I have also been President of the College Philosophical Society and an art and theatrical critic of a daily paper," he proudly announced, before writing an intimate profile: "I am six feet two inches high and twelve stone weight naked and used to be forty-one or forty-two inches round the chest. I am ugly but strong and determined and have a large bump over my eyebrows. I have a heavy jaw and a big mouth and thick lips—sensitive nostrils—a snubnose and straight hair." (When it came time to describe Van Helsing in *Dracula,* Stoker echoed this description, giving the Dutch doctor a "hard, square chin," a "large" mouth, "sensitive nostrils," bushy eyebrows, and red hair.) He included a physical description because he knew Whitman was "a keen physiognomist." Whitman had been to a phrenologist to have the bumps on his head examined. "I am a believer of the science myself," Stoker wrote, "and am in a humble way a practicer of it. I was not disappointed when I saw your photograph—your late one especially."†

As to his personality, Stoker admitted to a "secretive" nature, an insightful appraisal for his age. It was a character trait he never relin-

* Stoker gave two accounts of how he first came to read Whitman's poems. The most accurate surely was in the 1872 letter, but when he wrote his recollections of Irving thirty-three years later, he minimized the event, noting only how an outraged student gave him *Leaves,* which he read with enjoyment under the spreading elm tree still standing on the college green.

† Phrenology, a system of physiological psychology often associated with bump-reading to interpret character, was popular during the first half of the nineteenth century. It was brought to Britain by Johann Kaspar Spurzheim, a disciple of phrenology's founder, Franz Joseph Gall. Stoker's appreciation included the entire body, particularly facial features.

quished. "I am equal in temper and cool in disposition and have a large amount of self control and am naturally secretive to the world," he confessed. "I take a delight in letting people I don't like—people of mean or cruel or sneaking or cowardly disposition—see the worst side of me. I have a large number of acquaintances and some five or six friends—all of which latter body care much for me. Now I have told you all I know about myself."

Stoker loved words. "I love all poetry, and high generous thoughts make the tears rush to my eyes, but sometimes a word or phrase of yours takes me away from the world around me and places me in an ideal land surrounded by realities more than any poem I ever read." Later, in his romantic novels, Stoker created mystical lands with craggy settings to control wayward characters.

Then, in an apologetic vein, he concluded: "I don't know whether it is usual for you to get letters from utter strangers . . . even if you do not read my letter it is no less a pleasure to me to write it. . . . You will not laugh at me for writing this to you. It was with no small effort that I began to write and I feel reluctant to stop, but I must not tire you any more. . . . How sweet a thing it is for a strong healthy man with a woman's eyes and a child's wishes to feel that he can speak so to a man who can be if he wishes father, and brother and wife to his soul."

Stoker never posted this letter. He intended to copy the draft over, but it remained in his desk drawer for four years out of a feared or repressed anxiety over revealing what should be concealed—a proper Victorian reaction, which finds pivotal outlets in *Dracula*. When Lucy writes Mina about her love for Arthur, she feels her candor out of control. Her words echo Stoker's letter to Whitman: "I do not know how I am writing this even to you. I am afraid to stop, or I should tear up the letter, and I don't want to stop, for I *do so* want to tell you all."

Meanwhile the Whitman acolytes grew apace, gathering influential supporters along with the usual nay-sayers. Then, on Valentine's Day 1876, there was a meeting of the Fortnightly Club, an organization of educated Dublin gentlemen. To honor the patron saint of romance, ladies were invited, and a Whitman paper was presented, according to Stoker, by a man of "some standing socially; a man who had had a fair University record and was then a country gentleman . . . and a brilliant humorist." This speaker confined himself almost entirely to the "Children of Adam" poems and, in Stoker's opinion, made a strong and incisive attack. "But he went too far," Stoker criticized, "in challenging the existence in the whole collection of poems for mention of one decent woman—which is in itself ridiculous, for Walt Whitman honoured women."

After this "gentleman" of note left the podium, Dowden debunked his theories and Stoker offered an impassioned rebuttal. "Spoke—I think well," he wrote in his diary before tumbling into a restless slumber. Suddenly he remembered the letter to Whitman and, fired by the debate, sat up in the cold dawn to write a second letter. He boasted to Whitman: "I had the privilege of putting forward my views—I think with success. The four years which have elapsed have made me love your work fourfold, and I can truly say that I have ever spoken as your friend. You know what hostile criticism your work sometimes evokes here, and I wage a perpetual war with many friends on your behalf." The intervening years had "not been uneventful," Stoker wrote, although he had "felt and thought and suffered much in them," but had "much pleasure and much consolation—and I do believe that your open earnest speech has not been thrown away on me or that my life and thought fail to be marked with its impress. I write this openly because I feel that with you one must be open." The four-year interval had tempered Stoker's prose; he would soon be thirty.

All Whitman's admiring letters had, he said, the "same impertinence, and pertinence . . . the same crude boy confidence, the same mix-up of instincts, magnetisms, revolts. . . . the curious, beautiful self-deception of youth." Shortly after receiving Stoker's letters, Whitman replied. "You did well to write me so unconventionally, so fresh, so manly, and so affectionately, too," the poet said. "I too hope (though it is not probable) that we shall one day meet each other. Meantime I send you my friendship and thanks. . . . My physique is entirely shattered—doubtless permanently, from paralysis and other ailments. But I am up and dressed, and get out every day a little. Live here quite lonesome, but hearty, and good spirits. Write to me again." Stoker wrote Whitman brief notes, but never again unburdened himself so intimately on paper.

Years later Whitman remarked to his friend Horace Traubel that Stoker "was a sassy youngster. What the hell did I care whether he was pertinent or impertinent? he was fresh, breezy, Irish: that was the price paid for admission—and enough: he was welcome!" The description of Whitman as "father, and brother and wife to his soul" delighted the old man. "Beautiful!" Whitman exclaimed, "he is youthfully self-conscious: sees things in their exaggerations! . . . How sweet, indeed! where there is love, why not? why not?" He told Traubel, "I call that an extraordinary occurrence: that he should have let himself go in that style: or [is it] all studied out—even the spontaneity? It all sounds easy and informal to me—not verbally stiff in the joints anywhere: I was, I am, inclined to accept it for just what it pretends to be. I may be gullible, deceived, fooled: yet I am confident I have made no mistake." Whitman was not mistaken. The letter of 1872 was free of repression, but it was a voice needing validation.

Stoker thought he was "writing to me," said Whitman, but he was really writing to himself. "I could not but warmly respond to that which is actually personal: I do it with my whole heart." Here Whitman touches on a complex erotic situation, a kind of phobia that regulates all male-male relations. Stoker was learning that entry into adult masculinity was also an entry into the fear of one's own femininity, illustrated so aptly in the scene in which Count Dracula dismisses the vampire women to claim Jonathan Harker for his own: "This man belongs to me!"

Despite Whitman's ill health, Stoker and Dowden were determined to entice him across the Atlantic. Tennyson had corresponded with Whitman and invited him to England to lecture. Dowden urged him to extend his stay and visit Dublin. Stoker decided that he and Dowden would share the arrangements. "Dowden was a married man with a house of his own. I was a bachelor, living in the top rooms of a house, which I had furnished myself. [He had moved to 30 Kildare Street.] We knew that Walt Whitman lived a peculiarly isolated life, and the opportunity which either one or other of us could afford him would fairly suit his taste." But Whitman's stroke in 1873 left him unable to travel.

With this news Stoker resigned himself to never meeting the poet. But he had autographed copies of *Leaves of Grass* and *Two Rivulets*, and later when he read Whitman's description of Lincoln's death in *Memoranda During the War* was inspired to study the American president and the Civil War. Stoker eventually lectured on the subject on both sides of the Atlantic.

Whitman's influence on *Dracula* was profound. As Stoker had written, Whitman was "father . . . to his soul," an image reflecting a strange puzzle, particularly since the vampire at times resembles Whitman. Each has long white hair, a heavy moustache, great height

WALT WHITMAN at thirty-five in 1854, the year before he published *Leaves of Grass*

and strength, and a leonine bearing. Whitman's poetry celebrates the voluptuousness of death and the deathlike quality of love. Particularly evocative is Whitman's poem "Trickle Drops":

> Trickle drops! my blue veins leaving!
> O drops of me! trickle, slow drops,
> Candid from me falling, drip, bleeding drops,
> From wounds made to free you whence you were prison'd
> From my face, from my forehead and lips,
> From my breast, from within where I was conceal'd, press forth red
>     drops, confession drops,
> Stain every page, stain every song I sing, every word I say, bloody
>     drops . . .

Similar images vividly explode in *Dracula,* daring the reader to admit: sex is worth dying for.

## Chapter 3

# DRAMA CRITIC

S toker read the hoardings announcing Irving's return to
Dublin in 1871 as Digby Grant in the Vaudeville Company's
staging of James Albery's comedy *Two Roses.* He queued up
outside the Royal for his pit seat and saw the play three times. Irving
built his characterization on Chevalier Wykoff, a Philadelphian of
eccentric parts who was a former agent for Napoleon III. The actor
copied the aging dandy right down to his flamboyant smoking cap
with a trailing yellow tassel, a sartorial touch that marked "that epoch
in the history of ridiculous dress out of which in sheer revulsion of
artistic feeling came the Pre-Raphaelite movement," Stoker archly
observed.

Irving's days as a provincial player were at an end. On his return
to London, an American from Baltimore with the exceptional name
of Colonel Hezekiah Linthicum Bateman leased the Lyceum as a
showcase for his four daughters and hired him as the leading man.
Irving convinced Batemen to produce *The Bells,* adapted from the
French play *Le Juif Polonais* (The Polish Jew), by Erckmann-Chatrian,
the story of a respectable Alsatian mayor, Mathias, who kills a Jew for
his money and, although unsuspected, is haunted by the sound of the
bells on his victim's sleigh. On November 25, 1871, Irving's Mathias
electrified the first-night audience, catapulting him to stardom. It was
a role forever linked with his name.

The curtain rises on the interior of an Alsatian inn. A woman
knits, men drink and brood, the fire blazes. Outside snow falls. There

is a sinister foreboding. Suddenly the gale breaks a window, shattering a tray of glasses. The door opens and Mathias enters in a long, snow-flecked cloak, otter-skin cap, and gaiters and spurs, carrying a large riding whip.

"It is I! It is I! At last! At last!" After these opening lines the play's tension never relaxes.

"We were telling the burgomaster," a character says, "we haven't

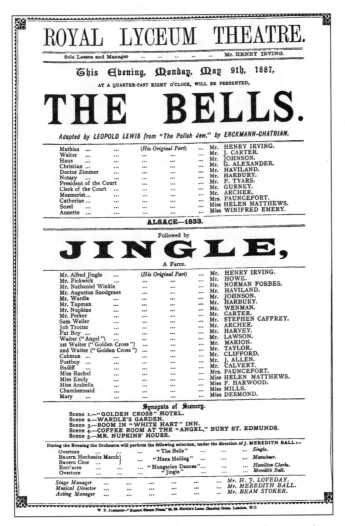

*THE BELLS.* Stoker watched Henry Irving perform Mathias, the role most associated with his name, 778 times.

seen such severe weather as this since what is called the Polish Jew's winter."

"Oh, you were talking about that were you?" replies Mathias. "Talking about that, eh."

The sound of jangling bells is heard offstage but only by the audience. Mathias reacts with a haunted look, communicating the horror of his hallucination. "The bells, the bells," he cries. "Don't you hear, the sound of sledgebells on the road?" The bells haunt Mathias until the last act, practically a monologue, when he has a nightmare in which a sinister mesmerist puts him into a trance before a tribunal of judges: he blurts out the truth before his horrified family at his bedside and dies from self-induced terror.

Watching *The Bells* was a cathartic experience for middle-class Victorian audiences, who related to a person like themselves (rather than someone rich or poor) being thrust into villainy for his family's sake and then losing out to a guilty conscience. It was a rip-roaring sermon. Stoker, who would see Irving perform Mathias hundreds of times, never forgot that first glimpse of "terror, the greed in his face." Everything about the performance was "so wonderful, powerful and weird."

Stoker saw in Irving a Promethean presence, an actor who radiated a mesmerizing power. He raved to his friends that Irving surpassed Sullivan, even Kean and Macready. Digby Grant "took the town," he said. When again no reviews appeared, he sought out Dr. Henry Maunsell, editor and joint-proprietor, with Sheridan Le Fanu, of the Dublin *Evening Mail,* located in Parliament Street. Published from 1823 to 1962, the *Mail* was a bastion of Tory unionism, an anti-Catholic newspaper that articulated the ambitions and demands of the city's middle-class Protestants. In a typical jibe, it once ran a parody of an announcement from the Vice-Regal Lodge about a levee: "There will be a Rosary at the Lodge on the evening of Monday the 20th inst. The ladies and gentlemen who attend are requested to bring their own beads." To be sure, anti-Catholic attitudes sold one-penny papers.

It was the appropriate newspaper, however, for Stoker to seek redress from for Irving. It was then the custom to have reviews written by the regular staff; there were no specialists and no budget to pay them. Stoker gladly accepted an unpaid position as drama critic, with no byline (the standard policy) and no editorial interference; he was allowed to direct public attention where he wanted. His first review was of Goldsmith's *She Stoops to Conquer,* which opened the Gaiety Theatre on November 27, 1871. For the next five years his unsigned reviews appeared under the heading "Public Entertainments" in the oversize four-page broadsheet.

Clerking at Dublin Castle passed the days, and work on his master's degree in pure mathematics bogged down, eventually taking three years to complete. More and more, Stoker drew oxygen from the theatre. It was splendid to walk along the River Liffey, turning into Hawkins Street for an opening night at the Royal. As the *Mail*'s critic on the aisle, he visited backstage, attended opening-night parties, chatted with the cast. He studied Shakespeare and always read the play before reviewing a production. He was the most educated drama critic in Dublin, and found his power addictive. Had Shaw and Stoker met at this time they would have shared common interests. Also left behind in Dublin by a wandering family, Shaw had taken refuge not in the theatre but in the music that once filled his Hatch Street home. He learned to play on his mother's discarded piano and taught himself the technical knowledge necessary to be the music critic he would first become in London.

Stoker abandoned acting and gave up auditioning for minor parts in university productions to linger around backstage, learning how the gaslight men created chiaroscuro moods, watching the artists paint scenic drop cloths. He discerned hidden critical insights and felt secure giving fatherly advice to nervous young actresses. He inhaled the theatre's fragrances, the pungent odors mingling with the redolent: the mildewed velvet curtains, the chalky face powder, the vinegary fish suppers, the pomades of jonquil and jasmine. He discovered a backstage family with whom he felt important and accepted.

Reports of this seduction reached the Stokers in Europe, where their transient life never kept them in one place for long. Their letters arrived from Switzerland and France, and in the winter from Italy, where they went for Abraham's health. Little is known of Charlotte's activities beyond shepherding her family from one place to another. Life was now filled with modest *pensions* and frugal meals; there were few opportunities for reforming, although the family may have befriended other British expatriates as they exchanged English newspapers in the lounge after dinner.

Like other middle-class parents of their time, Charlotte and Abraham looked to the professions, not journalism or the theatre, as rightful careers for their sons. Nothing uplifting could be said about journalism, filled as it was with rowdy, uneducated louts, and the theatre was worse, with its Pandora's box of temptations. In their shabby sitting rooms Stoker's parents read their son's exuberant letters and worried he might be jeopardizing his civil-service career with frivolous pastimes. Soon a fatherly sermon arrived at Kildare Street, cautioning Stoker about actors, who were "very agreeable" but not "desirable acquaintances to those not connected with their own profession (if I may call it), because it may involve expense and other matters which are not at all times advantageous. Under the circumstances I believe such acquaintanceship is better avoided." An oblique warning, perhaps, against the temptation of pretty young actresses.

That the theatre lacked respectability was hardly news. Its tawdry reputation was attractive to those who, as his father warned, were willing to risk "moral infection." No matter how talented actresses were, they were little better than prostitutes, despised by decent people. And actors? They were clowns, no more important than jesters had been to kings and queens. Not until 1824 was the 250-year-old law classifying actors as "rogues" and "vagabonds"* erased from the statutes. Half a century later respectability was not even a consideration. As late as 1898 Clement Scott, the Lyceum's official praiser, wrote that it was "nearly impossible for a woman to remain pure who adopts the stage as a profession . . . there is no school on earth so bad for the formation of character."

---

* The first Vagrant Law relating to "rogues, vagabonds and sturdie beggars" passed in 1572, included players and wandering minstrels not associated with a noble house or unlicensed. Other unlawful occupations were gamblers, palmists, jugglers, peddlers, tinkers, counterfeiters, scholars of Oxford and Cambridge begging without a license, and shipmen pretending losses.

Being a drama critic allowed Stoker to appreciate theatre on his own terms. Sitting on the aisle left, he learned to discern the best in acting, as well as to appreciate the importance of lighting, costumes, and set design. Even though he knew the texts, he brought a fresh eye to each performance. The legacy of his invalid years was an almost childlike capacity to marvel at the spectacle of life on stage, an enthusiasm shared by Oscar Wilde.

Ever since the Act of Union, theatres had hired London stock companies as cheaply as possible for the season. To attract an audience, a star (or couples like the Charles Mathewses, the Charles Keans, or the Herman Vezins) arrived one day and performed the next. With the bill changing up to six times a week, there was little time for a full rehearsal, and the visiting actor had to fit into the stock staging and be prompted with the right lines at the right time. Such substitutions resulted in more than a few mishaps. The harried actors often got the parts jumbled up, speaking Shakespeare's lines in the farce, or putting the farce into dramas or comedies.

Stoker found a group of friends at the *Mail* every bit as disreputable as those in the theatre. Shabby and smoke-filled, the newsroom was a raucous all-male bastion, offering the kind of camaraderie Stoker enjoyed so much at college, although of a lower intellectual order. Once established at the paper, he decided to instigate a major reform: an earlier deadline for first-night reviews. The *Mail* had one press run after midnight on a slow press that printed two pages, one side at a time, on a primitive contraption of wheels and pulleys. It was impossible for Stoker to see a play, rush to the office, and write a review in time for the next morning's paper. Under this schedule reviews of Monday performances were not being published until Wednesday. "This was very hard," he complained, "upon the actors and companies making short visits . . . and a sad handicap to enterprise and to exceptional work." Stoker persuaded the editor to move the deadline forward an hour on important opening nights. He was justly proud, as he put it, to have "helped largely to effect a needed reform as to the time when criticism should appear."

Reviews ranged from one paragraph for a pantomime to a whole column for Shakespeare. Stoker wrote fast and never shed his journalistic speed; most of his novels, with the exception of *Dracula,* were retyped first drafts. For a novice, his criticism was surprisingly knowledgeable and enthusiastic—even indignant. Always a wordy writer, he could be brief and incisive, as in his critique of Ava Cavendish as Juliet: "a wonderful illustration of passion, unrestrained by prudence, and of love, pure and unmixed with sordid calculations." Beyond critiquing a particular performance, he studded reviews with comments designed to educate and manipulate. When *Cymbeline* played to poor houses, he scolded theatregoers, asking that they appreciate intellectual drama. When those in the upper gallery or the "gods," packed "thick as herrings in a barrel," were raucous, he urged restraint.

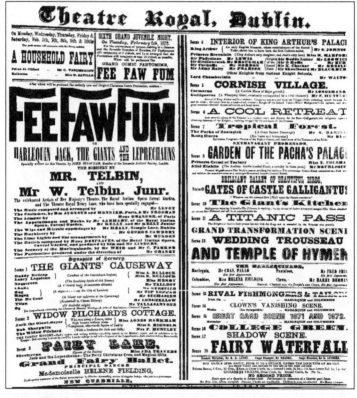

THEATRE ANNOUNCEMENTS ran on the same page as Stoker's weekly reviews.

When the front rows pushed toward the outer bar to see the stage, and the back rows howled and threw anything at hand, he sympathized about the difficulties of enjoying a performance.

During this time Stoker honed his father-confessor persona, an avuncular role he played throughout his life. "Uncle" Bram—an affectation he encouraged—was a good listener; actresses of all ages trusted him with their problems, their dreams. This demeanor shielded him from unwanted intimacies while promoting platonic relationships. The only letter comparable to his Whitman unburden-

## Public Entertainments.

### THEATRE ROYAL—THE PANTOMIME.

Saturday night's performance brought to a conclusion the seventh week of *Fee Faw Fum*, and it is no small test of the merits of the piece, as put upon the stage of the Theatre Royal, that it was played to a full and appreciative house.    When we consider that the dresses *alone* of the pantomime cost nearly £1,000, we can imagine at what an outlay Mr. Harris must have produced the piece in its present magnificence.  A manager who shows his willingness to trust to the public for the reward of his trouble and expenditure, and who does his best to please, is never disappointed; and we see no reason why Mr. Harris should prove an exception to the rule. ——

### BENEFIT OF THE CLOWN.

We understand that Mr. Harry Hemming takes his benefit to-morrow night; and we have no doubt that a crowded house will prove substantially how great a favourite he has· become in Dublin.  The success of a pantomime depends in no small degree on the    clown,    whose    province    it    is    to    arrange,

DUBLIN *EVENING MAIL*. As the paper's drama critic, Stoker wrote short snippets on pantomimes as well as discourses on Shakespeare.

ing was written to Helen Barry after her Covent Garden debut in
1872 as the Princess Fortinbrasse in Dion Boucicault's musical drama
*Babil and Bijou*. Six years Stoker's junior, Barry had a meteoric beginning, earning £15 ($75) a week—a salary actresses dreamed of
only in old age. Barry confided her determination to set herself "free
from misery. Fate seems inclined to smile upon me *now*," she wrote.
"I know there must come practical experience before I can hope to
be very good in my line of business."

The twenty-six-year-old Stoker replied in a fourteen-page cau-
tionary sermon on the theatre. As he had jousted for a felicitous tone
with Whitman, Stoker asked: "Since I have your permission may I
talk to you like a father. I am not a bit spoony [romantic] about you,"
he declared. "I say this lest you should ever misconstrue my purpose
in writing so often. . . . This style of beginning a letter may seem
strange but a correspondence which is neither business, amatory or
platonic requires some preliminary explanation." He dismissed her
inexperience. She had "risen like a rocket, and there is an old saying
about coming down like a star . . . you will have many enemies who
will decry your successes & exaggerate your failures." He urged her
to study plays as a whole, to research historical characters, to rehearse
as often as possible, and "to express real power by conscious passiv-
ity, to show your audience what you are about to do rather than simply to do it." He rightly advocated how "the potential is always
stronger than the actual."

Friendships, he advised, should be among theatre folk. "Whatever your inner life may be—and unhappiness never leaves a heart
quite free from pain—never forget that a *sorrow has not lost its sting till
we can look* at it with complacence & yet judge the present by the
standard of the ideal. You may think I am rhapsodising about the
actor's profession as a noble one, but I know quite enough of it to see
its many scary shadows." Speaking from his heart, he feared (as he
had with Whitman) that Barry might find him impertinent. "I know
that you know a great deal more of life than I can possibly know &
that you have felt distress that I have not heard of," he wrote, "but
sympathy can do a great deal to supply want of experience. I know
full well what it is to have a yearning for excitement, to feel a dull
aching void that cannot be filled."

Was lack of a romantic life creating that "dull aching void"? As an eligible bachelor with a decent position, Stoker was on many invitation lists. Tall and graceful, he was much in demand as a dance partner; his waltzing expertise was noted with approval at the season's balls. One partner recalled how her "heart used to jump in my dancing days when Bram asked me for a waltz. I knew it meant triumph, twirling, ecstasy, elysium, giddiness, ices, and flirtation!" He evidently made quite an impression, but there is no hint that he favored any one young lady at this time. He preferred to be ubiquitous but elusive.

It was a chilly November evening in 1873 when Stoker strolled into the Royal to escape the rain. The house was sparse with only a few hundred persons scattered about "like the plums in a foc'sle duff," he recalled. A visiting company was performing *Adrienne Lecouvreur*, a "somewhat machine-made play of the old school." The lead actress immediately absorbed his attention. "She was like a triton amongst minnows, very handsome; of a rich dark beauty, with clear cut classical features, black hair and great eyes that now and again flashed fire." This tenebrous actress, ten years Stoker's senior, ignited a friendship that lasted until his death, thirty-nine years later. She was called Geneviève Ward, but the name meant nothing to him. During the intermission, he admonished the manager that she was too good for such an audience. "She is fine; isn't she," he replied. The manager had seen her debut in Manchester as Lady Macbeth and signed her on the spot for Dublin. For the next week Stoker watched her in *Medea*, *Macbeth*, *Lucrezia Borgia*, *The Actress of Padua*, and *The Honeymoon*.

A fantastic story of abstruse success, her life would have played well as melodrama. Her father was the well-connected Colonel Samuel Ward; her mother's father was Gideon Lee, briefly mayor of New York from 1833 to 1834. They were in the vanguard of Americans who earned their wealth from financing the building of a new country and spent it in the grand hotels and spas of Europe. Geneviève was eighteen when the family wintered in Nice and she met Count Constantine de Guerbel of Nicolaeiff, a member of an old Swiss family that had emigrated to Russia in the time of Peter the Great.

In the Riviera's gilded ballrooms young ladies dressed in taffeta and tulle whispered and giggled behind fans while darting chaste glances toward the aristocratic young men, handsome in fitted, gold-embellished blue tunics, who had fortunes to share or fortunes to acquire, who smoked and gossiped and challenged one another in that hearty male way. Count de Guerbel had his fortune and desired only conquest. Breaking away from his colleagues, he crossed the gleaming floor, bowed deeply, and asked Geneviève to dance. She clasped his right hand, lifted an iridescent cascade of moiré silk, and was waltzed, twirled, and exhibited with such reckless abandon that the ample grandmothers, mothers, and spinsters, uncomfortable in their gilt chairs, awakened to romance.

De Guerbel asked permission to call on Geneviève, and following the protocol visits, proposed marriage. They wed in a civil ceremony that, according to custom, was considered a betrothal, and then parted, the bride-to-be remaining with her mother while the count went off to Paris to arrange a Russian Orthodox wedding. Months passed. Geneviève received no loving note from her rakish, impetuous count. Finally gossip reached the Riviera that he was planning to marry the daughter of the Russian ambassador at Naples. Summoned to France to avenge his daughter's honor, Colonel Ward rallied influential friends, who consulted the czar, who ordered the count to Warsaw for the wedding.

The bride wore black and held a lighted candle to become the Countess de Guerbel on November 10, 1856. During the ceremony her father kept his hand on a gun jammed into his military belt. Afterward the couple walked arm in arm down the long aisle of the Orthodox church to the entrance, where Colonel Ward covered the bride's shoulders with a black cloak and rushed her into a waiting carriage that hastened to the border with special exit papers. The astonished count was left standing on the church steps. The countess never sought a divorce and never made claim to her husband's estates following his death after years of debauchery.

Reinvented as Madame Ginevra Guerrabella, she became an acclaimed soprano, touring Europe and the United States. All her energies went into her career; all her love went to a succession of dogs; and from the time she fled Warsaw, her mother never left her side. During a stopover in Cuba, she collapsed with diphtheria, lost her singing voice, and was forced into drama. She studied with the incomparable Italian teacher Madame Adelaide Ristori, with whom she was often compared. Like the flamboyant Ristori, Ward spoke in precise rhythmic cadences, creating a bellowslike sonority that filled the stage.

"Will be a great actress," Stoker wrote in his diary. A few years after they met, Ward took a sabbatical from acting to study the French theatre in Paris. Letters begged Stoker to visit. Why wouldn't the *Mail* send him to Paris for her debut? she asked. Sometimes her mother added a coaxing postscript: "a plate, knife & fork are always marked Bram." As much as he wanted it, it is unlikely that he asked the *Mail* to pay his expenses.

Stoker continued to work at Dublin Castle, but considered friendships within the civil service too boring. Many an evening he hoisted a few pints with other *Mail* reporters after the paper was put to bed, but these chaps also bored him with their talk of women, sports, and politics. He stayed in touch with his Trinity classmates, the debaters and athletes he had known through the years, but even with them there was an awkwardness. They were growing up, courting and marrying, moving from apprenticeships to responsibility, while he remained a carefree theatre buff. He wanted to share his backstage gossip and anecdotes with grateful listeners, so he gravitated to the Saturday "at homes" of Sir William and Lady Jane Wilde, Oscar's parents.

The Wildes lived at One Merrion Square, the most splendid of Dublin's Georgian squares. Fitzwilliam and Mountjoy squares had quiet charm, but Merrion was poised and stately. Located near Trinity, the Shelbourne Hotel, and Stoker's Kildare Street flat, No. One was a nexus to the city's social and intellectual power. Only the depressed George Moore could have called it "melancholy Merrion Square . . . a land of echoes and shadows." A corner house with balconies and a staff of six, it was the most pretentious residence on the square. On the other side, at number 18 (now number 70), lived Le Fanu, Stoker's employer.

Oscar Fingal O'Flahertie Wills Wilde entered Trinity in 1871, when Stoker was in his final year. Stoker nominated him for The Phil, but Wilde was never very active. He despised muddying himself on the playing fields and had little in common with the athletic Stoker, seven years his senior, whose friends preferred the athlete to the aesthete and were a bit suspicious of the latter. Wilde's main attraction at college was his mentor and tutor, the classical scholar J. P. Mahaffy, but he was quickly bored with Trinity and provincial ideas. The Dublin quad was too small a pond for the Oscar who came to fame in London, and Oxford beckoned.

Stoker also knew Oscar's older brother, Willie, who was prominent in The Phil. Lacking creative talent, Willie was slovenly in person and dress, unlike his clothes-conscious brother, but equally amusing as a conversationalist. He drank too much, wore a full beard to differentiate himself from Oscar, did well at Trinity, and was called to the bar, but preferred the nonconformist life of a Fleet Street journalist. Lady Wilde once told George Moore's father that Willie had a first-class brain but Oscar would turn out "something wonderful."

At Merrion Square Stoker breathed in the latest cultural and political crosscurrents. Irish hospitality welcomed everybody and anybody, as long as they contributed originality and scabrous wit. The buffet table was excessive and constantly replenished with food and drink (Oscar said it was a restaurant, not a salon). The Wildes lived far beyond their means, giving these gatherings an air of personal anarchy. One well-fed guest recalled that Merrion Square "was a rallying place for all who were eminent in science, art, or literature. Dr. Shaw, the versatile sarcastic Fellow of Trinity and a brilliant writer, was frequently seen. H. J. Fitzpatrick, the well-known biographer, seldom failed to show his melancholy aristocratic face. Dr. Tisdall gave some of his delightful and mirth-inspiring recitations."

Oscar used this stage to test his dramatic entrances and exits, to refine his mezzo-voiced witticisms and *bons mots*. His eccentric parents were more talented than unconventional, but bizarre stories and gossip overshadowed Sir William's many achievements as well as Lady Wilde's contributions to Irish history. Arguably the more fa-

OSCAR WILDE as an Oxford undergraduate in 1876, when he was courting Florence Balcombe, whom he called Florrie

mous of the two was Jane Francesca Wilde, the chatelaine of Merrion Square. Dressed in gypsy costumes with outlandish headdresses and clunky cheap jewelry, she careened among her guests, speaking one or another of the ten languages she had mastered; she particularly enjoyed playing the coquette role with her sons' college friends. She was her husband's equal in wit and intellect—and a full head taller. Stoker would have agreed with Oscar's pronouncement in *The Importance of Being Earnest* that "All women become like their mothers. That is their tragedy. No man does. That's his."

"Speranza," her *nom de guerre* in the fight against the British, taken before her marriage, was her preferred name; her inflammatory anti-English poetry urged the Young Irelanders to burn down Dublin Castle, to make the British throne totter: she was at her best with vicarious suffering. Her lyrical attacks on British injustice found echoes in Oscar's *Ballad of Reading Gaol*. Her articles on how to blow up bridges, buy rifles, and make bullets were published by Charles Gavan Duffy, editor of the *Nation*. At Duffy's 1848 treason trial for publishing seditious articles—in particular, "The Hour of Destiny" and ("*Jacta Alea Est*") "The Die Is Cast," both written anonymously by Speranza—the author created a sensation by making herself rather than the defendant the fount of sedition. She rose in the gallery—all statuesque six feet—and shouted: "I, and I alone, am the culprit, if culprit there be." Trials were, rather ominously, a family addiction.

Dublin accepted Speranza as a second Madame Récamier. Staying through luncheon, dinner, and supper, guests of the Wildes wandered through rooms lit by lamps and candles; windows were shuttered and closely curtained even on sunny afternoons. Speranza needed a Bohemian atmosphere that encouraged bawdy talk. She informed one guest that the term *respectable* was never used at Merrion Square: only tradespeople were respectable. "We live in a bad prosaic age, but not in an age of good prose" was a Speranza aphorism, which Oscar later refined.

Lady Wilde was an odd mixture of genius and mischief, a mercurial role model for her sons and a phenomenon for Stoker, who admired—but feared—strong, capricious women. Her philosophy was succinct: an epigram was better than an argument, the paradox was the essence of social wit, and insignificant people should avoid anecdotes. Once when Stoker introduced her to a young woman whom he described as "half English and half Irish," she replied: "Glad to meet you, my dear. Your English half is as welcome as your Irish bottom." If a guest asked how she managed to gather such interesting people, she snapped: "By interesting them. It's quite simple. All one has to do is to get all sorts of people—but no dull specimens—and take care to mix them. Don't trouble about their morals. It doesn't matter they haven't any." One visitor suggested he bring a famous London newspaper correspondent. "By all means," said his hostess. "But a co-respondent would be a bigger draw. See if you can't get one."

Speranza enjoyed putting people in their place. Her greeting to the daughter of a third-rate novelist was typical: "Welcome, my dear. You resemble your intellectual father, but you do not have his noble brow. Still, I see from the form of your eyelids that you have marked artistic qualities . . . I hear you have a lover. This is a pity, since love puts an end to ambition. But don't on any account bind yourself until you have seen more of men." Visitors arrived at Merrion Square to see Speranza step out of the pages of *Nicholas Nickleby* as Mrs. Crummles, the tragedy queen.

One guest noted her peculiar dress: "Round what had once been her waist, an Oriental scarf, embroidered with gold, was twisted," while "her long, massive handsome face was plastered with white powder; and over her blue-black glossy hair was a crown of laurels. On her broad chest were fastened a series of large brooches, evidently family portraits, which came down almost as low as the gastronomical region, and gave her the appearance of a perambulating family mausoleum." The towering, overweight hostess, only thirty-seven at the time, walked like a ship at sea, the sails filled with wind. Still, Speranza's "faded splendour was more striking than the most fashionable attire," Anna, Comtesse de Brémont observed, "for she wore that ancient finery with a grace and dignity that robbed it of its grotesqueness."

This Byzantine atmosphere overwhelmed Sir William, who after a polite stay left the drawing room to his garrulous wife to join his colleagues in the study where they drank whiskey, discussed politics, and dissected the latest scandals, to which the host had contributed his fair share. A man of prodigious appetites, energy, and erudition, Sir William was at heart a sentimentalist with a roving eye and a need to prove his manhood. Short and simian, he was most unattractive, once crudely described as a "little creature, who, apparently unshorn and unkempt, looked as if he had been rolling in the dust." The Wildes were an odd-looking couple indeed.

As soon as Sir William retreated downstairs, Stoker followed; he found a corner chair and listened. Sir William had toured Egypt during the prearchaeological period, in 1838. He saw Cleopatra's Needle lying as it had for centuries beside Pompey's Pillar, and began a campaign to bring the obelisk to England; in 1878, two years after his death, the monument was transported—with many setbacks and much fanfare—to its present site, on the Thames Embankment. Outside a tomb at Saqqara he found a mummy that had been pulled out of its coffin, packed it up, and sent it home to Ireland. Stoker would use the mummy story as the framing device for his seventh novel, *The Jewel of Seven Stars.*

An expert on Irish prehistory, Sir William was the author of the seminal work *Irish Popular Superstitions,* published in 1852, which was completed thirty-six years later, with the publication of his wife's *Ancient Legends, Mystic Charms and Superstitions of Ireland.* Countless Irish authors before and after Stoker have been seduced by the shimmering Gaelic past of their country, still one of the most superstition-ridden lands in Europe. And vampire tales are very much a part of that legacy. The Dearg-due (the red bloodsucker) was said to tempt men with her beauty and then suck their blood. Irish fairies were bloodless, feared by children as bogeymen who would abduct them for their blood. Even before Stoker imagined life as a vampiric writer, he had a vampiric heritage.

Appointed surgeon oculist to Queen Victoria in Ireland in 1863 and knighted the following year, Sir William advanced new techniques for cataract operations, giving his name to "Wilde's cone of light" and "Wilde's cords." Notoriety followed nobility. Before his marriage Sir William had fathered three illegitimate children (whom

SIR WILLIAM WILDE, 1875. In the 1870s Stoker was a frequent visitor to the Wildes' house on Merrion Square in Dublin.

he acknowledged and supported), but he was perhaps ill served with his involvement in an unsavory court case. As soon as he had a "Sir" before his name, Mary Travers, a frequent patient, claimed that two years earlier he had raped her while she was under laudanum. After such an interval an allegation of rape could not be taken seriously, so Travers wrote scurrilous letters to the newspapers. In response, an outraged Lady Wilde wrote to Travers's father, a Trinity don, claiming his daughter was making "unfounded" charges. Travers sued Lady Wilde for libel, and the court upheld the charge (some incriminating letters were produced as evidence) but ignored the plaintiff's plea of outraged innocence, awarding her a farthing in damages. Sir William survived the incident—in fact, his practice increased as his randy reputation was celebrated—but the scandal took a toll on his health. While Stoker was at Trinity, he could not have avoided hearing a smoking-room ballad with this verse:

> An eminent oculist lives in the Square.
> His skill is unrivalled, his talent is rare,
> And if you will listen I'll certainly try
> To tell how he opened Miss Travers's eye.

Being the genial man-about-town, Stoker loitered backstage, traded jokes with fellow journalists, and accepted any and all invitations. Lacking focus or goals, he changed his address five times in seven years, moving from 43 Harcourt Street to 30 and then 47 Kildare Street, back to 43 Harcourt, then to 119 Lower Baggot Street, and ended up at 16 Harcourt Street. He read poetry and wrote; in 1872 he sold his first story, "The Crystal Cup," to *London Society.* It was a good time for short story writers with something to say; but Stoker, still edging toward maturity, kept recycling hackneyed plots and themes. No one would have called him an original writer. Not until *Dracula.* The seven years spent plotting that novel was an exceptional commitment, for he usually dashed off stories and novels to pay debts.

Early in the century, monthly magazines interested in opinion and the arts were founded as alternatives to the more intellectual reviews and quarterlies. Suddenly there was a burst of publishing, opening up outlets for general-interest writers. *Blackwood's Edinburgh Magazine,* founded in 1817 and affectionately known as "Maga," was considered the most prestigious. *Macmillan's,* associated with the eponymous publishing house, came out in 1856, followed the next year by *The Cornhill,* a lavishly illustrated magazine to be edited by Thackeray, and *Temple Bar,* which accepted light, sensational fiction.

In 1873 Stoker sent a story called "Jack Hammon's Vote" to *Macmillan's, The Cornhill,* and *Temple Bar.* In time he received three rejection slips. The following year he sent the manuscript to *Blackwood's,* with an ingenuous note admitting that the story had been turned down elsewhere. "I am anxious to see if you will add to the number," he challenged, enclosing the manuscript in a stamped envelope "to save you the trouble of doing so in case you will not read it." Stoker instructed the editor that a reading would take only twenty minutes, but if that was too much, he "had better return it unopened." A novice in query-letter protocol, Stoker emphasized insecurity rather than self-confidence. When nearly a year passed without a reply, he optimistically wrote: "Of course if you think of accepting it at any future time I shall be most happy to let it rest with you." The next month a rejection letter fell through the slot at Harcourt Street.

Doubtless there were other rejections before 1875, when three stories were serialized in *The Shamrock.* The third, called "The Chain of Destiny," establishes Stoker's favorite themes: romances, curses, and villains. Invited to a spooky gothic house, the motherless narrator is fussed over by a maternal figure who decides to find him a wife; in his bedroom an ominous portrait appears and disappears. A character called "the phantom of the fiend" auditions for *Dracula* (or *Macbeth*), uttering such lines as "Tomorrow, Tomorrow, and Tomorrow. The fairest and the best." With its uneasy dreams, visions, and ghosts, there is a tingle to the plotting: the reader enters the zone of unpredictability. The first Stokerian happy ending has the girl boldly proposing marriage. Derivative and overwritten, "The Primrose Path" recycles the old story of the Irishman who seeks a better life in London (this time as a theatre carpenter), falls in with bad company, drinks, gambles, and ends up killing his wife. In "Buried Treasure" the hero risks

*THE SHAMROCK.* Still known as Abraham, the novice author had three short stories serialized in 1875.

his life underwater; this story has the flair Stoker achieves often in short stories but seldom in novels.

The published son sent copies to Switzerland. "Some of what you had in *The Shamrock* I liked very much," wrote his sister Matilda in understated Victorian style. Sir William liked the stories (Stoker sent them to everyone). He was now writing unsigned commentaries for the *Warder,* a weekly Le Fanu–owned paper, which championed Irish Toryism. He applied for the position of editor of a new evening newspaper, the *Irish Echo,* and through his youthful self-effacing enthusiasm was offered another nonpaying job, though there he had the opportunity not only to write but to sell advertising. Nearly finished with his master's studies, Stoker juggled his gratis positions at the *Echo* and *Mail* with full-time paid clerking at Dublin Castle.

The *Echo* set out to be radically different: it would publish the latest world news and stock prices for half the price of competing penny newspapers, but without political news or opinion—not a prudent move in Dublin, where to breathe, much less to read, meant taking sides with either Tory or Catholic machinations. It was an inauspicious beginning. Shortly after the first issue appeared, on November 6, 1873, there was a name change to *The Halfpenny Press* (another journal was calling itself the *Echo*). By the time his parents commented on this precarious position, he had resigned. "It is very well written and managed," wrote his mother. Matilda added, "I hope when the 'Echo' is in a more flourishing condition you will be resuming your post as editor."

Unaware that his son's journalism was unsalaried, Abraham took a firm stand about the future. "I am sure the pay was never equal to the amount of trouble it entailed on you," he wrote, "in addition to which the Government have a great objection to any of their officers being connected with a newspaper, even thou' it may not at all be a political one." He also warned: "I know how very jealous these Commissioners are of a man doing anything outside his official duties." Abraham hoped his son would be promoted to senior clerk, the post he had held at retirement. "I was very glad to hear that Lane has gone into the church," he noted, "as his leaving will of course make you next in succession to a Senior place."

But Stoker did not want to stagnate for half a century at Dublin Castle as his father had. He reevaluated available options. In 1874 he planned to visit his family in Clarens, but stopped off in Paris to see Geneviève Ward. He never made it to Switzerland. "We were very sorry you could not come to us . . . how did you like Paris?" his mother asked evasively. Evidently very much. He told his father he wanted to give up Dublin Castle, go to London, and write plays.*

---

* Stoker's Paris visit led to the short story "The Burial of the Rats," which includes the passage: "In this year I was very much in love with a young lady who, though she returned my passion, so far yielded to the wishes of her parents that she had promised not to see me or correspond with me for a year." Stoker's previous biographers identify a "Miss Henry" as his love interest during this trip.

Abraham quickly put an end to this wayward plan. "You know that there are few men of your standing now in the castle who have a larger income," he wrote, "and you can also guess how many competitors there would be if a vacancy took place tomorrow in your office." Stoker considered applying for the post of Dublin city treasurer, but his father dissuaded him, pointing out that only an advanced Liberal or Roman Catholic would be elected. This was Abraham's last extant paternal advice: he died on October 12, 1876, at Cava di Terreni, near Naples. Stoker went to Italy for his father's interment at the English Cemetery; his mother and sisters did not return with him, choosing to remain abroad. Stoker's surrogate father, so to speak, Sir William Wilde, had died six months earlier.

Abraham Stoker had been a caring though detached parent, but by the time his seven children were born, he was an old man. Financial burdens had diminished his health, and at seventy-seven he was worn out with worries and fatigued with frequent changes of lodgings. Shortly after his father's death, Stoker dropped his Christian name and became Bram Stoker. It was another turning point.

## Chapter 4

# HENRY IRVING

"I am here to do Your bidding, Master. I am
Your slave, and You will reward me, for I shall
be faithful. I have worshipped You long and
afar off. Now that You are near, I await Your
commands, and You will not pass me by, will
You, dear Master, in Your distribution of good
things?"

—Renfield to Dracula

I
n the four years since Stoker saw Irving as Digby Grant, the
actor had fulfilled his promise. He was the talk of London. It
was said there were only two other men at whom people in the
street turned to look: Prime Minister William Ewart Gladstone and
Cardinal Henry Edward Manning. With his emaciated profile, dark
wavy hair, finely cut features, and a curiously cut coat with flowing
collar and skirt, Irving was an eccentric figure indeed. But was he
worthy of inheriting the mantle of Garrick and Kean? Or was he
simply a fine-tuned, well made-up melodramatic villain, better with
stage grimaces than with the pure sounds of Shakespeare? Irving was
a chameleon: at once strange and magnetic, graceful and awkward,
often melancholy, sometimes impish. He defied description.

On one thing, however, most critics and theatregoers agreed: he
had an odd way of speaking. He dropped consonants. Irving was
brought up in Cornwall, so he had a natural tendency to short *a*'s and
hard *o*'s. He was not a noble enunciator of Victorian English, much

less Elizabethan English. In *Macbeth,* the words "trammel up the consequence" became in his mouth "tram-mele up-p the cunsequence," with a sharp division of the two *m*'s, brief stops after the first, second, and fourth words. In *The Bells,* his Mathias was heard to say "Tack the rup from mey neck" for "Take the rope from my neck." Irving's grandson defended such pronunciations as deliberate rather than an uncontrollable impediment. "Rightly or wrongly," said Laurence Irving, the actor "strove to make words convey not only an idea but an emotion."

Caricaturists made fun of Irving's walk, attributing to him bent knees and back, or a dragging leg, like the aesthete in *Iolanthe.* Ellen Terry's son, Gordon Craig, said Irving's gait in private life was perfectly natural, but when he stepped "upon the boards of his theatre, at rehearsal, something was added to the walk—a consciousness, a springing motion, sometimes it wasn't really walking, but dancing. He was essentially artificial in distinction to being merely natural."

Irving should have chosen another profession, Henry James opined: "Nature has done very little to make an actor of him. His face is not dramatic; it is the face of a sedentary man, a clergyman, a lawyer, an author, an amiable gentleman—of anything other than a possible Hamlet or Othello. His figure is of the same cast, and his voice completes the want of illusion. His voice is apparently wholly unavailable for purposes of declamation." He was "picturesque," to select one word. "You can play hopscotch on one foot," James pontificated, "but you cannot cut with one blade of a pair of scissors, and you cannot play Shakespeare by being simply picturesque."

A more sympathetic observer, Max Beerbohm, praised Irving's "sense of humour—of sardonic, grotesque, fantastic humour. He had an incomparable power for eeriness—for stirring a dim sense of mystery; and not less masterly was he in evoking a sharp sense of horror." This latter power most certainly attracted Stoker, who wrote that Irving was a "histrionic genius" and deserved "not only the highest praise that can be accorded, but the loving gratitude of all to whom his art is dear!"

It was perfect timing when the actor returned to Dublin to play
Hamlet in 1876. Fatherless and patronless, Stoker needed a new hero,
and Irving was there at the optimal emotional moment. Fate, as
Charlotte had often told her son, was not to be ignored. Refined in
London, this realistic—but controversial—Hamlet mesmerized
Stoker. "Irving is in face and form," he wrote in the *Mail,* "of a type
of strongly expressed individuality such as Hogarth has touched
upon in his comparison of 'character and caricatura.' " Irving's physical appearance, he continued, "sets him at once above his fellows as
no common man; but his physique is somewhat too weak for the
heavy work which he has to go through. Thus at times there is a vari-
ance between voice and gesture, or expression which is manifestly
due to want of physical power . . . the voice lacks power to be strong
in some tones, and in moments of passion the speech loses its clear-
ness and becomes somewhat inarticulate."

As this review illustrates, Stoker was not blinded to Irving's flaws.
He criticized the actor's willingness to appear before the curtain after
every act. "He would do well to refuse to answer such calls, as they
detract from the dignity of the character which he acts." But Irving
never took this advice, from Stoker or anyone else. Applause was his
addiction and his abuse.

Still, the review pleased Irving, and he invited Stoker to dine
with him that night in his suite at the Shelbourne Hotel. Irving con-
gratulated the young critic for his astuteness in recognizing how he
played Hamlet as a mystic. They talked until daybreak, forging an almost sacred bond. By the time Stoker reviewed *Hamlet* for the third
time, he was searching for imperfections, finally criticizing how the
king took off his crown and turned his back to Hamlet to await
death: too convenient, too ordinary a stage direction. He said it reminded him of the old nursery rhyme "Dilly, dilly, dilly ducks, come
and be killed." By way of doggerel, Stoker had paraded his wit, but
he was also sending messages to Irving that he had standards.

When they dined again the next evening, Irving said he wanted
to give Stoker a special gift. The tribute was a recitation of Thomas
Hood's poem *The Dream of Eugene Aram.* Most Victorian schoolboys
orated this story of greed, death, and retribution in drafty school
halls, but Irving performed in the intimate warmth of a hotel suite

with an audience of twelve men in evening dress. Aram was an English eccentric, a mild-mannered schoolteacher who kills a feeble old man for his gold and dumps his body in the river. When the corpse is uncovered after the riverbed dries, he hides it again under mounds of leaves, only to have the wind scatter them away, as if the very forces of nature conspired to expose his crime. Finally, after agonies of remorse, Aram gives himself up to the law and the hangman. A crescendo of the melodramatic morals so dear to teachers, the confession includes the lines:

> Two sudden blows with a ragged stick,
>     And one with a heavy stone,
> One hurried gash with a hasty knife,—
>     And then the deed was done:
> There was nothing lying at my foot
>     But lifeless flesh and bone!
>
> Nothing but lifeless flesh and bone,
>     That could not do me ill;
> And yet I fear'd him all the more,
>     For lying there so still:
> There was a manhood in his look,
>     That murder could not kill!

In acting out the battering of the old man, a frenzied Irving tore the white necktie from his throat without realizing what he was doing. "The recitation was different, both in kind and degree, from anything I had ever heard," Stoker recalled, "and in those days there were some noble experiences of moving speech." Stoker was stunned to see Irving reach outside himself to become a murderer, to be "face to face with his Lord; his very soul aflame in the light of his abiding terror."

"So great was the magnetism of his genius, so profound was the sense of his dominancy that I sat spellbound," he continued. "Outwardly I was as of stone; nought quick in me but receptivity and imagination. That I knew the story and was even familiar with its unalterable words was nothing. The whole thing was new, re-created by a force of passion which was like a new power." Irving's incarnate passion was so intimate, Stoker said, that "one could meet it eye to eye within touch of one's outstretched hand."

At the end Irving collapsed in a swoon. There was silence. Then "something like a violent fit of hysterics" overpowered Stoker. "I was no hysterical subject. I was no green youth; no weak individual, yielding to a superior emotional force," he recalled. "I was as men go a strong man, strong in many ways," a representative of that "aim of university education *mens sana in corpore sano.*" Not surprisingly, Stoker's reaction mimics the veneration he first felt on reading Whitman's poetry: he had an impressionable disposition. "Seemed much moved by the occurrence" was Stoker's diary notation on Irving's reaction to his outburst. An expert in manipulating sensations, Irving had on this evening intruded on Stoker's immaturity. "The effect of his recitation upon Stoker," wrote Laurence Irving, "was all that Irving had hoped. . . . Though Stoker did not know it, at that moment the course of his life was changed." Gordon Craig believed that Irving deliberately cultivated the powers of hypnosis in order to exercise control over his fellow actors and the audience.*

Stoker was not alone in succumbing to Irving's power. As the actor built his empire, others surrendered their lives and careers to him. Stoker, however, believed he was special: he had found a friend. "Soul had looked into soul!" he wrote. "From that hour began a friendship as profound, as close, as lasting as can be between two men." Stoker indentured himself to Irving in the same way as Renfield bound himself to Dracula. At the conclusion of the evening Irving went into his bedroom and returned with an inscribed photograph. The ink, still wet, read: "My dear friend Stoker. God bless you! God bless you!! Henry Irving. Dublin, December 3, 1876."

---

* When Algernon Swinburne recited his "Dolores," he created such an ecstatic state that several listeners fell to their knees. This 1866 poem includes such vampiric lines as:

> By the ravenous teeth that have smitten
> Through the kisses that blossom and bud,
> By the lips intertwisted and bitten
> Till the foam has a savour of blood.

Trinity recognized Irving as an important actor. Stoker saw to that. Students and professors honored him with a dinner in the dark, richly paneled dining hall. Stoker called his performances "a school of true art, a purifier of the passions, and a nurse of heroic sentiments," attracting "a portion of society, large and justly influential who usually hold aloof from the theatre." This was not an official university tribute, but for an actor—in a profession still considered on the fringes of proper society—to be so honored by any academic group was rare indeed. When Irving replied, his dark saturnine eyes engaged the scholars looking up at him from long, polished tables.

"When I think that you, the upholders of the classic in every age," he intoned, "have thus flung aside the traditions of three centuries, and have acknowledged the true union of poet and actor, my heart swells. . . . I trust with all my soul that the reform which you suggest may ere long be carried out, and that body to whom is justly entrusted our higher moral education may recognise in the Stage a medium for the accomplishment of such ends."

Irving wanted acting to be as respected as medicine, the law, or the church, and he would make this happen. "What you have done to-day is a mighty stride in this direction. . . . We seek our reward in the approval of audiences, and in the tribute of their tears and smiles; but the calm honour of academic distinction is and must be to us, as actors, the Unattainable, and therefore the most dear when given unsought." That evening, as Stoker predicted, marked the beginning of a new era in the history of the Victorian stage.

On December 11 Stoker organized a University Night at the Royal. All five hundred seats were occupied in the protocol of academe: the university dignitaries in front, followed by civic leaders, alumni, and faculty; in the pit students wearing crimson rosettes trumpeted bugles and horns. As each fellow, professor, or well-known college character entered, he was cheered according to his popularity. When Irving made his appearance as Hamlet, the pit rose to greet him "with a cheer which somewhat resembled a May shower," Stoker said, "for it was sudden, fierce, and short, as the burst of welcome was not allowed to interrupt the play."

After the final curtain Irving returned to express his gratitude. The whole house rose simultaneously. He did not attempt to quell the demonstration: he relished adulation; humility was not in his lexicon. Then, as if on an invisible cue, the audience sat down and Irving presented one of his trademark farewells. "Every fibre of my soul throbs and my eyes are dim with emotion as I look upon your faces and know that I must say 'Goodbye.' Your brilliant attendance on this, my parting performance, sheds a lustre upon my life."

Wearing a fur-collared overcoat, black wideawake hat, and furled umbrella, Irving later emerged from the stage door, where a phalanx of students awaited. They had unharnessed the horses from his carriage, tied long ropes to each side, and were jostling one another for the honor of pulling the carriage up Grafton Street to the entrance of the Shelbourne. Hundreds more joined in, waving, running alongside the carriage, chanting "Irving! Irving!" and trying to catch a glimpse of the actor. Stoker had orchestrated no less than a coronation with a royal procession. Pedestrians took cover in doorways and side streets. When the students arrived at the hotel, Stoker said "cheers rang out across the great square and seemed to roll away towards the mountains in the far distance." Generous to a fault, Irving wanted to bring the celebration inside, but Stoker—not for the last time—dissuaded him from such imprudent, conceited folly.

More important to Irving, however, was that Dublin had repaid an old debt. In 1860, when he was twenty-one, he played Cassio in *Othello* at the Queen's Theatre, replacing the favorite juvenile lead, George Vincent, who had been dismissed for insubordination. As Cassio, a role Vincent never performed, all went smoothly. But two nights later his entrance as Laertes in *Hamlet,* a Vincent part, was greeted with whistling and stamping, tarryhooting and stick thumping. Irving never forgot the "howl of execration from the pit and gallery." He went through his part "amid a continuous uproar . . . groans, hoots, hisses, catcalls, and all the appliances of opposition. It was a roughish experience that!" Irving soon learned that Vincent had recruited a gang of hooligans to take revenge on the manager as well as his successor—the usual gambit when an actor was given "the bird"—but he was not mollified, even when the audience cheered him to the rafters after the final performances. An actor never forgets a hiss! So insecure was Irving that he waited until 1891 before admitting to Stoker that Dublin had been the place of his greatest censure; some believed this experience explained his obsessive drive for fame and respectability.

By the time Irving departed on the Channel ferry, Stoker had shored up many memories to see him through the dullness of Dublin Castle. One day the chief clerk interrupted his daydreams and called him into his office: Stoker had been appointed Inspector of Petty Sessions and was given a salary increase. This position involved traveling with the magistrate's court to rural areas where there was no sitting judiciary. Away for weeks at a time, he missed opening nights; reluctantly he resigned as unpaid drama critic of the *Mail*. But he was rewarded in other ways. He experienced rural Ireland and witnessed how farmers in the countryside suffered under the English landlord system. He watched hearings that ranged from stealing, unpaid rents, and the avoidance of taxes to dog attacks on cattle. Out of these experiences came his first novel, *The Snake's Pass*, published in 1890.

Everywhere Stoker traveled he found the courts lackadaisical: clerks made up the rules as they went along. He set about to reform and unify the system, gathering together diverse data into what he called his "dry-as-dust" first book: 248 pages ponderously entitled *The Duties of Clerks of Petty Sessions in Ireland*. Stoker read through documents accumulated since 1851, writing extracts on how clerks should deal with pawnbrokers and paupers, peddlers and lunatics, stray cattle and lost stamps, deserters and mutineers. There are numerous entries on the licensing of dogs, a reminder of the preeminence of sheep and cattle. Beyond its practical worth at that time, the book today opens a window through which mid-nineteenth-century Ireland can still be seen.

Stoker advocated uniform filing of papers and the use of dots instead of "O's" in money columns. His goal, he wrote, was "to formulate a code for the collecting and the collating of an immense mass of materials, the major part of which, having been once carefully examined, need never be referred to again." He urged future clerks to record their experiences and continue to systematize his work. Later, in *Dracula,* he would urge his characters to record their adventures: to explain the unexplainable.

Six months into this obsessive project, Irving arrived in Dublin. Following the rousing welcome given him the previous year, the actor pledged to return for a special reading in June. He performed extracts from *Richard III, Othello,* and *Eugene Aram.* Chanting students again paid tribute, this time chairing Irving through the streets. Being carried aloft in a chair, a time-honored university tradition, was neither comfortable nor safe. Worried that Irving might fall face-forward, Stoker advised him to entwine his fingers in the hair of the bearers on either side of him, to prevent them from moving in different directions. Irving probably pulled more than a few hairs to get his way. How could he have resisted?

On this trip Irving was accompanied by the Lyceum's stage manager, H. J. Loveday. Born to theatrical parents—his father was musical director at Drury Lane during Edmund Kean's reign and his mother, an actress—he was a solo violinist who had risen to stage

H. J. LOVEDAY, the Lyceum's stage manager, who never tried to abate Irving's spending on spectacular productions

manager and musical director at Liverpool's Alexandra Theatre before moving on to the Lyceum. A repository of theatrical history, Loveday could describe every nuance, gesture, and inflection of Kean's performances—invaluable information as Irving refined his interior style. This was the first meeting of what wags would call the Unholy Trinity.

The three men talked late into the night. Irving was in the mood to articulate his theories on acting. He rejected the views of Denis Diderot, who, in *The Paradox of Acting,* maintained that good acting required a complete absence of sensibility, a lack of feeling; he preferred French actor François-Joseph Talma's argument that a great actor needed the union of sensibility and intelligence. Irving told his friends he reached for "a double consciousness" in which all the proper emotions are available to him but he is "alert for every detail of his method." Those actors who bring feelings to a part excelled over those who "imitated" emotions based on observations and the feelings of others. Commenting on Polonius' speech "To thine own self be true," Irving argued that a man cannot be true to himself if he does not know himself, if he mistrusts his own identity, if he puts aside his special gifts in order to be an imperfect copy of someone else. Whenever Irving replied to a question about acting theory, he always quoted his primary rule: "If you do not pass a character through your own mind it can never be sincere."


Departing for England, Irving waved goodbye from the ferry railing, holding up a fox terrier called Trin, a gift from adoring Trinity students. Two weeks later Stoker spent his holiday in London watching Irving rehearse the melodrama *The Lyon's Mail.* They dined and talked endlessly. Being with Irving, said an ebullient Stoker, was a "positive quiver of intellectual delight." Knowing that Stoker wanted to publish, Irving arranged a meeting with James Knowles, the owner and editor of the prestigious magazine *The Nineteenth Century.* This was a curious—but brilliant—gesture for Irving, a man driven by self-interest, but he wanted an acting manager, not a frustrated writer. In the end Stoker was both.

At the meeting Stoker told Knowles he had written reviews, editorials, and short stories. The editor scrutinized him carefully, talked some, and then interrupted: "What are you smiling at?"

"Are you not dissuading me from venturing to come to London as a writer?" Stoker replied.

"Yes! I believe I am."

"I was smiling to think," Stoker said, "that if I had not known the accuracy and wisdom of all you have said I should have been here long ago!"

After a few more exchanges, Stoker inquired: "You are, if I mistake not, a Scotchman? And yet you came to London. You have not done badly either, I understand! Why did you come?"

"Oh!" Knowles quickly recovered, "far be it from me to make little of life in London or the advantages of it."

Knowles said the usual words of encouragement: send him some suitable articles.

Intellectually Stoker wanted to be a writer, but emotionally he was committed to wherever life in the theatre took Irving. It would be some years before *The Nineteenth Century* carried his byline.

Stoker and Irving were together again in Dublin when the actor returned for a repertory season in the fall of 1877. His Hamlet was better than ever. A "wild, fitful, irresolute, mystic, melancholy prince that we know in the play; but given with a sad, picturesque gracefulness which is the actor's special gift," went Stoker's review. They dined at Corless's and watched the wrestling matches in Phoenix Park. One evening after Irving had exhausted himself in *The Bells,* they supped alone at Stoker's Harcourt Street rooms. Irving entrusted his plans to Stoker: he would break his contract, lease the Lyceum, and be an actor-manager. He asked Stoker to renounce his civil service pension and join him in this lofty venture; he would share, the actor promised, in fortune and misfortune. Deftly, Irving stroked Stoker's vanity: he needed someone of his intellect, energy, and enthusiasm to take over the front of the house. "London in view!" Stoker jubilantly wrote in his diary on November 22, 1877.

The following June he was back in London for the opening night of *Vanderdecken,* written for Irving by the Irish playwright W. G.

Wills. Based on the Flying Dutchman legend, which Stoker wove into the tapestry of *Dracula,* the play was too long. Stoker offered to stay over and put it right. That weekend at Irving's apartment they trimmed and tightened. Satisfied with their labors, they dined at the Devonshire Club, smoked, talked, and heard the chimes at midnight. Back in Dublin in July for a two-week tour at the Royal, Irving and Stoker were virtually inseparable. Stoker's older brother Thornley offered Irving the hospitality of his house, and at one point bizarrely asked for—and received—a lock of the actor's hair. For the star-struck Stoker, the hours alone with Irving were without equal: "We understood each other's nature, needs and ambitions, and had a mutual confidence, each towards the other in his own way, rare amongst men."

Stoker felt a deepening friendship while Irving saw the time as a probationary period, a time to test Stoker's loyalty and stamina. If Irving left Stoker with the impression that he would be the premier knight, he was manipulative; Stoker would soon learn the pain of sharing the limelight with London's most celebrated actor. Six weeks later Irving summoned Stoker to Glasgow and triumphantly announced that he had the Lyceum and could offer him the position of acting manager, better described as business manager. Stoker immediately resigned from Dublin Castle, forfeiting all pension rights. Sealed was a Faustian pact: Stoker to be sycophant and friend, Irving to be genius and autocrat. Stoker told his mother, and she huffed: "Manager to a strolling player?" When Stoker left Glasgow on November 25, 1878, after accepting Irving's offer, he agreed to be in Birmingham on December 14. Typically, Irving wanted more. Two days later, he wrote from Sheffield, "I would like you to be with me a week sooner than we talked of. Say Tuesday, Dec. 10— at Birmingham."

Stoker barely had time to conclude unfinished business and court a beautiful young girl. The concept of the brave and gallant woman as represented by Mina is as central to *Dracula* as it was to Stoker's life. He wrote about sweet but spunky women, even as he surrounded himself with theatrical flirts and viragoes. Speaking through one of his alter egos, Stoker has Van Helsing, in his curious Dutch accent, tell Mina how his life has been devoted to work, with little time for friendships. Meeting her had given him hope that "there are good women still left to make life happy—good women whose lives and whose truths may make good lesson for the children that are to be."

Professor Henry Higgins's lament "Why can't a woman be more like a man?" is answered by Stokerian characters from Mina to Miss Betty to Stephen Norman: all heroines with a woman's heart and a man's brain. Stoker acknowledged the existence of female desire in a male body, and in Mina illustrates the divisions of the human body and psyche into masculine and feminine components. In *Lady Athlyne,* he writes that "each individual must have a preponderance, be it ever so little, of the cells of its own sex; and the attraction of each individual to the other sex depends upon its place in the scale between the highest and lowest grade of sex. The most masculine man draws the most feminine woman, and so down the scale till close to the border line is the great mass of persons who, having only development of a few of the qualities of sex, are easily satisfied to mate with anyone." Stoker's concept of bisexuality was before its time, as was his depiction of assertive, independent women. Many of his novels pivot on the conflict between the illicit and the irresistible, evoking an underlying fear of women. Curiously, after *Dracula,* all the monsters in Stoker's supernatural hierarchy are women: sexual women with voracious appetites.

It is not known when or where Stoker met his bride-to-be, when their courtship began, when he proposed marriage, or whether she (like his heroine Stephen Norman) did the asking. Like so many *rites de passage* in Stoker's life, here there are mysterious gaps. But Stoker had altered his career, completed his first book, and "not least," as he put it in his Irving memoir, "got married, an event which had already been arranged for a year later." His former professor Edward Dowden, on hearing of Stoker's marriage (had he not been invited?), was nonplussed. The wedding was "a good surprise," he wrote. The position with Irving would give him "abundant matter on shaping an interesting life," and all his friends were engaged in writing dramas that "through your influence are to be acted immediately at the

Lyceum." Stoker, too, looked forward to wielding such influence, but that role would be forever denied him.

If Stoker saw himself as "the most masculine man," then Florence Balcombe was his feminine counterpart. Eleven years younger, she was the pretty but penniless neighbor who lived at No. One on The Crescent. Her dowry was ethereal beauty. Tall at five feet eight, with a patrician profile, gray-blue eyes, and fine brown hair, she was fragile where he was robust, talkative where he was shy, curious where he was distracted. They made a striking couple. Everyone thought her admirable, but like *Dracula*'s Lucy, she attracted too many promiscuous gazes.

The third of five daughters in a family of seven, Florence Anne Lemon Balcombe was born to Lt. Col. James Balcombe and his wife, Philippa, on July 17, 1858, in a house on the Falmouth moor, where her family lived when her father's regiment was called to India. "Lemon" was for her great-grandfather, and "Florence"—her father's generation had fought in the Crimea—for either Florence

WATERCOLOR by Oscar Wilde, inscribed on the mount: "For Florrie. September 1876. View from Moytura House. Oscar F. Wilde"

FLORENCE ANNE
LEMON BALCOMBE
as drawn by Oscar
Wilde, 1876

FLORENCE BALCOMBE as she looked at seventeen, when Wilde was
smitten with her exquisite beauty

Nightingale or the town of Floriana in Malta where the colonel was stationed in 1857.

Florence earned an exclusive place in Victorian literary history as Oscar Wilde's first infatuation. Wilde called her an *"exquisitely pretty girl . . .* just seventeen with the *most perfectly beautiful face I ever saw and not a sixpence of money."* They first met during the summer of 1876 during Wilde's vacation from Oxford's Magdalen College. Later Wilde visited Clontarf to read his essays, at Florence's invitation, and she fondly signed one note "Believe me ever yours." In August Wilde and his artist friend Frank Miles (who later drew Florence) took a fishing trip to Galway, staying at Moytura House, the Wildes' summer home in County Mayo. There they sketched the rainbow hills. A rather amateurish watercolor of the view from Moytura over Lough Corrib was presented to Florence on Wilde's return. On holiday the following May, he reported to classmate Reginald Harding that Florrie was "more lovely than ever."

Nine months before her wedding, Florence received a note from Bournemouth. In it Wilde recalled that she had sent him a card in Athens the previous Easter "over so many miles of land and sea—to show me you had not forgotten me." He regretted not being in Dublin, adding ambiguously, "The weather is delightful and if I had not a good memory of the past I would be very happy." When news of her betrothal reached him, Wilde gravely asked for the return of his Christmas gift, a gold cross inscribed with his name. "Worthless though the trinket be," he wrote, "to me it serves as a memory of two sweet years—the sweetest of all the years of my youth—and I should like to have it always with me. . . . Though you have not thought it worth while to let me know of your marriage, still I cannot leave Ireland without sending you my wishes that you may be happy; whatever happens I at least cannot be indifferent to your welfare: the currents of our lives flowed too long beside one another for that." In a Wildean flourish, he concluded, "We stand apart now, but the little cross will serve to remind me of the bygone days, and though we shall never meet again, after I leave Ireland, still I shall always remember you at prayer."

Florence asked him to retrieve the cross at 16 Harcourt Street, where Stoker lived. Wilde replied it was "quite out of the question;

it would have been unfair to you, and me, and to the man you are
going to marry." He suggested as "the only suitable place" her parents' home on The Crescent. "We should part where we first met."
As to the cross, Wilde told her there was "nothing 'exceptional' in
the trinket except the fact of my name being on it, which of course
would have prevented you from wearing it ever, and I am not foolish enough to imagine that you care now for any memento of me. It
would have been impossible for you to keep it." A postscript alludes
to the nature of the meeting, which offended Wilde. "I am sorry that
you should appear to think," he wrote, "that I desired any clandes-
tine '*meeting:*' after all, I find you know me very little."

Florence asked for the return of her letters. Wilde sent the "enclosed scrap I used to carry with me: it was written eighteen months
ago: how strange and out of tune it all reads now." The sour notes of
misunderstanding indicated that there might not have been a meeting or an exchange of the "trinket." (A gold cross inscribed with
Wilde's name has not surfaced in any collections; whereas a gold crucifix plays a critical role in *Dracula*.)

Wilde was justifiably miffed. Judging from his letters, he appears
to have been fond of Florence, although he surely never thought of
marriage. As an eligible bachelor he had little to offer: he squandered
the modest inheritance from his father on expensive tastes; he had no
focused ambition other than poetry, but as Yeats observed, "we Irish
are too poetical to be poets; we are a nation of brilliant failures." Indeed Wilde was a footloose undergraduate, whereas Stoker was a
civil servant with a career. The stern Colonel Balcombe, with five
unmarried daughters, must have appreciated the security of Stoker's
position as Inspector of Petty Sessions. Even Lady Wilde used Stoker
as an example of probity. "He never gets into debt, and his character
is excellent," she told Oscar, who might have retorted that he at least
was taller.

If, as Stoker wrote, the wedding date was advanced a year, Florence allowed herself to be courted by two suitors at the same time.
That she attracted both men reveals more about their attitudes toward women than it does about her character. Both were obsessed by
the notion of chaste womanhood, and she posed no threat to the ide-
alized mother figure they sought. Florence's niece Eleanor Knott

wondered whether her grandfather "sounded the retreat, or did Florence decide. She was always, I think, very level-headed. My Mother used to say in later years: 'If Florence had married him [Wilde], it (the 'downfall') would never have happened.' I am not so sure. No woman could have permanently curbed that restless mind."

In *Dracula,* Lucy writes Mina that she picked the lackluster Arthur Holmwood (the most prosperous and prestigious of her three suitors) because "we women are such cowards that we think a man will save us from fears, and we marry him." Perhaps Florence made the same choice. Like Lucy, she was desirable and unhappy with her social standing.

And so, in the austere, if fashionable, St. Ann's Protestant church on Dawson Street in downtown Dublin on December 4, 1878, nineteen-year-old Florence Anne Lemon Balcombe wed thirty-one-year-old Abraham—then known as Bram—Stoker. The honeymoon was forgotten as the newlyweds rushed to Birmingham at Irving's command (echoed in Jonathan Harker's postponed wedding to Mina when summoned by Count Dracula to Transylvania).

Arriving in Birmingham a day early (the sign of an eager knight), the couple joined Irving at the Plough and Harrow, "that delightful little hotel at Edgbaston," Stoker recalled, "and he was mightily surprised when he found that I had a wife—*the* wife—with me." When Irving was in Dublin in the fall of 1878, Stoker said they took drives together every day and dined at restaurants with Thornley and his wife and at friends' homes or Stoker's lodgings. Traditionally these meals were topped off by a discussion of the day's events, in which, as Stoker put it, they told each other "the many things which had befallen us in our respective spheres of life."

Was Florence unmentionable because Stoker knew of the bitter estrangement between Irving and his own wife, also called Florence? The story of how she had ridiculed his success in *The Bells* and he had walked out on her was common gossip in theatrical circles. Or was the omission merely due to the Victorian code of privacy, whereby only fallen women were discussed in the company of men? That trumpets did not precede her mattered little; she had chosen wisely. Florence walked through the columned portico of the Lyceum and entered London society.

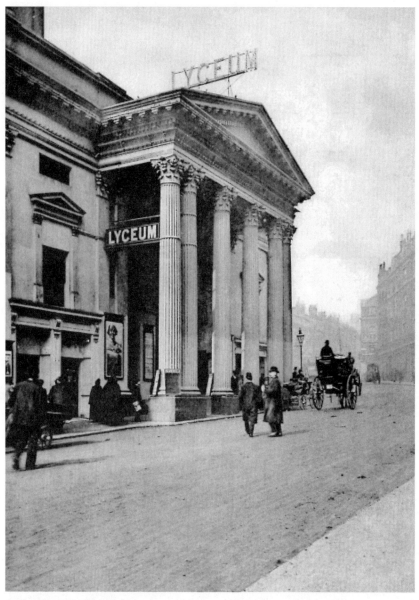

THE LYCEUM THEATRE as it looked during the management of Irving, Stoker, and Loveday, known as the Unholy Trinity

## 2

*London Limelight*

(1878–1884)

*Chapter 5*

# THE LYCEUM

The Stokers rented a top-floor flat at 7 Southampton Street, near the Lyceum and on the periphery of Covent Garden's bustling, noisy market. They had six unfurnished rooms for £100 a year. Planning to move her salon to London, Lady Wilde envied their find for its size and price. Anything Florence needed for her kitchen—fruits, vegetables, pots and pans—was available right outside the doorway, sold by some of the capital's thirty thousand costermongers. Stoker's weekly salary of £22 ($110) allowed for a housekeeper; but it was not the best residential neighborhood. Narrow streets leading from the Lyceum hid decaying tenements, dingy shops, and taverns. The street gutters overflowed with the odors of urine and grease, of vinegar and beer. The social armor of a four-wheeler or brougham shielded the middle and upper classes from the worsening social conditions. Carriages rumbled past the mullioned glass of shop fronts, scattering peddlers, pickpockets, prostitutes, and porters.

Dracula tells Jonathan Harker that he longs "to go through the crowded streets of your mighty London, to be in the midst of the whirl and rush of humanity, to share its life, its change, its death and all that makes it what it is." At this time London had more than three million residents; it was said that the city was home to more Irishmen than Dublin, more Scotsmen than Aberdeen, more Jews than Palestine, and more Roman Catholics than Rome. From all over England and Ireland more continued to migrate, exchanging rural and agricultural failures for urban and industrial challenges. Workers crowded the East End slums, areas hemmed in between railway viaducts, where some 80,000 transients found shelter nightly in commercial lodging houses notorious for unsanitary conditions and loose morals.

Almost a hundred miles of sewer had been built, but the Thames was still the main waste outlet as well as the main source of drinking water, contributing to frequent cholera outbreaks. Child abuse and child prostitution were widespread. Muggers and garroters roamed the streets. Humanitarians eased their consciences by proclaiming that suicide was no longer considered homicide. Gustave Doré's paintings depicting the East End's wretched conditions contrasted starkly with *The Illustrated London News*'s drawings of bejeweled ladies alighting from horse-drawn carriages for a West End first night. More than distance separated the deprived from the entitled. It was a vibrant city to walk about in, and unless accompanied by Florence, Stoker went everywhere on foot. One of his first stops was the British Library located in the British Museum on Great Russell Street, to obtain a ticket (as it was then called) for the domed blue-and-gold Round Reading Room, where recently published books such as Thomas Hardy's *Return of the Native* and James O'Grady's *History of Ireland: The Heroic Period* were available to readers.

The Stokers' arrival in the city coincided with the libel trial brought by the expatriate American painter James Whistler against John Ruskin, the acknowledged arbiter of British taste. Ruskin had attacked Whistler's *Nocturne in Black and Gold,* a moody night scene with fireworks. "I have seen, and heard, much of cockney impudence before now," Ruskin wrote, "but never expected to hear a coxcomb ask two hundred guineas for flinging a pot of paint in the public's face." A battle ensued to determine the nature of art and individual aesthetics. Dressed in a double-breasted suit of navy-blue serge, Whistler parried and fenced with the attorney general until he drew blood. Admitting that his painting had taken but two days to complete, he was asked: "The labor of two days, then, is that for which you ask two hundred guineas!" "No," replied Whistler triumphantly, "I ask it for the knowledge of a lifetime." The jury found Ruskin

THE ROUND
READING ROOM
of the British Library,
where Stoker did his
research. Every reader
had a chair; a folding
desk; a small hinged
shelf for books, pens,
and ink; a blotting
pad; and a hat peg.

guilty of libel but fined him only a farthing, which Whistler wore on his watchchain.

Frequently seen around the Lyceum, Whistler had painted Irving as Philip II in Tennyson's *Queen Mary.* When Stoker was introduced to him as a genius with numbers, the artist, then facing bankruptcy, asked for help with his finances. Stoker was flattered; he agreed that "no artist can properly attend to his own business." Stoker was ready to offer advice, but soon bailiffs carted away Whistler's furniture while the bemused artist served his guests pancakes with maple syrup. Whistler left for Venice to escape creditors, did a series of brilliant drawings there, and returned to London to find a new posturer in his place. His name was Oscar Wilde. Approving of a Whistler witticism, Wilde once remarked, "I wish I had said that." "You will, Oscar; you will," replied Whistler.

Stoker had left a castle in Dublin to enter a temple in London, a Grecian edifice with six towering Corinthian columns topped by three flaming torches. Originally built in 1771 for exhibitions, concerts, and other entertainments, the building was variously occupied by a public debating society, Count Zambeccari's air balloon, and Madame Tussaud's waxworks. Licensed as a theatre following the 1809 Drury Lane fire, the Lyceum staged some intriguing productions, including Mrs. Glover's female Hamlet. Also staged there was James Robinson Planché's melodrama based on John Polidori's *Vampyre,* called *The Vampire, or The Bride of the Isles,* which introduced the vampire trap: a spring-controlled floor opening or door cut into the scenery that allowed the demon to appear and disappear. The vampire trap surprised and terrified audiences and became part of stagecraft design.

Fire leveled the Lyceum in 1830. What Irving inherited was the rebuilt 1,500-seat theatre of 1834, in the block between Wellington, Exeter, and Burleigh streets. The Burleigh Street entrance was reserved for the comings and goings of the Irving-Stoker-Loveday triumvirate. When they signed the lease, in 1878, the Lyceum was the crown jewel of the Strand, surrounded by the Adelphi (home of melodrama), the Theatre Royal, Drury Lane, the Royal Opera House, and Covent Garden. Gilbert and Sullivan were at the Savoy, chorus girls at the Gaiety, coryphées at the Alhambra, and comics at the music halls. Arthur Wing Pinero and Henry Arthur Jones were the promising dramatists. At this time, Piccadilly and Leicester Square—today's West End—were distant from the new railway stations that brought patrons from the country; the subway, or tube, did not open until 1906.

After the Unholy Trinity inspected the Lyceum, they set about changing the mood. In their new decor, sage green and blue predominated, emulating the shimmering peacock; the ceiling was pale blue and gold; gaslit candles in wine-colored shades flickered off gilt moldings; escalloped shells shielded the footlights' golden glare. From the vestibule to the ascending staircase to the gilded auditorium, the Lyceum atmosphere was half museum, half church, unlike any other experience in Victorian England. "Faith is to be found more often in a theatre than in a church," Stoker observed. Formal dress was *de*

THE LYCEUM. A first-night audience awaits horse-drawn hansoms under the theatre's columned portico.

*rigueur* in the boxes, stalls, and dress circle, even though Henry James lamented that "these things testify to the theatre's being a fashion among a certain class, and the last luxury of a few, rather than taking its place in the common habits of the people, as it does in France."

The Lyceum programs announced that Henry Irving was sole lessee and actor-manager; Stoker was listed on the final page as acting manager. The actor-manager designation was a peculiarly Victorian legacy inherited from the inestimable David Garrick. Garrick, born in 1717 of French-Irish extraction, was called by his illustrious tutor Samuel Johnson "the gaiety of nations." An inspired Hamlet, Lear, and Richard III, he was followed by Edmund Kean, born in 1789, the illegitimate son of theatre folk. A relentless Bohemian with dazzling black eyes, Kean was known for using the old methods of pauses and dynamic modulations. In his play *Trelawney of the Wells,* Pinero calls

Kean a "great gypsy." Once he played the weak and vacillating
Richard II with the violence and passion reserved for Richard III; his
*King Lear* was the first in a century played with the Fool; his greatest
role was Shylock. Garrick and Kean died before the royal patent mo-
nopoly—whereby only two London theatres, Drury Lane and
Covent Garden, were licensed for "legitimate" performances, or
nonmusical drama—was broken in 1843, placing theatres on a somewhat equal footing.

Playwrights no longer had to placate government interests and
minor theatres had fewer restrictions, but managers faced the new
problem of competition. Theatres and audiences were segmented,
comedy at one place and tragedy at another, with classics at the
Lyceum. Irving never desired money for himself: he needed it to afford spectacular productions so that he—and all actors—would be
considered the equal of artists by the British establishment. To that
end, he demanded realism in acting and staging. He was inspired by
George II, duke of Saxe-Meiningen in Germany, a progenitor of the
modern theatre, who controlled all aspects of production and, like
Irving, created three-dimensional details. Working along the same
lines were Victorien Sardou in France and Augustin Daly in the
United States. Edmund Kean might have put minor characters into
armor made of zinc or tinsel, but not Irving, who insisted that real
food be served at banquets, real trees bloom in gardens, and real gold
leaf adorn regal crowns. That the theatre was capable of creating any
effect through staging, lighting, and costumes was Henry Irving's
most enduring legacy.

Irving wanted to impress the well-bred, not the wealthy. He wanted
respectability but needed applause, and was reluctant to follow the
path of Squire and Marie Bancroft, actor-managers who had run the
riffraff off to the music halls. He insisted the Lyceum maintain separate entrances and architectural distinctions to keep box holders from
rubbing shoulders with those headed for the pit benches or the
gallery. A classless theatre such as the Bancrofts created was dull, said
Irving. When Marie Bancroft (in frustration over being typecast as a
boy in burlesque parts) took over the rundown Queen's Theatre in

DAVID GARRICK
was considered the
greatest English actor
before Henry Irving.

EDMUND KEAN's
Shylock was the
model until Irving
reinterpreted the
role in 1879.

1865, renaming it the Prince of Wales's, she diminished the pit, raised prices, and scheduled drawing room comedies and dramas, thus eliminating an audience that spat orange pits on the floor, got drunk on ginger beer, and brought along broods of bawling children. Row by row the pit was stripped of its power, replaced by light blue stall seats covered with lace antimacassars. "Of all that has been accomplished in the way of rendering the English stage elegant and refined," observed historian Edwin Hodder, "both before and behind the curtain, the Bancrofts have been the pioneers."

Not everyone agreed. Many—certainly including Stoker, who had spent his youth in the pit—liked the popular theatre of Shakespeare. To understand nineteenth-century theatre is to understand the pit (short for orchestra pit). Located at the back of the stalls, it had immense power: it was the theatre's backbone. Any performer who said "The pit rose at me" knew success, and the manager had a hit. In the pit were students, artists, and writers, who came to devote all their energies to the stage, and they were quite simply a more responsive audience than the socializing patrons in the stalls, dress circle, and boxes. A spiked barrier prevented enthusiastic pittites—always ready to wave hats and handkerchiefs—from climbing into the sedate stalls where unemotional patrons waited for the play to resume. Any variation in pit management triggered a riot. Irving abandoned advance booking of the pit; "It did not applaud," he complained.

The fierce struggle at the pit door, the jostling to get into the worst of the crush, was one of the pleasures of youthful theatregoing. "When ribs and breastbone were on the verge of collapse," recalled Shaw, "and the stout lady in front, after passionately calling on her escort to take her out—if he considered himself a man—had resigned herself to death, my hopes of a place in the front row ran high." Those who threw rotten vegetables gathered off the pavements of Covent Garden were in the gallery or the "gods," rowdies who waited for suggestive lines like Lady Macbeth's "to bed—to bed—to bed" and yelled "Go along, ninnie, and I'll be after yea." After queuing for hours, spectators rushed the doors and received a square metal medallion, which was given up at the entrance and put on a spindle for counting. Overbooking frequently led to fights. A common abuse was for the gallery doorkeeper to unscrew the knob at the top of the brass banister and slide down medallions to be resold.

But the Lyceum drew reverent audiences. On the opening night of *King Lear,* a critic noted that Irving (who often sandblasted Shakespeare) had cut so much that, "seated in the sixth row of the stalls, not far from the middle, I heard practically nothing of the mad scenes. . . . The audience in the pit and gallery cannot have heard one-fifth of Lear's words; and I know of no stronger testimony to Mr. Irving's prestige and personal magnetism that they sat still and silent and respectful throughout uttering no syllable of protest."

"Are you a university man?" an Oxford don once asked Irving, who claimed the hard stage of a country theatre as his alma mater. "No," he replied, "but I employ a secretary who was." A secretary? Not only did Stoker supervise the front of the house, where he directed a staff of forty-eight, but he also ran errands and wrote endless letters in Irving's name. He estimated that in his twenty-seven years with Irving he wrote at least half a million letters, an arduous task that transformed his once readable—though cramped—script into an undecipherable undulating scrawl.

Stoker, in fact, was *the only* university man at the Lyceum, but class-conscious London barely noticed: his were Trinity degrees after all, and the Anglo-Irish, although considered separate from the native Irish, were always looked on as outsiders in London. Stoker had a proper British accent, but often put on a Milesian brogue, for he believed with Shaw that "it is a distinction to be an Irishman, and accordingly the Irish in England flaunt their nationality."

Stoker found celebrity—even reflected celebrity—irresistible. Thrown into the upper strata of London society, he had more than a few moments of insecurity and panic. He was often short-tempered and had difficulty handling criticism, particularly from Irving, who burdened him with so many menial chores that he often felt as harried as he had in Dublin while working two jobs and attending university. In *Dracula,* the count's main interest in Jonathan Harker is his knowledge of English law, custom, and language, paralleling how Irving drained Stoker intellectually and emotionally. A close relationship between any two people, in fact, almost always involves vampiric exploitation.

Sadly, Irving never appreciated his colleague's flair for innovation, which made the Lyceum such an efficient operation. Stoker was the first to number expensive seats, which made advance booking advantageous. He stopped the practice of the house staff's upgrading customers' seats and pocketing the difference. Instead of the box office issuing complimentary tickets, he did so personally and had them printed on cardboard to resemble invitations to elite social events. By advertising upcoming plays, Stoker's management made possible the financial projections necessary to plan, promote, and sell a season— rather than a show a night. In truth, his business acumen helped to mold the modern theatre.

For Stoker, the stalls, dress circle, and boxes were annexes to the Royal Enclosure at Ascot, recalled author Horace Wyndham, "and one almost had to be proposed and seconded before the coveted ticket would be issued." Indeed, patrons expected to be treated with the panache dispensed at private clubs. At the box office, Joseph Hurst, always in morning coat, kept a daily seating plan with the names of all reserved ticket holders, a time-consuming procedure not followed by every London theatre. Hurst was inordinately proud of it, for it prevented double booking and gave him the location of patrons in case of an emergency, or the need to deliver a telegram or return a lost glove.

Stoker was Henry Irving's shadow and called him the "Chief" or the "Guv'nor" like other members of the company. Irving was an intensely private man and revealed himself to few people. Max Beerbohm observed that he "seemed always to be watching, and watching from a slight altitude. I think [he] wished to be feared as well as loved . . . he was not going to let the 'good fellow' in him rob him of the respect that was his due." Control was critical, and he seldom let down his guard. At the Lyceum, he was what "Napoleon was in the midst of his army," reflected Gordon Craig. "No ruler is either fool enough or cruel enough to be an altruist. What he cares most for—cares solely for is the thing over which he has come to rule."

One of Shaw's snide asides observed that Irving "would not have left the stage for a night to spend it with Helen of Troy." From the time an uncle gave him £100 to buy the necessary stage properties (swords, wigs, buckles) for provincial tours, Irving had little time for anything except the theatre; but in 1863 he fell in love with Nellie Moore, a young actress in his touring company. They saw each other for five years, and marriage seemed a possibility when—and if— Irving could afford it. When she was twenty-three, recognized as the most promising and attractive actress on the London stage, an ideal mate and leading lady, the relationship ended. It was rumored that another man entered her life. In January of 1869, Nellie was gravely ill with scarlet fever, it was said, but a botched abortion was suspected. Irving stayed at her bedside until she died, clutching his violets, the symbol of faithfulness. He never stopped loving her, and photographs of the couple pasted back to back were found in Irving's pocket after his death.

During his estrangement from Nellie Moore, Irving met Florence O'Callaghan, statuesque daughter of Surgeon-General Daniel O'Callaghan of her Majesty's Indian Army, whose Irish roots went back to the tenth-century king of Munster. It was one of those chance encounters so dear to novelists. Irving, on his way to a party at the home of Clement Scott, then drama critic of the *Sunday Times,* went to the wrong house in Linden Gardens. Florence immediately recognized Irving and understood the mistake; she was attending the same gathering and asked him to escort her. Rebellious and frivolous, Florence became smitten with the romantic idea of an actor husband, particularly since the choice would infuriate her parents. Repeatedly, Irving refused invitations to dine at her home; his thoughts were only of Nellie. When Florence learned that the relationship was over, she resumed her bold overtures. News of his daughter's infatuation reached O'Callaghan in India, and he made the mistake of so many parents before and after him: he facilitated the romance by prohibiting future meetings. When Nellie died, Florence was ready to take her place. For Irving, it was a rebound marriage when they wed in July of 1869.

Irving's prospects were not the best. Even before marrying, he anticipated unemployment at the end of a touring contract. He man-

aged a villain's role at the Haymarket, but the play flopped, and all he
salvaged were a few good notices. He also noticed a change in Florence, hinting at a lack of understanding about the caprices of the theatre. Irving complained to her: "Nothing I think could so soon dull
affection in man or woman as indifference." Seeking reassurance, he
pleaded, "You at first lavished on me such love that if I became
spoiled—the fault is all your own. But you still love me as you did—
don't you my darling?"

A Victorian husband expected his wife to play a marginal, supporting role: to welcome him at the door, to run his home, bear his
children, and be a gracious hostess to his friends. After years of shabby
touring hotels, Irving anticipated relaxing at home after the theatre,
when he was at his convivial best. It is not known why Florence rejected this covenant. Perhaps she found the theatre crowd too loud,
too vulgar for her Anglo-Indian standards. Or if she wanted her husband to herself, she failed to understand that Irving's family was the
theatre: he needed his players around him. Whatever the reasons,
there was a breach, and Irving found bachelor quarters. When Florence gave birth to a son, whom they named Henry, the proud father
hoped for a more harmonious life. Early in 1871 she begged him to
return, but Irving wanted reconciliation on his own terms, and delayed their meeting until he had more money for a new home. En
route to Dublin in May of 1871, he urged Florence to have a photograph taken of their son, who now had a playhouse of wooden bricks
("I can see him seated on a little stool on the drawing-room carpet
trying to build his little castles on the floor," he wrote).

But Irving's dream of togetherness was not to be. On the night
of his greatest triumph, the opening of *The Bells,* Florence watched
tight-lipped as he mesmerized the audience. After the curtain fell,
everyone—from the pit to the gallery—sat in shocked silence, re-
covering from their participation in the violent departure of a tormented soul. Irving stepped before the curtain to accept round upon
round of applause. The pit rose and cheered. On the way home, an
ecstatic Irving put his hand on Florence's arm and spoke his
thoughts. "Well my dear, we too shall have our carriage and pair,"
echoing an earlier pledge of Edmund Kean following his triumph as
Shylock. As the story goes, Florence lashed out, demanding: "Are you

going on making a fool of yourself like this all your life?" Irving ordered the brougham to stop. He alighted, closed the door, and walked into the night. He never returned home and never again spoke to Florence, then pregnant with their second child. Irving impoverished himself to give her £8 out his £15 weekly salary. Not until Ellen Terry did a woman again engage his attention.

Ellen Terry was born somewhere between an exit and a curtain call when her parents played in Coventry in 1848. At eight she made her debut as Mamillius in *The Winter's Tale,* a performance witnessed with amusement by Queen Victoria. When she was twice as old, a radiant beauty with laughing gray eyes and an aureole of golden hair, she married the artist George Watts, shortly before his forty-seventh birthday. A precocious genius among British painters, Watts had effeminate good looks and an aesthetic manner that attracted patrons, in particular the determined Mrs. Thoby Prinsep, who collected people at Little Holland House in Kensington, where Watts and Terry lived after their marriage.

The hours spent posing for her husband gave Terry the regal carriage so admired on the stage, and the uncanny ability to become a setting, to harmonize within the stage. Max Beerbohm called her a Christmas tree decorated by a Pre-Raphaelite. A critic said that as Portia she was a Giorgione portrait. Victorian audiences wanted a stage that looked like a painting, and Terry brought to the Lyceum a well-developed sense of color, design, and the critical standards of the world of art beyond the theatre. She was "a dilettante," said a patronizing Laurence Irving, "upon whose judgment Irving came increasingly to rely."

It is generally thought that Terry's marriage to Watts was a sexless union; they separated after ten months. Terry returned briefly to the stage before bolting for country life and a six-year liaison with the married architect Edward William Godwin, with whom she had two children, later known as Edith and Edward Gordon Craig. Godwin was her great love; she doted on him with absolute devotion until financial problems forced her return to acting. The unappreciative Godwin left her and eventually married one of his students.

In 1877, Terry finally divorced Watts to marry Charles Wardell, an alcoholic ex-army officer and actor who used the stage name of Kelly. She called him "a man bulldog," and he provided the warmth and humor she craved. The marriage also made her respectable to the theatregoing public, but not to her parents. "It's a Princess marrying a cellarman," said her father. When Terry lived with Godwin, she was the target of gossip; through the Lyceum, she would rise to a kind of pure holiness. Oscar Wilde called her "Our Lady of the Lyceum," giving her a religious halo. It was prescient for Irving to have cast Terry as his leading lady; without each other, they would not have achieved their artistic potential. She joined Sarah Bernhardt, Helena Modjeska, Eleonora Duse, and Réjane as one of the foremost actresses of the time. For a star, though, she was temperamentally distinct, lacking malice or vanity—on and off the stage. She was the epitome of Stoker's good woman, and she had the same color gray eyes as Stoker.

Terry's success as Olivia in *The Vicar of Wakefield* had made her a popular London actress, and with some embarrassment, Irving recalled that at twenty-nine he had played an awkward Petruchio to the decade-younger actress's Kate. Many of Irving's "defects sprang from his not having been on the stage as a child," explained Terry, who had been a trouper for twenty-two years. On July 23, 1878, accompanied by his new terrier, Charlie (Trin had choked on a chicken bone), Irving visited Ellen Terry at her Longridge Road flat in Earl's Court. So reserved was his manner that Terry did not understand the purpose of the visit until final arrangements were settled by post: she was to be his leading lady, earning £42 a week to Irving's £60. Temperamentally, Irving and Terry were dead opposites: she light and gay, he dark and malevolent. But together they lit up the Lyceum.

She had grown up in the theatre, and to her it was a wondrous playground. Startled actors watched her slide down banisters, or catch hold of a bit of scenery being hoisted to the flies, hanging on with her lithe, strong arms until she was some forty feet above the stage. As a working mother she was overprotective and indulgent to her children, perhaps her greatest fault. She was beautiful but appeared ordinary; she was motherly but never looked maternal. An insightful woman, she observed—not without misgivings—how Irving

used Stoker like a servant. Stoker first glimpsed her talking with Irving in the passageway leading from the stage to his office. "Her face
was full of colour and animation," he recalled, "either of which
would have made her beautiful." She moved through the Lyceum,
he said, like embodied sunshine.

Stoker and Terry were the same generation (she a year younger),
and they became close friends. She was his "dutiful daughter" and he
was her "Ma," witticisms that perhaps softened the role Stoker often

ELLEN TERRY inscribed this photograph to Stoker, whom
she called "Ma." At right is the portly Fussie.

played as go-between. (Terry inscribed a photograph: "To my 'Ma'—
I am her dutiful child.") Their shared laughter floated contagiously
through the theatre—a bear and a nightingale at play. He said she
never struck a "wrong note," but conceded that she may have had
her faults. "She is a woman; and perfection must not be expected
even in the finishing work of Creation," he wrote, adding that "she
has to the full in her nature whatever quality it is that corresponds to
what we call 'virility' in a man." In *Dracula,* Stoker rewrites this concept. Van Helsing observes: "Ah, that wonderful Madam Mina! She
has man's brain—a brain that a man should have were he so gifted—
and woman's heart . . . one of God's women, fashioned by His own
hand to show us men and other women that there is a heaven where
we can enter."

It is odd that Stoker never dedicated a book to Ellen Terry, although he mentions her in *Dracula:* "Even Ellen Terry would not be
so winningly attractive as some of these grubby-faced little children
pretend—and even imagine themselves—to be." Neither did he
dedicate anything to Irving, although he named his son after him.
Such signposts were unnecessary: *Dracula* is all about Irving as the
vampire and Terry as the unattainable good woman.

# *Chapter 6*

# FIRST NIGHTS

"Do not fear, and do not rejoice as yet; for what
we wish for at the moment may be our
undoings."
　　　　　　—Van Helsing to Jonathan Harker

To inaugurate his Temple of Art, Irving planned a new production of *Hamlet*. He had taken the lease in September and
returned from the tour of the provinces only two weeks before opening night; he spent £4,000 on the renovations and the same
amount on the production. He demanded long rehearsals day after
day, night after night, doubling the pay for backstage crews. The costs
kept mounting and the theatre family kept growing: there were
ninety actors and extras, plus thirty offstage staff. Irving's disregard
for money unsettled Stoker, who noted opposite a receipt page in his
leather-bound account book the expenditures: £9,369.12s. By the
time the curtain rose, there was a bottom-line debt of more than
£15,000 ($75,000) against loans and box office profits.

Convinced that Irving's profligate ways should be concealed,
Stoker decided to keep the financial ledgers confidential. Only he
and Irving had access to the books secured in a large safe in Stoker's
office, and only Stoker possessed the key. The safe was the one object
he totally controlled. Not surprisingly, he wove it into his novel:
when Dracula is discovered in Mina's bedroom and destroys the
typescript compiled on him, one copy remains—locked in a safe.

HENRY IRVING
strikes a proud pose
following the
opening of the
Lyceum and his
triumphant *Hamlet*.

First-night preparations kept Stoker tearing about to oversee un-
done tasks in the front of the house; but he made time to be backstage, refusing to relinquish the behind-the-scenes exhilaration that
originally had lured him to the theatre. Known for surprise inspec-
tions (one actor said he could see through a brick wall), Stoker invariably ended up at the Green Room, where Irving held preliminary
readings.* For *Hamlet* he rehearsed in cloak and rapier and read
everyone's part—except Ophelia's. Ellen Terry watched as he threw

---

* In the Green Room—a name attributed to Cockney rhyming slang (on the green = on
the stage; greengage = on the green)—actors waited for their cues, gossiped, and postured
in front of the large mirror, always a feature. John Martin-Harvey recalled that when Irving made a rare appearance (his private entrance was shared only by Ellen Terry), a hush
fell on the group. "Humph!" he would grunt, and ask, "All right? Quite comfortable
here?" "Oh, quite, sir; very comfortable," everyone would hastily reply. "Behaviour was
impeccable," Harvey said, "and would have disappointed the kind of man who once said
to me in New York: 'Great times you have, I suppose, behind the scenes, eh? With the
champagne and the girls!' "

himself so thoroughly into the role that "his skin contracted and his eyes shone. His lips grew whiter and whiter and his skin more and more drawn as the time went on, until he looked like a livid thing." Irving was showing off, wanting Terry to understand that acting was not playing a part; he soon learned that Terry always played herself.

Irving demanded accuracy in every detail, no matter how trivial. Stoker recalled a rehearsal of the scene where Hamlet's mother, Gertrude, drinks the poison and Hamlet grasps the goblet to prevent Horatio's drinking from it ("Give me the cup. Let go. By heaven, I'll ha't"). When Irving flung the cup down, it rolled to the footlights; he watched it curiously, then ordered the prop man to have it fitted with bosses below the rim so it would not roll. He also ordered that the wine should not spill; colored sawdust would be substituted. "There is a sort of fascination in the uncertain movement of an inanimate object," Stoker remarked. Irving could not allow a rolling cup to divert the audience from *him*.

Ten days before opening night, Terry begged Irving to rehearse their scenes together. He demurred. Irving was building tension between the mystic Dane and his wistful Ophelia; at the same time he tested Terry's resilience, a technique he used with Stoker in Dublin. One day Irving showed an interest in her wardrobe, asking what she would wear. Pink for the first scene, she said, then amber brocade to tone down the color of her hair, and a transparent black dress trimmed with ermine for the mad scene.

Irving did not blink an eyelid, she recalled.

"I see. In mourning for her father."

"No, not exactly that. I think *red* was the mourning colour of the period. But black seems to me *right*—like the character, like the situation."

Irving asked her to present this idea to his production adviser, Walter Lacy, and when she did Lacy's face contorted at the word "black."

"Ophelias generally wear *white,* don't they?" he asked.

"I believe so," said Terry, "but black is more interesting."

The next day Lacy broached the subject again.

"You didn't really mean that you're going to wear black in the mad scene?"

"Yes I did," answered Terry. "And why not?"

"Why not? My God, madam, there must be only one black figure in this play and that's Hamlet."

Since Irving refused to deal with Ophelia's characterization, Terry visited a madhouse, where she observed a young girl staring at a wall. "I went between her and the wall," she recalled, "to see her face. It was quite vacant, but the body expressed that she was waiting. Suddenly she threw up her hands and sped across the room like a swallow." This movement and this expression became the starting point for her performance. Two days before opening night she cornered Irving after an orchestra rehearsal. "I am very nervous," she told him, "about my first appearance with you. Couldn't we rehearse *our* scenes?" "*We* shall be all right," he answered, "but we're not going to run the risk of being bottled up by a gas man or a fiddler," referring to the rehearsal risks. Irving wanted a spontaneous performance, but Terry, despite more years on the stage than Irving, deserved at least one rehearsal. What was Irving—who had reasons for all his machinations—plotting?

Unlike the great actors who preceded him, Irving never was a mentor or a teacher; supporting players were to be pale copies of him, not develop distinctive styles. Despite his sincere desire to elevate acting to an art, Irving curiously never felt a responsibility to give something back to the next generation. This attitude frustrated more than one talented young performer. But not John Martin-Harvey, who believed "Irving gave the actors he engaged every chance of making an impression in their parts, and it was because he saw that some were unable to do justice either to themselves or to their parts that he sometimes became savage. And the reason they so frequently failed was that they were taken out of a smaller *milieu* and put, as it were, into a large frame wherein they were either considerably diminished or altogether lost." That would not be Ellen Terry's fate.

When as a writer Stoker filled his tales with gothic palaces and ghostly portraits, he re-created the immutable images from his hermetic kingdom overlooking Dublin Bay. Routine binds invalids. The arrival of meals and visitors, the sounds of morning awakenings and night retirings, were the repetitive rituals of security and love on The Crescent. An echoing house portended emptiness. There should be a place for everything and everything in its place. Thus a dominant Stokerian literary leitmotif is ritual, which carried over into his work at the Lyceum. He made lists and devised schedules and did everything he could think of to make it an efficient theatre.

A lifelong squirrel, Stoker saved everything pertaining to Henry Irving. Envelope flaps with jottings survive, as do menus, tickets, passes, and programs. Deliberately he maintained a paper trail to honor Irving and the Lyceum but neglected himself. Jonathan Harker, Stoker's surrogate, is also a creature of habit: in Dracula's castle he winds his watch before going to bed and fastidiously folds his clothes. When Mina knits together "every scrap of evidence" concerning the vampire, she notes that "Dates are everything, if we get all our material ready, and have every item put in chronological order, we shall have done much."

Stoker's favorite lines from *Hamlet* were "If it be now, 'tis not to come; if it be not to come, it will be now; if it be not now, yet it will come—the readiness is all." The four words "the readiness is all" he called the "pearl amongst philosophic phrases." Behind the flash and glitter at the Lyceum, there was order: Stokerian order. The readiness was all at *Hamlet*'s first night on December 30, 1878, and for all the nights to follow.

Stoker checked first at the box office for any last-minute instructions on special guests or seatings. Then he inspected the theatre. In the stalls gaslight flickered on the rows of empty blue seats, illuminating the green baize safety curtain. It was an overpowering, quiescent atmosphere. Threading his hand along the cold brass railing, he inspected the pit, where he had spent years before moving to the stalls as a critic. In his best authoritarian voice, he called in turn to the ushers. "Mr. Jarvis." "Here, Sir," came the answer from the dress circle. He repeated the calls until the last usher from the top gallery replied. Every evening he followed the same procedure, he told his son, Noel, "so that, in case of fire or any other emergency, they will know my voice." Stoker enjoyed the utter power of his voice. He told Noel how it vibrated through the empty theatre, how it lingered as a last echo before the magic of illusion.

That first night, as the doors were about to open on what would become Britain's unofficial national theatre, the commanding figure theatregoers saw at the top of the Lyceum's majestic double staircase was Stoker, a towering column of black serge and starched white, elegant, poised, and nervous. On either side of the banister were the program attendants: small boys in Eton suits (the program girl was yet to come). Outside, long lines of carriages whose gleaming panels bore the crests of half of *Burke's Peerage* drew up to the portico. At the pit entrance, the queue was long but jovial as first-nighters warmed their hands over an open fire, jostling to improve their position for the rush to the door and the best seats.

At precisely 7:30 p.m., Stoker ordered the head usher to throw open the Wellington Street doors, turning calm to hubbub as the audience filled the vestibule. Stoker shook hands, smiled, bowed, and was gregarious to one and all. Although he knew few by name that evening, he soon learned to be obsequious to those who counted, those who could advance Irving's quest for respectability: he knew this was his mandate. Patrons recognized Stoker as the revered servant who had Irving's ear; they flattered one to reach the other.

When the pit was quiet, a thirty-piece orchestra played the overture to the first of a hundred nights of *Hamlet*. An opening at the Lyceum, a critic would later comment, was "theatrical court, with much the same *cachet* in the artistic, literary, and theatrical world as a presentation in court in other circles." Irving preferred a "good hearty house who have come to be pleased," but on this as all first nights the audience would revel in being critical. Peers and pittites knew their opinions would count when they gathered afterward at the Café Royal or the Lyceum Tavern. Those connoisseurs who had watched Irving create a mystic prince in his 1874 Hamlet would now see a mature melancholy.

On this evening Florence Irving was seated in the stage-left box. Although the couple were bitterly estranged and not even on speaking terms, Irving's offer of an opening-night box would always be accepted, and her presence, as she sat glowering like some hate-filled heroine from an Adelphi melodrama, never failed to unnerve him.

In the stalls Stoker seated his wife, Florence, and his brother George. In the prompt corner was the ever-patient J. R. "Jimmy" Allen, an ex–Indian Army enlisted man, who prepared the prompt books, timed scenes, and recorded the precise moment when each curtain rose and fell. Behind his stool was a hot water pipe where he would cluster potatoes at curtain time, turn them after the second-act curtain at 8:40, and continue shifting them with each act until his supper was done. Allen's love of ritual made him a favorite of Stoker's.

Irving said the *Hamlet* audience was with him from curtain time until curtain call, at midnight. Tennyson said Irving had not just improved upon his previous Hamlet but had "lifted it to heaven." Critics praised Terry's innocence, her vulnerability turned to derangement. The *Saturday Review* called her Ophelia (dressed in white sheeting with rabbit fur) "so perfect that every word seems to be spoken, every gesture to be made, from the emotion of the moment." At the curtain call, amid a litter of laurel wreaths and bouquets, Irving announced "he would do nothing that was not aimed to elevate his art and to increase the comfort of the public." But Ellen Terry was not at his side. It was said she had fled the theatre to wander along the Embankment (as some speculated, with the intention of drowning herself like Ophelia) but was brought back to Earl's Court, where Irving reassured her of their mutual triumph.

In fact, a trouper since childhood would never run from a curtain call. Terry knew the merit of her work and was never fragile about criticism. Was she paying Irving back for his detachment during rehearsal? Was she ill? Was she taking the initiative in an unconscious mating dance? Or was this story yet another Victorian myth? In any case, it is claimed the weeping Ophelia and the melancholy Hamlet became lovers that night. Ellen Terry's most recent biographer, Nina Auerbach, says this speculation marks "the chivalrous embarrassment that dogs biographers of Victorians. It seems indisputable that they played in their lives the flexible love that suited them more than their public union." Still, the impediments of their both being married, the difficulty of divorce by decree, and the stigma of Lyceum gossip kept them very discreet. They never broke the Eleventh Commandment of Victorian England: "Thou Shalt Not Be Found Out."*

Laurence Irving maintains that his grandfather sincerely loved Terry and "was prepared to sacrifice his jealously guarded independence for her sake"—even ask his wife to divorce him. But Terry had lived through one such illicit passion, with Godwin, and knew that the indignity of a divorce case in which Irving would be the guilty party was unwise. She was "level-headed enough to count the cost, financially and artistically, of such a scandal—a scandal such as had ruined Edmund Kean." Irving owed much to her intuitive wisdom. Perhaps there was little gossip because theatregoers found it difficult to see the stage Irving as a romantic figure when he clearly took his cue from Richard III:

> . . . since I cannot prove a lover,
> To entertain these fair well-spoken days,
> I am determined to prove a villain
> And hate the idle pleasures of these days.

Terry examines Henry Irving in her memoirs "as if he were a dream she could neither understand nor forget." She found his figure splendid, his face and aquiline nose noble, his smile delicate. Most of all she loved his blue-black raven hair flecked with gray, silken to the touch. Sometimes the ugly ear distracted her: "large, flabby, ill cut, and pasty-looking, pale and lumpy." She did not like it when he put brown makeup on his hands. That he was more interesting than anyone she had ever known made his indifference more painful. "He had precisely the qualities that I never find likable," she said. "He was an egotist—an egotist of the great type, *never* a 'mean egotist.' " Did Stoker or anyone else really know him? Terry said Irving never wholly trusted his friends and never admitted them to his consciousness.

---

* An earlier biographer, Marguerite Steen, bases her claim of their intimacy on a conversation she had with Terry in the actress's old age. Asked if she had been Irving's mistress, Terry said: "Of course, I was. We were terribly in love for a while. Then, later on, when it didn't matter so much to me, he wanted us to go on, and so I did, because I was very, very fond of him and he said he needed me."

Once Irving caught her sliding down the backstage banister and glared at her as if "she had laughed in church." Terry realized she was dispensable. "Were I to be run over by a steamroller tomorrow," she teased, "Henry would be deeply grieved: would say quietly 'What a pity!' and would add, after two moments' reflection: 'Who is there—er—to go on for her tonight?' " She wept, however, when Irving missed a performance during the opening run of *Hamlet*. "Stage very dismal," Stoker noted in his diary. "Ellen Terry met me in the passage and began to cry! I felt very like joining her!"

At the end of the Lyceum's first season, Stoker toted up the figures: they had taken in £36,000. Not an unworthy debut. A provincial tour was cancelled because Charles Kelly insisted on starring with his wife. To perform without Ellen Terry as an attraction would have been ill-advised, so Irving sailed off to the Mediterranean on the steam yacht *Walrus,* his first holiday in twenty-three years. His hostess was the remarkable Baroness Angela Georgina Burdett-Coutts, called "Queen of the Poor." As the favored granddaughter of the eminent banker Thomas Coutts, she inherited his wealth and a major share in his bank; she spent generously, building churches and schools and sending relief to the homeless of the Russo-Turkish Wars of 1875–78.

The baroness and her companion, Hannah Meredith Brown, doted on Irving. Mrs. Brown saw his *Hamlet* thirty times and left him a £5,000 legacy; it was she who pressed the baroness into lending him £1,500 for the first provincial tour. Through Burdett-Coutts, Stoker and his brothers George (known to her through Turkish relief work) and Thornley (through projects in Ireland) were admitted to a charmed circle, which included the fabled Dickens family. Before Charles Dickens's death, in 1870, the richest woman in England and its premier novelist worked together on various social programs, including a home for prostitutes, a sewing school, and a nursing school in London's East End. Stoker pays homage to the baroness's generosity by incorporating Bethnal Green and other East End locations into *Dracula*.

Among the *Walrus*'s guests were Thornley, signed on as ship's doctor, and Ashmead Bartlett, a dapper young man in his late twen-

GENEVIÈVE WARD in
costume for *Forget-me-not,*
her signature play, which
Stoker tailored to the
actress's lusty style

ties who had also worked with the baroness on charitable projects. During a moonlit evening, in an impetuous moment, Bartlett made amorous overtures to his hostess, never considering the consequences.* While romance bloomed for the baroness, Irving's thoughts never left his theatre.

Stoker was in charge of the Lyceum and enjoying every moment. The theatre was booked for a short run by his old friend Geneviève

---

* This May-September romance was the talk of London. The smitten baroness, planning a renewed life of travel and good works, swept this obscure young man along with her. They wed in 1881: she was sixty-seven; he was thirty. The marriage lasted twenty-seven years, until her death in 1906, and appeared not unhappy. He raised Yorkshire coach horses for hackney cabs until the automobile came along, took over his late father-in-law's seat in Parliament, and avoided the label of fortune-hunter: at their marriage—under a clause in the baroness's step-grandmother's will forbidding marriage to a foreigner—she forfeited a major part of her inheritance. Bartlett was American-born of British parents.

Ward, who for an opener selected *Zillah* by Palgrave Simpson, a play Stoker called "the oldest-fashioned and worst type of 'Adelphi' drama!, machine-made and heartless and tiresome to the last degree." When it closed after four performances, he advised her to perform a familiar role like *Lucrezia Borgia,* "to efface with all speed the recollection of a fiasco," and not to close for even one night, for "it will be a sign of weakness, theatrically speaking." The play was rushed into production while Stoker read into the night for the right script: he discovered *Forget-me-not* by Hermann Merivale and F. C. Grove, a drama that had been making the rounds for seven years. "With a little alteration in the first act, this would make a great success," he told Ward. She agreed, and he negotiated a five-year contract with a right of renewal.

Two weeks later Stoker's choice of material proved prescient. The part of the Marquise Stephanie de Mohrivart, a woman with a past, was ideally matched to Ward's imperious, passionate nature. She played Stephanie more than two thousand times, taking the play to the provinces and on tour to France and Italy, Australia, South Africa, and the United States. It brought her fame and a considerable fortune. After one performance Lady Wilde wrote: "You have waked me to new life." Everything had worked out brilliantly. Stoker as actor-manager had turned a discarded play into a *succès fou.*

Still, Stoker was never allowed to consider the Lyceum his. Every day a new batch of telegrams and letters arrived on his desk commanding changes. In August Irving suggested "it would be well to put our accounts into an accountant's hands. Let us begin with our eyes open . . . we shall find that our nightly expenses have been even more than we thought—really enormous." Stoker surely blanched when he read this: it sounded critical of his bookkeeping. But it was only Irving playing God. The new accountant was Charles Howson, a near-destitute old actor forced to eke out a living copying band parts at sixpence a time. In the Lyceum organization he was unimportant and paid only the smaller salaries and routine bills; but he was extremely jealous of Stoker, who refused to share with him the key to the big safe, which Stoker protected against all intruders.

Before the cruise Irving had planned to open the season with either *Venice Preserved* or *Othello.* But at the baroness's urging he de-

cided on *The Merchant of Venice*. She had many Jewish friends who
were offended by the way Shylock was caricatured on stage: Shylock
should have the dignity of a man like Sir Moses Montefiore, the phi-
lanthropist. At every port, the Levantine Jew drew Irving's attention.
Yes, he decided, Shylock should be played as courtly but complex, a
man of moods. So obsessed about Shylock was Irving that he refused
to finish the trip and was put ashore at Marseilles, where he caught a
fast boat-train to London. "When I saw the Jew in what seemed his
own land and in his own dress," he told Stoker and Loveday at dinner his first night back, "Shylock became a different creature. I began
to understand him; and now I want to play the part—as soon as I
can."

Stoker often said Irving had a "seeing eye" and was able to reproduce a "Chinese copy" of people he met, "every jot and tittle"
appertaining to the person. This he had done with the Levantine
Jews. By the time the sun rose behind St. Mary's-le-Strand, Irving
had roughed out designs. His enthusiasm would not be occluded.
With less than three weeks to opening night, everyone set to work.
Hawes Craven, the senior set designer, was instructed to change his
hat: usually the artist wore an old paint-splattered bowler, but in
times of pressure he would wrap a red handkerchief into a turban.


On November 1, 1879, Stoker triumphantly ordered the Lyceum
doors open for an unbroken run of 250 nights of *The Merchant of
Venice*. Shylock was the role most closely associated with Edmund
Kean, whose portrayal was considered flawless and textually accurate.
Irving's characterization broke with tradition: he did not wear the
red cap required for Jews by Venetian law, and he portrayed Shylock
as an intellectual, with gray hair and beard and a pale countenance.
As costumed by Irving, Shylock looked regal, with a dark brown robe
and tunic, a brocaded striped sash, a glint of gold earrings, and a
square black cap with a yellow bar. The snuffling usurer was replaced
by a heroic saint, which, to some, upset the balance of the play.

After one performance a blind man remarked that he heard no
sound of the moneylender in Shylock's opening line: " 'Three thousand ducats, well!' It is said with the reflective air of a man to whom

HENRY IRVING as Shylock. His was a regal intellectual, not an obsequious moneylender.

money means very little." Not everyone understood this new Shylock, but theatregoers took the opportunity to dissertate upon earlier Shylocks. "He was quite right!" said Irving of the blind man's criticism, and he improved the intonation of the line. "The audience should from the first understand, if one can convey it, the dominant note of a character!"

When the curtain fell on the hundredth night of *The Merchant of Venice,* the Lyceum celebrated. The stage was struck and transformed into a pavilion of scarlet and white, lit by two immense chandeliers with lily-shaped bells. Greenhouse flowers were everywhere. Stoker meticulously drew a seating plan for 350 prominent guests, including the earls of Dunraven, Fife, and Onslow and other peers, as well as judges, admirals, MPs, artists, writers, playwrights, and critics. Each guest received a copy of the play (as arranged by Irving), bound in white parchment with gold lettering. The official Lyceum caterers, Messrs. Gunter, served a seven-course meal; the menu was elaborately designed in the Japanese style, with pictures of leaves, kingfishers, and butterflies. An invisible quintet played during supper. Epicures and gluttons marveled at the elaborate feast spread out in the excess that Irving felt befitted his company.

Speeches followed dinner, and toasts followed speeches. When Irving proposed the queen's health, the voices of a concealed boys' choir sang the national anthem. The decanter of port passed to the

ELLEN TERRY costumed as Portia. She found Irving's heroic Shylock splendid, but not good for Portia.

left, and cigars were plentiful. Oscar Wilde insisted on reading a sonnet to Ellen Terry, extolling her beauty and wisdom as Portia. Irving realized he could stage galas more impressive than any London hostess's and more interesting than the Garrick Club's. The Lyceum became not only the most important drama venue but the most coveted supper invitation as well.

At season's end Stoker and Irving vacationed in Southsea, on the coast near Portsmouth. They were relaxed and pleased with themselves. The Lyceum's reputation was everything they had wished for back in Dublin. They chartered a small boat and headed out of the harbor; suddenly there was an explosion, and a column of water burst from beneath the boat, nearly overturning them. Stoker looked curiously at the dead fish popping to the surface. Unknowingly, they had sailed into a minefield being used for naval training maneuvers off Fort Monckton. The boatman urged a hasty retreat. Irving adjusted his eyeglasses and lit a cigar. "Why should we come away?" he asked. "We are, I take it, about as safe as we can be. The mines here have been fired and we don't know where the others are. Let us stay where we are and enjoy ourselves." So they swayed in the small boat while the mines around them were set off. It was an exhilarating time, and Stoker never forgot it.

Being anywhere with Irving was contentment for Stoker, who felt complete in his company, safe and protected. But Stoker's loyalties were soon tested. Florence was pregnant and none too happy about her bloated figure. Irving, who had refused to attend his second son's christening, stood as godfather for his namesake, Irving Noel Thornley Stoker, born on December 31, 1879. Stoker had bestowed honor and responsibility, but to Irving it was only a performance; in fact, he stole away Stoker's family life. But Stoker was a willing victim; he much preferred Irving's company to an evening in front of the fire with Florence cradling their newborn. In his maturity, Noel dropped his first name, saying he resented Irving for having monopolized his father. There were no other children.

The situation may have suited Florence. She had any number of fascinating escorts, including the playwright W. S. (William Schwenck) Gilbert. Motherhood did not content her; neither did ladies' tea parties nor needlework nor any feminist cause, such as the

Society for Rational Dress, which involved Wilde's wife, Constance. By all accounts, Florence was an enchanting hostess and made a comfortable home for her husband and his friends, when they were there. In every way, she was a social asset. And by Victorian standards the marriage, although lacking passion, was successful.

Stoker's most recent biographer, his great-nephew Daniel Farson, describes a loveless, frigid marriage, with Florence enamored only of her own beauty. Farson claims Florence refused to have sexual relations after Noel was born, driving her husband to prostitutes. According to Farson, Stoker " 'enjoyed' the reputation of being a 'womaniser', reputedly famous for his sexual exploits," and died of syphilis. Farson speculates that Stoker contracted the disease in Paris, where "so many 'faithful' husbands, such as Charles Dickens and Wilkie Collins, had gone for discreet pleasure before him."

There is now sufficient medical opinion to cast doubt on syphilis as a cause of death or even a factor in Stoker's medical history. As to his amorous adventures, it is hard to visualize him leaving Irving at dawn to pick up a prostitute on the Strand before arriving home for breakfast. Being in a touring company provided abundant opportunity for dalliances, but Stoker must have been discreet—or uninvolved—to have left no whiff of gossip.

*Chapter 7*

# THE BEEFSTEAK ROOM

"He took my arm, and we went into the next
room, where I found an excellent supper ready
on the table. . . . After supper I smoked, as on
the last evening, and the Count stayed with me
chatting and asking questions on every
conceivable subject, hour after hour. . . . All at
once we heard the crow of a cock coming up
with preternatural shrillness through the clear
morning air. . . ."

—Jonathan Harker's journal

Following the Lyceum's first season, Stoker explored the backstage lumber rooms filled with the rubbish of half a century.
Nestled among the mounds of rotting peacock feathers was a
rusty grill—a legacy of the eccentric Beefsteakers, formed in 1735 at
Covent Garden by the famous harlequin John Rich and the scene
painter George Lambert. When Lambert was too busy to lunch out,
he broiled a beefsteak over the fire for his guests, and soon a group
of regulars formed. Eschewing the ordinariness of the word *club,* they
christened themselves the Sublime Society of Beefsteaks. "What a
fine, old, fruity, Tom-and-Jerry air there was about that original
title!" recalled actor John Martin-Harvey. Some of the early names in
a membership restricted to twenty-four were William Hogarth,
Samuel Johnson, and Richard Brinsley Sheridan.

After Covent Garden burned in 1808, the Beefsteakers convened

THE BEEFSTEAK ROOM. Royalty and actors alike supped at the Lyceum's oak-paneled dining room, hidden behind a backstage stairway.

in the old Lyceum; after it too burned in 1830, they met at the Bedford Coffee House until returning in 1838 to the rebuilt Lyceum. There they dined in Gothic splendor, with the original gridiron—dug out of the charred ruins of two theatres—suspended from the ceiling. Placed over the cooking grate were appropriate lines from *Macbeth*:

> If it were done when 'tis done, then 'twere well
> It were done quickly.*

---

* The Sublimes thrived backstage until 1867, when membership dropped to eighteen (the younger generation found the uniforms and whimsical customs too antiquated). Disbanded for nine years, they reconvened in 1876 as the Beefsteak Club, meeting in rooms near the Savoy Hotel. In 1896 they moved to 9 Irving Place and are still meeting there. They are the true successors to the Sublimes—not, as often noted, the Lyceum's Beefsteak Room. When Stoker opened the room, the Beefsteak Club had been in existence for three years.

Dressed in blue coats and buff vests with brass buttons impressed with a gridiron and the motto Beef and Liberty, members had a full view of the kitchen and the white-clad cooks as they slapped hissing beef on hot pewter plates and piled on baked potatoes, Spanish onions, and beetroot. Tankards of porter and punch were served. The only second course permitted was toasted cheese with port, and smoking only after the song and toast of the day. New members were blindfolded during an initiation rite that included kissing the "book," a beef bone concealed in a napkin.

While Irving cruised the Mediterranean, Stoker rebuilt the oak-paneled suite, reinstating the original gridiron to the beamed ceiling. A modern kitchen range was installed to provide more varied fare than the rump steaks of old; crystal flutes of Heidsieck 1874 replaced pewter mugs of stout. Armor lined the sides of the room; walls were hung with Irving's collection of pictures: portraits of David Garrick, Edmund Kean, William Charles Macready, and later Whistler's full-length portrait of Irving as Philip II and Sargent's of Ellen Terry as Lady Macbeth.* It was christened with a champagne supper for the Unholy Trinity the evening Irving returned from the cruise with his intractable plans to play Shylock.

Few Victorian memoirs fail to mention dining there. Most evenings after the performance—unless Irving supped at the Garrick—there was a gathering of wits backstage. "It was a charming old place," recalled Gordon Craig, "not too large, but somehow more of a little hall than a room, and yet cosy. . . . You reached this delightful haven from the stage by mounting long staircases, which might belong to some dusty building of the time of Dickens—anything but a primrose way. It was so peculiarly of a theatre, this old magic room." At Beefsteak dinners Stoker basked in Whitmanesque comradeship; for Irving there was another stage for him to dominate. If not in the

---

* Irving never cared for the Whistler portrait, a Velásquez-like image rather than a true rendering. Shaw, however, said "this ghostly impression" was more like Irving than the posthumous statue outside the National Portrait Gallery. Sculpted by Thomas Brock and erected in 1910, it was the first to honor an actor. Draped in academic robes, Irving looks regal, the aristocrat of the theatre who he yearned to be back in Dublin. During Whistler's bankrupt period, the painting ended up in a shabby shop, where Irving found it and bought it for only £100. After Irving's death, it was sold at Christie's for more than £5,000. It is now in the Metropolitan Museum in New York.

limelight, he would be the generous host. Every evening proved the measure of Macbeth's banquet toast: "To the general joy o' th' whole table."

When the cast inhaled aromas of roast chicken and beef wafting through the passages during the last act, they knew the Guv'nor was entertaining while they made do with a pint and a pie. Privileged guests made their way through the dimness to the dining room, located their placecards according to Stoker's seating plan, and waited. Tall, gaunt, and somber—flanked on one side by the unobtrusive figure of Loveday and on the other by the burly, pushing Stoker, always in a mortal hurry—Irving triumphantly entered, often still in costume. If he had raised his right hand and proclaimed, "Let the games begin," no one would have registered surprise. Martin-Harvey recalled that he once tiptoed to the door to peek at the blazing baronial fireplace and imagined Irving's "clear-cut alabaster profile outlined against the sombre oaken panelling, looking back, as he might do, upon his obscure childhood, his long struggle for recognition"—then quickly scurried off, fearful that "the ubiquitous Stoker" might catch him.

Since the table sat only thirty-six, the group often migrated to the stage. Asked to draw up an invitation list for a garden party, Stoker stopped when he reached five thousand. "The range of his guests was impossible to any but an artist," Stoker noted; "the ordinary hospitalities of the Beefsteak Room were simply endless." As were the expenses. Still, these evenings went beyond the scraping of knives and forks and the emptying of crystal decanters. They were a time for pithy toasts and witty anecdotes; the conversation rivaled any in London. Irving and Stoker were instinctive hosts. They knew it did not suffice to spend lavishly; it was more important to cultivate and promote affinities among guests (for example, not to seat a critic next to an author), to keep conversations going, to fence a topic uncongenial to any particular guest, and to prevent private dialogues between neighbors.

Stoker was often called upon to speak. His close friend Hall Caine observed that those who knew him only through the theatre hardly knew him at all. "His true self was something quite unlike the personality which was seen in that environment," Caine recalled in a posthumous tribute. "Some hint of this would occasionally reveal itself among the scarcely favorable conditions of a public dinner," Caine wrote, "when, as a speaker (always capable of the racy humor which is considered necessary to that rather artificial atmosphere), he would strike in the soft roll of the rich Irish tongue, a note of deep and almost startling emotion that would obliterate the facile witticisms of more important persons." With this hearty male bonding the Beefsteakers created a "homosocial" world of masculine privilege in which women were used as pawns. In Stevenson's *Dr. Jekyll and Mr. Hyde,* critic Elaine Showalter detects "the shadow of homosexuality that surrounded Clubland and the nearly hysterical terror of revealing forbidden emotions between men that constituted the dark side of patriarchy."

A frequent Beefsteaker was Oscar Wilde, flushed with success after taking a first in "Greats" (the final examination for honors in humane letters) at Oxford and winning the coveted Newdigate Prize for his poem "Ravenna." (On hearing of this, the perennial curmudgeon Gilbert snapped, "I understand that some young man wins this prize every year.") This was the beginning of Wilde's swaggering stage, and he was hard at work inventing himself, appearing often with Lillie Langtry, the mistress of the Prince of Wales. Wilde haunted the Lyceum. Seen at *Othello,* he amused everyone, leaning languidly from one box, greeting friends in the stalls, and reappearing in yet another box. Gossip columns reported Wilde and Stoker were seen shaking hands throughout the theatre. If there was any lingering rivalry over Florence, it did not show in the Stokers' welcome, particularly after Wilde married Constance Lloyd in 1884. Wilde definitely had a place on their social calendar and accepted invitations even when his wife was out of town. Florence, who like Wilde was a consummate snob, enjoyed the reflected celebrity of her former suitor's growing cult.

Before his marriage, Wilde lived at One Tite Street, Chelsea, with his artist friend Frank Miles, a gardener who cultivated lilies long before Wilde thought of adopting them as an aesthetic symbol. Wilde may have urged the Stokers to move to this burgeoning artistic community, for in 1881 they leased 27 Cheyne Walk, a narrow four-story house on a curved terrace overlooking the Albert Bridge. The Chelsea Embankment, built seven years earlier, had perfumed the area where previously the Thames and its sewage washed up to the doorways. Thomas Carlyle had moved to Cheyne Row in 1834, and not far away, at 16 Cheyne Walk, lived the ailing painter Dante Gabriel Rossetti and on occasion the irrepressible poet Algernon Swinburne.

Sharing the Stokers' new home was youngest brother George, born the same year that Bram first walked. Through Stoker's influence George was a consulting physician to the Lyceum (he saved Ellen Terry from blood poisoning by lancing an infected thumb during a performance of *Twelfth Night*) and the Honorary Medical Officer of the Actors Benevolent Fund, positions that made him a member of the Lyceum family. A decorated medical officer, who served in the Russo-Turkish Wars and the South African Wars, he specialized in diseases of the throat, making him an ideal actors' physician.

George's book, *With the Unspeakables; or Two Years' Campaigning in European and Asiatic Turkey,* provided background for *Dracula*'s opening chapters, which so admirably evoke the geography, customs, and ethnic complexities of Transylvania, the "land beyond the forest," a country Stoker called "one of the wildest and least known portions of Europe." A country he never visited. Fertilized with "insider" references, *Dracula* was written as much to amuse Stoker's circle as to tell a multilayered morality myth that explored Victorian culture and companionship. Frequently Stoker uses names and places connected to friends or theatre life; it is not accidental, then, that the *Demeter,* which carried the count and his coffins, sails from Varna, where George Stoker had traveled.*

---

* Although a specialist on clergyman's throat, George Stoker is best remembered for developing an oxygen treatment for sores, burns, and other diseases, based on a Zulu practice he observed of exposing wounds to fresh air.

From Cheyne Walk's windows, Stoker and two-year-old Noel watched the boats and ferries on the Thames, the four-wheelers or "growlers" (because of the noise they made on the macadamized cobblestones), and the chimney sweeps with their bundle of rods and circular brushes on the street. The butcher's boy delivered meat to the kitchen on a wooden tray, and the housekeeper paid Italian organ-grinders, stilt dancers, and bands to move on. It was a varied, vivid parade, so different from Stoker's Clontarf vista of distant clipper ships. The Cadogan steamboat ferry stopped a few steps from Stoker's front door and took him to London Bridge and on to Waterloo, where he alighted and walked to the Lyceum.

Around the corner from Cheyne Walk, at 146 Oakley Street, lived Lady Wilde. The blinds were still drawn in the fashion of Merrion Square and the doyenne ensconced in artificial splendor "in an old white ball dress, in which she must have graced the soirees of Dublin a great many years ago," recalled Violet Hunt, the twenty-one-year-old Pre-Raphaelite beauty who followed Florence Stoker in Oscar Wilde's affection. Wilde describes the scene in *Lord Arthur Savile's Crime:* "It was certainly a wonderful medley of people. Gorgeous peeresses chatted affably to violent Radicals, popular preachers brushed coattails with eminent skeptics, a perfect bevy of bishops kept following a stout primadonna from room to room, on the staircase stood several Royal Academicians disguised as artists." After Wilde's infamy and exile, his lover Lord Alfred Douglas had his say about the salon, describing it as "a house of opulence and carouse; of late suppers and deep drinking, of

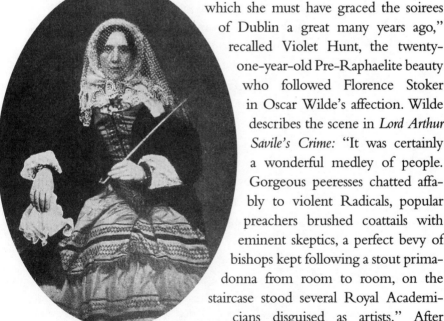

LADY JANE WILDE as an old woman. She died in 1896, at the age of seventy-five, while her son was imprisoned in Reading jail.

careless talk and example." Wilde's mother, he said, was a woman of "spotless life and honour, but had a loose way of talking which might have been a danger to her sons."

Sir William's legacy could not support the glitter of past Merrion Square salons, but Speranza managed to mix diverse English and American personalities: Ruskin and Browning, Oliver Wendell Holmes and Bret Harte, Frances Hodgson Burnett and Gertrude Atherton. People stopped by to stare at Oscar, whose costumes were as titillating as his mother's. One Sunday, Lillie Langtry said, he wore light-colored trousers with a black frock coat and a brightly flowered waistcoat, accessorized by a white silk cravat pierced with an old intaglio amethyst—and lavender gloves. Florence's sister, Philippa Knott, was invited, the only Dublin friend present. Lady Wilde "made me the guest, so to speak, of the afternoon, introducing everyone to me," she recalled. "Oscar came in and fell (tripped?) over a footstool, and complained of the dimness of the light, the only illumination being some small lamps with red shades."

At this time, Stoker added Tennyson and Gladstone to his personal pantheon. Dion Boucicault's creaky standby *The Corsican Brothers* was staged with William "Breezy Bill" Terriss, an adventurous young man who landed on the stage with the good looks of a Byron. During a dueling rehearsal, Terriss noticed that the limelight tracked only Irving, who was a great stylist as a fencing exponent. Terriss put up his sword and announced: "Don't you think, Guv'nor, a few rays of the moon might fall on me—it shines equally, ye know, on the just and the unjust." Like most autocrats, Irving respected a challenge; the lighting was changed, and company sycophants had something to think about.

The spectacular scene in this play was a masked ball set at the Paris Opera. Tiers of boxes were suggested by painted flats with openings; behind each one was a well-dressed extra leaning forward on a velvet ledge. On a backstage visit, Gladstone was intrigued by this arrangement and asked to be an extra. Warned to keep out of sight, he popped his head out at the first burst of clapping; when the play was interrupted by cries of "Bravo Gladstone!" he stood up and took a bow. Thereafter he sat out of sight in the O.P. (opposite prompt) proscenium corner.

Stoker and Gladstone immediately took to each other. A man of peculiar interests, the prime minister loved cutting down trees and rehabilitating prostitutes, a task he masked as charitable work. He would approach women in the Haymarket, engage them in long monologues, and talk them into momentary goodness. These women attracted him (on that there is little disagreement), and to curb his passions, he indulged in self-flagellation. To relax, he went to the theatre, where Stoker said he found "an intellectual stimulant— either an excitement or a pausing time *before* some great effort, or a relief of change from fact to fancy *after*." An admirer of Florence Stoker (he called her "the beauty"), Gladstone liked to talk politics with Stoker, who bore a striking resemblance to Charles Stewart Parnell, the Irish nationalist leader. Gladstone spent most of his public career trying to avert an Irish calamity and saw the Protestant Ascendancy, from which Stoker sprang, as "some tall tree of noxious growth, lifting its head to Heaven and poisoning the atmosphere of

WILLIAM EWART GLADSTONE in the mid-1880s. The British statesman often sought Stoker's opinion on the Irish troubles.

the land." Stoker supported home rule but never spoke out loudly for it, probably because the apolitical Irving—playing devil's advocate—mocked him about it.

Even after many years together, Stoker was overly sensitive when ridiculed by Irving. Asked one night to swell the crowd in the masked-ball scene, he selected from the rack in his office (always laden with costumes for such occasions) a black-and-white domino suit and a magnificent black feathered hat. "I was lurking at the back when Irving came hurriedly up the stage," he recalled, and "his laughter came explosively." Stoker had mingled where extras, positioned for height, were all children. "In the painted perspective you looked fifty feet high!" Irving taunted, and laughed again. So chagrined was Stoker at this stage bumble that he purged the incident by noting it at great length in his Irving book.

During the run of *The Corsican Brothers,* based on the novel by Alexandre Dumas *père,* Irving and Stoker discussed the implications of doubles in life, in literature, and on the stage. Stoker, like Wilde and Twain, found the doppelgänger theme irresistible: the unseen face in the mirror. With the publication of *Dracula,* Stoker joined Le Fanu and Charles Robert Maturin to form the Irish triumvirate of gothic writers. Maturin's *Melmoth the Wanderer,* published in 1820, is a purportedly moral work on the theme of the Wandering Jew, but it abounds with satanism, cruelty, and masochism, while Le Fanu's vampire tale, *Carmilla,* combines lesbianism and vampirism in a dreamy fairy-tale setting. Both empathize with the doppelgänger myth.

*Melmoth* fascinated Stoker, as it did Scott, Baudelaire, and Balzac. After Wilde's release from prison, he traveled under the alias of Sebastian Melmoth, adopting the name of his favorite martyr and his great-uncle's solitary wanderer. Beyond the obvious doubles in *Dracula,* Stoker creates some intriguing schizophrenic situations. Mina and Lucy, for example, have daytime and nocturnal counterparts. By day they are consciously allied with the antivampire forces; by night they are unconsciously controlled by Dracula. Both suffer guilt because of their repressed attraction to Dracula. Mina, after sucking blood from his chest, repeatedly refers to herself as "unclean."

A more typical tale, *The Corsican Brothers* is the story of twin

MRS. HENRY DICKENS AND STOKER. The author
with the wife of Charles Dickens's youngest son, dressed for
a costume ball in selections from the Lyceum's wardrobe

brothers joined together at birth who, when surgically separated, re-
tain a psychic bond. In Corsica, a land of strange happenings and
stormy passions, bizarre things are not always considered so. "The
story is so weird that it obtains a new credibility from unfamiliar *entourage,*" said Stoker. Irving's double when he shared the stage with
his twin was Arthur Matthison, a bit shorter but with similar features.
Matthison, however, firmly believed that he *was* Irving's double, and
this became the source of endless jokes, a sacred theatrical tradition.
Stoker said that young Henry and Laurence, Irving's sons, were
coached to go up to Matthison and call him Papa.

ALFRED, LORD TENNYSON. The future poet laureate
at the age of thirty, romanticized in a lithograph by J. H.
Lynch of an oil portrait by Samuel Laurence

On their first meeting Tennyson complained to Stoker: "I am seventy, and yet I don't feel old. I wonder how it is!" Stoker then quoted
as a reason Tennyson's lines from "The Golden Year": "Unto him
who works, and feels he works,/ The same grand year is ever at the
doors." Still the leading Romantic poet, closely followed by the
younger Swinburne and Browning, Tennyson like Whitman was a
bit of a recluse, the best-read unseen poet. Swarthy, scraggly, rustic in
speech and manner, he was "like a creature of some primordian
British stock," said Henry James. Stoker appraised Tennyson's appearance and pronounced him a "fighter," observing that at times he
lifted his upper lip, showing the canine tooth, which was a mark of

the military instinct. Canines, of course, are the vampire's forks. "Of all the men I have known," Stoker added, "the one who had this indication most marked was Sir Richard Francis Burton." Stoker first met the explorer in 1879 on the boat train to Dublin.

Tennyson had written a new play, *The Cup,* inspired by Plutarch; unfortunately, it had such a trite plot that when the Lyceum produced it, spectacular sets were ordered to divert the audience. Edward Godwin, Ellen Terry's former lover, built a Temple of Artemis and designed embroidered costumes for the supporting players. When Godwin ignored the leading lady's wardrobe, Stoker "went off, hotfoot," he said, and found, "through turning over a whole stock of old material at Liberty's, an Indian tissue of a sort of loosely woven cloth of gold, the *wrong* side of which produced the exact effect sought for." Extras for the temple scene included one hundred vestal virgins, and on opening night, January 3, 1881, one of the virgins was Florence Stoker.

Overwhelmed by the thought of his adored Ellen Terry ("Your love is more wonderful even than a crystal caught in bent reeds of gold," he told her) and his beloved Florrie sharing the same stage, Wilde sent Terry two crowns of flowers. "Will you accept one of them," he wrote, "whichever you think will suit you best. The other—don't think me treacherous, Nellie—but the other please give to Florrie *from yourself.*" Wilde was most romantic when he added, "I should like to think that she was wearing something of mine the first night she comes on the stage, that anything of mine should touch her. Of course if you think—but you won't think she will suspect? How could she? She thinks I never loved her, thinks I forget. My God how could I!" How Wilde dramatized life: he had seen Florence many times since his triumphant arrival in London.

At Cheyne Walk Stoker cherished ritual: he breakfasted in bed, took the eleven o'clock ferry, arrived at the Lyceum, caught up with correspondence, and worked the rest of the day with Irving. Being fastidious, he preferred to dress at home, where hot water was plentiful and a relaxing bath necessary before the long night. Young Noel watched as his father put on his dress suit and told him stories of the

FLORENCE AND
NOEL STOKER, in a
photograph taken
around 1884

Irish pixies. Noel left one vivid memory of his father as a "red-bearded giant, who used to lie at full length on the drawing room carpet, and let me climb about his chest." On the rare occasion when he did not dine with Irving, Stoker returned home to a solitary late supper warmed on the kitchen coals. Florence did not wait by the fire to greet her husband and share the day's events. On Sundays he was there for her "at home" gatherings, well attended by Chelsea's writers and artists and theatre friends.

Stoker's days began and ended with a ferry journey, and with every departure he anticipated adventure. On September 14, 1882, as the *Twilight* approached Oakley Street, Stoker's daydreams shattered when an elderly man jumped off in a suicide attempt. Leaning over the railing of the moving boat, he pulled on the man's coat, trying to drag him closer, but the man persisted in keeping his face under water. Stoker stripped off his coat and vest, dove in, and, swimming against the tide, managed to sustain the old man until a boat came. Rushed to Cheyne Walk and stretched out on the dining room table, he died despite George Stoker's attempts at mouth-to-mouth resuscitation.

For this heroic act (which some called foolish behind his back: he could have been drawn under the boat), Stoker received a bronze medal from the Royal Humane Society. He had risked his life to rescue a never identified man in his sixties. *The Penny Illustrated Press* praised his "gallant act." *The Entr'Acte,* known for its satirical swipes at theatre personalities, depicted the drenched Stoker (hat and dripping jacket in hand) greeting Irving, who said: "Bravo, Stoker! We pretend to be heroes on the stage, but you really *are* one!" (One wonders what Irving *really* said.) The same publication had its fun in its "Merry-go-Round" gossip column, noting: "Mr. Irving is fortunate in having for his manager a muscular Christian like Mr. Bram Stoker. Should the popular tragedian ever get out of his depth, he knows that his faithful Bram is ready to take the necessary header, and be to the rescue."

This was Stoker's finest hour. In novels he bestows the same medal on his alter ego, Harold, who rescues a child from a moving transatlantic steamer in *The Man,* and on the ship's captain in *Lady Athlyne.* He exulted in having his name and picture in the newspapers, but Florence was distraught over a sodden elderly man expiring on her mahogany table. She now loathed Cheyne Walk and wanted a new address. There were probably other reasons as well. The Victorians loved changing residences, and 17 St. Leonard's Terrace— overlooking a park—was a more desirable Chelsea address. An 1808 terrace house that resembled Stoker's Georgian birthplace, it featured a setback that allowed hansoms and broughams to drive to the front door—an elegant touch not lost on Florence. Once they moved in 1886, Stoker continued to take the Cadogan ferry, which was only ten minutes away for a brisk walker like himself. He ordered a bicycle custom-made to suit his large frame for transportation during the warmer months. Florence and Bram had number 17 to themselves: George Stoker had wed Agnes McGillycuddy and moved to nearby Cadogan Terrace.

———

STOKER'S RESCUE of a suicidal man who jumped from a Thames ferry
was acknowledged by the Royal Humane Society with a bronze medal.

In his new home Stoker started to write. He unearthed from an old cardboard trunk his Dublin notebooks, from a time when he tinkered with drafts of fairy tales, when he tried to dramatize his mother's Sligo stories, to capture images of the looming cholera epidemic—or the plague, as he re-creates it in *Dracula*. When he completed "The Invisible Giant," he wrote seven more stories, which were published as *Under the Sunset* by Sampson Low in 1881; they were dedicated "To my son whose angel doth behold the face of the king." The book title refers to a land that is visited only in dreams, a land guarded by angels, "a beautiful country which no human eye has ever seen in waking hours . . . those who go there in dreams, or who come in dreams, come and go they know not how."

In Stoker's land there is a good king and his palace, and the King of Death and his castle, not unlike Dracula's castle. The invisible giant, with its "grim, spectral hands," represents the plague (a harbinger of the sickness of the Un-Dead). Another character, the Shadow Builder, can (like Dracula) pass "through the vapoury walls of his abode," and "sometimes from a sleeping body the Shadow Builder summons a dreaming soul; then for a time the quick and the dead stand face to face, and men call it a dream of the Past." That dreaming soul was Stoker, an invisible giant himself, and these stories marked the beginning of his vampiric motif.

Not gruesome like the Grimm brothers' or fanciful like Hans Christian Andersen's, the tales are almost biblical, permeated with allegories of good and evil and an atmosphere of dreamlike unease. Real terrors (serpents, giants, mandrakes, dragons, sharks, crocodiles, vultures) collide with abstractions (lies, anger, purity, love, sin, obedience, peace, harmony). A favorite Stokerian theme, the quest for goodness, is ever present. But any child falling asleep to the admonition "the things which we do wrong—although they may seem little at the time, and though from the hardness of our hearts we pass them lightly by—come back to us with bitterness, when danger makes us think how little we have done to deserve help, and how much to deserve punishment" was not likely to ask for an encore.

"The Wondrous Child," however, has the whimsy associated with bedtime stories. Perhaps a filtered scenario from Stoker's sickly childhood, it tells of a brother and sister (Thornley and Matilda?)

THE INVISIBLE GIANT. This illustration by the Rev.
William Fitzgerald depicts a child (not unlike Stoker) looking
out a window at approaching pestilence: "In the sky beyond
the city she saw a vast shadowy Form with its arms raised. It
was shrouded in a great misty robe that covered it, fading away
into air so that she could only see the face and the grim, spectral hands" (*Under the Sunset,* 1960, Borgo Press edition, p. 51).

who have a new baby at home, but want one of their own. They find
one in a parsley patch. When they fight, the baby dies. When they re-
pent, the reborn baby speaks, tames cruel animals, and is a wondrous
child and playmate: an angel preaching love and harmony. Illustrations by the Rev. William Fitzgerald, a Trinity classmate of Stoker's
who became a parish priest, and W. V. Cockburn range from surreal
and haunting to macabre.

*The Spectator* praised the writing and illustrations—"Children of this year of grace have a new and generous friend"—but said the tales, like *Alice in Wonderland,* were better suited for adults. Ever-witty *Punch* advised: "Get *Under the Sunset* (awkward position). It's very pretty to look at as to binding, pictures, and general get-up . . . it's rather too goody-goody . . . and there's not very much to laugh at . . . perhaps somewhat above the heads of those who are only three feet and a half high." Now part of London's cultural establishment, Stoker never had a book panned; something positive was always said.

Before premiering *Romeo and Juliet* in 1882, the Lyceum underwent major renovations. At a cost of £12,000, sixty seats were added to the dress circle and two hundred to the pit, now made comfortable with padded cushions. Nightly receipts were increased, but at a sacrifice to the interior's graceful symmetry. The stage, however, now accommodated three-dimensional architectural elements, such as steps, platforms, and columns, allowing a mix of movable scenery with painted flats, cloths, and borders.

For this production, Stoker said, "it was necessary to give something of the luxury, the hereditary feud of two dominant factions represented by their chiefs, of the ingrained bloodthirstiness of the age of the Italian petty states." To this end, 135 extras were hired and Irving rehearsed them as carefully as he did actors. There were peacocks (dead) on the banquet table, azalea trees (live) in the background, draperies of silver brocade, and strolling musicians. "It was very sumptuous, impressive and Italian," said Terry, and in it "Henry first displayed his mastery of crowds. The brawling of the rival houses in the streets, the procession of girls to wake Juliet on her wedding morning."

More and more, the potential of using colored filters for stage lighting fascinated Irving, who constantly experimented with different combinations. Stoker kept scrupulous notes and later christened Irving the "father of modern stage lighting." Although not the first to do so, Irving consistently darkened the auditorium during a performance; he trained his stagehands to change scenes in the dark wearing silent shoes and black clothing. Electricity he viewed with suspicion, using it only for special effects and some house lights.

Ellen Terry, whose makeup was designed during the gaslight era, always preferred its "thick softness with the lovely specks and motes in it, so like *natural* light, which gave illusion to many a scene." Although barely perceptibly, gaslight actually moved, giving life and depth to flats. Carpenters tapped gently on the foliage cloths to enhance this shifting. Limelight spots best illuminated Irving, whose acting techniques relied heavily on facial expression: a step toward cinematic close-ups. Electricity gave complexions a deathly pallor and changed red lips to purple. Scenery painted with gaslight in mind (usually with a predominance of blue) did not pass scrutiny in the cool light of the electric arc.

During readings in the Green Room, Irving said the line "Thou canst not teach me to forget" was the keynote of the play. Once started, he went on with "fiery zeal to other passages," Stoker recalled, "till at last the pathos of the end touched him to his heart's core . . . and in speaking the words [he] wept." In the Beefsteak Room, rehearsals continued. Following one supper Irving asked Stoker to demonstrate how he would carry the body of Paris into the tomb. Using Loveday as Paris, Stoker stood astride him, lifted him by the upper hips, and flung him over his shoulder. Liking the look of it, Irving asked Stoker to do it to him so he could understand the motion. Switching places, Irving was less successful with the 170-pound Stoker, and realized he was too slight to carry off this maneuver.

Still undecided, Irving consulted George Stoker, who had lifted many a wounded soldier. What was the easiest way to carry a dead body, Irving asked? Easy, George said, and hoisted his brother on his back in the manner of a butcher carrying a dead sheep. Efficient, Irving observed, but not aesthetically pleasing. Finally it was decided to drag the body to the entrance and change the scene to show Irving dragging a dummy down the stairs to the crypt. The time and energy spent on this one action typified Irving's obsession with detail.

The live body of Paris was the Oxonian Frank Benson, one of the first university men to make a reputation on stage. Benson arrived in London with a classical profile, talent, and a brash know-it-all attitude. Lacking the humility expected in a young player, he ran afoul of the *other* university man, who slapped him down. Benson had the revisionist idea that wearing makeup hampered facial expressions. On his first exit he ran into Stoker, who bellowed that his face looked dirty from the front. "I have a theory . . ." began Benson. "Theory be damned!" Stoker interrupted. "You can't go on the stage of this theatre with a dirty face."

Never missing an opportunity to pontificate, Stoker told Benson that "acting is different from everyday life. . . . I have won many a bet from actors that they could not go out of the room and return, and say in a natural voice: 'Good-evening. Very fine day to-day, is it not?' Not one in a hundred can do it. It requires self-control, humour and conquered self-consciousness—in a word, technique." Benson left the Lyceum after one role but achieved success; perhaps he heeded Stoker's advice.*

When *Romeo and Juliet* opened, on March 8, 1882, the Prince and Princess of Wales were in attendance. Florence Stoker arrived with W. S. Gilbert and his wife. Gilbert's libretto for *Patience,* satirizing Oscar Wilde's aestheticism, had London laughing. Irving's estranged wife, Florence, always ready with subacid comments, was in her usual box; later she wrote in her diary: "jolly failure—Irving awfully funny." When Edwin Booth played Hamlet, she asked Irving for tickets: "I would like to have the two sons of Henry Irving see an actor." She taught Henry and Laurence to call their father "the antique" and Terry "the wench." A raging bitterness consumed her. Perhaps she regretted her impetuous dismissal of Irving's fame; by rights she—not Terry—should have been the Lady of the Lyceum.

At forty-two Irving was not a believable Romeo. There was no acting technique available to capture the spontaneity and appearance of youth. His performance drew some generous appreciation, but most reviewers relished the opportunity to attack. "I am sorry you

---

* Benson organized Shakespearian touring companies referred to as the nurseries of the English stage. Following his curtain call at the Drury Lane Theatre on May 2, 1916, Benson, clad in the bloodstained robes of the murdered Julius Caesar, was knighted by King George V as he knelt in the private room behind the royal box. Twenty-one years earlier, Irving had been the first actor knighted.

don't realize," Terry told one offensive critic, "that the worst thing Henry Irving could do, would be better than the best of anyone else." Her Juliet was damned with faint praise, and the play was never revived. Spectacular staging, however, filled seats for seven months, and on the hundredth night the stage was transformed into a moonlit garden for another banquet.

Back in Dublin, when Stoker made his Faustian pact with Irving to be acting manager, when he married in haste, had one child, and left his wife to make her own society, he knew Irving was his master, as he had once called Whitman his master. Stoker was there to fill the actor's empty hours, to sit up with him until dawn. That Stoker found this companionship endlessly rewarding in itself was obvious, but that he was not rewarded in kind was the disappointment of his life. Irving talking, Stoker listening; Stoker making astute comments, Irving appropriating them. Few realized that Irving's pride prevented him from giving credit to Stoker or anyone else whose ideas promoted his career.

Sometimes Irving needed a crowd. He wanted the Lyceum family with him to celebrate Christmas in 1882. Something special must be planned, he commanded. Stoker suggested home-cooked food. "There's no place—or no dinner—like home," he convinced Irving, who ordained a cooperative meal with assigned parts: Irving to serve the wine, Stoker to chop and carve, the property man's wife to roast, an usher (with culinary talents) to produce soup, fish, and vegetables. A suggestion to order ices from Gunther's, in case the pudding was a failure, was indignantly voted down. How a home-cooked meal must have thrilled and terrified Irving, a man who ate only anonymously prepared food.

What a wonderful concept! A communal dinner where all were equal, working together, waiting on themselves. But Irving's ego spoiled everything. Boasting of his minions cooking glorious food, he invited mocking epicures to taste. The family group grew to thirty. "The more the merrier!" Stoker said ingenuously.

When the soup tureen was placed before him, Irving recalled that he lifted the cover with the anxious pride of a Wellington firing the first shot at Waterloo. "The chance simile of a battle holds good," he said, "for the soup was awfully smoky. Somebody said that it tasted like a chimney on fire. The fish was worse. The roast beef uneatable. The pudding as hard as stone. What little appetite remained to us was lost while carving the meats and passing the plates around." The cuisine may—or may not—have been memorable that Christmas Eve, but Irving's generosity was. Each member of the company received a basket containing a goose with all the trimmings and a bottle of gin. After port and ripe Stilton, a roulette table was produced, and the Guv'nor distributed canvas bags with £5 in silver pieces for all his guests.

How different would be the following Christmas, when the company would dine on oyster pie, cold beef, and jellies in the dining car of a train headed for Baltimore. Irving announced he was going to bring the Lyceum, its players, sets, costumes—even the limelight men—on a six-month tour of America. Stoker's first thoughts were of Whitman.

*Chapter 8*

# AMERICA

"He [Dracula] seemed to have been prepared
for every obstacle which might be placed by
accident in the way of his intentions being
carried out. To use an Americanism, he had
'taken no chances. . . .' "
—Jonathan Harker's journal

A series of engravings on the art of fencing lined the dark, winding staircase leading to Irving's rooms at 15A Grafton Street, near the Royal Academy of Art. Over his bed hung a carved seventeenth-century Flemish crucifix, a reminder of the stern theology implanted in him by his aunt. There were portraits of actors but none of himself. A well-worn tiger skin was stretched in front of the fireplace. Books covered the floor. Swords and walking sticks clustered in one corner. Near the window was a long pier mirror, in which he created facial expressions and a character's makeup. Even after greasepaint became available, Irving continued to use watercolors, adhering to the practices of his youth.

Stoker could be summoned to Grafton Street several times daily. Such was Irving's temperament that if a question arose (even a minor one) or he otherwise needed instant gratification, off went a messenger with orders or queries for Stoker: "Look around in the morning before going to the theatre." "Bring tonight's speech with you." "Give me two fivers for a £10 note." "Please send up here at once a pint of clear turtle." "Don't forget Hatton at dinner. Put him up at

BRAM STOKER
at the age of thirty-
seven, in 1884, the
year he met
Walt Whitman

our end." "You will find in my drawer a large printed copy of speech. Please send it by bearer." "Put special advert in Evening Express." "Do you remember name of Venezuelan commissioner?" "Unless you have arranged for supper tonight why not have it at Garrick?" "Drop Pinero a line asking him to make a reading tomorrow—if he can?" "Supper for 16 or 18—wonder if Mrs. Stoker will come?"

Stoker wrote most of Irving's speeches. The homilies were similar at each stop on a provincial tour, but every address was personalized: what was said in lofty Edinburgh was different from what suited industrial Liverpool. Though an excellent extemporaneous speaker,

Irving never rose unprepared; even for toasts he used notes, often written on menu cards by Stoker. Reverent or raucous, toasts celebrated the ending of an indulgent meal, a time when those who had imbibed too much needed no encouragement to fill, raise, and drain another glass. Toasts were followed by replies to toasts. A typical evening required salutes to the queen, to the Prince and Princess of Wales and the rest of the royal family, to the Immortal Memory of Shakespeare, to Henry Irving (and sometimes the absent Ellen Terry), and to the local hosts.

Irving's demands on Stoker were relentless. "Go see Stoker!" Irving bellowed to favor-seekers. Once Irving overheard him trying to discourage an elderly woman's request for a job. "Why not let her take care of the theatre cats?" he suggested. "We have three women taking care of the cats," Stoker replied. "Well," said Irving. "You must find her something. Let her look after the three women that are looking after the cats." Irving delighted in divine ordination, but such indulgences put unnecessary burdens on the Lyceum's budget.

Irving's celebrity necessitated largess and an entourage. He employed three journalists of varying talents, each jockeying to be first knight and attempting to undermine Stoker's power. On the recommendation of Baroness Burdett-Coutts, Louis Frederick Austin, a clever Irish journalist, came on as Irving's secretary. The official historian was Joseph Hatton, London correspondent for *The New York Times,* who would write *Henry Irving's Impressions of America.* Austin Brereton, an unlikable and pretentious freelance writer, was sent to New York to make advance plans for the tour. Stoker realized he was in the midst of a power struggle. All the new journalist knights enhanced the Lyceum's reputation with articles and books, but none ever rivaled Stoker for ability.

Writer Horace Wyndham observed how "Stoker was down in the box-office doing unobtrusive, but uncommonly useful, work. As a matter of fact, if Stoker had not been on the bridge, the Lyceum ship would have foundered a lot sooner than it did." Irving "surrounded himself with a greedy host of third-rate parasites," Wyndham added; "these merchants called themselves 'literary advisers,' . . . they were, however, merely able hacks, whose sole business it was to write speeches full of classical quotations and historical allusions, which Irving delivered to awe-struck gatherings in the provinces and America." Stoker had "more brains than the entire pack put together and hated the sight of them." He once told Wyndham "if he could have made a clean sweep of the lot, the Lyceum treasury would have been saved thousands a year."

Stoker, who had fond memories of his five years as a reviewer, felt comfortable with the principal critics. Clement Scott of the *Daily Telegraph* and *The Theatre* was the Lyceum's main praiser, in a field of criticism considered the least reputable. Conflicts of interest did not worry him; nor did they trouble Irving, who, in 1878 before the Lyceum's first season, bought *The Theatre* for £1,000 and offered it to Scott to edit. Though Scott never returned a quarter of the profits, as agreed, he provided consistently good reviews, which was better. In Dublin, Stoker had written constructive criticism, but too often London reviews were colorful descriptions, with no thought given to improving the drama or acting. Many critics were successful or frustrated playwrights who used reviews to get even or to obtain favors; others were corrupted by managers and ambitious actors; some, like the egocentric Scott, became so inextricably involved with a specific theatre that objectivity was impossible. Replying to a comment that all drama critics could be bought, Wilde quipped, "Perhaps you are right, but judging from their appearance, most of them cannot be that expensive." Once Irving's popularity with the public was assured, his grandson said he exploited "the venality of the press in furthering his aims while striking ruthlessly at those who undermined his goals to make acting respectable."

Representing a new school of criticism, William Archer of the London *Figaro*—and later *The World*—avoided all social contact with actors. Lest he compromise his role as critic, he refused performing fees for his translations of Ibsen. He came to know Shaw when they had adjacent seats in the British Library's Round Reading Room, and he became one of the playwright's most percipient critics. Archer later joined with Harley Granville-Barker in making the Royal Court Theatre in Sloane Square a repertory venue that celebrated ensemble acting, not a particular actor. Like Henry James,

Archer refused to take the Lyceum as seriously as most of his contemporaries did. To him, Irving was just another actor, good in some roles, mediocre in others. The *Figaro* in 1879 was not a major publication, but it enraged Irving to lose control of any opinion.

Yet another type of critic was the Harvard-educated lawyer, poet, and biographer William Winter of the New York *Tribune*. Considered the dean of American drama critics, Winter glorified Irving while deriding the modern, realistic movement in theatre. He called the plays of Ibsen and Shaw "social sewer" drama. "A loyal friend and an abusive foe, too prone to prejudice to be a very profound critic" was Laurence Irving's assessment of Winter. Stoker was impressed that the critic had been a personal friend of Henry Wadsworth Longfellow.

America was not a vast cultural wasteland, but information about it was not readily available in London. Stoker was disappointed when among the many volumes in the Round Reading Room he found no standard source "from which an absolutely ignorant stranger could draw information." At that time, the British "did not know much about America," Stoker observed, "and perhaps—strange as it may seem—did not care a great deal." Eventually he located a copy of the "Sessional Orders of Congress," and kept building a reference library ranging from school texts to books of etiquette.

Since the early 1800s British and American actors had crisscrossed the Atlantic for star appearances; some even toured, but never with full productions. Because of a dearth of English-language playwrights, both countries relied heavily on the classics and the French drama. Players, however, faced comparison with the greatest actors of the past in roles that were familiar to theatregoers of both countries. In making the crossing, American actors sought endorsements of their talents from the land of Shakespeare, while English actors sought the unrestrained adulation of a new country eager for cultural refinement. Stoker's friend J. L. Toole, who had performed in America, reported that most of the New York press was "a blackmail ring . . . they will write up anyone for money," but admitted that any initial prejudice against English actors "wears away." A "certain

WILLIAM CHARLES
MACREADY, the successor to
Garrick and Kean, was hounded from
America after the Astor Place
riot of 1849.

class of busybodies," noted the pragmatic Stoker, always tried "to make mischief between American and English."

There were American theatrical dynasties—the Davenports and Sotherns, the Drews and Wallacks—to rival those of Britain. American audiences had seen Edmund Kean in 1820, followed by Charles Kemble and his daughter Fanny in 1832 and William Charles Macready, forever associated with the Astor Place riot. On the night of May 10, 1849, Macready played Macbeth at the Astor Place Opera House, while nearby the preeminent American actor Edwin Forrest was performing in the same role. Some 15,000 rioters disrupted Macready's performance, leading to military intervention, twenty deaths, and scores of injured. Still debated, reasons range from anti-British feeling handed down from the American Revolution and kept fresh by the insults and abuse of British writers on American manners, to a rivalry between the two egocentric actors, to the most probable cause: Americans blamed Macready for the poor reception Forrest had received during an 1845 British tour. This bloodshed focused attention on the importance of the American actor—a message not lost on Irving, who alternated with Edwin Booth as the Lyceum's Iago and Othello and leased his theatre to Lawrence Barrett during his own company's tours.

The Lyceum offered America—and Canada—not only Irving and Terry but an entire company, with spectacular sets and costumes. It was a pioneering concept, all new, and as Ellen Terry said, "to be new was everything in America." During eight tours—totaling four years—the Lyceum traveled by train from New York City to San Francisco and from New Orleans to Montreal, covering more than 50,000 miles (more than twice around the equator, Stoker calculated), hauling trainloads of scenery through storms and floods, and never canceling a performance, even during the Blizzard of 1888. Stoker made sure the caravan moved on time, which "was the kind of work he thoroughly enjoyed and at which he excelled," said Irving's grandson. Transporting Dracula's fifty boxes of earth by land and sea was routine after the American tours.

For its first trip it took three months to wish the Lyceum bon

MR. IRVING IS PACKING UP.

THE LYCEUM'S AMERICAN TOUR in 1883 captivated the press. A cartoon from *The Entr'Acte* features, from left, Loveday, Stoker, Irving, and Joseph Hatton.

voyage. The sad farewells made it seem that the company was leaving England forever, with the same poignancy and forlorn hope as Ford Madox Brown depicted in *The Last of England,* his exquisite painting of an emigrating family. The long goodbyes began on July 28, 1883. As the mournful strains of "Auld Lang Syne" filled the theatre, Stoker joined hands with the company on stage, and handkerchiefs waved in an unbroken line from the stalls to the gallery. There was a supper on stage for fifty, attended by the Prince of Wales and his retinue of dukes and peers, as well as James Russell Lowell, the American ambassador. And there was a farewell dinner hosted by British and American actors at the Garrick Club, and a banquet at St. James's Hall for five hundred of London's most important figures (with their wives discreetly hidden in the galleries to hear the postprandial speeches). Stoker had a prominent seat near the head table; he saved the program and marked his name with an X.

Sir William Pearce, the shipping magnate, invited the Unholy Trinity, along with Ellen Terry and her son, to cruise the Scottish coast aboard *The Lady Torfrida* before embarking for America. A gale-force wind was lashing black water into foam when they boarded the dinghy to row out to the steam yacht. "It seemed like madness going out on such a night in such a boat *for pleasure,*" Stoker recalled. "It was just about as unpleasant an experience as one could have, and yet all the time we were a merry party." Irving sat stolid and made casual remarks such as he would have made at his own fireside; "I really think he enjoyed the situation—in a way," said Stoker. Then a light flashed and they glimpsed the yacht rising high from the water. "We were pulled, jerked, or thrown on board I hardly knew which," Stoker said, "and found ourselves hurried down to our luxurious cabins where everything was ready for our dressing." Stoker and Irving seemed destined to ride out rough seas. Perhaps Irving enjoyed these adventures because he never appeared in *The Tempest*—the part of Prospero was not written for him. Stoker, on the other hand, surely had more than a fleeting thought about diving into the water to save his friend, a bravado reprise of his ferry rescue.

Before leaving England, Stoker settled Irving's two sons at the

BANQUET AT ST. JAMES'S HALL before the company sailed to America. The ladies, including Ellen Terry (center), watched from the balcony.

Marlborough school; visited Irving's blind aunt, Sarah Penberthy, in Cornwall; and wrote a Stokerian fan letter to Thomas Hay Sweet Escott, professor of classical literature at King's College. "It is a rare thing even with the most accomplished scholar to catch in a biographical sketch the *cachet* of the central figure," Stoker wrote in response to an Escott article on Irving, "and so reproduce it in the music of words as to give even the blind a chance of seeing and knowing what is before them. . . . I am emboldened to write to you for out of my own love for the man, I feel my heart warmer to you." A cynic might ascribe ulterior motives to such a letter, but Stoker was often spurred by the emotional moment only.

The Stokers then set off for Dublin, where Florence and Noel remained with Grandmother Balcombe during the six-month American tour. A local society columnist observed him at a D'Oyly Carte touring production of *Patience,* and recalled the days when Stoker "talked to the old ladies and got supper for half-a-dozen fair ones together by diving his tall form hither and thither amongst the crowds. . . . Everybody made room for Bram—his coming was like a charge of cavalry."


In Liverpool, Ellen Terry and Henry Irving waved farewell to hundreds of fans from the deck of the S.S. *Britannic* on October 11. Terry said she remembered only Oscar Wilde arm in arm with Lillie Langtry, in Neronian coiffure. ("Curly hair to match the curly teeth," Terry heard a passenger quip, referring to Wilde's ugly teeth, which he shielded with his hand when he talked.) Stoker waved his handkerchief from the quay; he sailed later on the slower *City of Rome,* shepherding tons of equipment for twelve plays, some hundred performers and technicians, and three wigmakers, brought along to tend 1,100 new wigs.

Also aboard the *Britannic,* entrusted to the ship's butcher for care and feeding, were Charlie, the now old and nearly blind successor of Trin as Irving's best friend; and Fussie, Terry's snappy and alert terrier. All the intimacy Irving withheld from people he lavished on his dogs—the link between him and humanity. "If you liked dogs— more especially if dogs liked you," actor Johnston Forbes-Robertson

NORTH RIVER FERRY, during the tour of 1896. Walter Collinson, with his hand to his mouth, is at the far left, with Irving center and Stoker on the right.

observed, "and you got on well with Fussie and took a real interest in his rheumatism, Irving would suffer you almost gladly; and that is about as far as his friendships went."

Weaned away from Ellen Terry with table treats, particularly biscuits soaked in champagne (no more chicken, which had been Trin's downfall), Fussie became a theatre legend. Most American hotels banned dogs, and Irving walked out if the terriers were not welcome. One evening in Detroit he was too tired to argue and allowed Fussie, now Irving's since Charlie's death, to sleep in the stables, sending his dresser, Walter Collinson, to keep him company. The following evening Fussie was registered when Irving told the manager the hotel already admitted animals: it was overrun with rats. That evening

Fussie supped on terrapin and other delicacies in Irving's sitting room; they always sat opposite each other, simply adoring each other. Occasionally the portly, self-indulgent Fussie would thump his tail on the ground to express his pleasure.

Much adored and coddled, Fussie had a habit of wandering off and getting lost, causing panic in the company. When he was left behind in New York, Irving stopped the train outside the station and waited until a small white-and-brown object was seen plodding steadily along the tracks following the company to California. Left behind again at Southampton, "he could not get across the Atlantic," Terry said, "but did the next best thing. He found his way back from there to his own theatre in the Strand," arriving at the backstage door—after a seventy-mile trek—a tired and hungry pilgrim. After this long separation Irving expected their reunion to be a delight. The homecoming was planned for the Café Royal. "Fussie burst into the room while the waiter was cutting some mutton," Irving wrote Terry, "when, what d'ye think—one bound at me—another instantaneous bound at the mutton, and from the mutton nothing would get him until he'd got his plateful. Oh, what a surprise it was indeed! He never now will leave my side, my legs, or my presence." But poor Fussie's greedy appetite would be his undoing.


Henry Irving wanted America to fall at his feet and fill the Lyceum's coffers. Ellen Terry wanted to survive what she feared was "a strange, barbarous land." Stoker longed to see Whitman's "weather-beaten vessels entering new ports" and, of course, Whitman himself. More than anyone else in the company, Stoker wanted to experience America, not just pass through it. A delegation of American actors and journalists met the ship as it lay anchored off Staten Island for quarantine inspection. Following a press conference, where Irving passed out his private stock of cigars, the Lord and Lady of the Lyceum were escorted to New York's first theatrical center, at Union Square. To avoid gossip, they stayed at separate hotels—he at the Brevoort House, a fashionable, English-style hotel near Washington Square; she at the Hotel Dam (or, as she called it, the Hotel Ahem!). Stoker and the rest of the company stayed at the less expensive Hotel

Brunswick at Fifth Avenue and Twenty-seventh Street. That first evening Irving took his favorite lady to a minstrel show.

The Lyceum's first American venue was an antiquated theatre in a downtown area no longer fashionable. New York's population had moved northward and the theatres had followed—to Madison Square and Long Acre Square (renamed Times Square in 1904). The Star Theatre's history reflected these changes. In 1861 Lester Wallack built a 1,605-seat theatre at Broadway and Thirteenth Street and named it after himself; it became known for mounting British comedies and melodramas. In 1882 he moved uptown and built another theatre at Broadway and Thirtieth Street, ten blocks from the Metropolitan Concert Hall (later opera house). Wallack's was leased and renamed the Star. In the fall of 1883, when the Lyceum opened downtown, the uptown competition was from Ouida's *Moths* at Wallack's, Ada Rehan and John Drew in *Dollars and Sense* at Daly's, and Madame Nielson in Gounod's *Faust* at the Met.

Still sparkling downtown, though, was Delmonico's, with its heavy mahogany doors, rich Moorish decorations, and antique-filled rooms. The Unholy Trinity raised many a glass there. Opened in 1862 in the former three-story Grinnell mansion at the northeast corner of Fifth Avenue and Fourteenth Street, the restaurant was imbued with the elegance of the early days of New York's first millionaires; it hummed with luncheons and banquets, before-theatre dinners, and after-theatre parties. The imperial table settings could have graced an Englishman's castle, but invitations were quintessentially American. "Will you come and take a chop with me, Mr. Irving and a few friends at Delmonico's," Albert Pulitzer wrote to Stoker, who much preferred that "great American bird," the wild canvasback duck, cooked so lightly "you must carry it through a moderately warm kitchen." The legendary chef Alessandro Filippini had made this gamy marine fowl the prize of the table. At that time a dinner for eight at Delmonico's with caviar, roast duck, wine, and champagne cost $82, while the catering charge for meals served on the Lyceum's touring train was kept to seventy-five cents per person.

The Lyceum opened with *The Bells* to avoid comparison with an American favorite by doing Irving's signature *Hamlet*. Certain New York idiosyncrasies, however, were not anticipated. One such was

THE STAR THEATRE on New York's lower Broadway as it looked in 1900, two years before it was torn down

speculators, organized teams of men and boys who descended on the box office and within an hour snapped up 3,360 tickets (for $7,200), reselling the average $2 ticket for $10 to $15. There were empty seats and double-booked seats. Had he been there, Joseph Hurst, who supervised ticket sales at the Lyceum, would have been shocked at such chaos in his tidy domain. Few in the stellar audience that crowded into the Star Theatre on that opening night could have imagined the trouble and confusion backstage. As Irving applied his Mathias makeup Stoker rushed into the dressing room with news of the seating problems and the weather: it had started to rain, heavily. Arriving to buy tickets, patrons were shunted to speculators; hems of gowns were streaked with mud, horses were high-strung, tempers frayed and flared.

When Irving spoke his prophetic announcement "It is I! It is I!" there was only a murmur, a polite welcome, not the usual inspiring applause. Stoker's actor friend Toole had neglected to mention that

American theatres had no pit or gallery; the audience saved their
tributes for the final curtain, showing little appreciation at the end of
acts. Irving was stunned. Stoker tried to calm him as he paced the
dressing room after the first act. "It's a frost, a damned frost," Irving
muttered. "Those Yankees are icebergs . . . I might as well play to a
churchyard!"

He need not have worried. *The Bells,* as always, was a brilliant
showcase for his talent. Following a rousing curtain call he felt welcomed to America. "No display of morbid spiritual vivisection has
been seen upon the stage that approaches, or even resembles, the
dream of Mathias as acted by Henry Irving," wrote William Winter.
Not every role was applauded. Later, Charles I, not Irving's greatest
interpretation, was dismissed with: "If that unhappy monarch sput-
tered and strutted and forgot the dignity of a king as Mr. Irving did
last night, it was a charity to cut off his head." Other reviewers
praised the musical accompaniment, new to Americans. "The continuous music of the Irving plays, now suggesting the emotions of the
situation, now intensifying the effects of the acting, now dominating
the scene, now almost unheard in the excitement of the dramatic incident, was unknown," wrote one critic. "People said of Irving's first
productions 'Why, they are like grand opera!' "

To Philadelphia, a city with sensitive theatrical roots, according
to Stoker, went the honor of Irving's *Hamlet.* On opening night at
the Chestnut Street Opera House, Stoker made the newspaper, described as "tall and genial" with a "broad smile," familiar epithets for
him (or rather his position); but times would change—particularly
after *Dracula.* In London, Stoker was generally ignored by journalists,
but in a country built by immigrants—many of them Irish—class
distinctions were blurred. Reporters were content to interview the
acting manager if the actor-manager was unavailable.


The train journeys from city to city delighted Stoker; he thrived on
the strenuous schedule and the romance of the railroads. During his
confined childhood he had listened to the whistle of the Dublin-to-
Drogheda train as it rumbled over the Great Northern Railway
viaduct. The sound meant adventure, chance encounters, clockwork

chases, scenarios he used in his novels. When Jonathan Harker enters Count Dracula's room, he finds him lying on a sofa reading—what else?—*Bradshaw's Railway Guide.* There was little romance, however, in Irving's memories. As a provincial player, he practically lived in four-wheeled carriages, bumped about on hard seats, jolted and jarred with the continual stopping and starting. In winter passengers huddled together for warmth; at night candles brightened the dim light of oil lamps. Players lived on greasy chips and—if they could afford it—the fish to go with them.

In America, for the first time, Irving understood the meaning of first-class travel: a private parlor car with maid, porter, and cook, donated by the president of the Erie Railroad, provided unexpected luxury. Ellen Terry ate California grapes and—to keep in the American spirit—quoted Ralph Waldo Emerson. The cook kept the ravenous group supplied with every variety of cold meats and pastries for midnight suppers. The company and baggage followed in seven

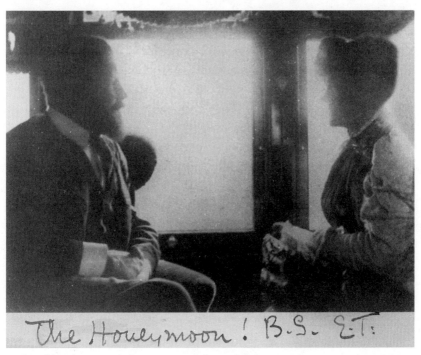

BRAM STOKER AND ELLEN TERRY in a train compartment rumbling through the American countryside. Terry wrote the inscription.

more cars. The trains ran at all hours and in inclement weather. Wheels frosted and cracked. Once an engine exploded and the driver was catapulted into a snowdrift. Floods washed out sections of the railway bed; a train caught fire entering the station. These major problems stood out among more mundane delays: burst pipes, frozen brakes, collapsed bridges. Stoker loved being in the middle of a crisis, ordering an efficient solution.

Scheduled by the leading impresario Henry Abbey, the tour was not well planned: it accommodated theatre managers, not the company. Stoker and Irving had not calculated distances between cities and the possibility for delays. On provincial tours, the five hours between London and Aberdeen were long and tiring, but that was a short trip compared with the eight-to-twelve-hour stretches between American cities. There was time—too much time—to enjoy the passing scene as the train pulled in and out of stations. Stoker noticed how the walls of buildings, the roofs of barns, and the sides of houses were plastered with advertisements for medicinal cures—an offensive disfigurement of the landscape, he said. In Britain one made money quietly.

Everyone complained about the convoluted schedule. The routing called for four weeks in New York, followed by two weeks in Philadelphia and Boston, a week each in Baltimore and Brooklyn, then two weeks in Chicago. There were stops in St. Louis, Cincinnati, Detroit, Toronto, Washington, New Haven, Worcester, Springfield, Hartford, and Providence, with return visits to Chicago, Boston, Philadelphia, and Brooklyn, ending with four weeks in New York. After returning to Chicago for a second week's run, the company was in Detroit for two performances, then up to Toronto for three nights and back to Boston. Irving and Stoker vowed to do the scheduling themselves next time and eliminate the unnecessary backtracking as well as Abbey, who pocketed $150,000.

The company never lacked for humorous diversions, particularly with Fussie backstage. At Haverley's Theatre in Brooklyn, during the last act of *Charles I* (when Charles says goodbye to his wife and children), an ebullient Fussie bounded onto the stage and, realizing his error, rolled over onto his back, whimpering, while carpenters called him from the wings. Finally the king's children picked him up (a good response) and kept him cowering between them until the curtain. Another time when Irving put on his hat and coat following a charity reading, Fussie thought the performance over and ran barking across the stage while John Drew and Maude Adams were acting. Drew was so shocked he departed from the text of *A Pair of Lunatics,* saying, "Is this a dog I see before me, his tail towards my hand? Come, let me clutch thee."

Fortunately Collinson kept track of the terriers; with daily logistical problems, Stoker refused to be a dog sitter. On leaving Brooklyn he had to have the scenery and costumes packed by midnight. Promptly at 1 a.m. they were floated across to Jersey City, and by 2 a.m. two large gondolas, three baggage cars, two Pullman sleepers, and the parlor and dining cars were moving toward Chicago. Stoker's obsessive nature made the Lyceum run on time, a talent he used to get the vampire hunters to Transylvania ahead of Dracula.

Wherever the train caravan pulled into the station, there were journalists. The Lyceum's tour had the grandeur of a royal visit, with endless publicity. Commenting on Irving's likeness to Oscar Wilde (recently lecturing in America), one reporter conceded that Irving was "more refined and manly." Asked about American women, Terry replied, "They can't be all so nice and pretty; I suppose I've only seen the nicest ones. And one thing I'll tell you which I have not seen; I've never set eyes on any Daisy Millers." "Of course not," replied the reporter. "Who ever heard of or saw a Daisy Miller outside of a book? That's a character you'll only find in James's novel, not in America."

To illuminate the Stoker-Irving relationship, one magazine writer created a make-believe Irving diary. On Stoker's speech writing: "People keep asking me why I come to Boston during the election. Stoker told me to say in answer: 'Because Boston is the most sensible city in America.' Clever chap, Stoker! Now what a judicious mixture of dignified self-esteem and subtle flattery there is in that phrase. Why between me and my diary, I believe I should fail were it not for Terry and Stoker. . . . That beggar Stoker went off to New York and forgot to write me a speech for tonight. . . . Feel better

now. Stoker is by me again." On Joseph Hatton, the writer shared
Stoker's opinion: "Hatton's an awful ass, when Stoker isn't about to
tell him so."

Throughout the tour there were suppers, banquets, and toasts. It
was reassuring for Stoker to see that clubbable Americans followed
British traditions. "The club in America is, indeed, to the masculine
wayfarer the shadow of a great rock in a lone and thirsty land," he
wrote. Stoker was impressed with how a properly introduced stranger
was welcomed, so different from the snobbery of London clubs. "I
often felt chagrin at the thought that we English can never repay in
a similar way this expression of American hospitality." In the vanguard were theatrical and literary clubs, not unlike London's Garrick, clubs like the Lotos, Century, and Lambs in New York and the
Hamilton in Brooklyn. The owner of the *Philadelphia Ledger* gave
Irving a wineglass that had belonged to George Washington; the
city's Clover Club gave him Edwin Forrest's silver watch, symboliz-
ing the death of old rivalries and a joining together of the British and
American stage. Delighted with this attention, Stoker saved all his invitations and had his menus signed.

Henry Ward Beecher, who collected $40,000 a year from his
congregation (a performer to equal Irving), invited them to his Ply-
mouth Church in Brooklyn to witness one of his rousing sermons.
The Toronto Toboggan Club initiated them into the sport, which
elated Terry. "I have never experienced anything so surprising," she
said; "it is like flying; for a moment you cannot breathe." They dined
at the White House with President Chester Arthur: "No ceremonious pomp, no show, and yet an air of conscious power," said Irving
(acting *ve-ry* upper-class) of the White House. He compared it to the
"modest country-seat of an English noble, or wealthy commoner."
Later Stoker identified an endearing—and enduring—national characteristic when he observed that since "Americans have no princes
of their own, they make princes of whom they love." And theatregoers had crowned Irving.

In Chicago the Lyceum competed with Mark Twain at the
height of his popularity. A friendship developed between Twain and
Stoker, and they met in New York at The Players Club on Gramercy
Park, where Twain rented an economy room and entertained.

Strolling up and down Fifth Avenue, they exchanged views on the conflicts of duality, on nightmares, and on the unconscious. Twain had an obsession with cleanliness, and his trademark white suit was a fetish, a way of dealing with forbidden and thus unclean thoughts. "Every man is a moon and has a dark side which he never shows to anybody," Twain once said. Although intrigued by the premise of *Dr. Jekyll and Mr. Hyde,* he believed otherwise: "the two persons in a man are wholly unknown to each other." Stoker had found a kindred spirit. At a dinner honoring the company at Delmonico's, Twain listened as Stoker told a story about a minister whose bombastic predictions of masculine glory are deflated when he learns that the infant to be christened is a girl. Twain roared and adopted the yarn on his lecture circuit.

At each city Irving made some three speeches, mostly prepared by his ambitious secretary, Austin, who informed his wife, "I have settled down to an understanding with Stoker and he has become remarkably genial and obliging." Initially, perhaps, but the tension between these two increased. It was natural for Stoker to resent Austin, as well as Hatton, who trailed about taking notes for his Irving book, in which Stoker is described as "bounding in (Stoker is always on the run)." In Boston Stoker met William H. Rideing, who published his poem "One Thing Needful" in *Youth's Companion* in 1885. He was paid £2 for this religious poem with such deathless lines as:

> One thing alone we lack!
> Our souls indeed
> Have fiercer hunger than the body's need.

Stoker was distracted and thought only of meeting Walt Whitman. The first Philadelphia stop, however, was too hectic for a visit, and a meeting was scheduled for the Lyceum's return. "I am not Shelley and you are not Godwin," Stoker had written Whitman back in Dublin, "and so I will only hope that sometime I may meet you face to face and perhaps shake hands with you. If I ever do it will be one of the greatest pleasures in my life." He was referring to Shelley's celebrated letter to the philosopher and novelist William Godwin that began their friendship in 1812. Whitman's poems of comradely love were no less controversial than they had been sixteen years earlier when Stoker read them under an elm tree at Trinity. Stoker had boasted how he helped make Whitman's work known "to many who were scoffers at first." But these readers were not the working-men, artisans, and farmers to whom Whitman addressed his poems, but British writers and intellectuals. Wilde championed Whitman at Oxford; Swinburne wrote the tribute "To Walt Whitman Across the Sea"; while the critic Edmund Gosse, with his "obstinate twist," saw Whitman as a sexual liberator.

Writer John Addington Symonds developed "the cult of calamus" with fellow-calamites, or Uranians, as homosexuals were then called, after the Greek god Uranus. Whitman's "Calamus" poems encouraged ardent physical intimacies, said Symonds, who wearied the poet with repeated requests for interpretations of the nature of "comradeship." Addressing him as "My Master," Symonds asked, "What the love of man for man has been in the Past I think I know. What it is here now, I know—alas! What you say it can and shall be I dimly discern in your Poems. But this hardly satisfies me—so desirous am I of learning what you teach." Exasperated by years of Symonds's badgering, Whitman tartly replied that these "morbid inferences" were "damnable," advising that his poetry about male love be read "within its own atmosphere and essential character."

Whitman had no intention of flouting his homosexuality or of supporting any related movements. When Wilde came to visit on January 18, 1882, during a break in his American speaking tour, he tried to seduce Whitman into the new aestheticism. Between glasses of elderberry wine and hot toddies, he compulsively talked on about young writers and artists, and Whitman's courage in publishing sexually ambiguous poems. Whitman would have none of it. But he admired the twenty-seven-year-old as "a fine handsome youngster," who was "frank and outspoken and manly." Wilde left behind a photograph, which he casually signed "To Walt from Oscar." Puzzled by the outcry over Wilde's posturing, Whitman wondered, "I don't see why such mocking things are written of him. He has the English society drawl, but his enunciation is better than I ever heard in a young Englishman or Irishman before."

WALT WHITMAN in the late 1870s

Stoker had to wait two years before his anticipated visit, which came on March 20, 1884. When Irving learned of the meeting and insisted on being included, Stoker hastily tutored him on *Leaves of Grass*. Whitman was impressed with Irving's gentle and unassuming manner; it falsified his view of actors as vulgar and undignified. Stoker saw an old man "of leonine appearance, burly, with a large head and high forehead slightly bald." Fascinated with the poet's look, he described how "great shaggy masses of grey-white hair fell over his collar. His moustache was large and thick and fell over his mouth so as to mingle with the top of the mass of the bushy flowing beard."

When Whitman heard the name, he quizzically asked: "Bram Stoker—Abraham Stoker is it?" They greeted each other, Stoker said, "as old friends—as indeed we were." Not that at ease with poets, Irving blurted out: "You know you are like Tennyson in several ways. You quite remind me of him!" Then, realizing a possible affront, added, "You don't mind that, do you?" Whitman laughed. "Mind it! I like it! I am very proud to be told so! I like to be tickled!" Irving retreated and Stoker sat down; meeting Whitman was akin to having an audience. They talked of Dublin friends, particularly Edward Dowden, his Trinity professor. There were many questions Stoker wanted to ask, questions similar perhaps to Symonds's, but Irving, hovering as he did, was inhibiting. Whitman asked Stoker to visit whenever he could. "Need I say that I promised," he noted in his diary. After his departure, Whitman remarked: "Well, well; what a broth of a boy he is! . . . He's like a breath of good, healthy, breezy sea air." But he disliked the change of name. Whitman said Stoker was born Abraham and should still be Abraham, "because of manhood and breath of humanity."

Stoker later wrote in his Irving book how he found Whitman to be all he had dreamed of back in Dublin: "large-minded, broad-viewed, tolerant to the last degree." He praised the poet's work tending the Civil War wounded, exclaiming: "No wonder that men opened their hearts to him—told him their secrets, their woes and hopes and griefs and loves! A man amongst men!" who spread "hope and comfort in the way only possible to one who walks in the steps of the Master!" A good title, Master, one that Renfield uses for Dracula. Whitman welcomed all this adulation. "The English theatrical people have always seemed to like me," he observed. "Irving has been here. . . . I have letters from Ellen Terry: then there is Bram Stoker—he has treated me like a best son." Whitman said he thought "the man Stoker repeats, fulfills, the boy." When Stoker's letters were reread to him, Whitman warmly remembered how Stoker "took a shine to me over there in Ireland and when he was in college. . . . I value his good will highly: he seems to have remained of the same mind, mainly, in substance, as at first."

Indeed, Stoker was a man, not a boy. Nearing forty, he appraised his youthful ambitions and decided to no longer neglect his writing. He began an Irish novel and wrote short stories, crowding even more into his daily schedule by studying for the law: he needed a life independent of Irving and the Lyceum. This was to be the vain struggle of his middle years.

HENRY IRVING as Mephistopheles in the spectacular Brocken scene from
Act IV of *Faust,* which employed 250 warlocks, demons, imps, and goblins

# 3

## Literary Overtures
### (1884–1895)

# Chapter 9

# MEPHISTOPHELES

"His eyes were positively blazing. The red light
in them was lurid, as if the flames of hell-fire
blazed behind them."

—Jonathan Harker's journal

The second American tour was a triumph for the Lyceum but
not for Stoker: the unique comradeship he had shared with
Irving had been forever altered by interlopers. The chatty
secretary, Louis F. Austin, was insinuating himself into Irving's inner
circle, and the fawner Austin Brereton was seeking to be the
Lyceum's press agent. Brereton wrote drama critic William Winter
that he was in "financial ruin" following a bad theatrical investment,
and asked for help in getting a position at the New York *Tribune,* ingenuously adding, "I write much better now than I used to." Stoker
smarted of humiliation with these two prowling about backstage;
whorls of anger turned inward, and avenging words percolated.

Planned by Stoker and Irving to shorten travel time, the second
tour opened in Quebec City on September 30, 1884, with *The Merchant of Venice.* They toured Canada and then headed down the East
Coast; new cities included Buffalo, Syracuse, Cleveland, and Pittsburgh, where the whole company celebrated Christmas with Irving
as paterfamilias at a dinner for thirty-four at the Monongahela
House. "We drank all the loyal and usual toasts and finished with a
sing-song," recalled Stoker. "There was much punch consumed that

night. The whisky for it was brought in great pitchers the size of those used in a wash-basin. I brewed the punch so I know." The plum pudding reeked of mothballs: it had been packed with the costumes. Irving had brought his own wine from the Lyceum's cellar. Terry recalled how they dined on "Henry's wine and Austin's wit."

The wit of Stoker's nemesis was never more evident than in the Christmas entertainment, for which he wrote satirical verses on the chief male members of the company. Pleased with his own cunning, Austin cooed in a letter to his wife that when the lines about Stoker began " 'I'm in a mortal hurry'—there was a yell of laughter that lasted several moments." Stoker "resented every joke of mine on *his* personality," Austin continued, "and was in a rage of jealousy because I had done something so successful. You would be amused by the petty jealousies of this expedition. This contemptible littleness seems to be fostered by the theatrical atmosphere."


Laurence Irving admitted how "poor strenuous Stoker must have suffered torments of jealousy. Irving, who enjoyed pulling the legs of his lieutenants and testing the extremes to which their eager assertions would carry them, got a good deal of sardonic fun out of their rivalries." To make matters worse, Austin claimed superiority to the other knights, bragging that he earned respect because he was neither "a tool" nor "a sycophant." Stoker and Austin were at odds again when Irving delivered a well-received speech to Harvard students on the art of acting in Sanders Memorial Theatre on March 30, 1885. By Austin's account this triumph was a collaborative effort between him and Irving, with his suggestions moving the actor to tears. Reporting this achievement to his wife, Austin crowed: "I am chiefly delighted about this business because that idiot Stoker wrote a speech for the same occasion and I was disgusted to find it on the Governor's table. When I read mine to Henry, he said: 'Poor old Bram has been trying *his* hand but there isn't an idea in the whole thing.' I said: 'I should be very much surprised if there was.' "

Stoker dealt with Austin's effrontery as best he could; he ignored him and thereby infuriated him. "The fact is," Austin noted, "Stoker tells everybody that he writes Henry's speeches and articles, and he wants to have some real basis for this lie. This is why he worried H.I. into putting his name to an article which appeared in *The Fortnightly Review,* a fearful piece of twaddle about American audiences that B.S. was three months in writing."* It was left to George Bernard Shaw to equalize this dispute. When Laurence Irving researched his grandfather's biography, Shaw answered questions about the Lyceum, but significant material was never published, including Shaw's observation that Stoker and Austin "were at home in good society, where they turned the conversation on to him [Irving] and talked him up." As speechwriters, Shaw believed they "made for him an entirely fabulous reputation as a man of profound learning. Like all the old actors, he slipped in the most puzzling way from complete illiteracy to the scraps of shrewdness and wisdom he had picked up from Shakespear [sic] and the plays he had acted."

Too young to know the protagonists, Irving's grandson had his information filtered through his father and Uncle Henry. At best, his feelings for Stoker were ambivalent, and with good reason: Stoker was the understudy for his grandfather and does not fare well in this biography, emerging as a social-climbing, stereotypical Irishman with little business acumen or humanity. As Laurence Irving saw the competition, Austin failed to differentiate between the extravagant loyalties of Stoker and Loveday. "Stoker, inflated with literary and athletic pretensions," he noted, "worshipped Irving with all the sentimental idolatry of which an Irishman is capable, reveling in the opportunities to rub shoulders with the great."

Stoker was "well-intentioned, vain, impulsive, and inclined to blarneying flattery," but Irving does concede he "was perhaps the only man who could have held his position as Irving's manager for so many years." Financier and Member of Parliament Henry du Pré Labouchère understood Irving's recklessness and begged him to be prudent, "to put by a certain sum, so as to be independent under all circumstances." But Irving kept plowing profits into one expensive production after another. "Had it not been for his old friend, Mr.

* Stoker's notes, drafts, and editing of numerous speeches for Henry Irving are in the Stoker Collection at Stratford-upon-Avon, proving Austin's braggadocio a lie. There are also more ideas than rhetoric in Stoker's drafts.

BRAM STOKER, 1885, drawn by
a popular cartoonist of the time,
Alfred Bryan

Bram Stoker," said Labouchère, Irving would have been "eaten out
of home and theatre very speedily." (Labouchère was responsible for
the amendment to the criminal laws under which Oscar Wilde
would be convicted in 1895.)

The stage manager H. J. Loveday was equally as self-effacing and
adoring as Stoker, according to Irving's grandson, but kept his domain the stage and had no other ambitions. Loveday saw Irving as
"divinely inspired" and allowed him to stage his spectaculars without interference. "In return, Irving treated Loveday with a trust and
affection which was never so apparent in his relations with Stoker."
Many in the Lyceum family saw Loveday as weak, a knight incapable

of disagreeing with Irving, but the young actor Martin-Harvey was not among them. He recalled that Loveday was "no fool and under his heavy eyelids lurked a world of humour. It was even said that at a convivial party, when the cup that cheers also liberates the carefully concealed truth, he would (occasionally) give a side-splitting imitation of Irving's more grotesque movements which would convulse the party." One loved him all the more, said Martin-Harvey, for "this humanity, this loyalty which was still not *quite* perfect." Between Stoker and Loveday, he wrote, "there was at times an open and often amazing hostility. Perhaps it was the old antagonism between fact and fancy." Some in the company resented Stoker herding them here and there "like helpless sheep, to make sure they were where they should be."

Stoker had watched 778 performances of *The Bells* and countless hours of *Vanderdecken;* with *Faust* in 1885, followed by *Macbeth* and *Cymbeline,* a theatrical legacy was waiting in the wings to become the architectural symbolism for *Dracula.* Irving's hypnotic evil power from *The Bells* is in the novel, and echoes from *Vanderdecken,* where Irving plays the sea captain doomed to sail around the Cape of Good Hope until Judgment Day (or until a woman who loves him sacrifices herself). As the Flying Dutchman, Irving's eyes were "like cinders of glowing red from out of the marble face," Stoker recalled; "in his eyes shines the wild glamour of the lost—in his every tone and action there is the stamp of death." The Dutchman asks: "Where are we?" "Between the living and the dead." And yet another demon beckoned.

Irving had wanted to play Mephistopheles for some time. In 1882 he asked W. G. Wills,* who had written *Vanderdecken* (none too well, said Stoker), to work Goethe's dramatic poem into a play. In preparation for the role, Irving researched wizardry—with Stoker looking over his shoulder. Following the seventh season, Irving decreed a

* Irish playwright William Gorman Wills, who adapted or wrote many plays for the Lyceum, started out to be a painter, and on the way to the theatre became a Bohemian. His studio was home to any stray cat or monkey or friend who needed a floor and a roof. Like Proust, he wrote in bed.

summer trip to Nuremberg to authenticate sets, costumes, and props. Stoker and Terry were there, as well as Joe Comyns Carr and his wife, Alice, Terry's costume designer. (The Carrs—he was editor of *The English Illustrated Magazine* and director of the Grosvenor Gallery, which had challenged the hegemony of the Royal Academy by exhibiting French paintings and the avant-garde in British art, as embodied by Whistler—brought a new cultural patina to the Lyceum: their aesthetic circle included Edward Burne-Jones, John Singer Sargent, Robert Browning, and Henry James.)

Led by Irving, the group strode down every cobblestone street, plunged into every shop, but not until they visited Rothenburg did Irving find the atmosphere he wanted. Hawes Craven, the scene painter, was summoned from London to sketch the quaint windows, old doorways, and flowered courtyards with wells at the center. In Nuremberg's old castle, they visited the torture tower displaying the famous Iron Virgin, a cabinet so constructed that when the door closed, spikes simultaneously pierced the eyes, heart, and genitals of the person enclosed in it. This visit inspired "The Squaw," Stoker's gruesome tale about a demonic cat instrumental in the accidental death of one Elias P. Hutcheson of Nebraska: "Happily the end was quick," Stoker wrote, "for when I wrenched open the door the spikes had pierced so deep that they had locked in the bones of the skull . . . he fell at full length with a sickly thud upon the floor, the face turning upwards as he fell." In a ghastly touch, the author concludes, "And sitting on the head of the poor American was the cat, purring loudly as she licked the blood which trickled through the gashed sockets of his eyes. I think no one will call me cruel because I seized one of the old executioners' swords and shore her in two as she sat."

Some anthologists rate "The Squaw" as Stoker's most grotesque short story, ignoring "The Dualitists; or, the Death Doom of the Double Born," published in the Christmas issue of *The Theater Annual* of 1887. This story was significant in Stoker's march toward *Dracula*: it foreshadows Renfield—one of the novel's most mysterious characters—and offers an appalling plot that illuminates Stoker's anomalous childhood and his anger toward the two Austins for siphoning off Irving's admiration. The plot concerns two young boys,

Harry and Tommy, who are given knives for Christmas. They develop a "hacking" obsession, working their way up from carpets to crockery to cats. Seeking a human target, they lure toddler twins onto a rooftop, where they hack away at their faces. The twins' father tries to stop the brutality and shoots at their attackers: "As the smoke cleared off and Ephraim recovered from the kick of his gun, he heard a loud twofold laugh of triumph and saw Harry and Tommy, all unhurt, waving in the air the trunks of the twins—the fond father had blown the heads completely off his own offspring."

When the boys throw the bodies from the roof, the impact of the fall crushes the twins' parents. In two short paragraphs Stoker unleashed infanticide and posthumous parricide, themes he would weave into *Dracula*. This story has the seeds of Stoker's own Oedipal repression: the battle of the sons against the father to release the desired woman, the mother. At the Lyceum there were rivalries as well, with Stoker, the Austins, and others competing for Irving's approval and affection. Both "The Squaw" and "The Dualists" have the kind of nasty deaths that small boys dream up for their enemies. Stoker, it seems, was still a small boy at heart.

Irving shared Stoker's interest in the macabre. Whenever they were in Paris, they visited the morgue (at this time open to the public), which Irving thought the most entertaining attraction in the city. He scrutinized the incoming victims, concocting tales of horror to account for the facial expressions. Afterward they went to the criminal courts to study the faces of the accused. Irving concluded that the innocent man generally looked guilty and hesitated when asked a question, but that his round, wide-open eyes corrected the bad impression. In the *Dracula Notes,* Stoker jotted down: "Count Dracula in prison picks out murderer," but did not develop this plot twist.

On December 19, 1885, theatregoers witnessed the most spectacular production ever mounted on a Victorian stage. The special effects—counterfeit apparitions, tinsel storms, angelic visions, heavenward ascents, descents into a sulfurous inferno, trapdoor vanishings, a ladder of angels, electric swords, and mysterious mists—are still replicated in twentieth-century musicals. A full-size organ was built into the stage;

a peal of bells was cast for £400. When Faust signs his compact with Mephistopheles in his own blood, the book shines with a strange light. Thunder was produced by dropping different-size cannonballs onto a boilerplate and then down a chute. So complex was the staging that each of the four hundred ropes used by the scene shifters was given a name to avoid confusion.

Walpurgis Night on the Brocken in Act IV guaranteed success—even though it did not advance the plot. The scene opens with Mephistopheles and Faust appearing in dim twilight over the top of a rocky peak. During rehearsal, with only black, white, and gray as colors, Stoker worried about the scene looking artificial. Irving promised that the stage would be transformed when Mephistopheles appears in a flaming scarlet costume,* a rapier at his side, a yard-long cock feather in his cap, and a pronounced limp to match his inner malignancy. "It will bring the whole picture together in a way you cannot dream of," he told Stoker, "and you shall see too how Ellen Terry's white dress and even that red scar across her throat will stand out in the midst of that turmoil of lightning!"

What Stoker saw on opening night was a lurid vermilion Mephistopheles emerging from a cleft in the rocks, Faust clinging to him in fear. Lightning flashed, thunder rolled, and the air filled with inhuman sounds. A flight of witches on broomsticks crossed a yellow moon; owls flew into the stormy night. At the height of the frenzy 250 warlocks, demons, imps, and goblins pranced about and danced. Irving's apocalypse stunned London. A *Dracula* foreshadowing occurs at the moment when Faust defies the devil and is silenced with: "I am a Spirit!" ("I am Dracula; and I bid you welcome"). In deliv-

---

* In medieval times, the devil wore black; red was reserved for papal robes. An early mention of the costume comes in a poem published in 1760 by David Lloyd:

> To suit the Dress demands the Actor's Art
> Yet there are those who over-dress the Part,
> To some prescriptive Right gives settled things,
> Black wigs to murd'rers, feather'd Hats to Kings
> But Michel Cassio might be drunk enough,
> Tho' all his Features were not grim'd with Snuff.
> Why shou'd Pol Peachum shine in Sattin Cloaths?
> Why ev'ry Devil dance in Scarlet Hose.

Charles Kean wore red tights, black doublet and trunks with red slashes, and a black cloak for *Faust* in 1854. Irving's all-red costume was perhaps a first.

HENRY IRVING as Mephistopheles. The actor created his own makeup for every part, and was perhaps the first to wear an all-red costume.

ering this line, it was said Irving "seemed to grow to a gigantic height, and to hover over the ground instead of walking on it." More than one Lyceum company member noticed how during this play the Guv'nor's usually generous nature changed into "a sort of grim, malicious sense of humour . . . very nearly diabolical."

Stripping away the pandemonium, Henry James sniffed that the Witches' Sabbath had been reduced "to a mere bald hubbub of capering screeching, and banging . . . it is a horror cheaply conceived, and executed with more zeal than discretion." Another critic called the Brocken a "startling advance in the scene-painter's art." Rembrandt, Whistler, Dürer, and Gustave Doré, whose expressionist illustrations Irving favored, were invoked. The acting, however, fared badly. Clement Scott of the *Daily Telegraph* disliked Ellen Terry as Margaret: a pale, pathetic role. Irving's Mephistopheles was his own

creation, played with sardonic mockery and grotesque facial grimaces at odds with Goethe's plump and worldly Lucifer. Even Irving could not carry a play whose text deprived him of the
psychological nuances of a Mathias. William Archer of *The World*
characterized his performance as all hideous glances. "Hatred, malignity, and cunning dwell familiarly in his eye," he wrote. "Grim
humour lurks in his eyebrows, and cruel contempt in the corners of
his mouth." Was it a pantomime for adults? A travesty on Goethe?
In a show of Victorian hypocrisy, mothers who allowed their daughters to attend Gounod's opera refused to have them see Margaret
betrayed without music.


The long *Faust* run was a time of personal sadness for Ellen Terry.
Charles Kelly, her husband, from whom she had been separated for
four years, and Charles Reade, her surrogate father, died within three
months of each other, and were soon followed by Godwin, father of
her two children. Each night the role of the pure and betrayed Margaret offered her little range except for an Ophelia-like mad scene in
the last act. By now she realized that Irving banned plays without
suitable parts for himself. She would never be the hoydenish and independent Rosalind of *As You Like It;* still, she had played the witty,
sharp-tongued Beatrice to his Benedick in *Much Ado About Nothing.*
A line from this play—Hero describing Beatrice's approach:

> For look where Beatrice, like a lapwing, runs
> Close by the ground, to hear our conference

—embodied Terry's joyous spirit, on and off the stage.

Every night before the performance Irving brought roses to her
dressing room, and every night Stoker poked his head in with best
wishes to a "dutiful daughter," but one who made a virtue of late-
ness: in times of stress it released tension. Standing in the wings waiting for her cue paralyzed her with fear, so she "lapwinged" from her
dressing table, alighting onstage just in time for her line. "Worst 'tear-
girl' ever I knowed," her dresser said.

IRVING WITH ELLEN TERRY as the Vicar and Olivia in the Lyceum
production of *Olivia* in 1885. Irving allowed only portrait photographs of
himself. This pose was labeled "the only authorized photograph" of the Lord
and Lady of the Lyceum.

One evening, a few minutes before curtain, Terry had not appeared.

"Miss Terry dressed?" inquired Irving as he put his head in at the door.

"She ain't come yet, Guv'nor," murmured her dresser.

"Pity" was his only reply.

(Alice Carr recalled thinking how much Irving cared for his leading lady, for restraint was not his style. At the very last moment Terry rushed in, cheeks aglow.)

"That you, Henry?" she remarked demurely as Irving, watch in hand, came in just as she started to make up her face. "I've been down to the Minories to see a fellow who sent me a begging letter this morning. I just wanted to make sure it was genuine."

"The Minories!" Irving grunted. "A nice place for you at night. I suppose you didn't think of what would happen to the play if you had been attacked by some rough down there."

"Why, every man in the crowd knew me or had heard tell. I let down the window of the four-wheeler and shook hands with them all. It's because there were so many that I'm so late."

"Of course," Irving muttered laconically, "it's a good advertisement, but I do wish you wouldn't cut things so fine."

"Not two minutes to your entrance, Miss Terry," yelled the callboy wildly from the passage outside.

"If anybody bothers me I shan't come at all," she replied mildly.

"Two lines to your speech, Miss Terry, *if* you please."

At this cue Ellen Terry tore down the narrow staircase with her dresser holding her skirts and landed on stage, the innocent Margaret.


On the ninety-ninth night of *Faust,* Franz Liszt was in the royal box; for supper the Beefsteak Room chef made the maestro's favorite meal of lamb cutlets, mushrooms in butter, and lentil pudding. Stoker was fascinated with the seventy-five-year-old's long white hair (which he borrowed, along with Whitman's, for Count Dracula). He noted Liszt's appearance in his diary: "fine face—leonine—several large pimples—prominent chin of old man—long white hair down on shoulders—all call him 'Master'—must have had great strength in youth."

One evening Stoker brought seven-year-old Noel to see *Faust,* certainly a frightening play for a young child, but one who was probably tucked into bed with more terrifying tales. "The little chap was exceedingly pretty—like a cupid," wrote his father. When Stoker brought him backstage, Irving looked at Noel, took out his dark pencil, and rapidly made the boy up as Mephistopheles—"the same high-arched eyebrows; the same sneer at the corners of the mouth; the same pointed moustache." Stoker said it was a strange and pretty transformation. Perhaps. But was being made up as the devil fun for impressionable Noel, who by all accounts grew up solitary and shy?

*Faust* was performed 792 times. At a cost of £15,402 it was the Lyceum's greatest success; staging and visual effects rescued a weak script. Lighting innovations, such as the electric swords used for Faust and Valentine's duel, were the talk of London.* For some time, Irving had experimented with the effects of limelights and colored glass to produce fine gradations of light and shade. Lighting rehearsals—held after the play ended, and the limelighters had supped, and Irving and Stoker had finished their cigars in the Beefsteak Room, and the scene was up—started in the early morning hours. On stage, bowing to the Guv'nor, were the gas engineer, the limelight master, the electrician, and their staffs. The coordination of twenty-five limes—each projecting a beam of light—created the memorable Brocken eeriness. Colored glasses (red, two shades of amber, and four shades of blue) slid into the back of an individually operated lamp.

Irving designed the lighting sequences, and the limelighters made them perfection. Irving was so insistent about the use of limes and trained operators that he contested United States officials in 1893 in order to have his own staff admitted into the country as artists

---

* Colonel Gouraud (Thomas Edison's partner) created this primitive but impressive visual effect. Two metal plates (one positive, one negative) were attached to the stage floor. Each combatant had a metal plate on the sole of his right shoe; a wire went through the costume into the palm of the right hand to contact a piece of metal on a rubber glove. When the glove came in contact with the metal handle of the sword and the swords struck each other, sparks were emitted.

## LYCEUM THEATRE.

SOLE LESSEE AND MANAGER · · · · · · · · MR. HENRY IRVING.

*Faust 204 to 209*

### WEEKLY STATEMENT. 28 day of January 1887

Week ending Friday, the

| Date | | Play. | Gross Receipts. | Discount to Agents. | Nett |
|---|---|---|---|---|---|
| **1887** | | | £ s. d. | £ s. d. | £ s. d. |
| Jany 22 | Bal. Matinée | | | | |
| | Saturday | Faust | 294 9 . | 3 18 11 | 290 |
| 24 | Monday | do | 248 6 | 2 1 6 | 246 |
| 25 | Tuesday | do | 257 14 6 | 2 7 1 | 255 |
| | Wed. Matinée | | | | |
| 26 | Wednesday | do | 267 1 . | 3 1 2 | 263 |
| 27 | Thursday | do | 273 7 . | 1 18 4 | 271 |
| 28 | Friday | do | 233 11 6 | 2 . 6 | 231 |
| | TOTAL WEEK | £ | 1574 13 . | 15 52 | 1559 |
| | FORWARD | | 34,408 4 . | 351 18 11 | 34,056 |
| | TOTAL TO DATE £ | | 35,982 7 . | 367 71 | 35,615 |

EXPENDITURE.

| | Expenses (taking Average of Rent, &c.) | Expenses (Cash actually Paid.) |
|---|---|---|
| Rent / Taxes / Insurance | 600 . . | |
| House Staff | 47 19 . | 47 19 . |
| House Expenses | 24 13 9 | 66 13 . |
| Sundries | 11 1 4 | 11 1 4 |
| Printing | 25 13 . | 25 13 . |
| Advertising | 77 6 1 | 77 6 1 |
| Bill Posting | 76 1 6 | 76 1 6 |
| Salaries :— | 412 6 | 412 6 |
| Separa | 27 | 27 |
| Stage Staff | 45 . | 45 . |
| *Stage Expenses | 15 7 3 | 15 7 3 |
| Gas | 28 7 | 28 7 |
| Limelight | 35 5 | 35 5 |
| Orchestra | 77 14 . | 77 14 . |
| Total Working Expenses £ | 1121 . 7 | 1030 13 6 |
| †Production Account | | 13 11 |
| Expenditure on House | | 8 16 |
| TOTAL WEEK | | 1053 1 |
| FORWARD | | 26,021 5 1 |
| TOTAL TO DATE | | 27,074 6 5 |

Paint Room / Property / Gas / Wardrobe — Carpenter's Dpt.

| PROFIT AND LOSS ACCOUNT. | £ s. d. |
|---|---|
| Receipts for week | 1559 4 10 |
| Weekly current expense (A) | 1121 7 |
| Profit on Week, not including expenses of production | 438 4 3 |
| Total profit/loss on season to date £ | 8,541 3 6 |

Bills due ...

Amount to Credit ... 755 18 .

Total Debit ... Balance 755 18 / 1915

Cash in Bank / on Hand / Amount due ... 164 2 ...

Amount to Credit ... 815 5 5 / 247 5 5 / 8333

Total Credit ... 19,905 8 1

*Bram Stoker* Acting Manager.

4 day of Feby 1887

Night expenses £187

STATEMENT FROM *FAUST.* Every week Stoker toted up the receipts and
the expenses. His signature as acting manager is in the lower right-hand corner.

under the labor law. When they first visited America in 1883, the
Boston Theatre, said Stoker, was the only one with good lighting
equipment.* Martin-Harvey recalled how one of Irving's men
worked on his *Hamlet* at His Majesty's in 1916. Martin-Harvey
wanted a ray of light to linger on his hand, one finger of which, at
the end of the words "I doubt some foul play," pointed to the throne,
which the king had just vacated. " 'You see, my man,' I said to the
electrician, 'I want you to concentrate your light on my hand at this
moment, *after* the other lights are dimmed down. 'Yes, sir,' he readily
replied. 'On which *finger,* sir?' "

It was of "absorbing interest," said Stoker, with characteristic understatement, to watch Irving develop this new branch of stage art.

---

* After a demonstration of its brilliancy (for use in lighthouses) on a dark Irish night in
1825, limelight found its way into the theatre in 1857. Produced by the heating of lime, or
calcium oxide, in an oxyhydrogen flame, limelight was extremely bright and thus effective
as a follow spot or to create the effect of sunrises and sunsets or any romantic setting;
scenes were particularly written with limelight in mind.

For twenty years he sat in the stalls while Irving "thought of it, invented it, arranged it." One "insider" *Dracula* reference involves this interest: Lucy's fiancé, Lord Godalming, is named after the town of Godalming, thirty-four miles southwest of London, among the first to use electricity for public lighting in 1881; in keeping with Stoker's love of double meanings, Lucy symbolizes light or Lucifer.

One day Stoker exclaimed to Martin-Harvey: "It's worthwhile to have a theatre in London as an advertisement!" Following *Hamlet,* Irving was seen (not gaunt but beautified) in an ad with the legend: "To Beecham or not to Beecham that is the question, methinks I've heard they are worth a guinea a box (with apologies to our greatest poet and our most renowned actor)." More than ninety thousand translations of Goethe's poem were sold in the first months of the *Faust* run. There was a Mephistopheles hat, a Margaret shoe, an Ogden's "Demon Flake" tobacco, and Tom Smith's Lyceum Crackers. Irving sardonically observed: "I didn't know that the devil expected to be an instrument in the revival of trade, but the many forms of honest industry which he has been the means of stimulating are really quite bewildering." Not a week went by without some kind of Irving caricature being published. Had Irving, like any actor today, received a commission for the use of his image, Stoker's account book would have glowed with health.*

*Faust* was to travel to America, and Stoker was dispatched to New York in the fall of 1886 to make the preliminary arrangements. Crossing on the *Etruria,* he took part—as he usually did—in the shipboard entertainment, reciting "Shamus O'Brien." On the return trip he shared the spotlight with Buffalo Bill, who did mind reading. Stoker prided himself on these performances; they gave him the opportunity to be the actor he had originally wanted to be. He liked to

---

* Irving was included in every group caricature published by *Moonshine,* which specialized in theme satires showing the Victorian elite's wigs, feet, shirt collars, mouths, chins, backs. The magazine also had a series called "Days With Celebrities," which ranged from tasteless ("If They Had Been Hebrew," with big noses) to funny ("If They Were Fat," with Irving as Falstaff).

mention that Irving praised his recitations because he "anticipated words by expression, particularly by the movement of my eyes."

Although this trip was rushed, Stoker made time for a second visit to Walt Whitman. It was a cold November day when he arrived at Mickle Street in Camden and found a blazing wood-burning stove. The light was dim, the furniture shabby, and the floor littered with piles of newspapers, books, and old, soft-gray, wide-brimmed felt hats. Stoker was saddened to see Whitman older and feebler. His eyes were not so "quick and searching as before"; his hair was longer and wilder, shaggier and whiter. When he eased his bulk from a custom-made rocking chair, he moved about the room with difficulty. Stoker noted his costume: gray trousers and coat worn with an open shirt of unstarched coarse cotton, fastened with a big white stud and trimmed with "a bit of cheap narrow lace" on the collar and cuffs.

During their hour together, the discussion lingered on Abraham Lincoln, for whom Whitman "had an almost idolatrous affection," said Stoker. "I confess that in this I shared; and it was another bond of union between us." Back in Dublin when Stoker read *Memoranda During the War*, he was so impressed with Whitman's description of Lincoln's assassination that he assumed the poet had been there. Whitman explained he had been close by but had spent most of the night interviewing those who were in Ford's Theatre on April 14, 1865. It was a wonder, he said, there was "no holocaust, for it was a wild frenzy of grief and rage. It might have been that the old sagas had been enacted again when amongst the Vikings a Chief went to Valhalla with a legion of spirits around him!" Stoker wanted to add his thoughts about Lincoln, but the "breath of good, healthy, breezy sea air," as Whitman called him, was off in a mortal hurry. He held the poet's hand and vowed to return.

Before embarking for London, Stoker talked to the press about *Faust*. When a journalist from the New York *World* asked about Irving's acting, Stoker winked and said, "He is a perfect devil." Reviewing the New York production, William Winter grasped the nascent *Dracula* atmosphere when he wrote that *Faust* reminded him of "the shuddering lines" from Coleridge's "Rime of the Ancient Mariner":

As one that on a lonesome road
Doth walk in fear and dread,
And, having once turned round, walks on
And turns no more his head,
Because he knows a frightful fiend
Doth close behind him tread.

As he approached middle age, Stoker's infatuation with men of power continued, doubtless aided by his growing insecurity over Irving's affection. Stoker was still an exile, a child trying to find his way home. His latest hero was James McHenry, an Anglo-American who amassed a fortune from the Lake Erie–New York railway, and a major benefactor of the Lyceum. Stoker's correspondence with McHenry begins in 1879, with letters concerning loan repayments. Later they provide a rare insight into Stoker's feelings about his family: "Florence has suffered from a dreadful cold," he wrote, "which she is trying to get rid of before going to Ireland to bring home our little man who is there with his grandmother." Stoker compared himself to "a three year old except for the loneliness of being away from Florence." On a cold February morning during the 1885 American tour, he embellishes a letter with a drawing of a broken thermometer. "Washington died merrily to the tune of $15,000," he told McHenry, adding, "I am off on the 4:30 train to Boston to see if all is going as it should in the Hub. Florence and the boy are well but lonely."

Florence had never accompanied her husband on an American tour, although Loveday's wife was always at his side. Noel was young, the trip arduous, and the country unfamiliar; the thought of playing lady-in-waiting to Irving displeased her. When a San Francisco stop was planned, Stoker optimistically wrote McHenry, "I think Florence will come out—it would be after the winter and the trip would do her good." But that did not happen.

Moved by some subsequent public appreciation by McHenry, Stoker unburdened himself: "Since I pressed my dear father's forehead in the vault of the church at La Cava, there has been no other person than you who shared the love I had for him . . . and your conduct toward me the other day when you made me your guest of guests has made a fool of me." There followed a typical Stokerian ambiguity: "I have been fighting my own battles in my own way for twenty years & all I arrived at never seemed so worthy as now." These are wrenching emotions, with Stoker revealing a pathetic loneliness, an embarrassed gratitude over some token acknowledgment, some attention McHenry gave that Irving could not.

America fascinated Stoker. From the first Lyceum tour he worked to understand how this new country was different from its origins in England. He corresponded with Harry Furness, editor of the Variorum edition of Shakespeare, and James Whitcomb Riley, the Hoosier poet of Indiana. He reveled in America's freedom and openness, a welcome antidote to the strictures of Victorian England. After, as he put it, consulting "all sorts of persons—professors, statesmen, bankers, etc.," he delivered the lecture "A Glimpse of America" at the London Institution on December 28, 1885. Sampson Low, Marston, publishers of *Under the Sunset,* printed it as a shilling pamphlet the following year.

A bit of a curiosity, the talk was well received. The *Pall Mall Gazette* praised Stoker for his "keen eye for humorous touches," noting that "the salient and distinctive points of American life" had been so "accurately stated" that his experiences surpassed previous reminiscences. The explorer Henry Morton Stanley admired "my little book," Stoker boasted, saying "I have mistaken my vocation—that I should be a literary man!" Stanley told Irving it "had in it more information about America than any other book that had ever been written." James Whitcomb Riley exclaimed: "Good! Splendid! Keen! Sharp! Observant! Superb!" Stoker would receive no greater literary rave until his mother praised *Dracula.*

Today the "little book" seems insignificant for all the fuss, but at the time it provided information not readily available. It was dense with facts: America had 124,281 miles of railroad and 11,403 newspapers and periodicals; Texas had 170,099,200 acres, and there was a difference between a state and a territory, and it was complicated to understand how the electoral college was constituted. Stoker noticed the inadequacy of domestic service (considered one of the lower orders of work because of other opportunities), the swiftness of communication (ringing a bell in one's home summoned a messenger boy, a carriage, a policeman, or a fireman), and the quality of the plumbing. It was so expensive, Stoker joked, that it "is better for you to offer the entire freehold in liquidation of the debt rather than undertake to pay the bill." Stoker was a witty and informative lecturer: he had found a way to earn applause.

For some months he had been working on his first novel, *The Snake's Pass,* or as he called it, the "outdoor" book, because it was written outside during August vacations or wherever he found a spare hour and a comfortable waterfront spot during the American and provincial tours. Stoker filled this Irish romantic tale with shifting bogs, ancient superstitions, and, of course, buried treasure. At the same time, he kept notes on the company's touring misfortunes, the storms and blizzards, eventually turning these anecdotes into the short-story collection, *Snowbound: The Record of a Theatrical Touring Party,* published in 1908. He also recorded examples of slang, seeing it as a separate speech, which he would use in *Dracula:* The laconic Texan cowboy Quincey Morris proposes that Lucy "hitch up alongside of me and let us go down the long road together driving in double harness." Morris (who originally had a larger role) fits right into the cowboy denouement, when the trackers cut off Dracula's coffin at the Borgo Pass. In the terms of the Old West, Dracula and his female assistants are victims of a lynch mob, already assumed guilty. In fact, the novel is an early source in England of the use of the phrase *true grit* to mean manly.

In addition to the American accent, Stoker uses Romanian-English, Dutch-English, Cockney, Yorkshire, and Scottish. Renfield tells Quincey Morris that he should be proud of his great state: "Its reception into the Union was a precedent which may have far-reaching effects hereafter, when the Pole and the Tropics may hold allegiance to the Stars and Stripes"—a look into the future on Stoker's part about Alaska and Hawaii.

Stoker was making his way as a literary man. In *Dracula* he celebrates the redemptive powers of writing. Jonathan Harker must write or go mad. "I dare not stop to think," he tells his journal. Mina discovers that writing "is like whispering to one's self and listening at the same time. And there is also something about the shorthand symbols that makes it different from writing." As an author, Stoker learned to tell but not tell, to hide the personal behind a mask, to project feelings onto characters; in this way he survived shipwrecks, married the beautiful girl, and lived happily ever after. Fantasy *was* better than reality.

*Chapter 10*

# THE BLOODY PLAY

S toker's two Trinity degrees set him apart from those he commanded at the Lyceum; even though an Anglo-Irish education lacked the luster of Oxford or Cambridge, it counted for
something—but evidently not enough. At the age of thirty-nine he
decided to become a barrister, a lawyer who tries cases in a higher
court. He was admitted to the Inner Temple, one of the four Inns of
Court, and, following four years of not-too-rigorous study, was called
to the bar on April 30, 1890, the Witches' Sabbath, or Walpurgis
Night, the date he chose to open the second chapter of *Dracula,* later
deleted and published posthumously as the title short story in the
collection *Dracula's Guest.*

He was acquainted with the court system through his work at
Dublin Castle and research for his *Petty Sessions* book. He had written the laws of order for The Hist at Trinity, the Actors' Benevolent
Fund, a hospital, and numerous societies. To be called to the bar, he
needed only to dine in the student hall once during each of the
twelve terms and pass a written and oral examination. Lectures, although available, were not compulsory, and he did not attend. But
why the law? And why at this time? Stoker joked that he wanted to
avoid jury duty,* but the motivation most likely was to elevate him-

---

* The Inner Temple archivist I. G. Murray explains that barristers were exempt from jury
service under the 1870 Juries Act, but previously Stoker might have served (and not liked
it), and his theatrical working hours would not have been a valid reason for deferment.

self in the eyes of Irving. Or to please Florence, whose attentive escort, Gilbert, started his career as a barrister. For the twenty-five years Florence outlived her husband, she referred to him in publications only as a barrister—never as the author of *Dracula* or the acting manager for the late Sir Henry Irving. To be fair, Stoker himself was never immune to labels. On passenger lists his name was followed by "M.A.," a form he also used on business cards.

Although he never practiced the law and never tried a case, he did frequent the Inner Temple's library, a quiet place to write. Instead, he put the law to work in his novels. Van Helsing is a barrister, and Harker a solicitor (one who prepares cases for barristers and represents them before lower courts). Dracula, Harker quips, "would have been a wonderful solicitor." Beyond using his new profession to anchor a hero's intellectual standing, Stoker designed plots where characters—frequently lawyers—seek documentation to understand the rational or supernatural world. "I must watch for proof," Harker says, bewildered by the bizarre events at Dracula's castle. But at the conclusion there is not one "authentic document," everything is subjective, "nothing but a mass of type-writing."

As October and another American tour approached, Stoker eagerly anticipated the violent Atlantic crossings. There was nothing more sublime, he felt, than a storm at sea—the tremendous energy of winds, clouds, thunder, lightning, and driving rain. Gothic tales traditionally feature storms to heighten the cruelty being perpetrated; in *Dracula,* Stoker harnesses the unpredictable North Sea weather to scuttle the captainless *Demeter* in Whitby Harbor. "Masses of seafog came drifting inland—white, wet clouds, which swept by in a ghostly fashion," he wrote, "so dank and damp and cold that it needed but little effort of imagination to think that the spirits of those lost at sea were touching their living brethren with the clammy hands of death, and many a one shuddered as the wreaths of sea-mist swept by." Nearly one-fourth of the named sources for *Dracula* concern superstitions of the sea, including *Henry Lee's Sea Fables Explained and Sea Monsters Unmasked,* Fletcher S. Bassett's *Legends and Superstitions of the*

*Sea and of Sailors—In All Lands and at All Times,* and William Jones's *Credulities Past and Present.*

In dreams Stoker endured countless shipwrecks, but it was his wife and son who experienced the unthinkable. On April 13, 1887, Florence and seven-year-old Noel, accompanied by a companion, Mrs. Cassan Simpson, left Newhaven on the steamship *Victoria* en route to Dieppe and the train to Paris. On board were 120 passengers and crew. At 3 a.m., an hour before arrival, thick fog obscured a dangerous line of rocks under the lighthouse at Cap d'Ailly, a headland nine miles west of Dieppe. Awake and preparing to disembark, passengers heard no foghorn. The lighthouse keeper had fallen asleep and did not start the fire for the steam-powered light until 4 a.m. By that time it was too late.

As Florence secured her luggage, the *Victoria* crashed into the rocks, the bow ripped open, and water flooded the forward cabins, sinking the boat in two hours. Twenty drowned, fourteen in the panic of lowering the first of only four lifeboats, each built to hold eight or nine. Florence, Noel, and Mrs. Simpson made it into the third boat, crammed in with ten other passengers; a sailor, a steward, and a fireman from the crew rowed. She was quoted in the papers, and wrote an article for the Dublin *Evening News* recalling how the "whole forepart of the boat was under water, which seemed creeping steadily on towards us. The part we were on was high out of the water. We heard agonising shrieks from the second and third class passengers, who were still below, and in the grey light of dawn saw dim figures climbing the rigging. . . . They allowed the first boat to fill before she touched water and it upset."

Another boat was lowered with mostly men; no order of "Women first" was given. Crying "No more," a man tried to push Mrs. Simpson into the water as she got in. They rescued a young girl afloat on an oar but left an old man to drown, for there was no room. "His cries were heart rending," she wrote. For seven hours the crew rowed, trying to reach land. "As we went on, the sea got rougher and the wind fresher, the waves were tremendous. I do not know how it was they did not engulf us. And all the time we saw the shore and high chalky cliffs, with villages on the top of them here and there."

Approaching St. Valéry, they saw a black flag, a signal there was not enough water to cross the bar at the mouth of the small harbor. They continued to Fécamp. Noel was sandwiched between two passengers in the stern. "I wanted him beside me," Florence wrote, "but we dared not move. He began to ask me when we would land, and when he heard them talking about how far Fécamp was from St. Valéry, he said, "Mamma, I will ask Miss Collins when I go back to school." After three hours of drifting and rowing, a steam tug rescued them: they disembarked at five in the afternoon, twelve hours after the accident.

In print, Florence seemed more worried about appearance than survival. "I was dripping wet; my dress torn, and trailing; my hair over my face," she wrote. Noel had lost a shoe. When she received her trunk, the lock was broken. "Of course, my dresses were spoiled by salt water; half my linen stolen, and everything of value gone." She had hidden money in her corset. At Fécamp she sent her husband a telegram, but in the confusion it was never dispatched. For two days Stoker was ignorant of their fate; thereafter, for many summers, the family made pilgrimages to Fécamp to commemorate the rescue.

Despite—or perhaps because of—the April shipwreck, Florence crossed the Atlantic on the *City of Richmond* for the third Lyceum tour, in 1887. It was one of those turbulent crossings that mark the late fall. She was hysterical during the entire voyage and never went again. But her husband enjoyed showing her America, and his ego soared with compliments on her charm and beauty. Just as the rough seas had faded from memory, the company was trapped in New York for the Great Blizzard of 1888, which arrived on March 11 as a soft, gentle rain in the last days of winter and ended three days later with snow twenty-one inches deep. At the peak of the storm, winds gusting to eighty-five miles an hour sculpted drifts towering to twenty feet. New Yorkers cut tunnels through the snow and wore squares of carpeting on their feet and blankets around their heads. Storm-related deaths climbed to four hundred; many were buried in the snow.

Stoker never had experienced snow driven with the force and fascination of a white hurricane: it was more exhilarating than a

North Atlantic storm. He explored the silent, shrouded wonderland of a city, tramped to the Star, and herded a sodden company onstage. Most of the theatres closed, but Irving refused to cancel even one performance. Ellen Terry recalled how "discipline was so strong that every member reached the theatre by eight o'clock, some walking from Brooklyn Bridge." Proudly Stoker opened the doors to *Faust* only forty-five minutes late. "There was hardly any audience and only a harp and two violins in the orchestra," Terry recalled. The actor John Drew was out front, along with the mayor of New York and his daughter. "It was the oddest, scantiest audience! But the enthusiasm was terrific!"

During the rough crossing, while Florence remained in her cabin, Stoker drafted an American version of his Lincoln lecture; the subject had obsessed him since last talking with Whitman. Hero worship drove him toward a historical father figure, and compassion for the injustice of slavery—not a topic that rallied Englishmen to fiery discourse in the Beefsteak Room—distressed him. Even stranger was his desire to deliver such a talk in America. Earlier he had asked Thomas Donaldson for a copy of Whitman's lecture, which the poet sent to his future biographer on August 11, 1885, calling it "a full report of my Lincoln Lecture for our friend Bram Stoker." But Donaldson never posted the manuscript to England.

When Stoker stepped up to the podium in New York's Chickering Hall on November 25, 1887, he had to rely on Whitman's "Memoranda During the War"; Josiah G. Holland's *The Life of Abraham Lincoln,* published shortly after the assassination; and research done in the Round Reading Room on the Constitution, the Missouri Compromise, and the Dred Scott decision. But in annexing new experiences he stumbled. *The New York Times* critic noted Stoker had "delivered this lecture with great acceptance before unenlightened English audiences, and his utterances have been highly commended by the semi-educated English press." He snidely added, "On this side of the water, however, where Abraham Lincoln lived and died, and where American history is taught in public schools, a historical review of the life and times of the martyr-President, even when presented by Mr. Henry Irving's manager, is apt to fall flat." Stoker was stubborn about his passions.

The next month he visited Whitman but did not mention the lecture, hoping the poet had not seen the review. Another topic disturbed him. "It was a great pity," he told Whitman, not to cut "certain lines and passages out of the poems." He urged him to let his friends help; they will only "want to cut about a hundred lines in all—your books will go into every house in America. Is not that worth the sacrifice?" Looking more and more like King Lear (or as Edmund Gosse put it, "a dear old Angora tom"), Whitman reacted immediately, as though his mind had been made up long ago. "It would not be any sacrifice. So far as I am concerned they might cut a thousand. It is not that—it is quite another matter." Stoker observed that Whitman's "face and voice grew rather solemn." "When I wrote as I did," the poet continued, "I thought I was doing right and right makes for good. I think that all that God made is for good—that the work of His hands is clean in all ways if used as He intended! No, I shall never cut a line so long as I live!"

Stoker felt strongly about Whitman sanitizing portions of *Leaves of Grass* and spoke his mind; he could do no more. Whitman was not angry, only exasperated; he hobbled over to his bedroom, returning with an autographed photo of himself (just as Irving had done in Dublin) and the 1871 edition, which he presented to Stoker. Then they said goodbye for the last time. There would be no Lyceum tour between the spring of 1888 and the fall of 1893. Whitman suffered another stroke and died in 1892. (Two years later, when Stoker returned to Philadelphia, Donaldson handed him the Lincoln lecture delivered at the Chestnut Street Opera House on April 15, 1886. "This was my Message from the Dead," Stoker remarked sadly.)*

On his return to England, Stoker addressed the Sunday Lecture Society on December 16, 1888. Posters announced the topic as: "Abraham Lincoln: how the Statesman of the People saved the Union, and Abolished Slavery in the American Civil War." When

---

* When Stoker's library was sold at Sotheby's on June 20, 1913, the London *Daily Telegraph* commented the next day on the lack of interest in Whitman's Lincoln material. "Seven years ago there was a fight at Sotheby's for the three notebooks by Shelley, and an agent of an American bibliophile won them for £3000. Yesterday, in the same rooms, a collection of fragments in the hand of Walt Whitman, the 'poetic celebrant of Democracy,' came up, and the last work was only £16/10s." This was the Lincoln manuscript.

Stoker gave his "A Glimpse of America" lecture in 1885, he spoke of the Civil War, pointing out that the British knew little about it. "Now that the graves are hidden with the 'sweet oblivious of flowers,' " he said, "we can only know or guess what it was from the dry page of books and statistics of the ruin which it caused." Stoker adapted this lengthy talk for different audiences, later including in it the death of Whitman. Once he lectured with a bronze copy of the Volk life mask of Lincoln on the podium.* In the margin of the original manuscript he practiced writing Lincoln's signature.

Unlike the xenophobic *New York Times,* British critics were impressed with the far-ranging subject matter. *The Elocutionist* said Stoker "brought the rugged, genial star-souled unfortunate president well before the audience." The *Westminster and Lambeth Gazette* reported the lecture was "received by the rather small audience with decided tokens of appreciation." Stoker tended to orate a potted history of America and to offer such insights as "There is a common idea that all tyrants are cowards. This is quite false; history eternally proves the contrary—and the slave owners had all the courage of their convictions—the hands must be strong and the hearts be bold that rule a people by the lash" and such anecdotes as "Lincoln had feet of enormous size—uncommon even in a region where bare feet or Moccasins were the ordinary wear for some generations of pioneers." He also pointed out that Lincoln had gray eyes but stopped short of saying they shared the same color. *Macbeth* was Lincoln's favorite play, Stoker pointed out: it was all about equivocation, the president said.

Blazing fires fascinated Stoker only slightly less than forbidding mists and howling gales. He was, in fact, an incendiary addict. There was a standing Lyceum joke that whenever there was a fire within range he was off to it "hot-foot." And there were many theatre fires during the gaslight era. A curtain ignited during *Hamlet* in New York but was quickly extinguished and did not interrupt Irving's speech.

---

* Stoker and Irving had been subscribers in the drive to purchase Leonard Wells Volk's life mask of Lincoln for presentation to the Smithsonian; in return they received copies cast by Augustus Saint-Gaudens.

A few people started to rush out, however, particularly one man whom Stoker feared might start a panic. As he ran up the aisle, Stoker caught him by the throat and, by his account, hurled him to the floor. "At such times one must not think of consequences, except one, which is to prevent a holocaust," Stoker recalled pompously. " 'Get back to your seat, sir! It is cowards like you who cause death to helpless women!' " With fires providing opportunities for such melodramatic lines, is it any wonder that Stoker stayed primed for the fire bell?

Even for Victorian times, Stoker was overly courteous and gallant. He fretted about helpless women; yet most of his fictional heroines are far from helpless. In *The Shoulder of Shasta,* Esse carries a man to safety on her back. In *The Mystery of the Sea,* Marjory dies trying to rescue her father. He often told the story of how Gladstone's wife broke a blue cut-glass perfume bottle as she alighted from a brougham in front of the Lyceum; Stoker picked up the fragments off the path and later found her another of the same design. "She was greatly pleased at the little attention and did not forget it," he said. "Years afterwards, when I went to see her in her box, she held up the scent bottle and said: 'You see I have it still!' " And Martin-Harvey praised Stoker's extravagant manners toward the actor's young wife, who was starting her career as a Lyceum extra: "It was rather pleasant to see his hat fly off whenever he met her." In these small ways, Stoker was a romantic hero to himself.

He seldom took dinner at home. Irving thrived on mania after a performance, refusing to sleep, feeling that it should be "at arm's-length till it is summoned." At these times Stoker did not like to thwart the actor when "a friendly chat of no matter how exaggerated dimensions would rest him better than some sleepless hours in bed." After so many years together the two could read each other's thoughts. "I have sometimes seen the same capacity," Stoker said cunningly, "in a husband and wife who have lived together for long and who are good friends, accustomed to work together and to understand each other." But his own wife was neglected, even ignored, and Noel deprived of fathering during his formative years.

WILLIAM S. GILBERT, who wrote the words to Arthur Sullivan's music, was a frequent escort for Florence Stoker when her husband was working with Irving.

Florence was enough of a pragmatist to make the best of things, filling the evening hours in other ways than being in her husband's company. She refused to let marital neglect turn her into a wilting neurotic, cared for by servants, soothed by laudanum, and resurrected beautifully intact for formal dinners. But she needed to be surrounded by people and made sure they were never boring. W. S. Gilbert, so cruelly observant, so riotously gay, who also disliked Irving every which way, kept Florence entertained with his mordant wit. Wilde, whose enchanting *The Happy Prince and Other Tales* was published to far greater acclaim than Stoker's *Under the Sunset,* stayed in touch with her. "Will you give me the pleasure of accepting a copy of my book of fairy tales?" he wrote. "I hope you will like them, simple though they are; and I think you will enjoy Crane's pretty pictures, and Jacob Hood's designs. With kind regards to Bram."*

Florence seized on her anxiety about hurricanes, surging waves,

---

* Inscribed "Florence Stoker from her friend the author Oscar Wilde June '88," the book and letter brought $8,500 at Christie's, New York, in 1984.

and fog as convenient excuses not to accompany her husband to America; there were dreams about *The City of Richmond* tossing on the Atlantic and the *Victoria* crashing onto the French coastline. Still, she managed the turbulent English Channel for a Parisian shopping trip, or the Irish Sea to deposit Noel with one of his grandmothers. Charlotte Stoker had returned to Dublin in 1885 for her final story-telling years, perhaps frightening Noel as she had his father with ghastly tales of the cholera epidemic. Thornley was there to care for her, as was Margaret, who married William Thomson, a Dublin surgeon she met in 1875 during the family's Italian peregrinations. Matilda was studying painting in Paris and would soon wed—at the age of forty-three—Charles Auguste Petitjean, a minor French bureaucrat. Like most of the Stokers, she published from time to time and, it was said, had artistic talent.*

The year 1888 was a turning point for the theatre and Stoker. It was the year the Lyceum began the long-awaited production of *Macbeth,* and the year Jack the Ripper terrorized Whitechapel, bringing evil into the drawing rooms of Mayfair and Kensington. At this time Stoker conceptualized a story that would intermingle Shakespeare's dark psychology with contemporary evils. He also met Joseph Harker, a curious footnote to the *Dracula* legend.

Harker joined Hawes Craven and William Telbin at the Lyceum to form the most renowned trio of England's scene painters, whose careers stretched from the 1850s to the 1920s. All came from theatrical backgrounds, and all worked under the contract system (it was impractical to keep a scene painter on the payroll when a play like *Faust* went into hundreds of performances). For publicity only, Irving

* In April 1887 Matilda Stoker published in *The English Illustrated Magazine* a charming biographical essay about the "palmy days of fashion" in the Georgian Bath of 1770. It was based on letters of Dublin actor Richard Brinsley Sheridan to his first wife, Eliza Linley of Bath, that were rescued from the 1809 fire at the Drury Lane Theatre. When Oscar Wilde accepted the editorship of *Woman's World,* a monthly for—and partly written by— "women of culture and position," he told the publisher he thought the present publication "too feminine, and not sufficiently womanly," mentioning Matilda's article as an example to follow.

engaged the Royal Academicians Sir Edward Coley Burne-Jones and Sir Lawrence Alma-Tadema to design—respectively—productions of *King Arthur* and *Coriolanus,* but mostly he relied on Craven and his assistants.

In bringing the thirty-three-year-old Harker into the fold, Irving repaid an old debt: Harker's father had taken the eighteen-year-old Irving under his wing at Edinburgh's Royal Theatre. Harker worked on five scenes for *Macbeth,* painting towering battlements and gloomy castle walls of black, ponderous stone, and intricately carved wooden beams, labyrinthine passages, stairways, and galleries. Annexing any opportunity to smite Irving, Shaw praised Harker's scenery as often of a "much higher order of art, and enormously more skilled in its execution than either the play or the acting on which it was wasted."

The Lyceum painting room was a fantasy nursery where Noel helped Harker put gold leaf on his drop curtains and Ellen Terry's son, Gordon Craig, destined to be one of the major theoreticians of modern theatre design, learned his skills. Irving's sons, Henry and Laurence, did not have much of a backstage childhood; they came to acting in their maturity and not without parental dissent: Irving cautioned them that there was no school at which to train, that the Irving name would be a hindrance, and that "education is as beneficial to an artist as to a scholar. If you are ever to be an actor worth the name, you will need all your knowledge and strength and all your armour for the coming fight."*

Rather than wait for contracts, Harker decided to open his own studio in London. Irving offered him financial backing and commissions in all future Lyceum productions. Stoker arranged for him to lease studio space at Her Majesty's Theatre. And it was there that Stoker appeared one day, Harker recalled in his memoirs, and an-

---

* Both sons excelled at Marlborough. Henry (known as Harry) was persuaded to go to Oxford; after graduation he failed at his first attempt to go on the stage, later distinguishing himself as an actor and biographer. Laurence joined the diplomatic service and was posted to Paris and Moscow, but lacking the independent income to continue in the foreign service, he joined Frank Benson's touring company—billed as Mr. Lawrence—and later the Lyceum, in 1895. Harry appeared with his father when Irving and Terry shared the stage for the last time in *The Merchant of Venice.*

nounced that "he had appropriated my surname for one of his characters." This was Jonathan Harker, the only name from the Lyceum family used in *Dracula*. The secretive Stoker never revealed why.

Ellen Terry said she divided the years at the Lyceum into before *Macbeth* and after. Of all the productions, she thought it the most important. "I judge it by the amount of preparation and thought that it cost us and by the discussion which it provoked." For Irving, the play was the obvious choice after *Faust*. Both are northern, medieval, and gothic; both embody a diabolic element, with chiaroscuro settings— red and gray for *Faust,* brown and white for *Macbeth*. Terry tried to dissuade Irving from doing the role, which had been "roundly condemned" when he performed it with the Batemans in 1875, but his "imagination was always stirred by the queer and the uncanny," she said. He preferred playing versions of Mathias, creating a character who suffers gradual deterioration from supernaturally inspired evil passions.

Research took the group to Scotland to view castles and heaths and, ultimately, to commission Keeley Halsewelle, an associate of the Royal Scottish Academy, to provide archaeological accuracy. En route to Inverness, Stoker glimpsed Cruden Bay, a quiet fishing village north of Aberdeen, overshadowed by Slains Castle on a precarious headland overlooking the North Sea. Stoker thought the isolation, contorted rocks, and caves irresistible, and he made a note in his diary to return on a walking tour.

Irving's conclusions about Macbeth's nature had not changed in thirteen years; what had changed was his ability to project a character to an audience. He saw the Thane of Cawdor as a black-hearted rogue, a liar, a traitor, a craven who displays courage only when he is at bay. He was not the blunt, full-blooded barbaric warrior familiar to audiences, who fears neither man nor ghost. Murder is on Macbeth's mind when he first meets the three witches, who are but the emanations of his own thoughts. To Irving, a man capable of such damnable treachery and such horrible crimes could never have had any good in him.

As Lady Macbeth, Terry also discarded the accepted reading of the devoted wife who, for love of her husband, seeks to gratify him. Instead of a traitoress, a masculine termagant, a grim and gaunt tragedy queen, she made her a scheming and ambitious wife, fascinating and fragile, unaware of the evil in her husband. Defending her interpretation to critic William Winter, she said that everyone thinks her a *"monstrosity"* but she found her a *"woman*—a mistaken woman—and *weak*—not a Dove—of course not—but first of all a wife. I don't think she's *at all clever.* ('Lead Macbeth' indeed!—she's not even clever enough to *sleep!)"* She confided to Winter that she had never been able to discuss Lady Macbeth's character with Irving, for he lacked "knowledge of *womenfolk*—it is almost ludicrous his ignorance on that one subject. He has, I think, never given it his consideration!!"

Irving also rejected the traditional Rob Roy kilts and helmets in favor of Scandinavian costumes and heavy armor. Lady Macbeth looked more like the Queen of Sheba than the queen of Scotland in 1056. Immortalized in John Singer Sargent's portrait, her regal gown was crocheted of green silk and blue tinsel, overlaid with real green beetle wings. A border of Celtic designs was studded with stage rubies and diamonds. A heather-toned cloak of shot velvet was embroidered with flame-colored griffins. Wilde observed that "Lady Macbeth seems an economical housekeeper, and evidently patronizes local industries for her husband's clothes and the servants' liveries; but she takes care to do all her own shopping in Byzantium." During the winter of 1889, Terry arrived in costume for sittings at Sargent's Chelsea studio, prompting Wilde, who lived nearby, to muse that Tite Street, which "on a wet and dreary morning has vouchsafed the vision of Lady Macbeth in full regalia magnificently seated in a four-wheeler, can never again be as other streets: it must always be full of wonderful possibilities."*

---

* Sargent's portrait of Ellen Terry as Lady Macbeth holding a crown over her head was first shown at the New Gallery and then hung in the Beefsteak Room until Irving gave up the Lyceum. At the sale of Irving's possessions in 1905, the portrait was bought by the collector Sir Joseph Duveen, who presented it to the nation. It now hangs in the Tate Gallery.

ELLEN TERRY as Lady Macbeth. Her gown was
decorated with real beetle wings and studded with faux
rubies and diamonds.

*Macbeth* opened on December 29, 1888, at a cost of £6,600, and
ran for 151 continuous performances—the longest run in the history
of the tragedy, interrupted only by Queen Victoria's command that
Irving perform *The Bells* and the trial scene from *The Merchant of
Venice* at her Sandringham estate. The company's journey there
prompted a journalist to describe the ubiquitous Stoker, as he "hurried about—here, there, and everywhere. He manipulated bundles of

railway tickets; he did conjuring tricks with mysterious documents; and he finally pasted hieroglyphics on the windows of several compartments." He was, as usual, in a mortal hurry.

*Macbeth,* like *Faust,* was a success but as a spectacle. Audiences loved the realistic battle scenes but criticized the performances. Irving's Macbeth was almost effeminate in his lack of moral courage and moments of terror-stricken collapse. Often a severe critic, William Archer had the intelligence to understand Irving's method. "I have no quarrel with Mr. Irving's conception of Macbeth," he wrote. "During the greater part of the action, Macbeth is in a state of nervous agitation varying from subdued tremor to blue funk—he says so himself, and he should know."

Stoker's first Macbeth had been Barry Sullivan, who played him as fully resolved, from the beginning, to remove all obstacles in the way of his ambitions. The last scene was played on a bare stage with wings of wild rock and heather, and in the background, Dunsinane Castle, framed by a Gothic archway. Offstage trumpets blared and drums rolled, Stoker remembered, and "suddenly the castle gates were dashed back" and through the archway came Sullivan, sword in hand. "Dashing with really superb vigour down to the footlights he thundered out his speech: 'They have tied me to a stake; I cannot fly.' "

That castle, with the massive gates thrown back on their hinges by the rush of a single man, returned to him vividly when he saw the play as Irving had bewitched the text. All was different. Macbeth's victorious battle-weary soldiers were outlined against the low-dropped sun across a heath studded with patches of light glinting on the water. "The endless procession of soldiers straggling, singly, and by twos and threes, filling the stage to the conclusion of an endless array, conveyed an idea of force and power," said Stoker.

In one of his frequent melancholy moods, Irving asked his dresser, Walter Collinson, which was his best part. A former wigmaker, Collinson was a wiry, dapper little man with shrewd, kindly eyes veiled behind steel-rimmed spectacles, who for years had played San-

WALTER
COLLINSON,
Irving's dresser, was
probably the actor's
closest confidant after
Fussie, Irving's dog.

cho Panza to the forlorn knight. At first he hesitated, then pronounced *Macbeth*. This pleased Irving immensely, Terry recalled, for he fancied himself as Macbeth more than any other role.

"It is generally conceded to be Hamlet," Irving argued.

"Oh, no, sir," said Collinson, "Macbeth. You sweat twice as much in that."

The pathos of *Macbeth*—much like that of *Dracula*—arises from the inability of the doomed to escape their evil destiny. But in the end, who is Macbeth? Who is Lady Macbeth? Who is Dracula or Mina? They must materialize in the psychology of the viewer or reader. Terry made a notation on her working script about Macbeth: "A man of great *physical* courage frightened at a *mouse*," she wrote. "A man who talks and talks and works himself up, rather in the style of an early Victorian hysterical heroine. His was a *bad* Nature and he became reflected in his wife. M. must have had a neglectful mother—who never taught him the importance of self-control."

Many similarities exist between *Macbeth* and *Dracula*. Both center on a desolate, brooding castle, to which an unsuspecting stranger is lured and then "visited" in his sleep. Both have a sleepwalking scene. The protagonists, motivated by power and ambition, receive a kind of immortality from their covenant with supernatural forces, and die with their throats slashed. In both the foul contagion of evil is seen as an infectious plague to be destroyed by teamwork. Macbeth's three "weird sisters" are resurrected to tantalize Jonathan Harker with their "brilliant white teeth" and "voluptuous lips." *Macbeth*—also—is a bloody play: the word *blood* or *bloody* occurs thirty-six times.

Beyond plot parallels, evocative Shakespearian quotes reverberate in *Dracula*. "It will have blood; they say blood will have blood," Macbeth proclaims. Lady Macbeth says,

> I would, while it was smiling in my face,
> Have pluck'd my nipple from his boneless gums,
> And dash'd the brains out.

In *Dracula*, Lucy "flung to the ground, callous as a devil, the child that up to now she had clutched strenuously to her breast." Lord Siward, Earl of Northumberland in *Macbeth*, finds his counterpart in Dr. Seward. Both end with king and count trapped in their castles, where the ancient cathartic Celtic ritual of the severed head releases the world from evil. "Behold where stands / Th' usurper's cursed head," cries Macduff. "The time is free." The dying Quincey Morris points to Mina: "See! the snow is not more stainless than her forehead! The curse has passed away!" Stoker used echoes from his favorite Shakespearian play to frame *Dracula* and to create the consummate villain to tempt Henry Irving into a new role. When he cast Irving as Dracula, Stoker understood there was little difference between the Macbeths of the ruling world and the Draculas of the supernatural.

Through the centuries *Macbeth* has been the unlucky play; untold accidents and mishaps have plagued productions. The name Macbeth is never uttered backstage, except during a performance; it is referred to as "the Scottish play." *Dracula,* when it was finally staged, was considered a lucky play—financially, that is: whenever a company was in trouble, it exhumed the old count from his coffin and good fortune followed.

*Chapter 11*

# THE OCCULT

"There are mysteries which men can only guess
at, which age by age they may solve only in part.
Believe me, we are now on the verge of one."
—Van Helsing to Arthur Holmwood

As the nineteenth century ebbed, Victorians turned to table-rapping, séances, clairvoyance, mesmerism, palmistry, and all manner of crystal-gazing. Soothsayers, astrologers, and healers flourished. Such alternatives to rational science may have been paltry quackery to unbelievers; but Dickens, Tennyson, Carlyle, and Keats were impressed observers, if not occasional practitioners. Stoker himself was easily drawn to the controversial occult ideas of Egyptology, Babylonian lore, astral projections, and alchemy. He had always been intrigued by phrenology, and his eclectic library held books on Egyptology, a history of the Ku Klux Klan, and the five volumes of J. C. Lavater's *Essays on Physiognomy,* published in 1789.

The Victorians had great faith in science, and mesmerism (or animal magnetism), which swept England in the 1840s, was—or seemed to be—a science. Charles Dickens, who hypnotized his wife when she was unable to sleep, had been at the center of the mania, using the technique in his unfinished novel, *The Mystery of Edwin Drood.* Tennyson once breathed upon the forehead of a lady to remove a pain over the eye, then apologized because he had been smoking, but the hypnotized woman could neither hear nor smell him. Phreno-

mesmerism, which combined the skills of mesmerism and phrenology, became a fashionable parlor amusement in Victorian literary circles. At one party an inebriated phrenologist pressed the alimentary
zone on the head of a temperance lady; she was then seized by a need
for brandy and water.

Out of this fascination for mind control there developed a genre
of mesmeric novels, which borrowed the gothic staples of magic portraits and enchanted mirrors and added sudden aging and perennial
youth, keeping the shadow rather than the spectacle. Among many
titles were Daniel Dormer's *The Mesmerist's Secret* and Edward
Heron-Allen's *The Princess Daphne*. *Helen Davenant* by Violet Fane,
published in 1889, describes a murder committed under hypnotic
compulsion. Whitman's poems "I Sing the Body Electric," "The
Sleepers," and "Song of Myself" all hint at mesmeric mastery. Wilde
gave his only novel, *The Picture of Dorian Gray,* hypnotic nuances. "I
cannot help telling you things," Dorian admits to Lord Henry Wotton. "You have a curious influence over me." Wotton charms Dorian with his musical voice and "cool, white, flower-like hands,"
which move "like music" and have "a language of their own." Dominated by Wotton, Dorian sleepwalks his way from boyhood innocence to dedicated hedonism.

In *Dracula,* Stoker uses Lucy's sleepwalking to exonerate her
from making a pact with the devil: she is in a trance when she is
vamped and when she dies, making her, as Van Helsing explains, different from the other undead. During the race to Transylvania,
Mina's powers go beyond mere hypnotism to clairvoyance. Stoker
invokes the name of Jean-Martin Charcot, a French neurologist who
worked with Sigmund Freud in 1885 to establish a technique for the
study of hysteria through hypnotism,* leading to the founding of
modern psychoanalysis. Stoker also attended F. W. H. Meyers's enthusiastic talk on Freud's experiments at a London meeting of the

---

* Hypnosis was known to the earliest races of Asia; ancient yogis in India put themselves
into states of hypnotic ecstasy by the use of eye fixation before the time of Christ. Franz
Anton Mesmer (1734–1815) gave mesmerism its name, but Dr. James Braid in 1852 introduced the term *hypnosis* from the Greek ("to sleep"). Mesmer claimed that with the use
of magnetic wands, "magnetic fluid" could be directed at will to cure the ill. Braid advocated a theory of double consciousness. Using hypnosis, he reported successful treatment
of diseases such as aphasia and rheumatism.

Society for Psychical Research, a group that inquired into thought reading, mesmerism, apparitions, and haunted houses.

It was widely rumored—but never substantiated—that Stoker was a member of the Hermetic Order of the Golden Dawn, a secret society that practiced ritual magic, founded in 1888 by a London coroner and prominent Rosicrucian Freemason named William Wynn Westcott. Magicians, charlatans, and eccentrics of all kinds gravitated to this group; but Yeats, Constance Wilde, Florence Farr (the actress who dallied with Shaw), and Annie Horniman, who founded Dublin's Abbey Theatre, are the only names remembered today. The order's enduring legacy was occult fiction, examinations of the dark side of life, which can be said to have begun with *Dracula* and the creation of Van Helsing as psychic detective. According to R. A. Gilbert, historian of the Golden Dawn, Stoker was an outside observer with a number of close friends who were members, and he might have learned about the rituals if they broke the oath of secrecy. Scottish author J. W. Brodie-Innis, founder of the society's Edinburgh offshoot, Alpha et Omega, dedicated his 1915 occult novel *The Devil's Mistress*—somewhat ambiguously—"To the memory of my dear friend the author of 'Dracula' to whose help and encouragement I owe more than I am at present at liberty to state."

An artist and clairvoyant, Pamela Colman Smith was a member of the "Uncle Bramy" cult as well as of the Golden Dawn. Thirty-one years younger than Stoker, she illustrated the first modern seventy-eight-card tarot deck, still known as the Rider-Waite deck; another Golden Dawn member, Arthur Edward Waite, provided the text. Arthur Machen, a writer of supernatural tales, including *The Great God Pan,* called her deck the "most wonderful pack of cards that has been seen since the days when Gringonneur illuminated three packs for the amusement of King Charles VI of France in 1392." Smith accompanied the Lyceum on its sixth American tour, in 1899. En route to Liverpool on the *Menominee* she drew cartoons of the shipboard entertainment: for one Stoker wears a sailor hat inscribed "HMS Dracula." Later she collaborated with him on a portfolio book about the Lyceum and illustrated the first edition of his last novel, *The Lair of the White Worm.*

It is significant that while Smith was imagining the tarot designs,

MOONSHINE, a satirical magazine, always ran on its cover a caricature of a public figure inside a half-moon. The quote for this one, "I have immortal longings in me," from *Antony and Cleopatra*, was particularly apt for Stoker.

Stoker was plotting *Dracula*. Throughout the novel there is a strong undercurrent of the tarot, symbolic of the classical gnostic quest. Jonathan Harker, obviously, is the Fool, who journeys forth and encounters hazards; he is depicted on the cards as a young man carrying a knapsack and a rose, standing on a precipice with his dog. During his travels Harker meets the Magician (Van Helsing), the Empress (Mina), the Lovers (Lucy and Arthur), the Hermit (Seward), the Devil (Dracula), and the Hanged Man (Quincey Morris). The first

# DRACULA

6d.

BY

BRAM

STOKER

6d.

WESTMINSTER

Archibald Constable & Co Ltd

2 WHITEHALL GARDENS

THE 1901 CONSTABLE EDITION. The cover featured a tarot-inspired drawing taken from the scene where Jonathan Harker watches Dracula slinking down the castle wall.

paperback edition of *Dracula,* published by Constable in 1901, featured a tarot-inspired cover illustration: Harker watches from a castle window as Dracula (with bat wings) climbs down the wall.

Another occult devotee was Constance Wilde, whom Stoker talked with many an evening while dining at Tite Street or when the Wildes supped at St. Leonard's Terrace. When her youngest son, Vyvyan, was a year old, she joined the Women's Liberal Federation and became editor of *The Rational Dress Society Gazette,* a publication dedicated to eliminating tight-laced corsets, bustles, and high heels. A grave, mystical woman whom Wilde called his violet-eyed Artemis, she grew into adulthood desperately wanting love. Her letters to Wilde during their engagement are worshipful. "I have no power to do anything but just love you," she wrote; "my whole life is yours to do as you will with it."

Constance moved from spiritualism—a movement supportive of women's rights and a haven for radicals, teetotalers, vegetarians, dress reformers, and antivaccinationists—to Helena Petrovna Blavatsky, one of the great eccentrics of the Victorian age. Credited with bringing the word *occultism* into common use, she founded the Theosophical Society in 1875 and linked the spiritualist movement with the esoteric wisdom of Cabbala and Eastern religions. To encourage unconventional behavior, the society condemned civilization and good manners as "things rotten to the core." Madame Blavatsky set the tone with demonstrative affection for her chief disciple, Annie Besant, the socialist and freethinker.

It is odd to think of Constance Wilde belonging to such a group at a time when her husband's restlessness made him vulnerable to the seductiveness of seventeen-year-old Robert Ross, his first male lover. Constance soon left Madame Blavatsky for a more mystical atmosphere in the Golden Dawn. Initiated in 1888, she wore a costume rational dressers would have favored: a black tunic with a cord wound three times around the waist and red shoes. Her neophyte's motto, chosen to reflect the initiates' highest aims and beliefs, was *Qui patitur vincit:* "He who suffers, conquers." In one year she reached the rank of Philosophus, the highest grade in the outer order; to remain, she would have to move to the secretive second order, which ran the organization. But in 1890, with the publication of *The Picture of Dorian Gray* in *Lippincott's Monthly Magazine,* Constance withdrew from public life. "Since Oscar wrote *Dorian Gray,*" she complained, "no one will speak to us."

"Live! Live the wonderful life that is in you! Let nothing be lost upon you. Be always searching for new sensations," Lord Henry Wotton urges Dorian in the most famous decadent novel of the Decadent, Yellow, Naughty Nineties. Wilde rode the crest of a wave sweeping away the old order; even the most formidable conventions began to crumble when he brought homosexuality into the Victorian drawing room. Speranza always said her son would do something wonderful; now she was triumphant: "It is the most wonderful piece of writing in all the fiction of the day."

The doppelgänger motif whereby Dorian lives a double life—one respectable, the other soaked in sin—keeping him forever youthful while his portrait ages, impressed Stoker, who recognized the theme borrowed from *Melmoth the Wanderer,* written by Wilde's great-uncle Charles Maturin.* Like Dracula, Dorian makes a Faustian pact for immortality, experimenting with two forms of sexuality: love of women and love of men. Wilde went to the same well, drawing Dorian from the sources of the Dracula myth, but instead of a vampiric creature of the night, Dorian is a sophisticate who helps Wilde satirize the pretentious art world.

Even though Wilde provides a moral ending (Dorian stabs the portrait, returning it to its original vision of youth and transforming himself in death into a loathsome old man), *The Athenaeum* called it "unmanly, sickening, vicious." Wilde did not cloak Dorian's splendid sins in the supernatural, as Stoker did in *Dracula,* but he had warned readers in the preface that "all art is at once surface and symbol. Those who go beneath the surface do so at their peril. Those who read the symbol do so at their peril." As a pun, he uses his own name some thirty-four times—from *wild* to *wildest.* Stoker does the

---

* Charles Maturin was an oddity. He liked writing in company, and to indicate that he was in the throes of composition would place a red wafer on his forehead. If the conversation became so interesting that he was tempted to join in, he sealed his mouth shut with a paste of his own invention.

same. Jonathan Harker writes, "When I found that I was a prisoner a sort of wild feeling came over me" and later "a wild desire took me to obtain that key at any risk." Were these coded messages to his exiled friend?

No personality better epitomizes the waning century than Wilde, who brought comedy back to the London stage with *The Importance of Being Earnest*. Better than Stoker and Irving, he understood why the old theatricality of Victorian life was over. The cheering of the pit, which had so delighted Irving, was banished to the music halls. As critic Walter Kendrick points out, by the time of *Earnest*, "laughter was the only physical response that remained genteel." The nineteenth century was on its deathbed, and Wilde managed to make it laugh at itself. How Stoker must have envied his former rival—for a time.

Hall Caine was the only man with whom Stoker forged a relationship separate from Irving. A forgotten writer today well below forgotten writers, Caine was once as popular as Dickens (*The Christian*, based on the prodigal son parable, sold 250,000 copies). Although six years younger, he became Stoker's mentor, literary adviser, and writing coach, sharing interests in spiritualism and second sight. In the domelike expanse of Caine's forehead, and the Elizabethan slope of his beard, Stoker said he resembled Shakespeare. Contemporary photographs reveal a more demonic visage in the coal-black, burning eyes. Initially a critic for the Liverpool *Town Crier*, Caine owed his literary success to no less a mentor than Rossetti: in 1878, when the Stokers arrived in London, the twenty-six-year-old Caine was living with the ailing painter at Tudor House on Cheyne Walk.

Rossetti encouraged Caine to be "The Bard of Manxland," to write about the Manx customs of his birthplace, the Isle of Man. His first novel, *The Deemster*, published three years after Rossetti's death, was an immediate success. Caine recycled the same ribald plots that appealed to the passions of the 1890s—stories of illegitimacy and rivalry, with brothers or cousins or half-brothers falling in love with the same girl. Irving asked him to write a new version of *The Flying Dutchman;* instead Caine offered "The Demon Lover," a role too

HALL CAINE, to whom Stoker dedicated *Dracula,* calling him Hommy-Beg, Manx for "little Tommy." Caine was a novelist who popularized tales from the Isle of Man.

young for the fifty-six-year-old Irving. When Stoker created the more appropriate four-hundred-year-old demon lover, Irving sneered.*

A gifted storyteller (Stoker said he should have been Irish), Caine never left St. Leonard's Terrace without a session in front of the blazing rainbow fire of salt-impregnated timber. "As he goes on he gets more and more afire," Stoker recalled of one January evening, "till at the last he is like a living flame. His large eyes shine like jewels as the firelight flashes. We sit quite still; we fear to interrupt him. The end of his story leaves us fired and exalted too." Stoker was still the bedazzled boy excited by tales told with frenzy—as he had been years ago in Dublin by Irving's recitation of *Eugene Aram.* When Irving

---

* The Flying Dutchman, the Wandering Jew (a man who insulted Christ at his Crucifixion), and the vampire were all condemned to live until Judgment Day. The Dutchman legend mingles history—the story of Captain Hendrik Vanderdecken (The Cloaked One), whose ship ran into a gale off the Cape of Good Hope in 1680 en route from Amsterdam to Batavia—and myth: the captain defies God and for his punishment is condemned to roam the seas in a cursed phantom ship. In *Dracula*'s aborted second chapter, Harker plans to see Richard Wagner's opera *The Flying Dutchman* in Munich.

was around they all told spooky tales. One evening in Edinburgh the
trio started off with Shakespeare and ended—well, weirdly. Caine remarked how he once looked into a mirror and saw a reflection not
his own. Irving also noticed the tricks mirrors played, and he used
this illusion in the *Macbeth* ghost scene. Stoker neglected—as he often
did—to preserve *his* contribution. Perhaps it was a story of an undead
man who casts no reflection. In 1893 Caine dedicated *Capt'n Davy's
Honeymoon,* with fulsome tribute, to Stoker,* who reciprocated with
*Dracula,* but in code: "To My Dear Friend Hommy-Beg." Hommy-
Beg is Manx for "little Tommy," a name Caine's grandmother called
him.


Busy as Stoker was at the Lyceum, he made time for holidays with
his family. Florence loved Paris, and they took short trips there for
shopping. Amsterdam (Van Helsing's home) was another favorite
destination; they visited Nuremberg, and Stoker refers in *Dracula* to
the red-roofed houses in Whitby, "piled up one over the other, like
the pictures we see of Nuremberg." Admirers of Hans Richter's interpretations of Wagner, they attended the Wagner cycle in Bayreuth.
Stoker visited Italy and Switzerland when his family lived there, but
never traveled farther east than Vienna, never visiting Romania and
Transylvania. When an American journalist made this oversight an
issue, Stoker snapped (referring to the vivid, scene-setting opening
chapters): "Trees are trees, mountains are, generally speaking, mountains, no matter in what country you find them, and one description
may be made to answer for all."

The Yorkshire location of Whitby, however, is authentic. Stoker's
three weeks there in 1890 with Florence and Noel mark the creative

---

* "To Bram Stoker: When in dark hours and in evil humours my bad angel has sometimes
made me think that friendship as it used to be of old, friendship as we read of it in books,
that friendship which is not a jilt sure to desert us, but a brother born to adversity as well
as success, is now a lost quality, a forgotten virtue, a high partnership in fate degraded to
a low traffic in self-interest, a mere league of pleasure and business, then my good angel
for admonition or reproof has whispered the names of a little band of friends, whose
friendship is a deep stream that buoys me up and makes no noise; and often first among
those names has been your own. . . ."

genesis of *Dracula,* the first time he made notes on a supernatural tale about an undead man. A medieval fishing village that grew into a Victorian resort, Whitby—then as now—was a misty, mystical place, the port where Captain James Cook departed for his three voyages that changed the Pacific from imprecise myth to modern map. Stoker was one of many artists, actors, and writers—from Caedmon, England's first recorded Christian poet, to C. L. Dodgson, the future Lewis Carroll—who summered in Whitby and adjacent Robin Hood's Bay.

That August, following an eight-hour train trip from Kings Cross Station, the Stokers arrived at 6 Royal Crescent, where they had booked a suite overlooking the sea on Whitby's West Cliff. In *Dracula,* Mina and Lucy have rooms on what is now called East Crescent, with the East Cliff view of the bleached skeleton of the thirteenth-century abbey and the twelfth-century church of St. Mary's. Stoker took long walks along the rugged cliffs, bellowing at the sea (as was his habit). Amateur theatricals and traveling circuses staged at the Saloon occupied Florence and Noel. The Grand English Opera Company presented *The Marriage of Figaro.* There were dances, concerts, and teas at the Spa, Whitby's social center.

After a hectic Lyceum season Stoker preferred socializing with the local fishermen, who congregated at St. Mary's churchyard. They entertained with tales of shipwrecks and drownings. Stoker took notes on their distinctive dialect and recorded epitaphs and ninety-one names, mostly drowned sailors and master mariners, from the then 1,530 readable headstones. In *Dracula* he pokes fun at the lying tombstones, which say, "Here lies the body . . ." when the body lies under the Greenland seas. The old sailor Mr. Swales, referred to as Sir Oracle (from *The Merchant of Venice*), sounds a lot like Irving, a "most dictatorial person," Mina says. "He will not admit anything, and downfaces everybody." Stoker consulted Francis Kildale Robinson's *A Glossary of Words Used in the Neighbourhood of Whitby* for Swales's dialect; he copied out 164 words and used sixty-four, including *lich wake* ("corpse wake"), *kirkgarth* ("churchyard"), and *boh-ghosts* ("terrifying apparition").

Another discovery was the Whitby Library. With three thousand volumes, it offered more serious reading than popular novels. Stoker pulled from the shelf 0.1097, the call number—recorded in his *Dracula Notes*—for *An Account of the Principalities of Wallachia and Moldavia* by William Wilkinson, a representative of the English Levant Company. Reading about the Carpathians, he learned the following: "Dracula in the Wallachian language means Devil. Wallachians were accustomed to give it as a surname to any person who rendered himself conspicuous by courage, cruel actions or cunning." Dracula? Dracula! Stoker liked the meaning and the sound of the word: it was something to dream about.

Whitby was the ideal setting for the shipwreck that brings Dracula to England. Stoker incorporates the town's distinctive features: the 199 steps leading to St. Mary's church, the graveyard, the abbey, and the unpredictable North Sea weather. The *Dracula* storm recalls an earlier scene from Stoker's *Under the Sunset:* "Onwards it rushes, and terrible things come close behind; black darkness—towering waves that break in fury and fly aloft—the spume of the sea swept heavenwards—the great clouds wheeling in fury;—and in the centre of these flying whirling, maddening shadows, rocks the shadow of the ship." Mina notes the Whitby weather in her diary as "a brool over the sea that sounds like some presage of doom."

On a visit to the lighthouse a Coast Guardsman told Stoker about the *Dmitry*—a Russian brigantine out of the port of Narva, ballasted with silver sand from the Danube—which ran aground on October 24, 1885. At the library Stoker read the Whitby *Gazette*'s report of the event: "The piers and cliffs were thronged with expectant people, when a few hundred yards from the piers she was knocked about considerably by the heavy seas, but on crossing the bar the sea calmed a little and she sailed into smooth water. A cheer broke from the spectators on the pier when they saw her in safety." By morning the *Dmitry* was high and dry, embedded in the sand; a picture by the Whitby photographer Frank Sutcliffe, which Stoker saw displayed at the library, preserved the scene.

In *Dracula,* as the correspondent of *The Dailygraph,* Stoker

WHITBY LANDMARK. In *Dracula* (p. 87), Mina Murray writes in her journal: "The steps are a great feature of the place. They lead from the town up to the church . . . the slope is so gentle that a horse could easily walk up and down them." These are the 199 steps Mina races up when she discovers Dracula with Lucy.

rewrites the story, renames the ship the *Demeter,* and has Mina paste the clipping into her journal. Stoker's lyrical version shows he wrote well when given time:

The day was unusually fine till the afternoon, when some of the gossips who frequent the East Cliff churchyard . . . called attention

THE *DMITRY,* a Russian schooner out of Narva, was beached near Whitby's Tate Hill Pier in October 1885. In the novel, Dracula, in the form of a dog, jumps off the Russian vessel *Demeter,* of Varna, a real port but an anagram of Narva. Stoker loved codes.

to a sudden show of "mares'-tails" high in the sky to the north-west. The wind was then blowing from the south-west in the mild degree which in barometrical language is ranked "No. 2: light breeze." . . . Shortly before ten o'clock the stillness of the air grew quite oppressive, and the silence was so marked that the bleating of a sheep inland or the barking of a dog in the town was distinctly heard, and the band on the pier, with its lively French air, was like a discord in the great harmony of nature's silence. A little after mid-night came a strange sound from over the sea, and high overhead the air began to carry a strange, faint, hollow booming. Then without warning the tempest broke.

In the *Dracula* notes Stoker drew a diagram of a boat about to ram into Tate Hill Pier. For the correct use of *mares'-tails* and the ranking of a No. 2 light breeze he consulted the 1887 *Fishery Barometer Manual* by Robert H. Scott.

The Stokers watched the Grand Fete on the River Esk, an annual procession of decorated boats, and Stoker borrowed this image for the funeral of the *Demeter*'s captain. "Every boat in the harbour seemed to be there, and the coffin was carried by captains all the way from Tate Hill pier up to the churchyard." Like all Whitby visitors, he was drawn to the abbey, "a most noble ruin, of immense size, and full of beautiful and romantic bits," and the cemetery, "the nicest spot in Whitby, for it lies right over the town, and has a full view of the harbour and all up the bay to where the headland called Kettleness stretches out into the sea." He watched bats from St. Mary's church tower wheeling about, and marveled at the sunsets, "marked by myriad clouds of every sunset-colour-flame, purple, pink, green, violet, and all tints of gold."

Some of the Whitby notes were used almost verbatim. On August 11 he recorded a "grey day . . . all grey . . . grey clouds . . . July sea . . . sea mist . . . lost in grey mist . . . all vastness . . . brool over

WHITBY ABBEY was founded as a monastic site in A.D. 657 by St. Hilda. Stoker found the surviving thirteenth-century church "a most noble ruin."

the sea . . . life, a pre–life a presage . . . dark figure on beach here and there . . . men like trees walking through mist." In *Dracula,* this becomes a symphony in gray:

> Today is a grey day, and the sun as I write is hidden in thick clouds, high over Kettleness. Everything is grey—except the green grass, which seems like emerald amongst it; grey earthy rock; grey clouds, tinged with the sunburst at the far edge, hang over the grey sea, into which the sand-points stretch like grey fingers. . . . Dark figures are on the beach here and there, sometimes half shrouded in the mist, and seem "men like trees walking."

—a quote not from *Macbeth* but from Mark chapter eight.


That summer Stoker met the Pre-Raphaelite beauty and novelist Violet Hunt, daughter of Alfred Hunt, a respected watercolorist, and Margaret Raine Hunt, the first translator of *Grimm's Fairy Tales.* Violet invited the Stokers to tea at Broad Ings Farm, between Whitby and Robin Hood's Bay, and found Stoker a "nice healthy stalwart Irishman as sweetnatured and gentlemanly as it is possible to be." Over a plate of cakes he told the Hunts his off-the-record theatre stories: Ellen Terry had pathos but no passion; Tennyson had a villainous mouth. That evening Violet told her diary: "Bram is a dear, and Mrs. is so pretty and kind. Noel came and played in the low haystack at Broad Ings."

Violet dominated a notable salon at her home on Campden Hill in Kensington. Stoker's name was added to South Lodge's invitation list, and he was introduced to a group not associated with the theatre. Vivacious and flirtatious, Violet had a destructive passion for loving the married literati; at this time her lover was the diplomat-turned-publisher Oswald Crawfurd (she later moved on to H. G. Wells and Ford Madox Ford). Crawfurd's new illustrated magazine, *Black & White,* would publish Stoker's short story "The Secret of the Growing Gold." Violet appreciated, as so many women did, Stoker's avuncular attitude, opening one letter with: "You are only 'Uncle Bram' in moments of emotion." Social columns noted the Stokers' presence at Crawfurd's literary gatherings at Queen Anne's Mansions; Hunt's previous lover, the Royal Academician George Henry Boughton, arranged invitations for private views.

Also at Whitby in that summer of 1890 was George du Maurier, who had featured the Stokers in a *Punch* cartoon entitled "A Filial Reproof." It depicts Stoker and Florence relaxing in wicker chairs at a country-house garden party. Noel hovers behind his preoccupied mother. The caption reads: "Mamma to Noel, who is inclined to be talkative, 'Hush, Noel! Haven't I told you often that little Boys should be *Seen* and not *Heard*?'" Noel: "Yes, Mamma! But you don't Look at me!" Was Florence more distracted than most Victorian mothers? Probably not. But when writers excavated Stoker's marriage, this cartoon—and the sin-

**A FILIAL REPROOF.**

BRAM, FLORENCE, AND NOEL at a garden party, in a cartoon for *Punch* drawn by George du Maurier, author of *Trilby*

gle-child family—buttressed the rumor that she was a distant mother and a frigid wife. This was not the intent of Du Maurier, who seized as easily on blue china and aesthetic affectation for satire as on mothering. Florence, he said, was "one of the three most beautiful women in London." (The others were Lady Hare and Marie Spartali Stillman, a Pre-Raphaelite beauty who became a successful painter.)

Du Maurier was completing his second novel, *Trilby* (published in 1894), which introduces the mesmerist Svengali, an enduring mythic character to rival Dracula. Surely the two writers had tea at the Spa and discussed their protagonists as the band played softly. Was Dracula born from Svengali, as critic Nina Auerbach suggests, with his powers still further extended over time and space? There are striking parallels between the two novels. Both deal with the fear of female sexuality and the loss of innocence, and with brave men who rescue the mother figure from a foreigner's embrace. Trilby O'Ferrall has three suitors, Taffy, Sandy, and Little Billee; Lucy Westenra also has three. The tone-deaf, weak-willed Trilby becomes a great singer when hypnotized, and Lucy becomes voluptuous when bitten. Both books illustrate the male-bonding novels popular in the late 1880s, novels such as H. Rider Haggard's *King Solomon's Mines* (1885) and Arthur Conan Doyle's *A Study in Scarlet* (1887).

Svengali and Count Dracula—both looming mesmerists and demon lovers—join Mr. Hyde, Iago, Claggart, and Professor Moriarty as enduring evil icons. The third of a trio of literary Jews who entered the English language after Shylock and Fagin, Svengali is described as an "Oriental Israelite Hebrew Jew." Dracula has a "hook" and "beaky" nose. By featuring a sinister foreign seducer, both authors reveal a prevalent xenophobia over the influx of Eastern European Jews at the end of the century, but only *Dracula* elevates the desire—and fear—of the pristine middle-class to be violated by a dark outsider.*

Grandfather of Daphne, author of *Rebecca,* and father of Gerald,

---

* In press accounts Svengali has survived as the epitome of the ruthless influencer, sometimes linked with Rasputin or Charles Manson or even Henry Higgins. Strong personalities are described as having a "Svengali-like influence" or playing "Svengali to the first Trilby he would find." The ballet star Suzanne Farrell says of George Balanchine that "he was not a soulless Svengali, I was not his Trilby." Anton Walbrook and Moira Shearer were Svengali and Trilby in *The Red Shoes.* Stephen Ward was characterized as having a Svengali-like influence over Christine Keeler during the Profumo scandal.

the actor who gave his surname to a cigarette, Du Maurier modeled Svengali on George Vandeleur Lee, the talented but vulgar singing teacher who befriended Shaw's mother and is thought by some scholars to be his real father. Shaw rewrote the Svengali-Trilby relationship in *Pygmalion,* but in his version Eliza Doolittle's voice speaks truly only when she emerges from Henry Higgins's bullying presence to begin an independent life. Thirteen years Stoker's senior, the Paris-born Du Maurier, like the Irish-born Stoker, was an outsider in English society. They spent their careers at two of Victorian England's most famous institutions: the Lyceum and *Punch.* Dracula too understands the drawbacks of leaving the country of his birth. "Here I am noble; I am *boyar,*" he tells Jonathan, "the common people know me, and I am master. But a stranger in a stranger land, he is no one; men know him not—and to know not is to care not for."

The setting for *Trilby* is the Parisian Latin Quarter of 1855, where Du Maurier studied art until the loss of sight in his left eye at twenty-three forced him to abandon painting. Returning to London, he satirized the upper classes with *Punch* drawings featuring tall, Trilby-like, aristocratic women; it was said that he added two inches to the height of English women, whom he spiritually elevated—following Coventry Patmore, William Morris, and Rossetti—to secular saints whose beauty was adored and minds ignored. After three decades of ridiculing Victorian life, Du Maurier was disappointed when he was passed over for editor of *Punch:* his humor had not kept pace with the times.

Looking for other sources of income, he illustrated *Washington Square,* and Henry James urged him to write a novel. When the illustrated *Trilby* was published in the United States by Harper and Brothers following serialization in *Harper's Monthly,* it sold more than two hundred thousand copies, the first example of a best-seller created by promotion, distribution, secondary rights, and publicity. Suddenly there was a Trilby mania. Because the plot pivots on sublimation, the three artists admire, paint, and make plaster casts of Trilby's left foot (it was more acceptable to focus on a part of the body most distant from the genitals). *Trilbies,* in the plural, became synonymous with *feet.* The fedora-style snap-brimmed hat with a crease in the middle worn by Little Billee is still called a trilby.

———

Stoker's first novel, *The Snake's Pass,* was serialized in *The People* and several provincial papers. It is set in western Ireland, where he traveled as Inspector of Petty Sessions. The narrator, Arthur Severn, is a wealthy young Englishman intrigued with the legend of Shleenana-her, or the Snake's Pass, an opening leading down to the sea in the mountain of Knockcalltecrore, where French invaders were rumored to have lost a treasure in the mountain's shifting bog. Severn falls in love below his class; outwits the villainous moneylender, or gombeen man, called Black Murdoch (a Dracula precursor); and befriends Andy Sullivan (a young Van Helsing), the repository of all gossip and wisdom. Curiously, there is no dedication; by rights, it should have been dedicated to Florence, since *Under the Sunset* was inscribed to Noel.

Gladstone read the novel at a time when the prime minister's hopes of settling the centuries-old Irish troubles were shattered by Katharine O'Shea's divorce trial, naming as corespondent Charles Stewart Parnell, the leader of the Irish Parliamentary party.* A self-proclaimed "philosophical Home-Ruler," Stoker told Gladstone that he "was both angry at and sorry for Parnell's attitude." Gladstone replied: "I am very angry, but I assure you I am even more sorry." Stoker was flattered that in the midst of political turmoil Gladstone found time as Stoker recalled "to read—and remember, even to details and names—the work of an unimportant friend."

Stoker's writing habits—a page here and there on the run—were always better suited to the short story. He published three at this time—"The Man from Shorrox," "The Squaw," and "The Burial of the Rats"—all foreshadowing *Dracula.* He wrote an article for James Knowles's *The Nineteenth Century,* on the history of the strolling player, which dismissed critics of the actor-manager system (and of

---

* Kitty O'Shea and Parnell had three children together, but her husband looked the other way, hoping for political advancement and part of his wife's fortune. When neither came, he won a divorce in November of 1890. Condemned by the Irish clergy as an adulterer, Parnell was dethroned as the uncrowned king of Ireland, his cause destroyed, and his supporters splintered into feuding factions that exist to this day. Gladstone refused to support the Home Rule Bill if Parnell did not resign: he did not and was voted out by his party. He married Kitty but died a broken man in less than a year.

Irving). For the *North American Review,* he dissected "Dramatic Crit-icism," cuffing William Archer for his begrudging reviews of Lyceum productions. Archer had called the actor a "parasite upon the play," and Stoker asked in good debating style, "What, in the name of logic, is the critic, who earns his bread or pursues his mis-sion by writing of the actor?" Archer's response was that the critic "is not a parasite upon the actor, but a co-parasite with the actor upon the play."

Other critics said Stoker, as an acting manager, had no right to lecture them. One noted:

> You could not have wars without soldiers, but you could have plays—that is, plays could be written, printed, and read, as the works of the standard dramatists are read—even if every actor in the world were swept off the face of the universe to-morrow. But if, on the other hand, such things as plays did not exist, players would cease to exist. Therefore, it is evident that the actor has not an individual sphere of usefulness in the scheme of creation, but exists only in virtue of pre-existing plays. Therefore, he *is* a parasite, though it may not be civil to tell him so.

In 1891 Stoker involved himself in a risky business venture. Together with publisher William Heinemann he launched *The English Library,* to compete with the famed Tauchnitz series, considered the travel-ing Briton's oldest friend. Published from 1841 to 1943, Tauchnitz editions comprised the work of some 750 authors in 5,370 volumes. By private agreement in 1843, and later by continental copyright provisions, the first Baron Tauchnitz secured from Dickens, Trollope, and others advance proofs of work then at press, producing variant texts preceding those regarded as "first editions." Using this proto-type, Stoker bought—as moderately as possible—the rights for works by Hall Caine, George Meredith, Henry James, Kipling, Stevenson, Conan Doyle, and others. A Leipzig firm distributed the books, but the venture collapsed after a few years. Stoker tried to work outside the theatre but was always drawn back to the Lyceum.

For a long time Irving had fancied himself as Thomas à Becket, Archbishop of Canterbury. Stoker and Irving went to Aldworth to ask

Tennyson's permission to trim his long play, *Becket*. They listened to Tennyson read "The Charge of the Heavy Brigade" on a recorded cylinder, and Stoker borrowed the device for Dr. Seward, who used it to record case histories, particularly the curious habits of Renfield, his zoophagous patient. Back at the Lyceum Irving took two copies of *Becket* and cut out one-quarter of the text; he pasted the leaves on sheets of foolscap so Tennyson would not be disturbed by seeing passages crossed out in pen. Stoker took the script to Tennyson's summer home, Farringford, on the Isle of Wight. The eighty-three-year-old poet was too ill to object. "Irving may do whatever he pleases with it!" he told Stoker. "In that case, he will do it within a year." Stoker asked for a new, rousing speech for one scene. "But where am I to get such a speech?" Tennyson asked. Stoker pointed out the window to where the sea thunders night and day under one of the highest cliffs in England. "There it is! In the roar of the sea!" he replied.

In September of 1892 Stoker needed Tennyson's final approval, and with Florence returned to Aldworth. The poet greeted them in his study, sitting with his back to a large mullioned window. "He had on a black skull-cap, his long thin dark hair falling from under it," Stoker recalled. "Shall I live to see *Becket*?" Tennyson asked. His doctor warned that he might not. "Well, Irving will do me justice with the piece," he murmured and, turning to Stoker, pleaded: "Don't let them know how ill I am, or they'll have me buried in twenty-four hours." Then, after a pause, he added: "Can't they all let me alone? . . . I sometimes wish I had never written a line." Stoker demurred; his poetry had given pleasure to millions. "Well, perhaps you're right," agreed Tennyson, who as poet laureate for forty-two years had symbolized the Victorian age as much as the queen. He died on October 6, eleven days after the Stokers' visit.

Stoker commemorates Tennyson's *Demeter and Other Poems,* published in 1889, by naming Dracula's ship *Demeter.* Halfway through *Dracula,* there are three parental deaths—Mr. Hawkins, Lucy's mother, and Arthur's father—which symbolize the recent deaths of McHenry, Whitman, and Tennyson. "Goodbye, my faithful friend and second father," Harker says to Hawkins when he leaves for Transylvania. Stoker's father figures had abandoned him. Only Henry Irving remained.

# Chapter 12

# CRUDEN BAY

"There seemed a strange stillness over everything; but as I listened I heard as if from down below in the valley the howling of many wolves. The Count's eyes gleamed, and he said: 'Listen to them—the children of the night. What music they make!' "

—Jonathan Harker's journal

At forty-seven Stoker still wanted to be a literary man, but money as well as loyalty bound him to Irving. A writer's life, particularly a fledgling writer's, was not so comfortable. Florence entertained extravagantly, shopped expensively, and set her sights on a Winchester education for Noel. Little was set aside for retirement; in particular, there was no country house or seaside cottage. And Stoker longed for a solitary place to write. In 1893 he took a walking tour around the Scottish coast between Peterhead and Aberdeen, returning to Cruden Bay, the isolated fishing village he had glimpsed five years earlier during the *Macbeth* research trip. Attracted by the sandhills and meadows, the distant Braemar mountains, the rows of fishermen's cottages with their red-tile drying sheds, he took a room at the Kilmarnock Arms. The next morning he hiked over the two-hundred-foot cliffs to Slains Castle. The earthy smells recalled his invalid days when, nestled among grasses and flowers, he inhaled the outdoors. Wild rabbits scampered through the dunes as the sun rose over the North Sea. This was the furious contentment he wanted. The following summer he wrote in the hotel visitor's book, "Second visit—delighted with everything and everybody and hope to come again."

Cruden Bay means "blood of the Danes," a reminder of when blood flowed as Celt and Dane slaughtered each other in the days of Malcolm and Macbeth. Dominated by Slains Castle, ancestral home of the Errolls, one of Britain's most ancient families, the village was more feudal than Victorian. Known as altruistic landlords, the Errolls emerged from the mists of folklore into history in the tenth century, when they played a heroic and decisive part in the Battle of Loncarty against the Danes; they enjoyed political intrigue, fought hard, died young, fled into exile, or were beheaded.

When Samuel Johnson and James Boswell visited the castle during their Scottish tour in 1773, Johnson remarked on the "terrific grandeur of the tempestuous ocean," not that he would "wish for a storm: but as storms, whether wished for or not, will sometimes happen, I may say, without violation of humanity, that I should willingly look out upon them from Slains Castle." Sometimes called the inspiration for Dracula's castle, Slains was neither that spectacular nor Stoker's only model. As he traveled throughout Ireland as Inspector for Petty Sessions, there were many magnificent examples, particularly County Antrim's Dunluce Castle. But Stoker needed no granite muses: turrets and towers had been imprinted on his memory since childhood.

The 20th Earl Charles Hay received Stoker in the baronial dining room, where a regal portrait of the 19th Earl loomed over the stone fireplace. In Stoker's time, residents recalled how this earl walked through the streets—insisting all the villagers doff their caps or curtsy to him—dressed in a tweed suit of antique cut and a high Glengarry bonnet with a falcon crest. Stoker borrowed his character for "Crooken Sands," a story about a London merchant who believes the proper holiday attire to be Highland costume with kilt, sporran, brooches, and dirk. Also intriguing was the 21st Earl Victor Hay, who wrote *Ferelith,* a strange, sad novel about a woman in Slains Castle who has a child by a ghost. Stoker remembered such lines as

"I become intoxicated with the magic touch of his filmy arms. I drink red nectar from the gossamer lips."*

Published in 1895, *The Watter's Mou'*—a melodrama about Cruden Bay during the smuggling era (dedicated "To my Dear Mother in her loneliness")—was the first of three tales in which Stoker used local characters. The title refers to a natural cauldron formed by primeval fire or earthquake, a mouth where the tide rushes in. There Sailor Willy and his sweetheart Maggie are found dead in each other's arms. "The requiem," Stoker wrote, "was the roar of the breaking waves and the screams of the white birds." There is an obsessive interest in the area's rock formations; likewise in *Dracula,* Van Helsing observes that the "very place where he [Dracula] has been alive Un-Dead for all these centuries, is full of strangeness of the geological and chemical world."

Following the Lyceum's visit to California, Stoker wrote *The Shoulder of Shasta,* so called for the snowcapped peak of Mount Shasta, an extinct volcano. The one memorable scene—in a silly story of a young girl's infatuation with a rough-and-tumble frontiersman named Grizzly Dick, who like *Dracula*'s Quincey Morris, carries a Winchester rifle and a Bowie knife—has the heroine kill a bear. *The Athenaeum* put it right: "This story will not increase his literary reputation nor appeal to many readers. . . . This want of maturity and a sense of humour may be due to haste, for the book bears the stamp of being roughly and carelessly put together. Mr. Stoker can probably do much better than this; so perhaps the less said about 'The Shoulder of Shasta' the better for everyone concerned."

Stoker would do better. But his women characters with liberated views and romantic yearnings, vague reflections of the New Woman,

---

* In 1916 the eighty-room castle was sold to Sir John Ellerman, a shipping industrialist, who had the lead stripped from the roof in 1925 and sold as scrap. Today the granite walls still stand, making it a ghostly ruin. The fierce winds have erased the last traces of plaster, and there is the music of gulls and puffins swooping and screaming through the corridors. The 22nd Earl Jocelyn Hay did little to brighten the family name: his murder in 1941 scandalized Kenya's British colony.

were always more real than his heroes. The Beefsteak Room regulars, shocked over Richard von Krafft-Ebing's *Psychopathia Sexualis* (1886), which introduced *sadism* and *masochism* into the language, and Havelock Ellis's treatise on *Men and Women* (1894), were dismayed by the so-called New Woman appearing in the pages of novels by Olive Schreiner, Thomas Hardy, and the two Georges: Meredith and Gissing. Coined in 1894 by feminist novelist Sarah Grand, the term more accurately defined a style of living than a political perspective. The New Woman wanted sexual freedom, smoked cigarettes, drank in public, and wore men's clothing. It was only a matter of time, the Beefsteakers worried, before this New Woman stepped out of fiction, fiercely multiplying and threatening the male status quo. Someone—certainly not an Englishman—was to blame. Whitman was a convenient villain. After all, the poet of "barbaric yawp" had promised that sex—whether the "amativeness" of men and women or the "adhesiveness" of men and men—would be the means by which conventional culture would be transcended.

Stoker wove this iconoclastic character, an important shift in the literary portrayal of women, into *Dracula*—stopping short, however, of giving her authentic independence. Was Stoker for or against the New Woman? Contemporary feminists still debate that question. If Lucy's death ended the novel, there would be a strong case for calling *Dracula* an antifeminist novel. But the second half introduces the complex and charming Mina Murray Harker, who survives Dracula's vamping and is largely responsible for his entrapment and destruction.

The stereotypical New Woman—like Mina—was middle-class, educated, often working as a typist in an all-male office. (Remington, the American arms manufacturer, spurred this career opportunity by opening a British typewriter dealership in 1886.) A girls' schoolteacher of etiquette and decorum, Mina feels the pedantry of the course biting into her. "I feel so grateful to the man who invented the 'Traveller's' typewriter," she writes in her journal, probably referring to the portable Columbia typewriter, weighing six pounds, that became available in 1885. Rather than weaving like the Lady of Shallott, Mina produces a sixty-two-page manuscript overnight, with the information needed to track Dracula.

The sexually aware Lucy exhibits the other side of the New Woman: Dr. Seward plays "with a lancet in a way that made me want to scream," she tells Mina. In the Victorian world men dominated women, but in the vampire world the unthinkable happens: women try to enslave the men who once enslaved them. Despite her intelligence and courage, Mina was not an authentic New Woman, for her choices involved others before herself; but for Stoker, she was the ideal motherly woman, although unconsciously he preferred the irresistible Lucy. As Whitman predicted, the decadent dandy—as personified by Wilde's aesthetic cult—and the New Woman were twin apostles of social apocalypse.

In *Dracula,* Stoker metaphorically toys with the taboos of castration, deflowering, and adultery. Harker fears for his manhood if he can't escape the castle. "At least God's mercy is better than that of these monsters, and the precipice is steep and high. At its foot a man may sleep—as a man," he notes in his journal. After giving blood to his fiancé, Arthur feels as "if they two had been really married, and that she was his wife in the sight of God," prompting Dr. Seward to pledge the group to secrecy: "None of us said a word of the other operations, and none of us ever shall." Thus the men create a fabric of lies surrounding adultery.

Stoker is careful not to sully the sweet Lucy; the transfusions always occur while she is asleep. The morning after, she feels closer to the man who has given his blood, but she has not been involved in the exchange (a problematic solution today without the suitors knowing their blood type). Substitution of transfusions for sexual penetration are, in critic Nina Auerbach's words, "the most convincing epithalamiums in the novel."

Stoker's first New Woman reference is a casual comment. Mina and Lucy have walked over the cliff path from Whitby to the small fishing village of Robin Hood's Bay. They are having tea in an "old-fashioned inn, with a bow-window right over the seaweed-covered rocks of the strand," when Mina remarks that their appetites would shock the New Woman, whose insistence on sexual freedom included greater physical activity, such as bicycle riding.

A second reference indicates Mina's anxiety with advocates of sexual frankness. "If Mr. Holmwood fell in love with her [Lucy] seeing her only in the drawing-room, I wonder what he would say if he saw her now [as she sleeps]. Some of the 'New Women' writers will some day start an idea that men and women should be allowed to see each other asleep before proposing or accepting. But I suppose the New Woman won't condescend in future to accept; she will do the proposing herself. And a nice job she will make of it too! There's some consolation in that." Mina sees liberated women as aggressors (as did Stoker) making a muddle of things. Stoker's novels, however, return more than once to the conflict of women proposing marriage, which begs the question: Did the ambitious Florence do the asking?

Mostly, the Beefsteakers preferred tales of faraway brothels brought back by intrepid explorers. Arguments about the New Woman's threat to their masculinity were disturbing. Dracula's physical characteristics, in fact, are a composite of some of these adventurers. There was Irving's nose, of course; Franz Liszt's white hair and beard; and the gaze of Jacques Damala, a Greek actor married to Sarah Bernhardt. "I sat next to him at supper, and the idea that he was dead was strong on me," Stoker recalled of Damala. "I think he had taken some mighty dose of opium, for he moved and spoke like a man in a dream. His eyes, staring out of his white waxen face, seemed hardly the eyes of the living." Sir Henry Morton Stanley, the praiser of Stoker's book on America, also looked more dead than alive. Stoker recycled these impressions. After greeting Dracula, Harker observes that his hand is "as cold as ice—more like the hand of a dead than a living man."

By translating such books as the *Arabian Nights,* the *Kama Sutra,* and the Tantric text *Vikram and the Vampire,* another Beefsteak guest, Sir Richard Francis Burton, introduced new attitudes about the pleasures of sex to the Western world. Like Stoker he was interested in mesmerism and sexual deviance, intrigued by the unknowable and the unthinkable. Stoker found him "dark, and forceful, and masterful, and ruthless." He noticed that when Burton laughed, his "upper lip rose and his canine tooth showed its full length like the gleam of a dagger." Dracula first appears as "a tall old man, clean shaven save for a long white moustache, and clad in black from head to foot." His face recalls Irving's strong aquiline features, but the mouth is cruel, "with peculiarly sharp white teeth" protruding over the lips.*

One day in March of 1892 Irving arrived in the office he shared with Stoker and tossed a manuscript on his desk. "I wish you would throw an eye over that during rehearsal. It came this morning," he said. "You can tell me what you think of it when I come off!" Stoker read the play twice. "It is made for you," he said.

"So I think, too!" replied Irving. "You had better write to the author to-day and ask him what cheque we are to send. We had better buy the whole rights."

"Who is the author?"

"Conan Doyle!"

Originally called *A Straggler of '15,* which Irving changed to *Waterloo,* the play examines the last hours of Corporal Gregory Brewster, whose wandering thoughts keep returning to the day he fought under Wellington's command. The role gave Irving an opportunity to build a character study of great virtuosity; he played the role 343 times, refining an interpretation of senility until it ranked with his Louis XI. It opened at Bristol's Princes Theatre on September 21, 1894. Stoker told his diary, "New play enormous success. H.I. fine and great. All laughed and wept. Eight calls at end."

This was Doyle's first attempt at drama. Since 1891 he had been writing Sherlock Holmes stories for *The Strand Magazine;* but before the Holmes character appeared in *A Study in Scarlet,* weird fiction made up almost a third of his work, including a novella of psychic vampirism, *The Parasite.* Doyle has Holmes in *The Sign of Four* schedule a rendezvous at the third pillar from the left outside the Lyceum Theatre, where "a continuous stream of hansoms and four-wheelers

---

* Dracula is four hundred years old; most vampires look only as old as they did when they "died" and were buried. Otherwise Stoker's description is accurate as to folklore: the thinness and pallor, the red lips, sharp teeth, hairy hands, great physical strength, curved and crooked fingernails, rank and fetid breath (from ingested blood), and radium eyes. Victorians believed hairy palms to be symptomatic of a masturbator, one who wasted his vital fluid, and in the case of a vampire must take it from others.

were rattling up, discharging their cargoes of shirt-fronted men and beshawled, bediamonded women."

Stoker's original cast of characters for *Dracula* included a detective inspector called Cotford and a psychical research agent called Singleton, later Van Helsing. His first scribblings indicate a Holmes-like detective story, with a German professor of history named Max Windshoeffel for the Watson role. Doyle convinced Stoker to join him and twenty-two other authors in each writing a chapter (without any collaboration) for a murder story called *The Fate of Fenella*. The critics hooted. "The style of the book is extraordinary," one wrote; "all write in the same womanly style." Advising them not to try the form again, the reviewer concluded: "It is a joke, a very long joke."

Never interested in the occult even though it was fashionable, Florence took singing lessons. The "master describes me as 'earnestly progressing,' " she wrote her mother; "it is nice to find oneself appreciated. It's the only amusement I indulge in as I have so much to do now for Bram." Florence was not being honest with her mother, for she had a full social calendar, often escorted by Gilbert, whose reputation as a flirt was augmented by having Mrs. Bram—as Florence was affectionately called—on his arm at the theatre while her husband was busy at the Lyceum. Gilbert was a topsy-turvy character, a professional curmudgeon with genuine contempt for just about everyone and everything British, particularly the law. He looked like a cuddly teddy bear in a light gray suit, but beneath a scabrous exterior was a man so obsessively devoted to animals he could not step on a beetle. When *Who's Who* listed him as a "writer of verses and the libretti to Sir Arthur Sullivan's comic operas," Gilbert, who had refused to complete the book's questionnaire, demanded to know if this was an appropriate reference for a man who had written seventy original dramas.

Florence shared Gilbert's distaste for Irving, but for different reasons. Gilbert thought Irving arrogant, an actor who believed himself superior to any dramatist. Asked whether he had seen Irving's *Faust*, he replied: "Madame, I go to the pantomime only at Christmas." At one of Florence's gatherings, writer Horace Wyndham recalled a young actress asking Stoker to introduce her to Gilbert at an inopportune moment. In a worse temper than usual, Gilbert shook his head fiercely. "Don't want to know her," he growled. "Want to be left alone." A common Gilbertian retort was: "I shall place the matter at once in the hands of my solicitor." With the possible exception of Whistler, Gilbert was the most litigious artistic figure of the nineteenth century. At this time, the famed musical partnership of Gilbert and Sullivan and Richard D'Oyly Carte had ended acrimoniously, with Gilbert suing Carte for excessive expenses in staging *The Gondoliers*—in particular, £500 spent for new house carpets.

The Stokers often visited Grim's Dyke, Gilbert's mellow-brick Old English house designed by the stylish architect Norman Shaw. The estate featured a zoo with foxes and pigeons, cows and cranes, deer and donkeys. Two Persian cats and six dogs lived as part of the family, even eating with them in the dining room from their own bowls. Gilbert's favorites were Madagascar lemurs and monkeys brought back from India and bred by him into a colony of significant size. Florence took one as a pet, to sit on her shoulder. During dinnertime lulls, Gilbert criticized Irving and Stoker admired the vampire tale *The Last Lords of Gardonal,* written by Gilbert's father, William, a naval surgeon turned novelist. Stoker and Gilbert were both Inner Temple barristers, but only Gilbert had practiced, achieving the rank of Justice of the Peace. While Stoker incorporated legal issues into his plots, Gilbert satirized the system. He understood its primal connection with humor, and nowhere more so than in *Trial by Jury,* the first Gilbert & Sullivan collaboration.

Gilbert's letters to Florence were teasing. "I would write a letter to the Times," he told her, "only it would never do to allow it to be publicly known that you and I were in correspondence." Another time, he confided: "I feel that I shall never be sufficiently grateful to you for your self-denying kindness in spending three days with a helpless invalid—you, whose society is so much sought—& who can spend your time as agreeably as any lady in London. . . . My wife sends her love & I would if I dared." Irate, as usual, over Shakespeare, he complained to Florence: "I was as bored by the Tempest as I was by Richard II and Julius Caesar—three ridiculously bad plays. I dare-

FLORENCE STOKER photographed at a Dublin Drawing
Room Ball

say Shakespeare was a great poet. I am not qualified to express a technical opinion on that point, but I consider myself an authority on
dramatic work & I have no hesitation in expressing a professional
opinion that all his works should be kept off the boards." As Irving's
star dimmed, Gilbert's indignation turned to his successor Herbert
Beerbohm Tree. A favorite after-dinner sneer was the proposition:
"Do you know how they are going to settle the Shakespeare-Bacon
dispute? They are going to dig up Shakespeare and dig up Bacon and
let Tree recite *Hamlet* to them. And the one who turns over in his
grave will be the author."

Irving's angular appearance made him an exemplary Becket, Hamlet, or Mathias but never a Falstaff or a Romeo; now he desired the

ideal physical role of Don Quixote. All he needed was the perfect steed. Ordered to find this horse, Stoker located a starving, old nag outside London and arranged for it to arrive by train the day before opening night. Annoyed that he could not rehearse in full armor astride his charger, Irving used the prompter's chair, waving his umbrella in place of a spear. Stoker assured him the horse was perfection. "You can count its ribs," he said, "and its bones stand out like hat pins. It's ewe-necked and has a head like a camel."

On May 3, 1895, a telegram announced that horse and owner had arrived at Euston Station and were headed for the Lyceum. Irving went to his dressing room, put on his armor, and waited. When Stoker arrived onstage, he wore his special look of tragic disappointment. The police, he said, had ordered the horse shot and the man sentenced to a month's hard labor for cruelty to animals. Irving showed no emotion and ordered up a hansom-cab horse, which had to be made up for every performance to look like a bag of bones—the ribs painted and hollow flanks artistically suggested.

During *Don Quixote* rumors circulated that Irving was on the queen's birthday list. Gladstone had promoted a knighthood for Irving, but the actor rejected the suggestion on the grounds that it would be wrong to single him out before the acting profession as a whole had advanced in its status. Twelve years later Irving felt differently. During a lecture at the Royal Institution of Great Britain, he put forth a formal claim to have acting officially classified among the fine arts. Shaw felt the need to interpret: "What Mr. Irving means us to answer is this question: The artist who composed the music for King Arthur is Sir Arthur Sullivan; the artist who composed the poem which made King Arthur known to this generation died Lord Tennyson; the artist who designed the suit of armour worn by King Arthur is Sir Edward Burne-Jones: why should the artist who plays King Arthur be only Mister Henry Irving?" Even so, he would always be listed as Henry Irving in theatre programs.

A few weeks after this speech, Irving received a letter from Archibald Primrose, who had succeeded Gladstone as prime minister, announcing his knighthood. The Prince of Wales sent his congratulations. Irving and Stoker drove to Ellen Terry's house to tell her the news. The whole world rejoiced, said Stoker. Letters and telegrams flooded the Lyceum. Most fulsome were tributes from fellow actors, to whom Irving's honor brought a long-delayed dignity. That evening laughter and cheers rose from the pit when Irving as Don Quixote says, "Knighthood sits like a halo round my head." To which his housekeeper replies: "But, master, you have never been knighted." Normally Queen Victoria said no more than the traditional words of the ceremony, but as she laid the sword on Irving's shoulder, she added: "I am very, very pleased."

On the same birthday list was Thornley, then president of the Royal College of Surgeons in Ireland. Thornley had been the family's professional success,* garnering titles and appointments, while enduring a sad personal life. His wife, Emily, was mentally ill and sequestered in a distant wing of their Dublin residence Ely House with two women caretakers. Stoker focuses on insanity throughout *Dracula*. Van Helsing's cryptic reference to his wife, "me, with my poor wife dead to me, but alive by Church's law, though no wits, all gone—even I who am faithful husband to this now-no-wife," echoes Thornley's situation.

On May 25, the day the queen honored two who were closest to Stoker, Oscar Wilde's second trial on charges of gross indecency ended with a conviction. At the time he was supreme in the London theatre: *An Ideal Husband* and *The Importance of Being Earnest* were running concurrently. A veiled lady had delivered violets during the trial at the Old Bailey, and Laurence Irving suggests this was Ellen Terry, bearing Irving's favorite flowers. Before sentencing Wilde to two years in prison, the judge described him as having been "the centre of a circle of extensive corruption of the most hideous kind among young men."

Most of Wilde's friends deserted him. "Open the windows! Let in the fresh air," shouted Clement Scott in the *Daily Telegraph*. Hall Caine was horrified, exclaiming to his friends: "To think of it! that

---

* Stoker's two sisters were married. George had a flourishing London practice, while Tom, after twenty-five years in the international civil service, would end his career with the title of Secretary to the Governor of the North West Provinces, and retire to London. And the mystery brother, Richard Nugent, four years Bram's senior, who trained as a doctor, served in the Indian Medical Service, and married a doctor's daughter, emigrated in the new century to Cawochan Lake, British Columbia, where he and his descendants dropped out of recorded memory.

SIR THORNLEY STOKER,
the eldest brother at the time
of his knighthood, in 1895

man, that genius as he is, whom you and I have seen feted and flattered! Whose hand we have grasped in friendship! a felon, and come
to infamy unspeakable! It haunts men, it is like some foul and horrible stain on our craft and on us all, which nothing can wash out. It is
the most awful tragedy in the whole of literature." William Winter
wrote Augustin Daly: "There was always something terribly repul-
sive about that man and about his work. And now at last the world
knows what it is. He ought to be led out and shot." Irving felt contempt for the members of his profession who were riding to Lord
Queensberry's hounds. Irving was touched by Wilde's "childish love
of the romantic candle-lit theatre" that Irving had created. It was
more than tragic, then, that on the day the acting profession was elevated to an art, the playwright who created the modern comedy
was stripped of his dignity.

Willie Wilde went about London defending his brother. "Bram,
my friend, poor Oscar was *not* as bad as people thought him," he
wrote. "He was led astray by his Vanity—& conceit, & he was so 'got
at' that he was weak enough to be guilty—of indiscretions and fol-

lies—that is *all*. . . . I believe this thing will help to *purify* him body & soul. Am sure you & Florence must have felt the disgrace of one who cared for you both sincerely." Stoker's feelings about Wilde went unrecorded. It is curious, though, that five years after the playwright's death, when Stoker drew up a list of a thousand notable guests entertained at the Lyceum, there was no Oscar Wilde. A story still circulates that Stoker brought money to Wilde when he was destitute in Paris. It is pleasant to imagine Stoker arriving at the Hôtel d'Alsace and Wilde's surprise and pleasure at seeing him. They would go first to the Café de la Régence for Courvoisier, and Wilde would order a box of gold-tipped cigarettes. They would dine at the Café de Paris and talk of Trinity, of Florence and her beauty. That one evening they would be Dubliners.

From the time Wilde arrived in London, he maintained ties with Florence, sending her notes and flowers. What made Stoker uncomfortable, perhaps, was not jealousy but the psychological impulse

FLORENCE STOKER, in a portrait by Walter Frederick Osborne that was featured at the Royal Academy's summer show of 1895

called troilism, in which homosexual desire for someone is expressed in wanting to share a partner. Florence's last communication from Wilde was in 1893, when a performance of his play *Salomé* was banned by the Lord Chamberlain. A text was published in French, and Wilde sent Florence a first edition. "My dear Florence, Will you accept a copy of *Salome*—my strange venture in a tongue that is not my own."

At the time of Wilde's trials in 1895, Florence was vainly preoccupied; her portrait by Walter Frederick Osborne, a well-known Dublin artist, was shown at the Royal Academy's summer exhibition. "One of the *very best portraits* of the year, if not really the best," *The Athenaeum* noted, "is that of Mrs. Bram Stoker, sitting upon a white bearskin, with a warm grey background and mainly in half-tone." Draped in fur, Florence looks positively feral. Stoker accepted congratulations all around: for Irving, for his brother, for his wife. For Wilde there was only silence.

# Royal Lyceum Theatre.

Sole Lessee and Manager:

## HENRY IRVING.

# DRACULA

OR

## THE UN-DEAD.

FIRST TIME.

# 4

## *Dracula's Secrets*

### (1895–1912)

## Chapter 13

# SHAW'S DILEMMA

"All men are mad in some way or the other;
and inasmuch as you deal discreetly with your
madmen, so deal with God's madmen, too—
the rest of the world."
                              —Van Helsing to Dr. Seward

s Wilde exited Stoker's life, Shaw entered. The two
Dubliners had come a long way since that evening in 1871
at the Royal when they watched Irving become Digby
Grant in *The Two Roses*. From their seats in the pit they acknowledged a new style of acting: an interior voice that made audiences
think as well as feel. Later in London, Shaw envisioned Irving as a
Shavian character, someone who could "revive the rotting theatre of
that day." But Shaw misplaced his optimism: Irving's knighthood was
more an end than a new beginning.

A symbol of an outworn romanticism, Irving devoted his talent
to the classics, not to new dramatists; he denied a dying century and
a changing theatre. He declined Conan Doyle's offer to write a play
around Sherlock Holmes, which would have rejuvenated his career,
and unwisely agreed to *Peter the Great,* written by his son Laurence,
a Russian scholar, which flopped in its unrelenting gloom. The play
deserves a niche in theatre history, however, because the smitten playwright demanded that eighteen-year-old Ethel Barrymore play Eu-

GEORGE BERNARD
SHAW (1890s). He
disagreed with Irving
about the staging of
Shakespeare and the
direction of the modern
theatre.

phrosine, the czar's mistress, which led to an all-too-brief engagement between author and actress.

Shaw would refuse to attend Irving's funeral, riled at his "extraordinary insensibility to literature," bitter at an actor who he felt
misunderstood every word of Shakespeare. In one *Saturday Review*
article, Shaw said that twenty-five years ago Irving should have been
tied "up in a sack with every existing copy of the works of Shakespeare, and dropped into the crater of the nearest volcano." Shaw referred primarily to Irving's practice of adapting plays to suit his
talents.

To irritate, Shaw appeared at opening nights in bizarre mufti—
knickerbockers—instead of evening dress; he accepted Stoker's invitations to Beefsteak dinners but was conspicuous by his absence. He
turned his verbal enchantment on Ellen Terry, beginning a pillar-box
flirtation ranking with that of George Sand and Gustave Flaubert as
epistolary masterpieces between those unmet but not unseen. He at-

tempted to lure her away from the Lyceum with his new one-act play *The Man of Destiny,* an encounter between a twenty-seven-year-old Napoleon and a strange lady during the campaign of 1796.

Lamenting she had "no lovers, only loves," Terry observed how Shaw managed to substitute the physical act of love with "a lot of things to say." Terry was "a born actress of real women's parts," Shaw complained, "condemned to figure as a mere artist's model in costume plays which, from the woman's point of view, are foolish flatteries written by gentlemen for gentlemen." Irving promised to consider *The Man of Destiny,* but seven months passed before he offered Shaw his standard payment of £50 for a year's exclusive option. Not wanting to wait until 1897 for a production, Shaw proffered: if Irving produced a play by Ibsen, he could have his play free and clear. "But if you will excuse my saying so," said Shaw, who sought to cleanse the Victorian theatre of snobbish bardolatry, "I'm hanged if I'll be put off for Shakespeare."

Irving, of course, had no intention of producing *The Man of Destiny,* but he wanted a pyrrhic victory over his scornful critic. Shaw waited eighteen months to hear Irving announce from the Lyceum stage a production of Sardou's Napoleon play, *Madame Sans-Gêne.* Shaw asked for the return of his play to submit elsewhere, but Irving—still teasing—counseled forbearance, vaguely promising an 1898 date. Shaw waited to retaliate.

The time came when the first night of *Richard III* on December 19, 1896, did not go well. Irving was all leers and grimaces, creating a Satanic character lacking in subtlety. After dining at the Garrick Club, he returned to Grafton Street early in the morning. No matter what the hour, he always bathed before retiring, but this evening on his climb up the narrow stairs he slipped and struck his knee against a chest on the landing, rupturing the ligaments of his kneecap. The Lyceum closed for three weeks, but the psychic toll on Irving, who found himself an invalid forced to confront his invincibility, eclipsed the financial loss. Visitors listened to him mutter how it was far better to be struck down onstage in one's prime and glory than to linger off of it.

Shaw wrote a critique of the play in the *Saturday Review,* implying that Irving had been drunk. In some scenes Irving was not "answering his helm satisfactorily," Shaw observed, "and he was occasionally a little out of temper with his own nervous condition. He made some odd slips in the text, notably by repeatedly substituting 'you' for 'I.' . . . Once he inadvertently electrified the house by very unexpectedly asking Miss Milton to get further up the stage in the blank verse and penetrating tones of Richard." (Irving, like Van Helsing, had a way of hissing words to betray emotion.) No man enjoyed a fine brandy or a well-put-down bottle of Madeira more than Irving, but he was never a person who drank to intoxication. Shaw knew this.

"I am sorry that the article should have caused you any uneasiness," Shaw wrote Irving; "you are in some ways the most difficult subject a critic can tackle." Irving denied knowledge of the review. "I have never read a criticism of yours in my life. I have read lots of your droll, amusing, irrelevant and sometimes impertinent pages, but criticism containing judgment and sympathy I have never seen by your pen." Irving returned *The Man of Destiny* with a curt rejection note. But Stoker never stopped trying to bring Shaw and Irving together, either as artists or as collaborators.

By this time Ellen Terry was fed up with the adolescent bickering. "What I cared for more than for you or H.—or the parts," she wrote Shaw, "was the Play—and now—well, go your way." On Irving, she mused: "I think he has always cared for me a little, very little, and has had passing fancies, but he really *cares* for scarcely anyone. Indifference is personified in H.I. His hold upon *me* is that he is INTERESTING no matter how he behaves." Undaunted, Shaw chipped away at Terry's affection for Irving; he tempted her with the role of Lady Cecily Waynflete in *Captain Brassbound's Conversion*. "Your career has been sacrificed to the egotism of a fool," Shaw correctly admonished. After twenty-four years Irving still was unwilling to offer Terry the parts necessary to maintain her reputation.

Fed up with towering egos, Terry accepted Beerbohm Tree's invitation to join him in *The Merry Wives of Windsor* at Her Majesty's Theatre, which had supplanted the Lyceum as the center of theatrical fashion. Shaw was incensed, even more so when she agreed to one last provincial tour with Irving. "I recognize that you and I can never be associated as author and player," he wrote, "that you will remain

Olivia, and that Lady Cicely is some young creature in short skirts at a High School at this moment." Terry was adamant in her reply: "If you worry (or try to worry) Henry, I must end our long and close friendship. He is ill, and what would I not do to better him?" Irving continued to pay Terry £200 a week, making her, with the exception of Queen Victoria, the highest paid woman in England.

Stoker was in the middle of this feud, unable to influence or change the outcome. It was with great relief, then, that he once again signed the guest book at the Kilmarnock Arms in July of 1896, settling his family into a gabled suite overlooking the river. Here he wrote the last pages of *Dracula*. For decades there was speculation as to whether the coincidence of Irving and Thornley's knighthoods and Wilde's imprisonment put Stoker over the edge, triggering his vampire story. Clearly no one event, conversation, or personal frustration motivated *Dracula*. The novel's genesis was a process, which involved Stoker's education and interests, his fears and fantasies, as well as those of his

THE KILMARNOCK ARMS HOTEL in Cruden Bay, Scotland (as it looked in the 1930s), where Stoker stayed for two summers while writing *Dracula*

Victorian colleagues. He dumped the signposts of his life into a supernatural cauldron and called it *Dracula*.

His son later said the plot came to his father "in a nightmarish dream after eating too much dressed crab." (Mary Shelley and Robert Louis Stevenson also said they dreamed of *Frankenstein* and *Dr. Jekyll and Mr. Hyde*.) Perhaps Stoker did awake one night, swimming up from a purplish nightmare; in terms of how Victorian authors released libidinous energy onto the page, Harker's dream could well be Stoker's. The one constant—the pivotal dramatic point—throughout the working notes is Jonathan Harker's dream of passive seduction. "Young man goes out sees girls," Stoker wrote; "one tries to kiss him not on lips but throat Old Count interferes—Rage and fury diabolical—This man belongs to me—I want him—a prisoner for a time. . . ."

Sleep, trances, dreams, and nightmares drive the novel's action. "Mina is sleeping, and sleeping without dreams," her husband observes. "I fear what her dreams might be like, with such terrible memories to ground them in." By the end of the novel, it is Van Helsing who fights seduction by the vampiresses: "She was so fair to look on, so radiantly beautiful, so exquisitely voluptuous, that the very instinct of man in me, which calls some of my sex to love and to protect one of hers, made my head whirl with new emotion." There is a delicious ambiguity here with Stoker's phrase "some of my sex."

Vampires are usually bisexual, except in Stoker's novel, where apparently Dracula is the last male vampire (neither Renfield nor the Russian sailors attacked at sea are transformed). The notes show how Stoker struggled over the novel's homoerotic aspects: the phrase "This man belongs to me!" appears repeatedly. "The sexual threat that this novel first evokes, manipulates, sustains, but never finally represents," observes Christopher Craft, "is that Dracula will seduce, penetrate, and drain another male. . . . Dracula's desire to fuse with a male, most explicitly evoked when Harker cuts himself shaving, subtly and dangerously suffuses this text."

When Stoker plotted *Dracula,* he planned a mythic power struggle between two men, which eventually symbolized the struggle for dominance among all men. His was not an original concept. The first fictional vampire, Lord Ruthven, appeared in print seventy-eight years before Count Dracula, the name lifted from *Glenarvon,* Lady Caroline Lamb's roman à clef satirizing Byron. The author was John Polidori, Rossetti's uncle and briefly Byron's personal physician and lover: he died mysteriously at twenty-five, another self-destructive and almost forgotten personality of the Romantic period. Polidori's reputation like Stoker's rests on one work and one character: a vampire.

Lord Ruthven's story grew out of the celebrated winter house party in 1816 at the Villa Diodati, near Geneva, when Byron suggested that his guests write ghost stories. Mary Shelley created *Frankenstein;* Percy Bysshe Shelley tinkered with something based on his childhood; Byron considered a vampire story but, exhausted from laudanum, produced only "a fragment" about two schoolfellows traveling through Greece; while Polidori conjured up a skull-headed woman who is punished for peeking through a keyhole. Polidori's *The Vampyre,* based on Byron's discarded idea, appeared in *The New Monthly Magazine* of April 1819 and was initially attributed to Byron (Goethe called it the poet's finest work).

Polidori illustrates in this novella how the vampire who feeds off others fits right into a corrupt society. Lord Ruthven and Count Dracula step out of folklore into the real world and must cope with modern problems. Stoker's most successful innovation was to set the core of his story in Victorian England, a world immediately recognizable. Indeed, both authors reject the spooky trappings of Horace Walpole's *The Castle of Otranto* and Ann Radcliffe's *The Mysteries of Udolpho,* early shudder novels whose exotic, musty settings allow the reader's dreams and fantasies to wander guilt-free. Ruthven's successor was Sir Francis Varney, a Restoration nobleman, and the first vampire to wear a black cape. Labeled a "penny dreadful," *Varney the Vampyre: or, The Feast of Blood* was a 750,000-word saga written by James Malcolm Rymer and published in 1847, the year of Stoker's birth.

As a Trinity scholar Stoker was conversant with the vampire imagery in the eighteenth-century poetry of Goethe's "The Bride of

Corinth," Coleridge's "The Rime of the Ancient Mariner," and
Robert Southey's "Thalaba the Destroyer," as well as the next generation of Romantic poets—Shelley, Byron, Scott, and Keats—who
used the vampire not to frighten but to enlighten. In Keats's "La
Belle Dame sans Merci" there are images of the femme fatale, a version of Lucy. Stoker's Irish heritage also imbued him with stories of
the succubus, who seduces young men in their sleep, and her male
counterpart, the incubus.

More than poetry or fiction, however, Shakespearian images moti-
vate *Dracula*'s epic action. Stoker's chapter outlines read like a theatre
program; clearly, a dramatic version of the novel was on his mind
from the outset. Stage vampires had been popular since the Parisian
success in 1820 of Charles Nodier and Achille Jouffroy's *Le Vampire,*
which J. R. Planché adapted into English. Stoker saw parts of his
novel performed night after night on the Lyceum stage. Countless
times he heard Irving intone that most Draculian of speeches from
*Hamlet:*

> 'Tis now the very witching time of night,
> When churchyards yawn, and all hell itself breathes out contagion
> to this world. Now could I drink hot blood,
> And do such bitter business as the day would quake to look on.

Lucy identifies with both Ophelia and Desdemona. "I sympa-
thize with poor Desdemona when she had such a dangerous stream
poured into her ear," she writes to Mina after Quincey Morris's
proposal.

Both *Othello* and *Dracula* articulate the male anxiety over female
sexuality.

> Was this fair paper, this most goodly book
> Made to write 'whore' upon?

demands Othello. Both the murder of Desdemona and Lucy's staking erase evidence of a man violating another's woman. Mina begs

for the same end if she becomes a vampire. "Think dear, that there have been times when brave men have killed their wives and their womenkind," she urges her husband, "to keep them from falling into the hands of the enemy." Bedroom visitations recall *Cymbeline*. To prove he has dishonored Imogen, Iachimo secrets himself in a large chest in her chamber; he creeps out, looming Dracula-like over her while she sleeps, and turns down her nightdress to look for an intimate mark known only to a lover; he finds a crimson five-spotted mole (almost like teeth marks) on her left breast.

And what of the historical Vlad Dracula also called Vlad Tepes or—by the Turks—Vlad the Impaler, who shares the name but not the vampirism, a tyrant who reputedly feasted al fresco amid rows of impaled bodies. (Vlad IV's use of Dracula was inherited from his father, Vlad Dracul; the added "a" means "son of.") Stoker refers to Hungarian campaigns against the Turks in the fifteenth century, facts gleaned from his research in the Round Reading Room, but Dracula is not Vlad Tepes, only a novelist's interpretation. Raymond Mc-

VLAD TEPES, *voïvode* or prince of Wallachia in the fifteenth century, provided historical background for *Dracula*.

Nally, a biographer of the fifteenth-century ruler, believes there emerged from Stoker's research "a composite picture—admittedly sketchy—of an authentic historical character who bore at least some of the characteristics of the historical Dracula."*

Another ambiguous influence is Arminius Vambéry, an adventurer and master of obscure languages, who is mentioned by Van Helsing: "I have asked my friend Arminius, of Buda-Pesth University, to make his record; and . . . he must, indeed, have been that Voivode [Prince] Dracula who won his name against the Turk." Stoker met the Hungarian folklore expert at a Beefsteak supper on April 30, 1890. But there is no evidence that Vambéry initiated the vampire myth. Up to this date, the notes mention only: "describe old dead man made alive." If anything, the professor might have influenced the change of setting from Styria—the location of Le Fanu's *Carmilla*—to Transylvania. Stoker already was familiar with the writings of Emily Gerard, who had lived there for two years as the English wife of a Hungarian cavalry brigade commander. She found the region bubbling over with beliefs in ghouls, goblins, and vampires and, in 1888, wrote *The Land Beyond the Forest,* the title a translation of Transylvania.

Unraveling *Dracula*'s origins will continue as long as the novel endures; equally as fascinating, though, is Stoker's fixation on this one story. After all, he was a Grub Street hack, dashing off romantic adventures with little editorial revision. So it was obsessional, not to say unusual, for him to spend six years plotting *Dracula*. This novel obviously meant something more to him than a few hundred pounds. His first notes were made on March 8, 1890, on the completion of *The Snake's Pass,* his first novel; the last date recorded was March 17,

* In Stoker's time Transylvania was administered by Hungary as part of the Austro-Hungarian Empire, joining Wallachia and Moldavia as part of Romania at the end of World War I. Vlad Tepes, although born in the Transylvania town of Sighişoara, ruled over Wallachia to the south briefly in 1448, between 1456 and 1462, and, at the time of his death, in 1476. His castles were in Romania, but Stoker decided that Hungary was more steeped in vampire lore and so relocated Castle Dracula on the Borgo Pass connecting Transylvania with Moldavia.

1896, after publication of *The Watter's Mou'* and *The Shoulder of Shasta.* By February of 1892 he had sketched out a plot, placing events in the next calendar year. Initially he planned to kill Dracula on his birthday, November 8, but in the final draft the novel ends two days earlier.*

By the time he arrived in Cruden Bay, he had toyed with a varied group of characters and, more important, a format, even though derivative. The narrative owes much to Wilkie Collins's 1860 novel *The Woman in White,* considered the progenitor of the mystery novel, which also uses an epistolary structure and a familiar social setting. *Dracula* builds through a multiplicity of text, some in shorthand or undecipherable script (Stoker loved secret codes). Except for the frivolous tone of Lucy's letters, Quincey Morris's Americanisms, and Van Helsing's annoying Dutch-English accent, the voices are indistinguishable. Only the vampire speaks in the narrative form; all other information is filtered through written documents. Stoker makes clear the purpose of these overlapping texts in an anonymous preface (often omitted from some modern texts): "There is throughout no statement of past things wherein memory may err, for all the records chosen are exactly contemporary, given from the standpoints and within the range of knowledge of those who made them." In a brilliant touch, he enhances the present tense by featuring new inventions such as the Kodak camera, the portable typewriter, and the recording phonograph.

Stoker's affinity with the exchange and depletion of energy—so vital to vampire life—was a version of Edgar Allan Poe's short story "The Oval Portrait." An artist paints a portrait of his wife, but when colors are brushed on she is drained. When the portrait is finished, she is dead—a motif refined by Wilde in *Dorian Gray.* According to the notes, Stoker considered an artist character called Francis Ay-

---

* The notes were collected and mounted by Stoker's literary executor prior to a sale at Sotheby's on July 7, 1913. A Mr. Drake paid £2.2 for item 182. The Rosenbach Museum & Library in Philadelphia purchased the eighty-five pages of manuscript and typescript notes from a Philadelphia dealer on February 25, 1970. They are probably incomplete, since Stoker had a habit of writing on envelopes, stationery, menus, any flat surface; the executor did not attempt to arrange the bits and pieces in chronological order.

*DRACULA* MANUSCRIPT. Stoker's twenty-seven chapters in three books dated February 29, 1892, mention the Borgo Pass, Whitby, Dracula, and the flyman, later called Renfield.

town, who would complement a specific vampiric characteristic: painters cannot make a likeness of a vampire, or as Stoker put it, "however hard the artist tries, the subject always ends up looking like someone else." A fascinating plot twist that did not survive.

The main character was to be called Count Wampyr, but Stoker

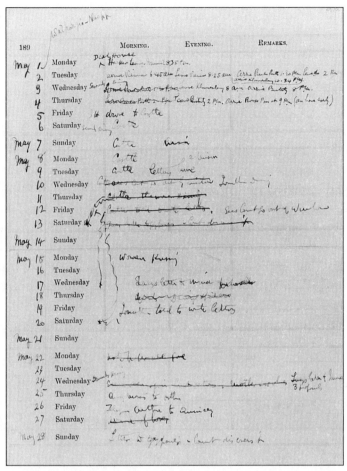

*DRACULA* DIARY. Stoker organized the book in a diary with days and dates corresponding to the year 1893. "Women Kissing" on May 15 refers to the scene when Jonathan Harker desires a vampiric kiss "with those red lips."

crossed out the old-fashioned spelling and substituted Dracula. On a page called *Historiae Personae,* he wrote *Dracula Dracula* on each side of the heading, and *Count Dracula* in the left-hand corner. As the notes progress, he refers to him as Drac. Omitted from the published novel was an intriguing dinner party for thirteen, hosted by "The Mad Doctor," as in a doctor who cares for the insane, who will emerge as Dr. Seward. Assigned a number, each guest makes up a strange incident, with the order of the numbers completing the story.

At the end Count Dracula appears. It is difficult to imagine where this scene could be placed in the existing plot, but its suitability for the stage was evident.

Beyond Aytown, other dinner guests not woven into the novel included a detective, a psychical-research agent, a German professor, and an American inventor called Brutus M. Moris (later Quincey Morris). At first Dracula's castle employs a deaf-mute woman and a silent man as servants, but Stoker decided the count should do his own cooking, even though he drinks rather than eats ("an excellent roast chicken," says Harker). Other walk-ons—an undertaker, his assistant, and a maid—were dropped. Renfield may have sprung from *King Lear*'s poor Tom, who pretends to be mad and consumes water animals. In the notes, Dr. Seward's patient is nameless, but in the typescript he is called Flyman (a pun not only on his food preferences but on the theatre: the flyman hoists drop cloths from the flies).

The significant change from working notes to published book is the beginning. Harker's extraordinary journey to Transylvania, a brilliant opening, was not the original first chapter. Stoker planned to start the novel on March 16, with correspondence between Mr. Hawkins and Count Dracula about the purchase of property in England. The second chapter was to commence on April 30, the Witches' Sabbath, when en route to Transylvania, Harker stops off in Munich to attend a performance of *The Flying Dutchman.* Both chapters were dropped, cutting 101 pages from the final manuscript. The second chapter, often referred to as the deleted first chapter, was published posthumously as the title story in *Dracula's Guest,* which inspired the film *Dracula's Daughter.*

In Stoker's mind, Dracula was the devil. In the Wallachian language, the word means "dragon" or "son of the devil." Also known to Stoker was the resonant Celtic phrase *dhroch fhola,* pronounced "druck ulla," meaning "of bad blood." Stoker makes the vampire's immortality a version of the Faustian pact: Dracula is both Faust and Mephistopheles, both dream and demon. In the 1890s the concept of Satan had come full circle, reverting to the biblical meaning of an invisible tempter. Stoker's demon, however, returns to the Middle Ages, with Van Helsing playing Grand Inquisitor and using the symbolic power of the holy wafer and the crucifix. Catholics exorcise vampires, while Protestants burn witches. Stoker found documented accounts of the devil vanquished in Britain by Catholic ritual in an 1875 book on witchcraft. The named sources in the notes include some thirty-two major reference books on the occult, the devil, medicine, sea legends, and the Carpathians. He delved into Sarah Lee's 1823 volume *Anecdotes of Habits and Instincts of Animals* for background on wolves, rats, and the blood-sucking vampire bat, known only in Central and South America (Quincey Morris's horse was drained by a vampire bat on the Pampas), and found in *The Devil: His Origin, Greatness and Decadence* what he needed to document the Scholomance, or Devil's Academy, that Dracula attended.

Most readers are puzzled by the ambiguous relationship the count has to the three vampiresses dressed as ladies, two dark and one fair. Are they his sisters, daughters, or wives? There is one hint. "You yourself never loved; you never love," one accuses him (in the manuscript this was originally written "You never loved yourself"). Dracula replies, "Yes, I too can love; you yourselves can tell it from the past." Once Dracula vamps his women he is no longer interested in them, only in the women of other men. There is also a vampire incest taboo. "And you, their best beloved one," Dracula explains to Mina, "are now to me, flesh of my flesh; blood of my blood, kin of my kin; my bountiful wine-press for a while; and shall be later on my companion and helper." Sexual excitement ceases after the immortal kiss. Harker vaguely recognizes the fair-haired one because she is Countess Dolingen, whom he first met in the deleted second chapter. This inconsistency was never caught in the editing process. An original line explains everything: "As she spoke I was looking at the fair woman and it suddenly dawned on me that she was the woman—or her image—that I had seen in the tomb on Walpurgis Night."

A typescript manuscript, perhaps the original manuscript, was not included among Stoker's papers auctioned at Sotheby's after his death; it was discovered in America, according to one story, and sold by a Dickens scholar to a private collector in California. It appears to

not feeling nearly as easy in my mind as usual. If this book

should ever reach Mina before I do, let it bring my good bye.

Here *Comes* ~~is~~ the Coach !

Jonathan Harker's ~~Diary~~ *Journal* (continued)

*The* Castle. May 5.

The grey of the morning has passed and the sun is high

over the distant horizon, which seems jagged whether with trees

or hills I know not, for it is so far off that big things and

little are mixed. I am not sleepy and as I am not to be call-

ed till I awake naturally I write till sleep comes. There are

many odd things to put down and lest who reads them may fan- *let me put down my dinner exactly. I'll tell you*

cy that I dined well before I left Bistritz on what they call

"Robber steak" - bits of bacon, onion and beef, seasoned with

red pepper ~~and~~ strung on sticks and roasted over the fire ~~in~~

~~the simple~~ ~~broohette" as the French call it~~ - like *in* the simple style of the

London cats'-meat! The wine was Golden Mediasch which pro-

duces a queer sting on the tongue which is however not dis-

agreeable & I had only a couple of glasses of this and no-

thing else ~~until supper with which I had two glasses of old~~

~~Tokay the oldest wine I ever tasted ; but I did not take as~~

~~much as I should have liked for I feared it might be too strong~~

~~and the Count might want to talk business at once. A roast~~

~~chicken was my support.~~

When I got on the coach the driver had not got into his

seat and I saw him talking with the landlady. They were evi-

PAGE FROM CHAPTER II of *Dracula,* taken from a privately owned manuscript purported to be the original typesetter's copy

be a ribbon copy, organized by the cut-and-paste method Stoker preferred. He either composed it on the typewriter or typed out an earlier handwritten version. There are three distinct holographs:
Stoker's, an editor's in blue pencil, and Thornley's notes on blood
transfusions and autopsies. Pages have been renumbered, and blank
spaces occur throughout the text. The number of fill-ins argues in
favor of the original-typescript premise; Stoker would have firmed
up names and places in an earlier draft. *The Un-Dead* appears on the
first page as the title.

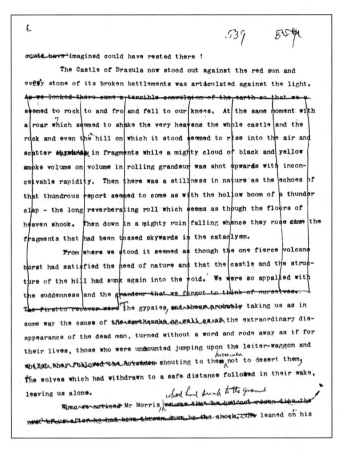

PAGE FROM CHAPTER XXVII of the manuscript, with an editorial cut eliminating the destruction of Dracula's castle

It is often assumed that Dracula was staked in the novel—so deeply imprinted is this violent film scene—rather than dying from multiple knife wounds, as Mina describes: "But, on the instant, came the sweep and flash of Jonathan's great knife. I shrieked as I saw it shear through the throat; whilst at the same moment Mr. Morris's bowie knife plunged into the heart." Dracula was spared the ritual vampire death because his staking would be a counterpart to Lucy's orgiastic death—except male to male—something too overtly suggestive for a novel in any genre.

The startling change from manuscript to novel, however, is the ending. Stoker destroyed the castle after Dracula's death, obliterating

all vampiric traces. But someone, at the last moment, deleted 195
words, including:

> As we looked there came a terrible convulsion of the earth so that we
> seemed to rock to and fro and fell to our knees. At the same moment,
> with a roar which seemed to shake the very heavens, the whole cas-
> tle and the rock and even the hill on which it stood seemed to rise
> into the air and scatter in fragments while a mighty cloud of black
> and yellow smoke volume on volume in rolling grandeur was shot
> upwards with inconceivable rapidity. . . . From where we stood it
> seemed as though the one fierce volcano burst had satisfied the need
> of nature and that the castle and the structure of the hill had sunk
> again into the void. We were so appalled with the suddenness and the
> grandeur that we forgot to think of ourselves.

Was this ending too evocative of Poe's *The Fall of the House of
Usher*? Did Stoker—or his publisher—have a sequel in mind? A series, perhaps, not unlike the Sherlock Holmes stories, with Van Helsing as psychic detective? In hindsight, it seems best to have only one
Bram Stoker's *Dracula* to look back on—and forward to. Still, what
taunts the reader is the lingering fear—or desire—that Dracula, if not
properly executed, will return and make good his contemptuous
boast: "Your girls that you all love are mine already; and through
them you and others shall yet be mine—my creatures, to do my bidding and to be my jackals when I want to feed. Bah!"

# Chapter 14

# DRACULA DEBUTS

D*racula* arrived at booksellers on May 26, 1897, bound in yellow, the color of the French novel that Oscar Wilde draws attention to in *The Picture of Dorian Gray.* Dramatic rights were protected with a prepublication copyright reading at the Lyceum on May 18 at 10:15 a.m. The script, divided into five acts, forty-seven scenes, and a prologue, was a cut-and-paste narrative produced from galley proofs. Everything was rushed, but rights—not craft—were at issue. The program announced *Dracula or The Un-Dead,* indicating that Stoker—listed as author and acting manager of the Lyceum—was still ambivalent about the title. Two days later, when he signed Constable's contract, it was *The Un-Dead;* six days later it became *Dracula,* a prescient change, for a novel called *The Un-Dead* would never have endured into the twenty-first century.*

Posters were plastered on the theatre hoardings half an hour before the performance, a usual procedure for such readings. Some crew members, performers, and wanderers off the street made up a meager audience. Cleaning ladies leaned on their brooms. The lime-light men sat silently in the wings. Except for castle drop cloths from

---

* Stoker earned no royalties on the first thousand copies of the six-shilling novel; then one shilling and sixpence for each copy up to ten thousand, and two shillings thereafter. At this time, contracts were usually executed at least six months before publication. Oddly, *Dracula*'s contract was signed six days before publication. Because Constable had published Stoker's two previous books, perhaps an oral agreement was legally executed when convenient.

*Macbeth,* the melodrama played on an empty stage. Among fifteen actors drawn from the company's supporting ranks was Ellen Terry's daughter, Edith Craig, the first actress to play Mina. Count Dracula was a Mr. Jones, most likely Whitworth Jones, whose roles veered toward an assortment of wizards, kings, and demons, including Mephistopheles. More than anything, though, Stoker wanted to woo Irving to a role he saw as the crowd-pleaser the financially strapped Lyceum needed, a role to celebrate the actor's consummate stage villains, particularly Mathias, Mephistopheles, and Iachimo. Somewhere in the creative process, Dracula became a sinister caricature of Irving as mesmerist and depleter, an artist draining those about him to feed his ego. It was a stunning but avenging tribute.

The reading concluded after four hours, and the crew pressed onto the stage to prepare for *Madame Sans-Gêne,* Irving's revenge on Shaw: *his* Napoleon play rather than Shaw's *The Man of Destiny.* Stoker approached Irving in his dressing room, where he was transforming his tall, ascetic body into the short, stout, full-faced emperor and asked: "How did you like it?" "Dreadful!" he replied. Already Irving, as emperor, was in character. Irving "simply would not give himself up to appreciation," explained Ellen Terry. "It was never any pleasure to him to see the acting of other actors and actresses." Or, it appears, a play written by his business manager.

Irving's repudiation of a vampire role was not unprecedented. In 1852, another Irishman, Dion Boucicault, wrote *The Vampire: A Phantasm Related in Three Dramas* for Charles Kean. When Kean declined the part, Boucicault stepped in and launched himself as an actor. Irving would have known this, as he knew everything about Kean's career, but his rejection, like everything about him, was more complex. Did he feel it beneath his dignity to star in a play written by an employee? Was the part of a mostly offstage villain too small? As the count or in one of his various forms (coach driver, bat, or dog), Dracula is present on only sixty-two pages out of a total of 390 in the first edition. The novel draws its strength from this absence; Dracula is more pervasive and dangerous when offstage or being described by others. Despite the countless hours Stoker spent trying to persuade Irving to be Count Dracula, the actor refused to consider a role that would set the standard for any future interpretation.

FUSSIE AND IRVING, sketched during the run of *Madame Sans-Gêne,* when the actor transforms himself into the squat emperor Napoleon

The reading did little for Stoker's self-esteem, but it did protect his dramatic rights. Concerned about the slovenly and slipshod nature of many "pirated" stage versions, he had urged the Select Committee of the House of Lords (then drafting the Copyright Law Amendment Bill) to give authors a say in the dramatization of their works. The reading also earned the imprimatur of the Lord Chamberlain's Office, whose blue pencils were renowned for crossing out offending passages to protect the morals of the theatregoing public. Nothing was amiss with this *Dracula.* The censor wrote Stoker he had devoted a day "to read, mark, learn, and inwardly digest the very remarkable dramatic version of your forthcoming novel; which I

should say amply fulfils the letter of the copyright law . . . and my official mind is satisfied that there is nothing unlicenseable in the
piece." *Dracula* was granted License #162, the play was shelved, and
no version was produced during Stoker's lifetime. In fact, theatrical
histories, biographies of Irving and Terry, any literature about the
Lyceum, including Stoker's two-volume *Reminiscences of Henry Irving,*
omit any mention of *Dracula*'s being performed there. Except for the
existence of the program, the reading might never have occurred.

When he opened the first edition, Stoker must have been disappointed. The novel looked shabby. The last-minute title change may
explain why the book was issued in a poor-quality yellow cloth
binding, with red rather than gilt lettering on the spine, front, and
back. Stoker's previous Constable books—*The Shoulder of Shasta* and
*The Watter's Mou'*—were handsome by comparison. The initial
printing was three thousand copies; no records survive on the total
number sold or whether there were reprints. The next printing was
a Constable paperback in 1901. Surprisingly, no American publisher
wanted *Dracula,* even though Stoker formerly had published with
Harper and with Appleton. To protect himself, he purchased the
copyright but never registered the required two copies. Thus,
through a technicality, *Dracula* has always been in the public domain
in the United States. Finally in 1899, Doubleday & McClure announced the first American edition, which followed serialization in
the New York *Sun* and other American newspapers.

It took until the late 1930s, after the silent film *Nosferatu* and Bela
Lugosi's *Dracula,* for French and German editions to be in demand.
Curiously, the first translation in 1901 was Icelandic, entitled *Makt
Myrkanna* (The Power of Darkness). Asked to write an introduction,
Stoker took the opportunity to make his story more believable. He
describes the characters as good friends and hints at a connection between the vampire killings and the Whitechapel murders of 1888.
"This series of crimes has not yet passed from the memory—a series
of crimes which appear to have originated from the same source," he
wrote, "and which at the time created as much repugnance in people everywhere as the notorious murders of Jack the Ripper. . . ."

DRACULA

2/- Net.    BRAM STOKER    2/- Net.

THE RIDER EDITION of 1925 used imagery similar to the Constable cover of 1910. The artist, Holloway, incorporated the shape of a phoenix into the folds of Dracula's cloak.

Stoker sent boxed, leather-bound presentation copies to important friends and—judging from replies—some five hundred yellow
books to everyone else. Readers found nothing sexually unsettling
about *Dracula*. No moralistic letters of outrage were published in the
London *Times,* for who would admit to understanding its hidden
messages? It was a horror story, nothing more. Favorably compared
with *Frankenstein, Wuthering Heights,* and *The Fall of the House of Usher,*
it was called weird and powerful, one of the best in the supernatural
line. *Punch* labeled it "a first cousin to Mephistopheles," admonish-
ing Stoker for venturing into a "domain where angels fear to tread."

Stoker flogged his books relentlessly. Edgar Pemberton from the
Birmingham *Daily Post,* told the expectant author he would write
"an appreciative notice after dipping into it," giving the impression
that book reviewers were page flippers rather than readers. The prestigious *Athenaeum* attacked it for lacking "constructive art in the
higher literary sense. It reads at times like a mere series of grotesquely
incredible events." They did allow Stoker "a certain degree of imaginative faculty, and many ingenious and gruesome details," and they
praised the beginning (as critics have through the years), which
promises "to unfold the roots of mystery and fear lying deep in
human nature."

Fortunately authors have mothers. "My dear, it is splendid,"
gushed Charlotte Stoker, "a thousand miles beyond anything you
have written before, and I feel certain will place you very high in the
writers of the day—the story and style being deeply sensational, exciting and interesting." To his mother, Stoker had surpassed all competitors. "No book since Mrs. Shelley's 'Frankenstein' or indeed any
other at all has come near yours in originality, or terror—Poe is
nowhere," she wrote. "I have read much but I never met a book like
it at all. In its terrible excitement it should make a widespread reputation and much money for you." Unfortunately it did neither during Stoker's lifetime. If *Dracula* had been published in 1818 at the
same time as *Frankenstein,* instead of at the height of literary realism
and naturalism, it would have been hailed as a Romantic milestone.

Gladstone received his book and a cautious note. "It is a story of
a vampire," Stoker explained, "the old medieval vampire but re-
crudescent today . . . the book is necessarily full of horrors and ter-

rors but I trust that these are calculated to cleanse the mind by pity & terror. At any rate there is nothing base in the book, and though superstition is fought in it with the weapons of superstition, I hope it is not irreverent." Then Stoker concluded in his typical sycophantish style: "I deem it a high privilege to be able to address you in the first person and to be able to put before you a book of my own, though it be only an atom in the intellectual Kingdom where you have so long held sway." Even at the age of fifty Stoker could not move beyond adolescent flattery to friendship.

The editor of *Harper's* wrote: "If I enjoy Dracula as much as I did your Irish book, I have indeed a treat before me." Mary Elizabeth Braddon, a sensation novelist who made her reputation with *Lady Audley's Secret* in 1862, found *Dracula* a page-turner. "I have done my humdrum little story of transfusion, in the *Good Lady Ducayne*—but your 'bloofer' lady . . ." Fellow barrister and author of *The Prisoner of Zenda* Anthony Hope Hawkins (whose surname Stoker borrowed for Mr. Hawkins) admitted: "Your vampires robbed me of sleep for nights." Arthur Conan Doyle added: "I think it is the very best story of diablerie which I have read for many years. It is really wonderful how with so much exciting interest over so long a book there is never an anticlimax."

*Dracula's* publication coincided with the opening of the New Gallery, which exhibited a portrait called *The Vampire* by Philip Burne-Jones, son to the Pre-Raphaelite painter Edward who had designed sets for the Lyceum's *King Arthur.* Painted in dark greens, whites, and crimson, the portrait shows a woman with long, flowing black hair and long, sharp teeth in a clinging nightdress, astride a contented-looking man collapsed across a bed. London was shocked, for the pantherlike woman resembled the actress known as Mrs. Patrick Campbell, with whom young Burne-Jones was besotted. It made for delicious gossip. Burne-Jones's cousin Rudyard Kipling enlivened the catalogue with a poem called "The Vampire." Acknowledging *Dracula,* Burne-Jones wrote: "As soon as I have a copy, I shall beg your acceptance of a photograph of my Vampire—a woman this time, so as to make the balance fair!"

That August Stoker returned to Cruden Bay, where he tidied up *Miss Betty,* the romantic novel completed but put aside while he wrote *Dracula.* To attract vacationers, the Great North of Scotland Railway built a pink granite hotel, finished with stepped gables and turrets, as well as a championship golf course overlooking the sea. Stoker was distressed to see advertisements touting Port Erroll as the "Brighton of Aberdeenshire." But the activity made it more exciting for Florence, who now socialized with the wives of the tycoons of Colman's Mustard, Bovril, Horlicks, and Coats Thread. She proudly mentioned that her son was studying at Winchester.

And the Stokers had a new address. In 1896 they had moved to 18 St. Leonard's Terrace, adjacent to their old home, where they had an extra floor but were four years away from electrification. During the season, they returned to Dublin for the Drawing Room Ball. Florence was, the society column reported, the "most lovely lady present." At this time Stoker borrowed £600—a substantial sum— from Hall Caine. To cover the debt (the equivalent of eight months' pay), he signed over a £700 insurance policy, noting he would "have to be re-examined medically as is always necessary before a new policy." Was the money to renovate number 18 to Florence's tastes, to subsidize the Lyceum, or to cover Irving's personal debts? The loan was repaid, but the significant fact here was Stoker's acceptable health in 1898.

During the last week of the provincial tour, Fussie died onstage in Manchester. A carpenter had thrown his coat with a ham sandwich in the pocket over an open trap. Nosing and nudging for the food, Fussie fell through and was killed instantly. When a stagehand retrieved him after the performance, every man took off his hat. Irving silently received the news and carried the body back to his hotel room. Ellen Terry saw him there eating supper, with Fussie lying on the rug, talking to the dog as if he were alive. The following day Fussie traveled back to London on the train, covered with a coat. Irving had the head stuffed, and the remains buried in the Hyde Park Dogs' Cemetery. When he returned to the Lyceum for the first time after Fussie's death, the crew and cast were apprehensive. Then an odd thing happened. The wardrobe cat, who had never been near Irving's dressing room, came and sat on Fussie's cushion. Walter

Collinson looked anxiously at the cat until Irving ordered him to get some food. Thereafter the cat was Irving's constant companion.

Five days after Fussie's death, "Breezy Bill" Terriss, once a minor player at the Lyceum, was murdered by an unemployed extra, Richard Arthur Prince, who had been on the Lyceum boards as a witch in the 1888 *Macbeth*. Prince blamed Terriss for his failure to receive a stipend from an actors' fund and followed him from his club through the dimly lit lanes of Covent Garden to the stage door of the Adelphi, where he stabbed him to death. Terriss was forty-eight and had been the stage victim of numerous assassins. He died in the arms of Jessie Millward, his mistress and leading lady in the American drama *Secret Service*. Bearing violets, Irving and Stoker visited Terriss's wife first and then his mistress.*

Stoker confounded present-day critics by following *Dracula* with an unworthy novel, *Miss Betty*, written in 1890 when he began the *Dracula Notes*. Hall Caine read the manuscript a year later and told his friend "the writing wants another revision," citing "repetitions, a few very modern colloquialisms & the like." He recommended "more suspense and less predictability." In 1895, at Anthony Hope Hawkins's suggestion, Stoker sent the manuscript to his publisher. "A slight sketch of a pure and amiable girl, but this itself won't sell a book," J. W. Arrowsmith replied by way of rejection. Doubtless other editors had similar thoughts before Pearson published it in 1898. The novel's pivotal dramatic point is a rescue from the Thames, a reminder of how Stoker once saved an elderly man. Even though watery rescue scenes play badly onstage, Stoker had his Lyceum copyright reading, using many of the same actors from *Dracula*. "A pretty little tale of a woman's devotion," reported *The Era*. Stoker had ignored all editorial advice. By rights, Constable should have

---

* One of the most famous theatrical mementos, the sword worn by Edmund Kean as Richard III in 1814, was passed down through two generations of actors to Irving in 1877; he in turn gave it to Terriss. Eventually, Ellen Terry's sister, Kate Terry Gielgud, gave it to her son John in 1938. John Gielgud presented it to Laurence Olivier in 1944 for his Richard. Olivier broke with tradition by keeping the sword and made no provision in his will for its disposition.

made amends for *Dracula's* shoddy presentation by taking *Miss Betty* and commissioning a vampire sequel. Obviously, there were unexplained problems between publisher and author.*

Stoker returned to his Cruden Bay stories. Then disaster struck. On the evening of February 18, 1898, the Bow Street police reported a fire at the Lyceum's storage area: two arches under the Chatham and Dover railway at a point on an elevated line in Southwark. Stoker had thought this location safe. It was isolated from neighboring buildings and spacious enough for the accumulated scenery of two decades; the Lyceum's basement, with its maze of gas tubing, could no longer contain it all, particularly the thirty-foot-high drop cloths, rolled on battens forty-two-feet wide. Initial insurance coverage was £10,000, when the value was five times that amount; in 1897, Irving called for frugality and Stoker reduced the policy to £6,000. Irving had a skewed way of saving money while Beefsteak entertainments continued unabated, with no concern for the price of claret and champagne. Destroyed was the scenery for 260 scenes of forty-four plays; gone were the Italian dresses and armor, the painted castles and temples and battlements; the Brocken Scene from *Faust,* the tavern scene from *The Bells.*

Following this ruination, Irving was stricken with pleurisy and pneumonia while performing in Glasgow. All his life he had been conscious of the force of the threefold emphasis. Now within a year three catastrophes had struck: the first—an injured knee—restricted his activity, the second destroyed his stock-in-trade, and the third undermined his health. Confined to bed for seven weeks, he leaned heavily on Stoker. "If there is anything to say tonight and tomorrow night—and there will be until next week," Irving told Loveday, "I should if I were you try Stoker on the stump. He's good with them lungs of his and would do anything you asked him."

During his convalescence in Bournemouth, Joe Comyns Carr visited and outlined a plan for a syndicate to take over the Lyceum.

---

* Apparently Stoker kept abstracts of all his reviews. The pages for *Miss Betty* have survived at Stratford. Twenty-seven British publications reviewed the novel. *The Irish Times* of February 26, 1898, loyally predicted that the "mantle of Robert Louis Stevenson seems to have fallen upon Mr. Stoker."

Such was Irving's depression that he signed away his theatre without consulting Stoker or Loveday. Due to sail for New York to arrange the next tour, Stoker was mortified that his opinion went unsolicited. He always grumbled he "had no part in the matter and no responsibility." The terms called for Irving to stay on as actor-manager and transfer all his interests to the syndicate, which would run the theatre as a limited-liability company responsible for the financing and production of plays. Irving agreed to give 100 performances a year, bearing 60 percent (a high figure) of the costs of new productions, and to tour four months in England or America. He received a cash settlement of £26,000, plus shares in the company, enough to solve his immediate financial needs.

It is difficult to believe Irving's being deeply in debt, but then he never heeded Stoker's warnings. He was an eternal optimist about money, but unsentimental when it came to satisfying creditors: he sold his collection of theatrical books and prints to cover personal

IRVING AND STOKER, behind him, leave the Lyceum from the Burleigh Street private entrance, where a horse-drawn hansom awaits.

obligations. The Lyceum, however, was far from bankrupt. Funds were obtainable; arrangements could have been made with Coutts Bank. There were other reasons for relinquishing control, reasons Irving denied: he was preparing to die. Only Stoker and Collinson knew the seriousness of his lung infection. Irving coughed up so much phlegm he went through five hundred pocket handkerchiefs weekly. He needed burnt brandy to accelerate his weak heart, sometimes taking it onstage to keep going. "Life lost part of its charm for him," Stoker said. "In those last seven years of his life I was not able to see so much of him as I had been in the habit of doing throughout the previous twenty."

Irving was a lonely man as only those who have resigned domestic ties to follow art must be. His habit of sitting up until after dawn clung to him, and he would seize upon anyone for company. A waiter at the Queen's Hotel in Leeds, recalled, "Ah, yes; Old Henry would keep me chatting for hours after supper till I almost fell asleep standing." He spent less time at the theatre. Stoker saw him at a new sunny flat at 17 Stratton Street, off Piccadilly, or in his hotel when on tour. The Beefsteak entertainments were replaced by an occasional weekend meal at the Garrick Club.

Stoker wistfully recalled "the old long meetings when occasion was full of chances for self-development, for self-illumination," the nights when they talked until daybreak, sharing "the secret chambers of the soul." (Jonathan Harker notes how his "diary seems horribly like the beginning of the 'Arabian Nights,' for everything has to break off at cock-crow—or like the ghost of Hamlet's father.") The time had passed, though, for recriminations. Stoker had put his unspoken grievances on the pages of *Dracula,* but Irving probably never read the book. Yet, after so many years of withholding, of waiting for the right moment to unburden himself, the realization that it would never be was a relief.

The theatre both had known and loved was part of history; gone forever were the Lyceum nights of fond delights. The changing world of entertainment went beyond avant-garde taste in Ibsen or Shaw or the rise of modernism. When Irving and Stoker refurbished the

Lyceum in 1878, there were seven legitimate theatres. By the turn of the century the number had doubled. Although theatres continued the tradition of actor-managers—Her Majesty's was the home of Herbert Beerbohm Tree, considered Irving's successor in Shakespearian roles; Charles Wyndham was at the Criterion; and three Lyceum graduates, George Alexander, John Martin-Harvey, and Johnston Forbes-Robertson, had companies and theatres of their own—the choice no longer fell between an Adelphi melodrama or a Lyceum classic. There were pantomimes, burlesques, and French comedies, and a new genre: the musical comedy. Chorus lines with beauteous chorines decorated the stages of Daly's and the Gaiety. As the century waned people wanted frivolity, laughter, and music.

After much agonizing, Ellen Terry decided to play one more Lyceum season, followed by a two-year farewell tour, to earn money for her old age. Irving begged her to be with him in America one last time. Of course she agreed, telling Shaw that she had "always thought to be *useful, really* useful, to any one person is rather fine and satisfactory." In fact, since Irving had sold his rights in the theatre Terry found him less autocratic; the only comment she ever gave on their parting was to say "that we never quarrelled, and that our separation could not be avoided." The inevitable had come for her as well as Stoker, who held Irving's coat and urged a slower pace.

Stoker hoped a truce with Shaw, crossed off the critics list after the *Richard III* debacle, would raise Irving's spirits. How gratifying for Irving to have Shaw approach him and admit the actor had given him much enjoyment over the years. Ever ingenuous, Stoker never understood how few people are capable of the generous act. Had Shaw offered his hand in tribute, Irving would have bitten it for insincerity. Optimistically, Stoker sent off tickets for the first night of *The Medicine Man* on November 2, 1898. "Personally I have only one desire concerning the theatres of this accursed metropolis," Shaw replied, "and that is to see them, with their actors, managers and all completely plunged into the blinding white hot heat of hell until anything theatrical is consumed out of them & nothing remains but a virgin art and a small heap of clinker representing the press." But he told Stoker he would review *The Medicine Man* if he attended, because "it is not decent to have first nights at the Lyceum without me;

it makes the front of the house ridiculous. Again, it produces an impression of a vendetta; and Irving and I are too eminent to indulge in such schoolboyishness in public." Indeed! But how they both loved it. For Shaw to free Terry from the "ogre's den" made the battle worthwhile.

Such was the power of *Dracula* that in 1898 Stoker was invited to write a biographical sketch of himself for *Who's Who.* Under "Recreations" he secretively noted: "pretty much the same as those of the other children of Adam." Stoker sleuths have enjoyed twisting this ambiguous phrase to suit the occasion, including a parallel to Cain and Abel. Here Stoker is referring to Walt Whitman's poem "Children of Adam," children who "know how to swim, row, ride, wrestle, shoot, run, strike, retreat, advance, resist, defend themselves. They are ultimate in their own right—they are calm, clear, well-possess'd of themselves." Stoker's allusion was his best projection of himself, only he wrote it in code.

That year Mark Twain, whom he first met in 1883 during the American tour in Chicago, arrived in London. Twain wanted to adapt the German playwright Philipp Langmann's strike drama *Bartel Turaser* and asked Stoker to be his English agent for dramatic works. Twain genuinely liked Stoker for himself, not for his proximity to Irving; the humorist found him an amusing companion and respected his business acumen. Although Stoker was as class-obsessed as any Etonian, he relaxed with Twain, letting his innate Irish charm drive his personality. Their discussions of dreams and dual personalities continued.

Twain was always a bit chagrined around Stoker and Irving, for they were among the investors in the ill-fated typesetter scheme he promoted in 1894, when Mergenthaler's Linotype was already in production. Shares of the Paige Compositor Manufacturing Company (face value, $100 each) were marketed at $50 a share because of their speculative nature. Stoker was the first to throw in dollars, buying twenty shares on an installment plan. "I am glad Irving takes a chance with you," Twain wrote, referring to Irving's $500. "Please

MARK TWAIN with his daughter Clara in the drawing room of the Chelsea
house in Tedworth Square, near the Stokers, which they rented in 1897

do not mention the price you are paying, for I have raised it higher
since, for what seemed good reasons." When Twain realized the venture was doomed, that his impractical dream had dissolved, he wrote
his business adviser: "Bram Stoker must be stopped from paying any
more installments." He refunded Stoker's $100 and asked him to
"tell Irving for me—I can't get up courage enough to talk about this
misfortune myself, except to you, whom by good luck I haven't dam-
aged yet—that when the wreckage presently floats ashore he will get
a good deal of his $500 back; and a dab at a time I will make up to
him the rest."

During the eight years Twain traveled and lectured in Europe and Asia, he lived at one point at 23 Tedworth Square, near the Stokers' St. Leonard's Terrace home. Twain was writing a new travel book, which he considered calling *Another Innocent Abroad,* a sequel to the book that made him famous, but eventually settled on *Following the Equator,* published the same year as *Dracula.* Twain's presentation copy of *Dracula,* catalogued after the humorist's death, had page eleven turned down and half the pages uncut—a sure indicator of readership in the days when book signatures came folded.

At least he read as far as his tribute where Van Helsing tries to convince Dr. Seward to suspend disbelief. "Let me illustrate," he says. "I heard once of an American who so defined faith: 'that faculty which enables us to believe things which we know to be untrue.' For one, I follow that man." Here Stoker rewrote Pudd'nhead Wilson's maxim "Faith is believing what you know ain't so," taken from *Pudd'nhead Wilson's New Calendar,* which Twain sent him in 1894. *Dracula,* perhaps, had more of an influence on Twain. His fragment "The Chronicle of Young Satan," written between 1897 and 1900, features a character who claims to have "seen the great bat that sucks the blood from the necks of people while they are asleep, fanning them softly with its wings and so keeping them drowsy till they die."

Invited to dinner at the Stokers' in January of 1897, Twain told the tale "about Commodore Vanderbilt & the young clerk from the Memphis wharf-boat." Twain tried to be of good cheer, but he still mourned the death of his eldest daughter, Susy, who had died of meningitis at age twenty-four the previous summer. In his never-ending grief, Twain turned his rage on everyone, including himself. Stoker understood these emotional outbursts and was sympathetic when he received an intemperate letter. Twain's other daughters, Clara and Jean, had asked for inexpensive four-shilling seats at the Lyceum to see *Cymbeline.* They were insulted, Twain claimed, by "a mangy cur," a "large blonde man with spectacles." He asked Stoker to dismiss the box office clerk immediately and demanded his name, threatening to make future use of him in print. "Perhaps he can imitate a gentleman's gentleman when people apply for boxes," Twain angrily wrote. "But in any case he is a hog; he was born a hog & will

SHIPBOARD ENTERTAINMENT on the Lyceum's 1899 tour was
illustrated by Pamela Colman Smith, the tarot artist. From left
are Irving, Edith Craig (Ellen Terry's daughter), Smith, Stoker, and
an unidentified woman. Stoker plays the ship's stoker, who shovels
the coal. He emerges from the engine room, but on the stage it was
called a vampire trap.

die one. But he shall not die uncelebrated if I can help it." In his genial manner, Stoker soothed the situation.

In October of 1899 the company sailed on the S.S. *Marquette* for the
sixth American tour; it was the only time Stoker and Irving crossed
the Atlantic on the same ship. During this voyage the storm-loving
Stoker experienced a hundred-mile-an-hour hurricane, which eerily
lacked rain. The roaring wind moaned like a banshee. "Tossing in
that frightful sea was awful," he recalled. "Most of those on board

STOKER with Pamela Colman Smith in a pixie costume and Edith Craig

were dreadfully frightened. Irving came out for a while and stood on the bridge holding on like grim death, for the shaking was like an earthquake. He seemed to really enjoy it." Ellen Terry came on deck and was so enraptured with the watery mountains turning to foam she stayed for hours. "I had to hold her against the rail," said Stoker, "for at times we rolled so that our feet shot off the deck." Inside, the rest of the company huddled together in the corridors; Stoker gathered the panicky women around him on the trunks, which were lashed to the railings, but during one pitch they broke loose, badly gashing his leg. He was still limping on the return voyage.

In America the author of *Dracula* was a curiosity, prompting one journalist to exclaim, "And Bram Stoker wrote it! Think of him.

# SIR HENRY IRVING'S MANAGER TALKS
## OF PLAYS, BOOKS, PICTURES AND WAR

Bram Stoker Visible But Thirty Minutes Each Day, But
Accomplishes Wonders.

### HE DISCUSSES CISSY LOFTUS AND ELLEN TERRY

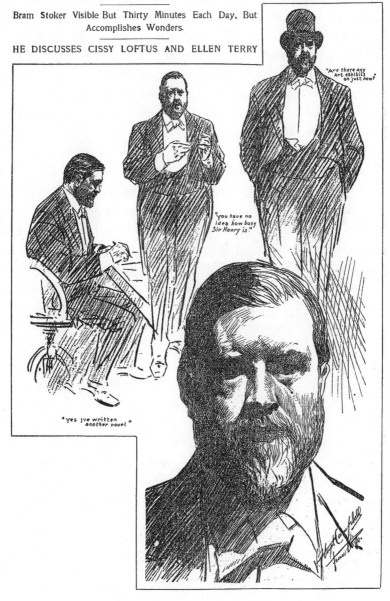

"Are there any
Art exhibits
on just now?"

"you have no
idea how busy
Sir Henry is."

"yes I've written
another novel"

A PHILADELPHIA NEWSPAPER gives the acting manager the kind of
publicity he never received in England.

He—a great shambling, good-natured overgrown boy—although he is the business manager of Henry Irving at the Lyceum, with a red beard, untrimmed, and a ruddy complexion tempered somewhat by the wide-open full grey eyes that gaze so frankly into yours! Why it is hard to imagine Bram Stoker a business manager, to say nothing of his possessing an imagination capable of projecting *Dracula* upon paper." Unfortunately, the story of Stoker's life! "Known merely as the astute manager of Sir Henry Irving's interests," another paper noted, "Bram Stoker is a writer of renown. His 'Dracula,' a weird story of a human vampire, is as vivid and thrilling as [Poe's] 'The Black Cat,' with vastly more detail."

There was a coldness between the Lord and Lady of the Lyceum on this tour. Irving had found a new companion, Mrs. Eliza Aria, a fashion writer who owned several bonnet shops in the West End. She was Jewish and immediately had Irving's ear when at a dinner she thanked him, in the name of all Jews, for his interpretation of Shylock. "But who is Mrs A?" Terry asked Shaw. "I only know she is 'a journalist' and 'a friend' of H. I.'s. I never set eyes on her and she has no idea I know of her. (This is fun, and would be better fun, if I knew something about her.) If you know her personally don't 'give away' that I know of her existence." Shaw replied that she is a "good sort."

Mrs. Aria had that rare quality of being an astute listener, one who commented and advised with acuity and intelligence. She was witty and knew how to be useful. Her husband had walked out five years after their marriage, a turn of events that did not displease her (his first comment following the wedding was "I wonder what has won the Lincoln handicap?"). With her, Laurence Irving said his grandfather found "a humour and temperament perfectly complementary to his own." Once a welcomed third party in the Terry-Irving relationship, Stoker now was excluded, chilling his humor and his heart.

# Chapter 15

# FAREWELLS

Oscar Wilde died on November 30, 1900, Queen Victoria on January 22, 1901. "I was a man who stood in symbolic relations to the art and culture of my age. . . . I awoke the imagination of my century so that it created myth and legend around me," wrote Wilde in *De Profundis,* explaining his ambition to raise Victorian aesthetic standards by illuminating how art reflects life. For the three and a half years Wilde lived in Europe after his release from prison, he was mostly shunned; if former friends recognized him in a café, they walked the other way. He was forty-six when he died and, as he put it, dying beyond his means, with his taste offended: "My wallpaper and I are fighting a duel to the death," he quipped. Both Wilde and Count Dracula were thoroughly modern men, belonging to future centuries.

In 1902 Charlotte Stoker died at the age of eighty-three. Her eyesight had failed, and she feared the darkness; she told Bram she hoped God took her before she went blind. Her prayers were answered, and she did not suffer. " 'Euthanasia' is an excellent and a comforting word!" Dr. Seward remarks. "I am grateful to whoever invented it." Burial at St. Michan's in Dublin meant Charlotte's body would be preserved for some time: decay was delayed by an atmospheric phenomenon in the crypt, built in the eleventh century on the site of a prehistoric oak forest. His mother's death did not curb Stoker's fictional search for his own lost or hidden female self, and in

STOKER AND IRVING (seated second from right and standing second from right, respectively) at one of the many luncheons they attended to promote and raise money for the Lyceum

his characterizations of women, he continued to see an alter ego reflected in the responsive eyes of another.

Gaslight had added to the Lyceum's financial problems, and to comply with stricter regulations, the theatre needed to make substantial alterations. When the London County Council made an inspection, the theatre was refused certification. Rather than invest in safety, the shareholders sold their interests. The Lyceum closed and was put into receivership. Maintaining that the syndicate had squandered its funds, Irving rallied Loveday and Stoker to save the theatre. But it was impossible to raise more capital.

Irving scheduled a double bill of *Waterloo* and *The Bells* on July 3, 1902, to mark the coronation of Edward VII. A reception onstage followed for the visiting rajahs, tribal chiefs, and potentates from the far-flung empire. Irving and Stoker wanted everyone to remember why the Lyceum had been the center of theatrical fashion. For the penultimate time, Stoker's voice was heard backstage as he bellowed out orders to an army of carpenters to gut the stalls and pit, and cart away seats. Upholsterers laid a field of crimson carpet flecked with gold fleurs-de-lis; the stage was draped in scarlet; florists arrived with a jungle of palms, exotic flowers, and shrubs. Chandeliers were hoisted aloft while over the proscenium—outlined in colored electric lights—glowed an enormous Union Jack surmounted by a crown. How fitting that Irving, who needed only limelight to work his stage magic, decided to exit with the lights on.

When the last guest departed, Irving and Stoker were left alone on the littered stage, where they talked, as in the old days, until dawn. The end of the Lyceum mandated appreciation of past triumphs. Perhaps Irving praised his acting manager, gave him credit for endless hours of work, made him feel indispensable, even said, "I could never have done it all without you." And then perhaps not. As they climbed down from the stage, Irving turned to Stoker and confessed for the first time that he felt "certain of one thing—mine is the only great Shylock." The Lyceum's farewell performance, appropriately, was a matinee of *The Merchant of Venice,* on July 19. After the final act Irving led Ellen Terry forward by the hand to acknowledge the applause. It was their last curtain call together as Lord and Lady of the Lyceum; for Stoker it was the thousandth performance of the play.

Irving soon realized how old age is a journey into a foreign land where one is constantly surprised by the impossible. Martin-Harvey saw him "as a man mortally tired, his star declining." Stoker calculated that from December 30, 1878, when the Lyceum opened with *Hamlet,* to the day of Irving's last performance in *Becket,* the public had paid more than £2 million to see him act. But Irving wanted one more role: Dante. Physically and temperamentally he inhabited the part; but he lacked the play. "A fine subject!" Tennyson once exclaimed, "but where is the Dante to write it?" Irving enlisted the veteran French playwright Victorien Sardou, who produced a muddled script, which Irving decided—as he had with *Faust*—to salvage with special effects and a teeming cast. He spent £12,000 on scenery and hired fifty players and three times as many spirits to arise from *The Divine Comedy*. It opened on April 30, 1903, at the Theatre Royal, posing an additional challenge, since Irving and Stoker were working in an unfamiliar theatre. Despite mixed reviews, *Dante* was scheduled to open the eighth American tour.

It was an ill-conceived itinerary, covering thirty-three cities in five months, but Irving needed to display his pyrotechnics one more time, to leave behind a legend and a legacy. Ellen Terry remained in London at the Imperial Theatre, having fulfilled her commitment to Irving. The company missed her joyousness as well as Fussie's backstage antics. *Dante* failed to attract an audience when it premiered on October 26, 1903, at the Broadway Theatre. Knowing the Italian poet was the last larger-than-life role he would create, Irving abandoned the play and sent the scenery to Canada, where it was given away to avoid customs duties. Nearing sixty-six, he fell back on parts originated thirty years earlier.

For the first time, everyone wanted the tour over before it began. Stoker rushed about tending to train schedules, baggage loading, caterers, the press—all the busywork he once enjoyed—but there was no Walt Whitman or James McHenry to visit. America no longer revived his exhausted soul. Journalists questioned him about his other career. "Mention was made of his literary achievements," one paper reported, "and the big man actually blushed—a proof of the modesty of high ability." In a mortal hurry, he crashed through a plate glass door in the lobby of Philadelphia's Chestnut Street Opera House, emerging without a scratch. "An Irishman's luck," he calmly remarked to a journalist.

The tour ended with *Louis XI* at New York's Harlem Opera House (later the Apollo Theatre), built by Oscar Hammerstein in 1889, at a time when speculators saw Harlem as a middle-class white suburb. Eight American tours had brought Irving a profit of $579,201 (£119,669), most of which had gone into new productions. Despite the failure of *Dante,* Stoker's little account book showed a profit of £32,000. Irving told the audience on March 25, 1904, that he would return before retiring in 1906, the year he and Terry celebrated their stage jubilees.

Stoker and Irving were in the provinces when the Lyceum's contents were auctioned, a funeral they were glad to miss. The cardboard models of hundreds of scenes went unsold, as did a dilapidated trunk filled with yellowing press clippings. Thirty-eight yards of crimson carpet used on special occasions for access to the Royal Box brought only £8. The last remnant of splendid nights of wine and wit disappeared with lot 112: four gothic doors and an iron grid from the Beefsteak Room. Then the demolition crew arrived to turn the grand old lady into a tawdry music hall.

Irving stopped dining at the Garrick Club: he could not discuss the Lyceum's demise. Supper guests invited to his Stratton Street flat found violets (picked by the host) on their plates. He took holidays with Eliza Aria and her daughter. There was no reason to summon Stoker, and the friendship faltered on both sides. Although still involved in the provincial tours, Stoker awaited an invitation to join another theatre company. At fifty-six, he had few fresh ideas to recommend him to a new generation of actor-managers. Irving was archaic, and Stoker along with him.

But Stoker knew the value of self-promotion and kept his name in the newspapers. He accepted an invitation to present prizes at the Glasgow School of Art Club, where his speech on "Art and the Stage" stressed that all the arts were allied in various ways and had much in common. "It represented the great world," Stoker said, "and what was done in the great world was done on the stage in little." A review noted he "spoke without a single note to jog his memory, but, this notwithstanding, his language was perfect, some of his sentences being masterpieces in their way." He agreed to sponsor a gold medal for the best imaginative figure composition, which he awarded in 1903 and 1904. The school provided the design and the dies, and Stoker paid for the gold. He received some publicity for his generosity but was spending money not easily earned anymore.

During this period he wrote "The Secret of the Growing Gold," a short story worthy of mention not only for its Poe-like quality but for its echo of the most ghoulish graveyard tale in all of literature: the death of Rossetti's wife, Lizzie Siddal. Now appreciated as an artist in her own right, Lizzie was a frail beauty with dazzling green eyes and radiant copper hair who died from an overdose of laudanum. Before her burial at Highgate Cemetery, a grief-stricken Rossetti nestled a gray notebook containing the only copies of his unpublished poems in the folds of her hair. (In *Dracula* Stoker uses Highgate as the site for Lucy Westerna's tomb, changing the name to Kingstead.) Seven years later, in 1869, Rossetti ordered an exhumation to recover the notebook. When the coffin was opened, Lizzie's hair, it was said, was still golden and growing. Inspired by this oft-told tale, Stoker wrote a story of a man who murders his mistress and buries her under the flagstones in the great hall of his castle; but her golden hair, seen only by him, grows through a crack, haunting him to death—a plot also reminiscent of *The Bells*.

Returning to Cruden Bay in 1902, Stoker moved from the Kilmarnock Arms to Whinnyfold. There he wrote *The Mystery of the Sea*, an exemplary novel in terms of characterization and scene setting, which resembles Alfred Hitchcock's 1935 British film *The Thirty-Nine Steps*. "When first I saw the place I fell in love with it," says the barrister Archibald Hunter, Stoker's alter ego. "The next year I came again, and the next, and the next," staying at the Kilmarnock. "And then I arranged to take a feu at Whinnyfold and to build a house overlooking the Skares." Stoker never built a house, as his narrator did, but rented "The Crookit Lum," so called because the chimney has a ten-degree list. Still standing, the cottage maintains its precarious position overlooking the North Sea.

Here Stoker spent the summers left to him, listening to the sea and writing in a hammock; when a cinder pit was excavated in the 1970s, his old ink bottles were unearthed. It is easy to see what charmed Stoker about Whinnyfold, a cluster of crofts shrouded in mist and facing the sea gales head on. Then, as now, the village belonged to another century. Entire families worked at what they called "sma' line" fishing from the bottom of the cliffs. The fishwife with a

THE CROOKIT LUM, overlooking the North Sea at Cruden Bay, was Stoker's summer retreat during his last years of ill health.

basket creel strapped over her shoulders was as familiar a sight as Stoker striding over the dunes on his marathon walks.

Stoker returns to his youth in *Mystery,* parting the curtain ever so slightly on his invalid years in Dublin. On discovering letters written in cipher, the narrator observes: "I knew something of secret writing, for such had in my boyhood been a favourite amusement with me." Later he comments: "I am never quite happy with the writer whose hand is exact, letter by letter, and word by word, and line by line. A hand that has no characteristics is that of a person insipid." Indeed, few had a more indecipherable script than Stoker.

For this novel, he immersed himself in Scottish history, reading up on witchcraft and second sight to create Gormala, who like a witch from *Macbeth* speaks in Gaelic runes. Train travel, so integral to *Dracula* (Harker observes "that the further East you go the most unpunctual are the trains. What ought they to be in China?"), commands the destinies of hero and heroine, who bound on and off the cream-colored carriages of the Great Northern line. In Marjory Drake (a descendant of Sir Francis, whom Stoker thought he resembled), he expands on the independent woman described in *A Glimpse of America* as "almost if not quite, as free to think and act for herself as a young man is."

Always stronger and more memorable than their male counterparts, Stoker's women characters frequently have names beginning with *M* (Maggie, Mina, Mimi, Marjory, Margaret), a tribute, perhaps, to "Mother" and sisters, Matilda and Margaret, his early caretakers. Women growing up without mothers was a cliché of Victorian novels, a plotting device that allowed characters to explore behaviors and make mistakes against which their mothers should have warned them, and *Dracula* was no exception (Mina is an orphan and Lucy becomes one).

Stoker's later novels were invariably compared with *Dracula,* although *Mystery* deserved better. "In the case of 'Dracula,' " wrote one critic, "I could not put the book down until I had finished it, in the case of 'The Mystery of the Sea,' it was an effort to finish the book before I put it down. . . . 'Dracula' was gruesome, but it was absolutely absorbing." Friends were supportive. J. W. Brodie-Innis found the ghosts "distinctly fine," and the American heroine "very fascinating." Arthur Conan Doyle complimented Stoker on the use of a cipher first described by Francis Bacon: "I've done a bit in cryptograms myself, but that knocks me out!" Still optimistic about dramatization, Stoker cut and pasted the novel into a five-act copyright performance.

After a quarter of a century of rushing to and from the Lyceum, Stoker now had time to write; he set the goal of a book a year. The next summer at the cottage with the crooked chimney he corrected proofs for *The Jewel of Seven Stars,* which he dedicated to "Eleanor [misspelling her name] and Constance Hoyt," two American sisters whose beauty impressed him when they were escorted about London for the season by their seventy-year-old grandfather, a friend of Irving's. Elinor Hoyt was seventeen and met Stoker only once. As

Elinor Wylie, poet and novelist, she never mentioned the dedication; after all, she was a well-bred lady, perhaps affronted by such a tribute from a virtual stranger. Stoker could have dedicated *Jewel* to Ellen Terry or his two sisters or any one of the "Uncle Bramy" cult; why he made this choice remains his secret.

*Jewel* resembles *Dracula* in that years of reading and research preceded it. From the time Stoker heard Sir William Wilde expound on his Egyptian adventures, he had in mind a book about mummies and curses; he borrowed the plot from Wilde, who had found a mummy outside a tomb and brought it back to Merrion Square. Stoker made his Egyptologist a Dutchman (like Van Helsing) and centered intrigue on an ancient Egyptian queen's wish for resurrection. Reviews said he had fashioned a "tale of mystery and imagination equal to anything that ever emerged from the fertile brain of Edgar Allan Poe." *Jewel* was even—strangely—called a "story which begins like a dime novel, and ends like a page out of Schopenhauer." Brodie-Innis, his conduit to the Golden Dawn, simply said, "It is not only a good book—it is a *great book*."*

Stoker spent the summer of 1904 completing *The Man,* an ornately layered romance notable for its New Woman heroine, Stephen Norman, who proposes marriage to the wrong man and spends the rest of the novel waiting for the right one. With insight, Stoker details a woman's revolt against the convention that she may love but must not speak. The man of the title, Harold An Wolf, resembles the author: a bearded giant and Trinity graduate (Cambridge, though, not Dublin) who takes honors in athletics, rescues a child from a turbulent ocean, and saves survivors from a burning vessel. In between he discovers a gold mine in Alaska, returns temporarily blind to the heroine, but regains his sight (echoes of Jane Eyre and Rochester) to marry her. As an alter ego, Harold ranks as Stoker's most omnipotent creation.

*The Literary World* predicted that the novel would "enhance the author's well-earned reputation." *The Outlook* disagreed:

---

* Two films were based on the novel: *Blood from the Mummy's Tomb* (1972), with Andrew Keir and Valerie Leon, and *The Awakening* (1980), with Charlton Heston and Stephanie Zimbalist.

> Like a miserly old lady with savings, Mr. Bram Stoker has hidden his treasure in a feather-bed. The mattress is so big that there is no casual groping with hands alone; we must get bodily inside it, and the feathers—disquisitions, excursions, sentiments, explanations, moralisations—swallow us up. And while we struggle through, there are all sorts of little feathers—slips in grammar, awkward associations of words and so forth—to add irritation to suffocation.

Stoker would have liked the language, hated the review.

That winter Stoker and Irving set off on the first of two farewell provincial tours. During a February snowstorm, en route from Bath to Wolverhampton, Irving caught a chill and collapsed with acute bronchitis. The company was disbanded, and nine cities were disappointed. The doctor sent Irving to Torquay for two months; he was to return only for the last performance of *Becket* at Drury Lane. Stoker spent hours acknowledging letters of condolence. By the time Ellen Terry visited Irving, they had not seen each other for several years. Her blond hair was silver, his dark hair white; their elegant hands were outlined in prominent blue veins. He looked like "some beautiful grey tree," Terry recalled. "His old dressing-gown hung about his frail yet majestic figure like some mysterious grey drapery." They looked at each other with devotion. "I'm glad you've come," Irving said. "Two Queens have been kind to me this morning. Queen Alexandra telegraphed to say how sorry she was I was ill, and now you—." Sitting beside his bed, she smiled and asked:

"What a wonderful life you've had, haven't you?"

"Oh yes, a wonderful life of work."

"And there's nothing better after all, is there?"

"Nothing."

"What have you got out of it all . . . ? You and I are 'getting on,' as they say. Do you ever think, as I do sometimes, what you have got out of life?"

"What have I got out of it?" said Irving, stroking his chin and smiling slightly. "Let me see. . . . Well, a good cigar, a good glass of wine—good friends." He paused to kiss her hand with courtesy.

"That's not a bad summing up of it all," she said. "And the end . . . how would you like that to come?"

"How would I like that to come?" Irving asked, then snapped his fingers. "Like that!"

In October the tour resumed at Sheffield. Irving was frail and walked slowly. When Stoker accompanied him to a luncheon at Bradford's Town Hall, Irving disguised his infirmity by halting to point at some landmark while he regained his breath. Against Stoker's advice he played Mathias that evening and collapsed after the curtain fell. Stoker said he "seemed tired, tired; tired not for an hour but for a lifetime." Without further discussion, Stoker ordered the sets and costumes of *The Bells*—the play that had made Irving famous—sent back

HENRY IRVING, then sixty-seven, in his last photograph, taken a few weeks before his death in Bradford in 1905

to London. The actor was relieved; he had done the part one more time to prove to himself he could do it. But the strain of gasping for breath, shaking in terror, turning cold and pale, and rolling his eyes upward into his skull was too great an effort for a dying man. The following morning, Friday, October 13, Irving admitted that the planned American tour would also be too much for him. Stoker was pleased to cancel all plans. "A kindly continent to me," Irving said, "but I will not leave my bones there if I can help it."

That evening the cast watched as Irving's frailty led to resignation: actor and character merged. During his last scene with John Salisbury, Becket says:

> My counsel is already taken, John.
> I am prepared to die.

And John replies:

> We are sinners all,
> The best of all not all prepared to die.

Becket's answer should be "God's will be done," but Irving changed it to "God is my judge." Later came Becket's last words: "Into thy Hands, O Lord, into thy Hands!" Then Irving collapsed—not as he usually did, with his head downstage, but upstage, toward the steps that led to the choir, which was another departure from his playing of the scene. After the curtain fell, he looked up at the cast surrounding him and asked, "What now . . . ?"

Irving came before the curtain, as was his custom, to thank the audience for their "inspiring welcome," and for their appreciation of "this great play by our great poet." His skin was the color of parchment, the shaggy eyebrows and histrionic mop of gray hair mussed, the pince-nez slightly askew on the famous aquiline nose; deep furrows bracketed the thin, stern mouth. For the last time, Irving gave his salute to those who had given him all he ever knew—or cared to know—of love. A cast member helped him to his dressing room, where he slumped into a chair; he sat looking into the mirror for a few moments before slowly wiping away his makeup. Stoker feigned

## Theatre Royal, Bradford.

Lessee · · JOHN HART.

MONDAY, OCTOBER 9TH. 1905, FOR SIX NIGHTS.

### FAREWELL TO HENRY IRVING

TUESDAY and FRIDAY NIGHTS, Oct. 10th and 13th at 7.30

## ⚜ BECKET ⚜

By ALFRED LORD TENNYSON.

ADAPTED FOR THE STAGE BY HENRY IRVING.

| | |
|---|---|
| Thomas Becket { Chancellor of England, afterwards Archbishop } | HENRY IRVING |
| Henry II. (King of England) | Mr. GERALD LAWRENCE |
| King Louis of France | Mr. H. B. STANFORD |
| Gilbert Foliot (Bishop of London) | Mr. H. ASHETON TONGE |
| Roger (Archbishop of York) | Mr. WILLIAM LUGG |
| John of Salisbury } Friends of { | Mr. MARK PATON |
| Herbert of Bosham } Becket { | Mr. JAMES HEARN |
| John of Oxford (Called the Swearer) | Mr. T. REYNOLDS |
| Sir Reginald Fitzurse } The Four Knights of { | Mr. FRANK TYARS |
| Sir Richard de Brito } the King's Household, { | Mr. G. GRAYSTONE |
| Sir William de Tracy } Enemies of { | Mr. L. BELMORE |
| Sir Hugh de Morville } Becket { | Mr. LESLIE PALMER |
| Richard de Hastings (Grand Prior of Templars) | Mr. J. ARCHER |
| The Youngest Knight Templar | Mr. STEVENS |
| Lord Leicester | Mr. VINCENT STERNROYD |
| Philip de Eleemosyna (The Pope's Almoner) | Mr. W. J. YELDMAN |
| Herald | Mr. H. R. COOK |
| Monk | Mr. A. GURNEY |
| Geoffrey (Son of Rosamund and Henry) | Master TONGE |
| Retainers | { Mr. A. FISHER   Mr. HAYES |
| Countrymen | { Mr. CHARLES DODSWORTH   Mr. R. BRENNAN |
| Servant | Mr. W. MARION |
| Eleanor of Aquitaine { Queen of England, divorced from Louis of France } | Mrs. CECIL RALEIGH |
| Margery | Miss GRACE HAMPTON |
| Rosamund de Clifford (Fair Rosamund) | Miss EDITH WYNNE MATTHISON |

Knights, Monks, Heralds, Soldiers, Retainers, &c.

### Synopsis of Scenery

PROLOGUE.

Scene 1—A Castle in Normandy. Scene 2—The Same.

ACT I. Scene 1—Becket's House in London. Scene 2—Street in Northampton leading to the Castle. Scene 3—The Same. Scene 4—The Hall in Northampton Castle.

ACT II. Scene—Rosamund's Bower.

ACT III. Scene 1—Montmirail, "The Meeting of the Kings." Scene 2—Outside the Wood, near Rosamund's Bower. Scene 3—Rosamund's Bower.

"*At Merton the Archbishop assumed the ordinary habit of the black canons of the Augustinian Rule, which dress he wore to the end of his life.*"—GRIM.

ACT IV. Scene 1—Castle in Normandy—King's Chamber. 2—A Room in Canterbury Monastery. Scene 3—North Transept of Canterbury Cathedral. Period—12th Century.

*The Scenery has been Specially Painted by Mr. Joseph Harker.*

*The Overture and Incidental Music by Sir Charles Villiers Stanford.*

*The Costumes, &c., from designs by Mrs. Comyns Carr and Mr. Charles Cattermole, R.I., executed by Mrs. Nettleship, August et Cie, and Messrs. L. and H. Nathan. Wigs by W. Clarkson.*

PROGRAM for *Becket*. Irving died on Friday the thirteenth. The scenery credit at the bottom goes to Joseph Harker, whose last name Stoker appropriated for his hero Jonathan Harker.

optimism: "You have been feeling the taking up of your work again after an absence of it for four months, the longest time of rest in your life. Now you have got into your stride again, and work will be easy!" Irving paused for thought and answered, "I really think that is so!" As Stoker prepared to leave, Irving stretched out his hand to say goodnight. Stoker grasped it. They never parted with this gesture. "Muffle up your throat, old chap!" advised Irving; "it is a bitterly cold night—you have a cold—take care of yourself. Good night. God bless you."

Irving lingered backstage to sign a charcoal study of himself drawn by a local boy, then deliberately and methodically washed his hands, as was his ritual. Bundled into a heavy overcoat, he entered a waiting cab with Collinson. Irving did not speak during the short ride to the Midland Hotel; on entering the lobby he stumbled and was helped to the nearest chair. Moments later he lost consciousness and slipped to the floor. Collinson cradled his head in his lap, crying softly: "He died in my arms!"

When Stoker arrived, he knelt over the body and put his hand over Irving's heart. The doctor shook his head. By the time Irving was laid out in his hotel bedroom it was morning. In his room, Stoker put on the appropriate frock coat and top hat and walked slowly to the Theatre Royal, where he ordered the advertisements for that night's performance blanked out. "It was all so desolate and lonely," he recalled, "as so much of his life had been. So lonely that in the midst of my own sorrow I could not but rejoice at one thing: for him there was now Peace and Rest."

The following evening during her performance in *Alice Sit-by-the-Fire* in Manchester, Ellen Terry broke down when she came to the lines: "It's summer done, autumn begun. . . . I had a beautiful husband once . . . black as a raven was his hair." The curtain was lowered, and the audience silently left the theatre. Terry voiced the thoughts of many when she said Irving's death in the vestibule of a provincial hotel "was more fitting for such a man than one where friends and relations weep." Throughout Britain flags were lowered to half-mast. The pillars of the Lyceum were wrapped in black crêpe; every London horse cab driver tied a black bow around his whip. Newspapers throughout the English-speaking world carried fulsome tributes. Irving's body lay in state in the dining room of Baroness Burdett-Coutts's home on Stratton Street while friends appealed to the dean of St. Paul's to bury the first knighted actor in Westminster Abbey. Their request was denied.

While letters of protest circulated, Irving was cremated at Gold-

STOKER, crossing the street, the day after Irving's death, in front of the Theatre Royal, where announcements for *Becket* have been blanked out

ers Green Crematorium (bodies had long ago taken up all the Abbey's ground space). In addition, Stoker asked King Edward for a public funeral from Buckingham Palace. "The request, the King says," replied the royal secretary, "must come from the people, and not from His Majesty." The old prejudices against actors were not so easily erased by the laying on of one sword. Fortuitous circumstances, it might be said, forced the dean to acquiesce. Threatened with blindness, the cleric called in Sir Anderson Critchett, the country's leading oculist. Critchett knew some members of the Irving delegation and reminded his patient that he had asked what favor might be granted for saving his sight. That favor was Irving's burial in Poets' Corner.

Stoker probably received more condolence letters than Irving's sons. He was family. One letter noted how he had given "up everything for him," how Irving's death broke "up a constant companionship,

as *well* as a friendship which can never be replaced." He was reminded how his "face always lighted up at the mere mention of his
name," how the alliance "seemed more like the disciples than anything else. You forsook all and followed him." Tom Stoker heard the
news, went directly to St. Leonard's Terrace to see Florence, and
telegraphed his brother that "though distressed and anxious she is full
of courage and thinks only of the distress you must feel." Florence,
of course, had no reason to mourn a man who had monopolized her
husband's time. A pragmatic Thornley forsook the niceties: "We are
filled with anxiety about your future and as soon as this urgent press
of affairs leaves you time, come over for Christmas."

Irving's estate of £20,527 was divided equally among his sons and Eliza Aria, with no bequest to Lady Irving. There were no to-kens of appreciation for Stoker, Loveday, or Collinson. Stoker bought his tangible memories: Bernard Partridge's portrait, drawn three months before Irving's death, showing him in one of his happy moods, and a portrait of Edmund Kean by George Clint, the only picture for which the actor ever sat, and one of Irving's most prized possessions.

The terms of the will outraged Florence Irving. She had thought herself a most proper estranged wife: no scandal ever touched her boring existence. She asked Shaw to prevent the Abbey burial. Ir-

BRAM STOKER, above and at left, looking his serious self

ving's longtime nemesis wisely advised that as the widow of a famous actor buried in Poets' Corner, she could obtain a civil pension by "lifting her little finger, but as the widow of an exposed adulterer no Prime Minister would dare to put her on the Civil List." Shaw refused to attend the funeral "on the public ground that Literature had no place at Irving's graveside." In his way, Shaw managed the last word.

On October 20, John Henry Brodribb, known as Henry Irving for nearly fifty of his sixty-seven years, was buried in Westminster Abbey with pomp and circumstance. The coffin was shrouded with a laurel pall so profuse it hung to the ground on all sides when fourteen pall-bearers marched. It was made by Eliza Aria. The establishment Irving had so assiduously wooed carried him to his last resting place, at the foot of Shakespeare and the side of David Garrick. Stoker, Loveday, and Collinson watched. Ellen Terry sat in the same Abbey pew she had occupied thirteen years earlier for Tennyson's burial, with Irving at her side. "No face there looked anything by the side of Henry's," she had thought then, and looked for his face at his own funeral. She imagined hearing him say, "Get on! get on!" in the parts that dragged. When the coffin was carried up to the choir, the sun pierced the solemn misty gray of the Abbey. It was a theatrical effect the Guv'nor would have applauded.

*Chapter 16*

# THE LAST WAVE

"We have been blind somewhat; blind after the
manner of men, since when we can look back
we see what we might have seen looking
forward if we had been able to see what we
might have seen! Alas! but that sentence is a
puddle; is it not?"

—Van Helsing

iographies, articles, and tributes followed Irving's death.
Stoker had his say in 1906 with *Personal Reminiscences of Henry
Irving,* two volumes of unobjective idolatry with occasional
insights into himself, but he could not (or would not) bring himself
to look critically at the Irving legend, such was his loyalty. Stoker tore
out pages from his jotting diary—the same document-splicing technique used in *Dracula*—and wove them into chapters. Like Mina he
produced a connected narrative, approaching Irving's life and career
with a sanguine quietness; anger can be life-affirming, but this he had
spent creating *Dracula.* "It is, I think, another sign of his love and devotion for his friend," his son said, "that, however long had been the
day—or night, the record in that diary was never deferred." Stoker's
account illuminated a remarkable theatrical career—so many famous
names, so many invitations, so many honors, so little insight.

Stoker kept the spotlight on Irving. As he wrote Whitman years
earlier, "a man cannot in a moment break the habit of comparative
reticence that has become second nature to him." There were a few

instances—later deleted—when his ego surfaced, when he went on at length about his influence over Geneviève Ward and Hall Caine. He omitted Oscar Wilde's name from a list of one thousand notables entertained at the Lyceum, and gave Shaw the middle initial *F* instead of *B*. To Irving, he proclaimed only allegiance. "Looking back I cannot honestly find any moment in my life when I failed him, or when I put myself forward in any way," he wrote. "In my own speaking to the dead man I can find an analogue in the words of heartbreaking sincerity [of Elizabeth Barrett Browning]:

> Stand up on the jasper sea
> And be witness I have given
> All the gifts required of me!

The reviews, of course, were mixed. Stoker had "built a monument more lasting than brass to his great and dear friend," said *The Sketch,* accurately predicting that *Dracula* would be "reprinted in the cheap series of 2000 A.D." *The Bookman* forecast disappointment for anyone expecting "an illuminating account of the making of a great actor, or an impartial estimate of his actual achievements." An idol builder, not a demythologizer, Stoker lectured throughout Britain, adding to the Irving legend. The only major biography to precede his was Percy Fitzgerald's *Henry Irving: A Record of Twenty Years at the Lyceum,* published in 1893. When Austin Brereton wrote *The Life of Henry Irving* in 1908, he diminished Stoker's importance, as he had during the American tours. In the preface he claims never to have consulted Stoker's book for "a fact, a date or an incident." Subsequent biographies by Gordon Craig and Laurence Irving, however, owe everything to Stoker: without his jotting diary there would be no record of where Irving was on any given day or what he did.

Stoker returned once to theatre management. An American opera singer, David Bishpham, hired him as acting manager for a West End musical of *The Vicar of Wakefield.* It closed within two months. As with Othello, his occupation was gone. He lived the restless life of the lonely mind, never focusing for long on one project; he went from

PROMOTION for the one-volume edition of Stoker's biography of Irving. The title changed to *Personal Recollections,* it was available for six shillings to "those ardent spirits in the gallery, whose judgment," the publisher wrote, "often crudely expressed of the plays and players of today would be so much more valuable were it founded on the study of the methods of the actors and managers of, let us say, a few years ago."

IN ONE VOLUME

SIX SHILLINGS NET

HENRY IRVING:

Personal Recollections

NEW EDITION IN ONE VOLUME

By BRAM STOKER

6/= NET          ILLUSTRATED.          6/= NET

WILLIAM HEINEMANN, LONDON

1907

organizing the English section of the Paris Theatrical Exhibition to modeling for Goldsborough Anderson's wall painting *William II Building the Tower of London.* He can still be seen in the former trading room of London's Royal Exchange—a russet-haired king astride his horse.

The Lyceum years had been amusing, and he missed the company of men. He joined the Dramatic Debaters, harking back to his Trinity days; he was active in the Society of Authors; he took up Irving's role as advocate for a Shakespeare Memorial; he was president of the Urban Club, and with Hall Caine formed the New Vagabond Club, whose first function honored his friend Gilbert. He was on the general committee for Ellen Terry's Golden Jubilee in 1906, contributing his reminiscences, titled "Fifty Years on Stage: An Appreciation of Ellen Terry," to *The Graphic.*

The celebration included a performance of Shaw's *Captain Brass-*

MURAL PANEL. In 1911, the year before his death,
Stoker modeled for the panel *William II Building the
Tower of London*, the fourth picture in a series of wall
murals around the trading floor of the Royal Exchange.

*bound's Conversion* at Chelsea's Royal Court Theatre with Terry as
Lady Cicely, the role Shaw wrote to woo her away from Irving. At
fifty-eight, Terry could not remember her lines. Shaw was generous.
"Behave as if you were more precious than many plays, which is the
truth," he wrote. "The only other point of importance is that you

look 25; and I love you." A future biographer of Wilde, Hesketh Pearson, called the Court, which introduced London to repertory theatre in 1904, "the most famous epoch in theatrical management since the days of the Globe on Bankside." The Court's success depended largely on the triumph of Shaw's plays and Granville-Barker's productions. Its avant-garde spirit continues to this day.

Shortly after this performance, Stoker suffered a stroke. He was unconscious for twenty-four hours; his walk and eyesight were permanently impaired; he could talk but needed the aid of a magnifying glass to write; he had gout—an infirmity he gives Mr. Hawkins, to explain why he cannot travel to Transylvania—and Bright's disease, a kidney ailment that poisons the blood. He was often bedridden, as in his youth. Florence was his nurse. To economize, they moved again in 1907, from 18 St. Leonard's Terrace to a smaller flat at nearby 4 Durham Place, a rambling Georgian dwelling, where Captain Bligh of the *Bounty* once lived. It is a measure of Stoker's capacity for friendship that invitations did not evaporate after Irving's death. The Stokers attended Conan Doyle's second marriage, to Jean Leckie; and for Churchill's wedding to Clementine Hozier, Florence sent boxed volumes of *Personal Reminiscences of Henry Irving.*


As a backlist title *Dracula* still earned royalties, but Stoker's income depended on journalism. He served briefly on the literary staff of the *Daily Telegraph* and wrote a series of profiles for the New York *World,* later published in London's *Daily Chronicle.* Notable friends— Gilbert, Conan Doyle, and Pinero—cooperated. A young Winston Churchill, then Under Secretary for the Colonies, agreed to be interviewed because of Stoker's friendship with his father. And, as he wrote, "because you are the author of Dracula," which appealed to "my young imagination." Thomas Hardy declined. "If I were to be interviewed there is nobody whom I should prefer than yourself for performing the operation," he wrote. Andrew Carnegie explained he was "a worn-out subject. Although if any man could dress it up appetizingly it would be your good self."

Lacking a forum in which to demonstrate his debating skills, Stoker joined the controversy over censorship, advocating the banning of lewd fiction. He addressed the Authors' Club and the White Friars' Club, and urged newspapers to refuse all mention of "unclean" books. "This abomination—the foully-conceived novel," he said, "has great vogue both in Britain and America, and belongs to the category of pestilences that must be stamped out." At issue were writers who once produced illicitly sold soft pornography and now pushed sexually explicit novels in the more liberal Edwardian marketplace. But to establish a censor, some said, would create for such books a *succès de scandale.* Although Stoker never named a particular book, he was probably referring to such erotic titles as *Colonel Spanker's Experimental Lecture* and *Birch in the Boudoir,* published in Paris by Charles Carrington.

PRURIENT NOVEL IS CONDEMNED, BRAM STOKER OPENS CRUSADE IN LONDON, read one headline. *Dracula,* of course, was absolved, for the erotic was cloaked in the preternatural. He put forth his views in "The Censorship of Fiction," published by *The Nineteenth Century & After.* Critics have particularly enjoyed dissecting the double entendre in this sentence, written eleven years after *Dracula:* "A close analysis will show that the only emotions which in the long run harm are those arising from sex impulses, and when we have realised this we have put a finger on the actual point of danger." Stoker encouraged self-censorship as the "first line of defense against such evils as may come from imagination—itself pure, a process of thought, working unintentionally with impure or dangerous materials."

Stoker was more subdued in his article "The Censorship of Stage Plays," where he opposed transferring censorship from the Lord Chamberlain's office to local authorities. The Lord Chamberlain himself never read plays; that was the task of underpaid clerks, who looked for blasphemy and explicit sex while letting subtleties on the same subjects slip by their blue pencils. Shaw had long objected to the appointment of "an ordinary official with a salary of a few hundred a year to exercise powers which have proved too much for Popes and Presidents." Local censors would be even more limited, Stoker warned.

Mark Twain returned to London in 1907 to receive an honorary degree from Lord Curzon, the new chancellor of Oxford University. America had celebrated him and now, Twain said, he had a final credential for immortality, "a loftier distinction than is conferrable by any other university." Twain's visit invigorated Stoker's spirits. Both men were lonely, in ill health, and devastated by loss: Twain never recovered from the death, in 1896, of his daughter Susy, and Stoker never forged a life after Irving.

Twain told journalists he had come to show Oxford "what a real American college boy looks like." After toasting his latest accolade at Windsor's Royal Garden Party, Twain and Stoker, accompanied by the American journalist Eugene Field, retreated to Brown's Hotel on Dover Street. The talk turned to the kaiser and rumbles of war, and then to witchcraft. "Fine," Stoker told Twain, "tell us some more; I have a short story on witchcraft in hand." Twain explained that "the only satisfactory way to do a witchcraft story is to filch it bodily from Balzac. The Frenchman got the thing down to perfection in one of his droll yarns—I know a shop in the Strand where you can buy a pirated edition—reproduced by the camera—for half a crown." When the trio assembled in the Doctor Johnson room of the Cheshire Cheese pub off the Strand to savor the famous meat pies, the topic was Shakespeare. Twain remarked that Voltaire had called Shakespeare "a drunken savage, an amazing genius and an indecent buffoon who had rendered English taste a ruined lady for two hundred years to come." Stoker called for a slate—there was no paper at the Cheese—and scrawled:

Opening of the Lyceum Theatre under Henry Irving
and Bram Stoker————1878
Death of Shakespeare————1616
Interval————262

"As you see," said Stoker, "Voltaire was out only a little more than half a century."

Stoker attended most of the parties and celebrations during Twain's stay in England. *Harper's Weekly* called the humorist "the most advertised man in the world." At the Savage Club Stoker heard him tell a longer version of the Scotch-Presbyterian christening story Stoker had told at Delmonico's in 1885. Twain gestured to Stoker, seated at the head table, and acknowledged his debt. Stoker bowed to the applause. Then Twain told the audience what a favorite the yarn had become on his many lecture tours. The New York *Tribune* once reported there being such a reaction that Twain "was forced to tell another story to satisfy his hearers."*

Even as Stoker strived to be taken seriously, journalists unearthed him and had fun at his expense. Seen with Violet Hunt at her club, Stoker was heard to comment on a hat trimmed with cherries. The ladies decided it looked like a confection. "It looks to me more like a tart," said Stoker. *The Tatler* purred about this "horrible dooble ongtong." In an item, "How to Humanize the Landscape," *Punch* suggested that on the golf course at "Stoke Poges and Bramshott two new pot bunkers be cut so as to represent the Olympian head (in profile) of Stoker in celebration of his 50th interview with Sir Oliver Lodge on the Psychical Significance of Vampires." Florence, who had converted to Catholicism in 1904, had her name listed in *The Catholic Who's Who* in 1910. This same year newspapers announced that Irving Noel Thornley Stoker and Nellie Sweeting, daughter of Dr. Deane Sweeting, were wed in St. Andrew's Church, Ashley Gardens, on July 30. The couple had been engaged for six years. Noel was a chartered accountant.

More often he read about the death of friends. Twain died on April 21, 1910. Before he slipped into a coma, he was still talking

---

* The tale, according to Stoker's brief version: "The house was full of the baby's kinsfolk, and the minister was betrayed into oratory—oratory of the spread-eagle kind, which is very dangerous, as it gets you into the clouds, and without a parachute you cannot get down. He took the child from the father. The little thing was about the size of a sweet potato. He held it in his hands till the silence should work, and then, 'Ah,' he said, 'I see in your faces disparagement. And why? Because he is little. Because he is little you disparage him. If there was more of him you would look into his future. But great are framed out of the little. The vast oak tree grows from the little acorn. He may be the greatest general. He may be Napoleon and Alexander compacted into one. He may be a poet, the greatest poet the world has ever seen: a Shakespeare, a Homer, a Shelley, a Keats, a Byron compacted into one. He may sing songs that may live as long as the land. He may become—'What's his name?'—this last to the father. 'Mary Ann,' replied the parent."

about Jekyll and Hyde and dual personality. In November, Thornley's wife died. Stoker had suffered a second stroke the previous May and could not travel to Dublin for the funeral. His personal physician, Dr. James Browne—educated in Belfast and Dublin—ordered him "not to take a sea voyage on any account" because the cold, wet weather would affect his leg. Browne's treatment for the legacy of two strokes was arsenic, strong soups, and no meat. Thornley was kept up to date on his health ("I can now stand for a few seconds at a time on the one leg and better still I am able to work, the book [*Famous Impostors*] is getting on. . . . Anyway happy memories are all anyone can ask for").

Stoker worried more about work than his health, complaining to Thornley that the previous year his royalties came to only £80—"Not much for a living wage, but there is hope that we can manage to pull through." Letters always stressed their misfortunes. "It is harder on poor Florence (who has been an angel) than on me," Stoker wrote. "She had to do all the bookkeeping and find the money to live on—God only knows how she managed." Stoker offered enough hints about his finances, short of asking for a loan. Just one of Thornley's Chippendale chairs (no drawing room was complete without the ball-and-claw, he always said) would have eased expenses at Durham Place. During this time, the brothers collaborated on designing a family coat of arms, with the motto *Quid verum atque decens: Whatever is true and honorable.*

Doubtless Thornley's side of the correspondence complained in kind about his own heart condition. After his wife's death he had retired at sixty-five and sold off many antiques from his Georgian residence. Ely House had been to him not so much a home as a series of connected rooms to fill with treasures. Like many passionate collectors he found acquisition more exciting than ownership. At dinner parties, when the light of a hundred candles reflected off the eighteenth-century silver displayed on mahogany credenzas, Thornley felt an affinity with the past. Frequent guests were fellow surgeon Oliver St. John Gogarty—the model for James Joyce's Buck Mulligan in *Ulysses*—and author George Moore. Arriving late for dinner, Moore would irritate by balancing his chair on its hind legs to admire what Thornley called "the excellent skin" of its glossy Chippendale wood and, with a sly smile on his pink porcelain face, ask his host: "A cancer, Sir Thornley, or a gallstone?" referring to Thornley's habit of buying an antique after being paid for an operation.

Gogarty recalled how one evening the "mahogany door burst open, and a nude and elderly lady came in with a cry, 'I like a little intelligent conversation!' She ran around the table. We all stood up. She was followed by two female attendants, who seized whatever napery was available, and sheltering her with this and their own bodies, led her forth, screaming, from the room." This sudden appearance of his wife upset Thornley, who asked his guests, particularly Moore, "as you are the only one who causes me grave misgivings," not to discuss the mortifying incident. "But it was charming, Sir Thornley. I demand an encore," said Moore.

The illness—real or imagined—that destroyed Emily Stoker is not known, although gossip said she had descended into schizophrenia, watched over by Florence Dugdale, a thirty-one-year-old New Woman cast in the mold of H. G. Wells's Ann Veronica. Drawn to literature and a life beyond teaching, she became Thomas Hardy's typist and, according to one Hardy biographer, thought Thornley would marry her following his wife's death. She always referred to the Stokers as "my dear lost friends in Dublin."

In February 1911 Stoker petitioned the Royal Literary Fund for a grant. In his request he noted earnings of £166 in 1910 from his only source of income: writing. Describing his medical condition, he said: "At the beginning of 1906 I had a paralytic stroke. Fortunately the stroke was not a bad one and in a few months I resumed my work. Just a year ago I had another break-down from overwork which has incapacitated me ever since. The result of such a misfortune shows at its worst in the case of one who has to depend on his brain and his hands." Henry Dickens, Charles's son, and Gilbert wrote in support. "This is not a mere formal backing on my part. I desire to support this application to the fullest extent," said Dickens. Added Gilbert, "I have enjoyed the privilege of Mr. Bram Stoker's friendship for about twenty-five years." The fund awarded him £100. "This, I fancy, is as much as is ever given except under special circumstances," he wrote Gilbert, who offered to help if Stoker decided to apply for a Civil List pension.

In the three supernatural novels published after *Dracula,* Stoker dismissed the male villain to concentrate on demonic women. *The Lady of the Shroud,* dedicated to Geneviève Ward, features an amateur occultist, Rupert Sent Leger, who is visited in his bedroom (Stoker's favorite vampiric rendezvous) by a mysterious lady. The suspense as to her origins covers the first three-quarters of the book, until it is discovered that she is Lady Teuta pretending to be a vampire to protect her country from the Turks. The one original scene in an otherwise boring book is the final rescue using airplanes.

Women who think like men but act like women return. Lady Teuta wields political and intellectual power. "Her woman's quick wit was worth the reasoning of a camp full of men," says Rupert. Like Mina she uses this power to support her family rather than her own interests. There is a noticeable aversion to seductive females and a preference for platonic unions. In *The Jewel of Seven Stars,* the hero says a woman can "unman" a man if he becomes too physically attached to her. The hunters in *The Lair of the White Worm* vow "our strong game will be to play our masculine against her feminine."

In *Famous Impostors,* a curious nonfiction excursion with an entire section devoted to women as men, Stoker attempts to prove that Queen Elizabeth never married because she was a man. He bases this on a report that Elizabeth visited Bisley, near London, in 1544, then became ill and died; unable to find a little girl, her governess supposedly dressed up a boy, who impersonated the princess for the rest of his life—a story that again illustrates the author's fascination with the masks people wear to survive. Editors found that the headlines wrote themselves: ANOTHER ELIZABETHAN HERESY, alluding to the controversy over who wrote Shakespeare; KING ELIZABETH; GOOD 'KING' BESS; WAS THE VIRGIN QUEEN A MAN?

In 1911 finances forced the Stokers out of Chelsea, where they had lived for thirty years; they took a small flat at 26 St. George's Square in Belgravia, a rectangular area that stretched to the Thames. It could not compare with Durham Place or St. Leonard's Terrace, but Stoker enjoyed the walk along the river to Vauxhall Bridge and the Tate Gallery. As his health failed, writing became an act of des-

BRAM STOKER
used a photograph of
this painting by
Goldsborough
Anderson to promote
the publication of
*Famous Impostors* in
America.

peration, and for the first time he put himself on a schedule. He
began writing *The Lair of the White Worm* on March 3, 1911, inscrib-
ing a date after each day's work, and completed it three months and
nine days later, on June 12.

A dark tale of womanhood, the novel stars Lady Arabella, who
dresses in white, speaks in sibilant sentences, and is a giant, primor-
dial worm—200 feet long and two thousand years old—who terror-
izes the Yorkshire countryside. To eradicate the ancient worm, the
hero, Adam Salton, concentrates his efforts against its lair, in a hidden
chamber in Lady Arabella's home. The hole is repeatedly and nega-
tively described in vaginal terms: its privacy, its darkness, the strange
moist fluids surrounding it, its odor. Salton delubricates it with sand
and destroys it with dynamite. The lair's destruction, however, occu-
pies only a small portion of an incoherent plot. And the symbolism
points more to Stoker's preparation for the arc of darkness from
womb to grave than a literary orgasm avoiding the dangers of sex.

The British film director Ken Russell interpreted the novel in

1989, using his signature camp style: fantasy sequences, snakes entwined around crosses, impalements, cavorting nudes, a dinner of pickled earthworms in aspic, and a hallucinatory sequence involving the rape of nuns—none of which is in the text. To some the film and book are the same. They are not. *Lair* became Stoker's most popular novel after *Dracula*. And it was his last. After it he decided to recycle published work rather than struggle with new ideas. Florence gathered together all his short stories, and he set about organizing three collections.

Dr. Browne urged exercise for his muscles, but Stoker preferred reclining to read and sort his legacy. On April 15, 1912, Florence burst into their bedroom with the news that the previous evening the luxury liner *Titanic,* the unsinkable ship, had ripped itself apart on an iceberg off Newfoundland on its maiden voyage from Southampton to New York. Such a disaster was beyond comprehension: 1,513 died, and only 705, mostly women and children, were rescued. The shipwreck of the century surpassed any of Stoker's fictional accounts. Florence shuddered when she recalled her own experiences with Noel on the shipwrecked *Victoria.* Stoker was reminded of his alter ego in *The Man,* who plunges into icy water to rescue passengers from a burning ship.

Despite his weakened condition, Stoker joined the whole world in "What if?" discussions. On board the *Titanic* were Conan Doyle's friend, the spiritualist W. T. Stead, editor of *The Pall Mall Gazette,* and some of the world's richest men: John Jacob Astor, Archibald W. Butt, Benjamin Guggenheim, and Isidor Straus. Who was to blame for this greatest civilian disaster at sea? Shaw pointed to the officers: there was panic when steerage passengers found no lifeboats on deck. Conan Doyle rushed to the defense of the late Captain E. J. Smith. Both, however, overlooked the one crucial factor in the accident: the weakness of the ship below the waterline.

On April 20, the date official inquiries into the disaster began, Stoker died quietly at the age of sixty-four, with Florence and Noel at his bedside. The death certificate, signed by Dr. Browne, gave three causes: "Locomotor Ataxy 6 Months, Granular Contracted Kidney.

Exhaustion." Because it reconciled with Stoker's overwork for Irving, exhaustion—a general term with no modern medical meaning—became the most-quoted cause of death. When Stoker's great-nephew Daniel Farson published *The Man Who Wrote Dracula* in 1975, he sensationalized his uncle's death. Curious about whether the drugs Stoker took for gout had stimulated *Lair*'s disorientation, he consulted the family physician, who examined the death certificate and diagnosed syphilis, interpreting "locomotor ataxy" as a euphemism for *tabes dorsalis* ("General Paralysis of the Insane"), or tertiary syphilis.

One of the prevalent diseases of the nineteenth century, syphilis, like tuberculosis, was frequently overdiagnosed. Anyone who led a dissolute life (hardly a description of Stoker) and showed signs of skin eruptions, an unsteady gait, or brain disturbances was suspect. Stoker told Thornley in 1910 that Dr. Browne was treating him with arsenic, commonly used as an antibiotic. At this time there were few means of treating syphilis, only bichloride-of-mercury injections and potassium iodide; no successful treatment was available until 1909, when Dr. Paul Ehrlich developed his "magic bullet," salvarsan, an arsenic-based drug. It is doubtful that Browne would have been able to obtain salvarsan; Ehrlich began clinical tests in the spring of 1910 but would not release his discovery for general use until more trials, although some unauthorized units were distributed worldwide by the manufacturer.

No matter what *Lair*'s altered states, Stoker was never the classic demented, psychotic personality associated with tertiary syphilis. Nonetheless, Farson accepted this diagnosis, and further speculated that Stoker contracted the disease sometime after Noel's birth in 1879, when his wife's purported frigidity forced him to seek out prostitutes. Stoker now had a tragic flaw. To some this explained the genesis of *Dracula* and its references to insanity and pestilence. Syphilis rather than renal failure was accepted as the cause of death. We shall never know whether Stoker ever had syphilis, but the medical evidence argues against his dying from that disease. Like most middle-class Londoners of his time, he died at home, not in a hospital, so there are no medical records. Dr. Browne was in attendance, and there was no need for an autopsy. Kidney failure would have been sufficient for the medical certificate, but it appears Browne was thorough and listed all possibilities. As a friend and fellow Irishman, he would have been callous to include a cause of death that hinted at syphilis. After all, the family's good name was at risk.

Some British medical experts contend that syphilis was not an issue in Stoker's death. Dr. W. F. Bynum, of The Wellcome Institute for the History of Medicine in London, explains that "locomotor ataxia generally referred to tertiary syphilis in Victorian times, but if Stoker had had a stroke it is quite possible that this was a misdiagnosis." Dr. R. B. Gibberd, a neurologist at the Charing Cross and Westminster Medical School, says the key lies in the time element of "six months" on the certificate: "If Stoker had locomotor ataxia for only six months before his death, then it is unlikely it was due to syphilis." Lack of coordination, Gibberd explained, was more likely due to the residual symptoms from two strokes.

Obituaries were widely published. The London *Times* noted that he had been ill for six years and called him "the master of a particularly lurid and creepy kind of fiction." The *Irish Times* praised him as "a typical Irishman of the best type." The *Daily Telegraph* said the author "had a genius for the extreme of improbability, to which he lent an air of weird fascination that gave some of his books the atmosphere of a dream, rather than a nightmare." Others ran in the *Daily Sketch, The Illustrated London News, The Graphic,* the *Daily News,* the *Daily Mirror,* and the Westminster *Gazette.* The Pittsburgh *Gazette* said his death did not attract the notice in America it deserved:

> Few "intimates" of the theatre in America will not recall this gifted and versatile man. It was Stoker who made smooth the pathway of Henry Irving in this country, and to his wit, good nature and splendid genius went the credit for the success of nearly all the social gatherings in which Irving was a feature. He was the finest and most tactful man that ever kept watch and ward at the gateway to stage greatness and reserve.

A month before he died Stoker made a final will, a simple document leaving everything to Florence. At probate this came to

£4,723. Among the small group of mourners at Golders Green Crematorium were Hall Caine, Geneviève Ward, Laurence Irving, Ford Madox Hueffer, and Violet Hunt. The stone casket was large enough to hold Florence's ashes eventually, but too small for an epitaph. These lines from Yeats would have been fitting:

> I have spread my dreams under your feet;
> Tread softly, because you tread on my dreams.

# Epilogue

"My revenge is just begun. I spread it over
centuries and time is on my side."
—Dracula

Forty days after his brother's death Thornley died. Florence inherited her husband's small bequest of £1,000. Florence Dugdale's share was £2,000, plus a one-sixth interest in the estate. Despite a forty-year age difference, Dugdale married Thomas Hardy in 1914, two years after the death of his wife. Hardy's recent biographer says of Thornley and Florence: "She may very well have, at the least, shown him sexual consideration. I mean, not to be too mock-delicate about the matter, that she may have masturbated the old man," thus relegating any other kindnesses (to Thornley's wife, for instance) as implausible for such a legacy. Florence Stoker was inclined to agree.

When Oliver St. John Gogarty's book *As I Was Walking Down Sackville Street,* with the scene of Emily Stoker running naked through the dining room, was published in 1933, Florence wrote Noel that "Aunt E wouldn't dream of showing her altogether to such an audience" and demanded that he extract an apology from the author. "If the story is true," she continued, "has not Gogarty betrayed a friend and a dead one at that by this breach of confidence," wisely adding, "of course one might by taking any notice, make too much of it." She signed her letter: "To H..ll with these annoyances!! I don't know why I am selected to fight the family battles!" Thornley's housekeeper, Betty Webb, whose share was £5,000, denied the event. Legal action was never taken.

Meanwhile Florence cleaned house. On July 7, 1913, Sotheby, Wilkinson & Hodge auctioned off 317 items, including the *Dracula Notes,* original manuscripts, seventeen volumes associated with Whitman, sixty signed presentation editions, the death mask and hands of Lincoln, and an important collection of David Garrick's letters. A book of Winston Churchill's illustrations was inscribed: "To

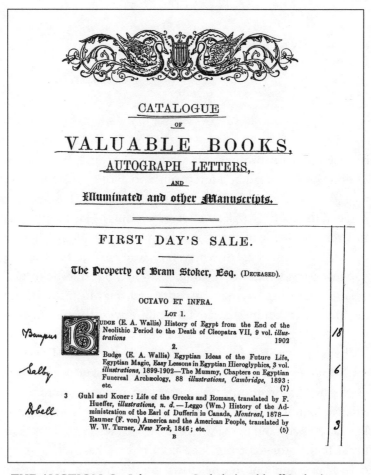

THE AUCTION. On July 7, 1913, Sotheby's sold off Stoker's books, presentation copies, and original manuscripts for *Under the Sunset, Snowbound, Personal Reminiscences of Henry Irving, The Lady of the Shroud, The Lair of the White Worm,* and the *Dracula Notes.*

Bram Stoker, October 31, 1899. Another Gentleman who belongs to both sides of the Atlantic," a reference to Churchill's American mother, Jennie Jerome. The sale added £400 to the estate. Florence held on to some autographed letters, waiting for the best prices ("I believe in pulling reserves," she said). In 1914, she published *Dracula's Guest,* the only story collection Stoker had time to organize before his death, including *Dracula*'s excised second chapter, which gives the volume its name.

Florence stayed on for two years at St. George's Square before moving to a better address, 4 Kinnerton Studios, now Braddock House, in Knightsbridge. Her life as an attractive widow was far from boring. She went on Hellenic cruises, to Foyles book lunches; took refuge in Catholic ritual at the nearby Brompton Oratory; and visited Seaview on the Isle of Wight, where Noel and his family summered. She surrounded herself with artifacts from the Wilde period, directing visitors' attention to the Moytura watercolor "that poor O. painted for me."

In her letters, Wilde is always "poor O."; thus she distanced herself with a kind of motherly affection. She wrote her sister, Philippa, how "Oscar's little water-colour creates much envy in the breasts of the Oscar cult." When she met the brother of Robert Ross, Wilde's first male lover, she reported: "He keeps in touch with Oscar & Willie's children, & is going to ask me to meet them." Florence was disappointed when Wilde's second son, Vyvyan, did not visit. "I wanted him to come & see me, being so fond of his Father," she wrote, "but he never turned up." She was an astute critic of Wilde's biographers. "The [Robert] Sherard book has left a nasty taste behind. I don't know why he wrote it, except to make money. 'Aspects of Wilde' by Vincent O'Sullivan is the best book I've read on poor O."

For companions she had a niece, Philippa Adams, and a Pekingese called Moonbeam. "I have never had a better time than I am having now, or surrounded by more congenial spirits, really the wits and brains who foregather here from time to time are quite remarkable," she told her sister. "I have been out no end this season, & lots of attention from both sexes, theatres & parties and dinners thrown in, but I enjoy every moment with a zest." After an evening at the Berlin Orchestra, she exclaimed: "Came home in comfort, my dear swain always has a car when he takes me out." It was "a mistake," she said, "to turn back the leaves of the book of our past. The present is so interesting."

One of the wits who visited Knightsbridge was the young Vincent Price, then studying to be an art historian at the Courtauld Institute. He recalled Florence as "frail and small and nearly blind with cataract-clouded eyes, holding court, surrounded by portraits from her youth." Noel would describe his mother as "an ornament not a woman of passion. People used to stand on chairs to look at her. She was still a very beautiful woman in middle age and when she was seventy-five."

This social idyll was disturbed in 1922, when Florence learned of an unsanctioned German silent film adaptation of *Dracula,* called *Nosferatu: Eine Symphonie des Grauens* (A Symphony of Horror), a fantasy with more spectral atmosphere, more ingenuity, and more imaginative ghoulishness than any of its successors; its central image, the cadaverous Max Schreck as Count Orlock, was more in keeping with the novel than any of the film vampires to follow.

Florence refused to pay for expert advice, but as her husband's literary executor she was able to join the Society of Authors for £1/10 a year. She sent off a check and received a welcome from G. Herbert Thring, secretary, who offered to help with any problems concerning her late husband's literary work. Little did he suspect that for the next fifteen years he would be besieged and berated by the widow Stoker. By return mail he received an advertisement and program for the screening that month in Berlin of *Nosferatu,* the first production of the Prana-Film company. The director was thirty-two-year-old Friedrich Wilhelm Murnau, who with scriptwriter Henrik Galeen emphasized the homoerotic aspects of the novel, concentrating on shadowy visuals and metaphors associated with the German Expressionism of the time.

As far as the Germans were concerned there were no copyright problems. The titles acknowledged Bram Stoker's novel as the source; characters' names were changed, and the plot was modified. Set in Bremen in 1838, the encounter is between a man and a woman, not two patriarchal figures. Nosferatu dies when Nina (Mina) sacrifices herself by keeping him with her until dawn; when the morning sun breaks into the bedroom, he dissolves.

Florence was a formidable adversary in this three-year battle, and her sense of entitlement made her most unpleasant. "I want to call your attention to the fact that the type of your letter was quite faint" she wrote Thring, "and being so blurred, I was obligated to have it read to me, which is not always desirable if the communication is a private matter." Another time she complained: "Your secretary omitted to *fasten* the envelope, it might have been lost in transit, it was very careless on her part." In July of 1922 Prana was on the verge of bankruptcy (publicity costs had exceeded film costs), and it seemed unlikely that any money was available for rights, although Thring thought it possible to obtain the film or an injunction against anyone who purchased it.

A month later he wrote Florence the case had become so complicated the society could not afford to continue counsel. Would she be willing to meet any expenses to solve the difficult legal points? Without hesitation, she agreed to pay £20 to the society's German lawyer, but negotiated the sum as an advance against recovered damages. Florence had discovered a latent talent: bargaining. By June of 1923, when there was still no settlement, Thring advised that other long-standing society members were more deserving of assistance.

Rather than withdraw the society's aid, Thring wanted Florence to accept defeat, which she was unwilling to do. She had powerful friends, not the least of whom was the publisher William Heinemann. Escorted by Noel, she attended the Society of Authors' annual membership dinner to bolster her cause. Thring was answering four to six of her letters a month. Demands scrawled in increasingly large letters on blue stationery constituted a postal bombardment. She asked for £5,000 in royalties and the destruction of all copies of the film. The bankruptcy case went to court in May of 1924, to be followed by fourteen months of appeals. "I am quite prepared to carry on," she informed him. When Prana's liquidator withdrew, the original film was said to be incinerated. "I am glad this matter is now at an end," Thring wrote Florence, with an audible sigh.

Nothing, of course, had ended. In October Florence read an announcement of a London Film Society showing of *Nosferatu*. "Surely the German film comes under the head of 'Stolen Goods,'" she wrote Thring. The society claimed that permission came from an American motion picture company called Universal, which owned the rights, but Florence assumed someone had sold the pirated German film to America. Thring advised caution. He did not want an action for libel if it could be proven the film was not a copyright infringement. Four years later this disputed print was again presumably destroyed. For nearly a decade Stoker's widow sought to suppress a seminal film that elevated the value of *Dracula* as no other dramatic adaptation ever has.

That chapter concluded, the long-suffering Thring was engaged to protect foreign book rights. A German translation was negotiated in 1908. But could she sell more German rights in Vienna? Florence asked. Would the Society of Authors collect royalties? Would they translate letters? French rights were sold for £20, Spanish for £12, and Tamil for £5. Foreign rights "are not worth much," Noel told his mother. To be sure, these were not large sums, but maintaining an adversarial momentum was the issue. Florence enjoyed testing wits with publishers and pirates. But what was her opinion of the novel she now so fiercely fought to protect? She surely read it; then again perhaps she never finished it. Her only comment occurs in the preface for *Dracula's Guest,* where she notes it "is considered my husband's most remarkable work."

A young Irish actor named Hamilton Deane, a member of Irving's touring company in 1899, produced the first play based on the novel. A copyright reading was staged in July of 1924 at the Grand Theatre in Derby. This time the censors—demonstrating that the silliest minds of all are those of literary or theatrical expurgators—pounced on the violence and sexual overtones. One banned the play. "I thought the novel tedious rubbish," he wrote, "when I read it 30 years ago or so and was not thrilled at all. The play is also rubbish, of course, but the details of it seem to me too disgusting for the stage. . . . It may be a strong measure to forbid the production, as a play, of a once popular novel, which has of course nothing whatever immoral in it, in the ordinary sense." Still, he could not condone horror for horror's sake.

"Dracula made my flesh creep in my youth, just as fairy stories of giants and bears did in my childhood," wrote another censor, unaware that Stoker's cut-and-paste version once passed muster. "But I never thought anyone would be so foolish as to try and dramatise it." Finally a decisive note was struck: "In view of the wide publicity given to this disgusting story in novel form, it is rather high-minded to stop its publication altogether." The Deane version was licensed, with the following alterations: Dracula's death was to be less violent, and Mina's neck was not to be penetrated.

*Dracula* opened at the Little Theatre on Valentine's Day 1927. "So well did Stoker do his job as a scarifier," one critic wrote, "that his ability penetrates into the play and actually overpowers Mr. Deane's appallingly pompous speech." This first dramatization caused more amusement than horror. "There is very little of Bram Stoker in it. But most of us jumped in our seats at least once in every act." *The Era* questioned "whether such a story can ever be as successful on the stage as it is in print"; still, "the ordinary Grand Guignol play is a nursery rhyme beside it." To mark the 250th performance, a special edition of one thousand numbered copies of *Dracula's Guest* was issued for presentation to the audience at the Prince of Wales Theatre. Inside the cover of the mystery packet was a black bat, powered by elastic, which flew out as the book was opened.

In later plays based on the novel, by John L. Balderston and Charles Morrell, the Lord Chamberlain's office again objected to sex and violence. Blue-penciled were scenes in which vampires are decapitated and their mouths stuffed with garlic: scenes should be played for more laughs and less horror. Thus a burlesque drama breezed through in 1930. Censors probably did not know what to make of this dramatization written in the form of Henry Wadsworth Longfellow's *Hiawatha*. It had more props than characters. Stoker was renamed Bramwell. Memorable lines included:

> I am Dracula the Vampire
> Very old and very cunning

First abroad in 1620
Still going strong like Johnnie Walker.

It did not take too much intelligence for the censors to rule that this version "avoids any of the original beastliness."

Negotiations for film rights followed. As monumental as *Nosferatu* will always be, it was part of a bygone silent era. Universal Pictures paid $40,000 for the rights to the 1931 Tod Browning film, starring the Hungarian actor Bela Lugosi; it paid $400 for the print of *Nosferatu,* but never destroyed it as instructed. Florence received about half after commissions and other fees, but it allowed her to live well off her husband's dreams.

Florence Irving died in 1935, at the age of ninety-one, at Folkstone. Some accounts of her passing described her as mad. Henry, her eldest son, had died in the shipwreck of the *Empress of Ireland* during a transatlantic crossing. For thirty years, on the anniversary of Irving's death, she played the role of the mourning widow. Newspapers reported how she visited Westminster Abbey to place a spray of red roses on his stone, with a card inscribed: "I shall remember while light lives yet, and in the darkness I shall not forget."

Florence Stoker died two years later, on May 25, 1937, of colon cancer at the age of seventy-eight. Her estate of £6,913 exceeded her husband's by some £2,000. She instructed that her ashes be dispersed on the Garden of Rest outside the Ernest George Columbarium at Golders Green. Noel took his mother's place in his father's stone casket on his death in 1961. Today Stoker's burial place is closed to the public, the 1,700 niches filled long ago; the central apse's colored mosaic is gritty and dark. There are cobwebs and a sense of peace.

Stoker's prediction that Geneviève Ward would be a great star was vindicated in 1921 when she was the second actress to receive the title Dame of the British Empire (the first was May Whitty in 1918). There was much resentment in the theatrical community about her preceding Ellen Terry, who became a Dame four years later. Terry died on July 21, 1928. Her name is still revered as the outstanding actress of the Victorian era. Irving's talent was never captured on film. Those who saw him as Mathias or Hamlet or Shylock were messengers for the next generation.

Laurence Olivier decided to become a great actor in defiance of Henry Irving. The precise moment was a performance of *King Lear* at the Biltmore Theatre in Los Angeles in 1931. Olivier was twenty-four. When he heard everyone praising Randle Ayrton's interpretation, comparing it to the Old Man (Irving), he vowed "to eradicate all knowledge of the Old Man from the public's memory forever. I was determined to become the Old Man myself. Let them impersonate me fifty years after my death." In 1977, the London Dracula Society unveiled a London County Council round blue plaque at 18 St. Leonard's Terrace, to commemorate the residence of *Dracula*'s author. Two years later Olivier and his third wife, actress Joan Plowright, moved in and lived there for five years.

The Lyceum closed as a legitimate theatre in 1939 with John Gielgud's *Hamlet*. Gielgud was Ellen Terry's great-nephew. To him Irving was a god. "I'd never seen him; I'd just read about him being Ellen Terry's partner. But the whole idea of this magnetic, strange man, whom I knew I could never be anything like, somehow appealed to me more than any past actor that I'd read about. I didn't try to copy. I only took note of all the things he'd done and looked at the pictures of him and so on."

After World War II, the Lyceum was a dance hall for forty years. Although plans are under way for a multimillion-pound restoration, the exterior—for now—is painted a harsh yellow. The interior smells of mold; weeds grow on the roof. The only legacy from Irving and Stoker's time is the Corinthian-columned portico. Even as a ruin the theatre commands attention. One can imagine Stoker at the back of the pit calling to each usher before ordering the Wellington Street doors open, the houselights dimming, and prolonged applause greeting Irving's entrance. Time has eclipsed the art of these performances, but Bram Stoker's *Dracula* endures.

# Acknowledgments

I owe my primary debt of gratitude to Bram Stoker's granddaughter, Ann Stoker, and great-grandson Noël Dobbs, whose hospitality and generosity during my stay in London to consult the Stoker Family Papers was a model for cooperation with a biographer. I am indebted to those who shared information and documents: Patrick Stoker, Stoker's great-nephew; Dennis McIntyre, Leslie Shepard, and David Lass, members of Dublin's Bram Stoker Club; Bernard Davies of the Dracula Society, London; and Jeanne Youngson of the Bram Stoker Memorial Association, New York.

I appreciate the special assistance of Nina Auerbach, Ray Bradbury, Dame Jean Conan Doyle, Bruce Francis, Sir John Gielgud, Benjamin Glazebrook, Richard Dalby, Sir Rupert Hart-Davis, Maurice Hindle, Robert H. Hirst, George Hoare, Merlin Holland, John McLaughlin, Raymond McNally, Senator David Morris, Margot Peters, and David Skal.

My thanks to the staffs of the following libraries and collections in the United States: Billy Rose Theatre Collection at Lincoln Center; the Theatre Collection of the Museum of the City of New York; the Berg Collection, New York Public Library; the Beinecke Rare Book and Manuscript Library, Yale University Library; The Pierpont Morgan Library; Dartmouth College Library; Princeton University Library; Library of Congress; Fales Rare Book Library, New York University; Rosenbach Museum & Library; the Free Library of Philadelphia's Theatre Collection; the Folger Shakespeare Library; the Harvard Theatre Collection; the Harry Ransom Humanities Research Center, the University of Texas at Austin; State University of New York at Buffalo, Rare Books Collection; Williams Andrews Clark Memorial Library, University of California. Special thanks to: Interlibrary Loan, Butler Library, Columbia University; Laura Fuderer, Theodore M. Hesburgh Library, University of Notre Dame; and Mary Huth, Rush Rhees Library, University of Rochester.

I am grateful to all those librarians who answered queries from Ireland and England: Trinity College Library, Dublin; National Library of Ireland; the British Library; Bodleian Library, Oxford; National Library of Scotland; University of Reading; University of Nottingham; the Theatre Museum, London. Special thanks to: Marian Pringle, Shakespeare Memorial Theatre Library, Stratford;

C. D. W. Sheppard, Brotherton Collection, Leeds University Library; Margaret Weare, Ellen Terry Memorial Museum, Smallhythe Place, Kent; and Kay Hutchings, Garrick Club Library, London.

To my friends, colleagues, and mentors who encouraged this biography, my first debt is to the astuteness of Victoria Wilson, my editor at Alfred A. Knopf, whose acuity helped this book to grow in depth and stature, and to Geri Thoma, the best and kindest of agents. My gratitude also to Lee Buttala, Victoria Wilson's assistant; to Allegra Huston of Weidenfeld & Nicolson, who loved the subject; and to my new British editor, Elsbeth Lindner.

I am very much indebted to my daughter, Deborah Belford de Furia, and Zach Sklar, Miles Merwin, and Mary Ellen Noonan for their careful reading of the manuscript, and to the meticulous copyediting skills of Candice Gianetti at Knopf. Members of the Biography Seminar at New York University offered constant encouragement. Colleagues at Columbia University, Professors Richard Blood and Melvin Mencher, always understood. Alf and Berthe Wallis and Robert and Joan Cook made my research in London more enjoyable by their presence. A grant from the National Endowment for the Humanities and a tenured faculty leave from Columbia provided time for research and writing.

Last but not least, this book is dedicated to Bill Kutik, my oldest and dearest friend, who was there at those moments when confidence flags and computers fail. He has lived through every emotional nuance of this book.

# Notes

The main repositories of material on Bram Stoker's life and the history of the Lyceum Theatre are the Stoker Family Papers; the Bram Stoker Collection of Irvingiana at the Shakespeare Memorial Theatre Library, Stratford-upon-Avon; the Brotherton Collection at the Leeds University Library; the Theatre Museum, London; Trinity College Library, Dublin; Folger Shakespeare Library, Washington, D.C.; the Rosenbach Museum & Library, Philadelphia; and Fales Rare Book Library, New York University.

The following short titles are used frequently in the notes (see Selected Bibliography for full citations of works not fully cited here):

*Actor-Managers:* Frances Donaldson, *The Actor-Managers.*

Bingham: Madeleine Bingham, *Henry Irving: The Greatest Victorian Actor.*

Craig: Edward Gordon Craig, *Henry Irving.*

*Dracula:* Bram Stoker, *Dracula* (London: Penguin Classics, 1993). Introduction and notes by Maurice Hindle; this text follows the first edition of 1897.

Ellmann: Richard Ellmann, *Oscar Wilde.*

Hatton: Joseph Hatton, *Henry Irving's Impressions of America.*

Irving: Laurence Irving, *Henry Irving, The Actor and His World.*

*Letters:* Rupert Hart-Davis, ed., *The Letters of Oscar Wilde.*

Ludlam: Harry Ludlam, *A Biography of Dracula: The Life Story of Bram Stoker.*

*Lyceum:* A. E. Wilson, *The Lyceum.*

Martin-Harvey: Sir John Martin-Harvey, *The Autobiography of Sir John Martin-Harvey.*

*Memoirs:* Ellen Terry, *Ellen Terry's Memoirs,* Edith Craig and Christopher St. John, eds.

*Reminiscences:* Bram Stoker, *Personal Reminiscences of Henry Irving.*

Shakespeare: William Shakespeare, The Tudor Edition, *Complete Works of William Shakespeare* (London: Collins, 1951).

Wilde: Oscar Wilde, *The Portable Oscar Wilde,* ed. Richard Aldington (New York: Viking Press, 1946).

*Whitman:* Horace Traubel, *With Walt Whitman in Camden.*

Folger: Folger Shakespeare Library, Washington, D.C.

Leeds: Brotherton Collection, Leeds University Library.

Rosenbach: Rosenbach Museum & Library.

Stoker: Stoker Family Papers, private collection.

Stratford: Bram Stoker Collection of Irvingiana, Shakespeare Memorial Theatre Library, Stratford-upon-Avon.

## INTRODUCTION

ix "I only slept": *Dracula,* p. 38.

xi "Childhood builds its": Bram Stoker, *The Gates of Life (The Man)* (New York: Cupples & Leon), p. 34.

xii "It is bad": Ibid., p. 53.

"a central document": Dijkstra, *Idols of Perversity,* p. 341.

"an embattled male's": David Skal, *Hollywood Gothic: The Tangled Web of Dracula from Novel to Stage to Screen* (New York: Norton, 1990), p. 28.

xiii "Van Helsing went": *Dracula,* p. 253.

## PROLOGUE

4 "To give strong": *Reminiscences,* vol. 1, p. 27.

"host's heart was": Ibid., p. 28.

5 "only terminated with": Ibid., p. 25.

"a kind of ": Richardson, "The Psychoanalysis of Ghost Stories," p. 427.

"All three had": *Dracula,* pp. 53–4.

7 "sex without genitalia": James Twitchell, "The Vampire Myth," *American Imago* 37 (1980): 88.

8 "Arthur took the": *Dracula,* p. 277.

"his face flushed": Ibid., p. 363.

"a child forcing": Ibid.

"He placed his reeking": Ibid., p. 370.

## CHAPTER 1
### The Dreamer

13 "There are bad": *Dracula,* p. 47.

"In my babyhood": *Reminiscences,* vol. 1, p. 31.

14 "When the nursery": *Reminiscences,* original holograph manuscript, Folger.

15 "If I lie": Ibid.

"ever-smiling": Abraham Stoker, "The Crystal Cup," *London Society* (Sept. 1872): 228.

15 "had been an": Bram Stoker, *The Mystery of the Sea* (New York: Doubleday, 1902), p. 89.

17 "fell upon the": Victoria Glendinning, *Anthony Trollope* (New York: Alfred A. Knopf, 1993), p. 163.

19 "seldom hesitated to": William Stoker, M.D., *Pathological Observations on Continued Fever, Ague, Tic, Doloreux, Measles, Small-Pox, and Dropsy* (Dublin, 1829), p. 188.

"the cheapest expedient": William Stoker, M.D., *Treatise on Fever, with Observations on the Practice Adopted for its Cure* (London: Longman, Hurst, Rees, Orme, and Brown, 1815), p. 20.

"The blood is": *Dracula,* p. 184.

20 "This early weakness": *Reminiscences,* vol. 1, p. 31.

21 "therein hangs another": notation on genealogical chart in Bram Stoker's handwriting, Stoker.

22 "It was said": letter from Charlotte Stoker to Abraham Stoker, Caen, France, May 6, 1873, Ibid.

"Mrs. Feeny": Ibid.

23 "The city sleeps": George Moore, *A Drama in Muslin* (London: Scott, 1893), p. 220.

27 "England is known": Charlotte M. B. Stoker, *On the Necessity of a State Provision for the Education of the Deaf and Dumb of Ireland* (Dublin: Alexander Thom, 1863), p. 5, Stoker.

"Any measure calculated": Charlotte M. B. Stoker, *On Female Emigration from Workhouses* (Dublin: Alexander Thom, 1864), p. 8, Stoker.

## CHAPTER 2
### Trinity Man

29 "He is a": *Dracula,* p. 27.

"At school I": Bram Stoker, *The Mystery of the Sea* (New York: Doubleday, 1902), p. 8.

"dull stone set": James Clarity, "Dublin," *The New York Times,* June 6, 1993.

30 "my big body": Bram Stoker, *The Mystery of the Sea,* p. 8.

"the only real": *Reminiscences,* vol. 2, p. 290.

"A brave man's": *Dracula,* p. 194.

32 "whose pedestrian feats": *The Daily Express,* Nov. 14, 1872.

"arose from the": Abraham Stoker, A.B., *College Historical Society Address,* Nov. 13, 1872 (Dublin: James Charles & Son, 1872), p. 9, Stoker.

33 "Its government, its": Ibid.

"At the close": Abraham Stoker to Chief Secretary, Dublin Castle, 1865, Stoker.

34 "every night since": Abraham Stoker to Bram Stoker, Nov. 1872, Ibid.

36 "He's as good": Ludlam, p. 23.

37  "mysteriously thrilling people": Holroyd, *Bernard Shaw: The Search for Love,*
    p. 57.

38  "the old weather-beaten": *Reminiscences,* vol. 1, p. 4.

    "a triumph of": Ibid.

    "a patrician figure": Ibid., p. 3.

    "painstaking and": Ibid., p. 7.

    "somewhat improved the": Dublin *Evening Standard,* Feb. 14, 1870.

    "I am glad": Charlotte Stoker to Bram Stoker, Nov. 1872, Stoker.

39  "Great Men, taken": Thomas Carlyle, *On Heroes, Hero-Worship and the
    Heroic in History* (London: Macmillan, 1904), p. 2.

    "modern squeamishness": Kaplan, *Walt Whitman,* p. 324.

    "Come, I will": Walt Whitman, "For You O Democracy," *Leaves of Grass*
    (New York: The Modern Library, 1957), p. 96.

40  "whole moral nature": unidentified newspaper clipping, May 12, 1871,
    Stratford.

    "Put it in": *Whitman,* p. 182.

43  "I do not": *Dracula,* p. 76.

44  "some standing socially": *Reminiscences,* vol. 2, p. 95.

    "Spoke—I think": Ibid., p. 96.

    "I had the": *Whitman,* p. 180.

    "same impertinence, and": Ibid., p. 217.

45  "was a sassy": Ibid., p. 182.

    "Beautiful! . . . he is": Ibid., p. 185.

    "writing to me": Ibid., p. 218.

    "Dowden was a": *Reminiscences,* vol. 2, p. 98.

47  "Trickle drops! my": Walt Whitman, "Trickle Drops," *Leaves of Grass,*
    p. 102.

CHAPTER 3
*Drama Critic*

48  "that epoch in": *Reminiscences,* vol. 1, p. 10.

49  "It is I!": Erckmann-Chatrian, *The Bells or The Polish Jew* (New York: De
    Witt, c. 1872), p. 20.

50  "terror, the greed": Dublin *Evening Mail,* Dec. 4, 1876, review of *The Bells*
    at the Royal.

    "took the town": *Reminiscences,* vol. 1, p. 10.

    "There will be": Hugh Oram, *The Newspaper Book: A History of Newspapers
    in Ireland 1649–1983* (Dublin: 1983), p. 49.

52  "very agreeable": Abraham Stoker to Bram Stoker, n.d., Stoker.

    "nearly impossible for": Michael Sanderson, *From Irving to Olivier* (London:
    Athlone, 1984), p. 11.

53  "This was very": *Reminiscences,* vol. 1, p. 14.

54 "a wonderful illustration": Dublin *Evening Mail,* Nov. 16, 1875, review of *Romeo and Juliet* at the Gaiety.

"thick as herrings": *Dublin Evening Mail,* Dec. 27, 1876, review of *Sinbad the Sailor* at the Queens.

56 "free from misery": Ludlam, p. 35.

"Since I have": Bram Stoker to Helen Barry, Sept. 1873, private collection. Quoted with permission.

57 "heart used to": *Percy Fitzgerald Scrapbooks,* Garrick Club, vol. 5, p. 158.

"like the plums": *Reminiscences,* vol. 2, p. 167.

59 "will be a": Ibid., p. 169.

Why wouldn't the: Geneviève Ward to Bram Stoker, Sept. 23, 1876, Leeds.

"a plate, knife": Ibid., Sept. 22, 1875.

"melancholy Merrion Square": George Moore, *A Drama in Muslin* (London: Scott, 1893), p. 225.

60 "something wonderful": Horace Wyndham, *Speranza: A Biography of Lady Wilde* (London: T. V. Boardman, 1951), p. 73.

"was a rallying": Wyndham, *Speranza,* p. 68.

61 "All women become": "The Importance of Being Earnest," p. 452, Wilde.

62 "I, and I alone": Terence de Vere White, *The Parents of Oscar Wilde* (London: Hodder and Stoughton, 1967), p. 111.

"We live in": Wyndham, *Speranza,* p. 70.

"Glad to meet": Ibid.

"By interesting them": Ibid., p. 76.

"Welcome, my dear": Ibid., p. 71.

63 "Round what had": Ibid., p. 77.

"little creature, who": Ibid., p. 81.

65 "An eminent oculist": Ellmann, p. 15.

66 "I am anxious": Abraham Stoker to Editor, *Blackwood's Edinburgh Magazine,* National Library of Scotland, Oct. 6, 1874.

"Of course if": Ibid., Aug. 19, 1875.

67 "Some of what": Matilda Stoker to Abraham Stoker, Sept. 1874, Stoker.

68 "It is very": Charlotte Stoker to Abraham Stoker, May 17, 1874, Ibid.

"I hope when": Matilda Stoker to Abraham Stoker, June 18, 1874, Ibid.

"I am sure": Abraham Stoker to Abraham Stoker Jr., 1874, Ibid.

"We were very": Charlotte Stoker to Abraham Stoker, Sept. 19, 1874, Ibid.

69 "You know that": Abraham Stoker to Abraham Stoker Jr., 1874, Ibid.

CHAPTER 4
*Henry Irving*

70 "I am here": *Dracula,* p. 135.

71 "trammel up the": Craig, p. 63.

71 "Rightly or wrongly": *Irving,* p. 298.

"upon the boards": Craig, p. 74.

"Nature has done": *Actor-Managers,* p. 47.

"sense of humour": Ibid., p. 54.

"not only the": Dublin *Evening Mail,* Nov. 28, 1876.

72 "Irving is in": Ibid.

"He would do": Ibid.

"Dilly, dilly, dilly": Ibid., Nov. 30, 1876.

73 "Two sudden blows": Thomas Hood, *The Dream of Eugene Aram, The Murderer* (London: David Bogue, 1841), p. 24.

"The recitation was": *Reminiscences,* vol. 1, p. 28.

"So great was": Ibid., p. 29.

74 "something like a": Ibid., p. 31.

"The effect of ": Irving, p. 279.

"Soul had looked": *Reminiscences,* vol. 1, p. 33.

"My dear friend": inscription on original photograph, Stratford.

75 "a school of ": *Reminiscences,* vol. 1, p. 36.

"When I think": Ibid.

"with a cheer": Ibid., p. 38.

76 "Every fibre of ": Ibid., p. 39.

"howl of execration": Ibid., p. 17.

77 "to formulate a code": Abraham Stoker, *The Duties of Clerks of Petty Sessions in Ireland,* preface.

79 "a double consciousness": *Reminiscences,* vol. 2, p. 20.

"If you do": Ibid., p. 23.

"positive quiver of ": Ibid., vol. 1, p. 49.

80 "What are you": Ibid., p. 45.

"wild, fitful, irresolute": Ibid., p. 48.

"London in view!": Ibid., p. 54.

81 "We understood each": Ibid., p. 60.

82 "Manager to a": family anecdote.

"I would like": Henry Irving to Bram Stoker, Nov. 27, 1878, Leeds.

"there are good": *Dracula,* p. 239.

"each individual must": Bram Stoker, *Lady Athlyne* (New York: Reynolds, 1908), p. 82.

"not least, got": *Reminiscences,* vol. 1, p. 61.

"a good surprise": Edward Dowden to Bram Stoker, Jan. 3, 1879, Leeds.

85 Floriana in Malta: Eleanor Knott to Rupert Hart-Davis, Nov. 11, 1957. Quoted with permission of Sir Rupert Hart-Davis.

85  *"exquisitely pretty girl"*: Oscar Wilde to Reginald Harding, Aug. 6, 1876, *Letters*, p. 24.

"Believe me ever": Florence Balcombe to Oscar Wilde, n.d., William Andrews Clark Memorial Library, Los Angeles.

"more lovely than": Oscar Wilde to Reginald Harding, May 1877, *Letters*, p. 36.

"over so many": Oscar Wilde to Florence Balcombe, April 1878, Ibid., p. 51.

"Worthless though the": [late 1878], Ibid., p. 54.

"quite out of ": Ibid., p. 55.

86  "we Irish are": H. Montgomery Hyde, *Oscar Wilde* (New York: Farrar, Straus and Giroux, 1975), p. 114.

"He never gets": Terence de Vere White, *The Parents of Oscar Wilde* (London: Hodder and Stoughton, 1967), p. 238.

87  "sounded the retreat": Eleanor Knott to Rupert Hart-Davis, May 5, 1957. Quoted with permission.

"we women are": *Dracula,* p. 79.

"that delightful little": *Reminiscences,* vol. 1, p. 61.

"the many things": Ibid., p. 59.

CHAPTER 5
*The Lyceum*

91  "to go through": *Dracula*, p. 31.

92  "I have seen": Horace Gregory, *The World of James McNeill Whistler* (New York: Thomas Nelson & Sons, 1959), p. 141.

"The labor of ": Ibid.

93  "no artist can": *Reminiscences,* vol. 1, p. 151.

"I wish I": Wilde, p. 657.

94  "Faith is to be": *Reminiscences,* vol. 2, p. 68.

95  "these things testify": John Pick, *The West End* (Eastbourne: John Offord, 1983), p. 58.

98  "Of all that": Ibid., p. 45.

"It did not": Ibid., p. 70.

"When ribs and": Bingham, p. 211.

99  "seated in the": Pick, *The West End,* p. 70.

"it is a distinction": Holroyd, *Bernard Shaw: The Pursuit of Power,* p. 383.

100  "and one almost": Horace Wyndham, *The Nineteen Hundreds* (New York: Thomas Seltzer, 1923), p. 117.

"seemed always to": *Actor-Managers,* p. 92.

"Napoleon was in": Craig, p. 97.

101  "would not have": *Actor-Managers,* p. 72.

102 "Nothing I think": Irving, p. 158.

"I can see": Ibid., p. 173.

"Well my dear": Ibid., p. 200.

103 a Christmas tree: Auerbach, *Ellen Terry: Player in Her Time,* p. 177.

a Giorgione portrait: *Lyceum,* p. 114.

"a dilettante": Irving, p. 316.

104 "It's a Princess": Bingham, p. 128.

"defects sprang from": *Memoirs,* p. 161.

105 "Her face was": *Reminiscences,* vol. 2, p. 190.

106 "She is a": Ibid., p. 199.

"Ah, that wonderful": *Dracula,* p. 302.

"Even Ellen Terry": Ibid., p. 229.

CHAPTER 6
*First Nights*

107 "Do not fear": *Dracula,* p. 391.

108 "All right? Quite": Martin-Harvey, p. 91.

109 "his skin contracted": *Memoirs,* p. 121.

"Give me the": "Hamlet," Shakespeare, p. 1071.

"There is a": *Reminiscences,* vol. 1, p. 76.

"I see. In": *Memoirs,* p. 123.

110 "I went between": Ibid., p. 122.

"I am very": Ibid., p. 121.

"Irving gave the": Martin-Harvey, p. 88.

111 "Dates are everything": *Dracula,* p. 288.

"If it be": "Hamlet," Shakespeare, p. 1070.

"pearl amongst philosophic": *Reminiscences,* vol. 1, p. 77.

"so that, in": *Noel Stoker Memoir,* Stoker.

112 "theatrical court, with": *Pall Mall Budget,* Dec. 24, 1885.

"good hearty house": Irving, p. 315.

113 "lifted it to": Ibid., p. 316.

"so perfect that": *Lyceum,* p. 112.

"he would do": Irving, p. 315.

"the chivalrous embarrassment": Auerbach, *Ellen Terry: Player in Her Time,* p. 181.

114 "Of course, I": Steen, *A Pride of Terrys,* p. 185.

"was prepared to": Irving, p. 479.

"since I cannot": "Richard III," Shakespeare, p. 701.

"as if he": Auerbach, *Ellen Terry: Player in Her Time,* p. 191.

114 "large, flabby, ill": *Memoirs,* p. 269.

"He had precisely": Ibid., p. 119.

115 "she had laughed": Ibid., p. 128.

"Were I to": *Actor-Managers,* p. 72.

"Stage very dismal": *Reminiscences,* vol. 1, p. 82.

117 "the oldest-fashioned": Ibid., vol. 2, p. 172.

"to efface with": Geneviève Ward and Richard Whiteing, *Both Sides of the Curtain* (London: Cassell and Company, 1918), p. 80.

"With a little": *Reminiscences,* vol. 2, p. 173.

"You have waked": Ward and Whiteing, *Both Sides,* p. 89.

"it would be": Henry Irving to Bram Stoker, Aug. 4, 1879, Leeds.

118 "When I saw": *Reminiscences,* vol. 1, p. 84.

"seeing eye": Ibid., p. 9.

" 'Three thousand ducats' ": *Memoirs,* p. 147.

121 "Why should we": Irving, p. 358.

122 " 'enjoyed' the reputation": Farson, *The Man Who Wrote Dracula,* p. 212.

"so many 'faithful' ": Ibid., p. 234.

CHAPTER 7
*The Beefsteak Room*

123 "He took my": *Dracula,* p. 36.

"What a fine": Martin-Harvey, p. 91.

124 "If it were": "Macbeth," Shakespeare, p. 1004.

125 "It was a": Craig, p. 175.

"this ghostly impression": Christopher St. John, ed., *Ellen Terry and Bernard Shaw: A Correspondence,* p. xxvi.

126 "To the general": "Macbeth," Shakespeare, p. 1014.

"clear-cut alabaster": Martin-Harvey, p. 92.

"The range of": *Reminiscences,* vol. 1, p. 310.

"His true self": Hall Caine, "Bram Stoker: The Story of a Great Friendship," *The Daily Telegraph,* April 24, 1912.

127 "the shadow of": Showalter, *Sexual Anarchy,* p. 107.

"I understand that": Mrs. J. Comyns Carr, *Reminiscences* (London: Hutchinson, n.d.), p. 85.

128 "one of the": *Dracula,* p. 8.

129 "in an old": Violet Hunt diaries, May 27, 1882, Olin Library, Cornell University.

"It was certainly": Oscar Wilde, *Lord Arthur Savile's Crime* (London: Penguin, 1954), p. 11.

"a house of opulence": Wyndham, *Speranza,* p. 74.

130 "spotless life and": Ibid.

light-colored trousers: Hesketh Pearson, *Oscar Wilde: His Life and Wit* (New York: Harper & Brothers, 1946), p. 43.

"made me the": Philippa Knott to Eleanor Knott, 1933. Quoted with permission of Sir Rupert Hart-Davis.

"Don't you think": Irving, p. 362.

131 "an intellectual stimulant": *Reminiscences,* vol. 2, p. 27.

"some tall tree": Ibid.

132 "I was lurking": Ibid., vol. 1, p. 165.

133 "The story is": Ibid., p. 159.

134 "I am seventy": Ibid., p. 201.

"like a creature": *Times Literary Supplement,* Oct. 2, 1992, p. 3.

him a "fighter": *Reminiscences,* vol. 1, p. 200.

135 "Of all the": Ibid.

"went off, hot-foot": Ibid., p. 207.

"Your love is": Bingham, p. 232.

"Will you accept": *Letters,* Jan. 3, 1881, p. 74.

136 "red-bearded giant": *Noel Stoker Memoir,* Stoker.

137 "Bravo, Stoker! We": *Entr'Acte,* Sept. 23, 1882.

"Mr. Irving is": Ibid.

139 "a beautiful country": Bram Stoker, *Under the Sunset* (San Bernardino, Calif.: The Borgo Press, 1960), p. 1.

"grim, spectral hands": Ibid., p. 51.

"through the vapoury": Ibid., p. 76.

"the things which": Ibid., p. 37.

140 "Children of this": *The Spectator,* Nov. 12, 1881.

141 "Get *Under the Sunset*": *Punch,* n.d., Stratford.

"it was necessary": *Reminiscences,* vol. 1, p. 93.

"It was very": *Memoirs,* p. 162.

"father of modern": Bram Stoker, "Irving and Stage Lighting," *The Nineteenth Century & After,* May 1911, vol. 70, pp. 903–12.

142 "thick softness with": *Memoirs,* p. 134.

"Thou canst not": *Reminiscences,* vol. 1, p. 96.

143 "I have a": J. C. Trewin, *Benson and the Bensonians* (London: Barrie and Rockliff, 1960), p. 23.

"acting is different": Sir Frank Benson, *My Memories* (London: Ernest Benn, 1930), p. 146.

"jolly failure—Irving": Irving, p. 389.

"I would like": Billy Rose Theatre Collection, New York Public Library, undated newspaper clipping.

143 "the antique": *Actor-Managers,* p. 91.

"I am sorry": Irving, p. 390.

144 "There's no place": Hatton, p. 257.

145 "The chance simile": Ibid.

CHAPTER 8
*America*

146 "He seemed to": *Dracula,* p. 291.

"Look around in": Henry Irving to Bram Stoker, various dates, Stratford.

148 "Why not let": Billy Rose Theatre Collection, New York Public Library, unidentified newspaper clipping.

"Stoker was down": Horace Wyndham, *The Nineteen Hundreds* (New York: Thomas Seltzer, 1923), pp. 117–18.

149 "Perhaps you are": Pearson, *Oscar Wilde,* p. 199.

"the venality of": Irving, p. 351.

150 "social sewer": William Winter obituary, Robinson Locke Collection, vol. 488, Billy Rose Theatre Collection, New York Public Library.

"A loyal friend": Ibid., p. 418.

"from which an": *Reminiscences,* vol. 2, p. 368.

"a blackmail ring": J. L. Toole, *Reminiscences* (London: Hurst and Blackett, 1889), p. 175.

"certain class of": *Reminiscences,* vol. 1, p. 88.

151 "to be new": *Memoirs,* p. 201.

152 "was the kind": Irving, p. 382.

153 "It seemed like": *Reminiscences,* vol. 2, pp. 45–7.

155 "It is a": Bram Stoker to Thomas Escott, July 20, 1883, Department of Manuscripts, British Library.

"talked to the": *Percy Fitzgerald Scrapbooks,* Garrick Club, vol. 5, p. 158.

"Curly hair to": *Memoirs,* p. 198.

"If you liked": Sir Johnston Forbes-Robertson, *A Player Under Three Reigns* (London: T. Fisher Unwin, 1925), p. 185.

157 "he could not": *Memoirs,* p. 217.

"Fussie burst into": Ibid., p. 219.

"a strange, barbarous": Ibid., p. 198.

"weather-beaten vessels": *Whitman,* p. 184.

158 "Will you come": Albert Pulitzer to Bram Stoker, n.d., Leeds.

"great American bird": Bram Stoker, *A Glimpse of America,* p. 43.

160 "It's a frost": Irving, p. 424.

"No display of": Brereton, *The Life of Henry Irving,* vol. 2, p. 22.

"If that unhappy": Ibid., p. 25.

160 "The continuous music": Michael R. Booth, *Victorian Spectacular Theatre 1850–1910* (London: Routledge & Kegan Paul, 1981), p. 97.

"tall and genial": Percy Fitzgerald, *Sir Henry Irving* (London: T. Fisher Unwin, 1951), p. 157.

163 "Is this a": *Memoirs,* p. 218.

"more refined and": Hatton, p. 320.

"People keep asking": *Life,* Nov. 20, 1884.

164 "The club in": Bram Stoker, *A Glimpse of America,* p. 16.

"I have never": Hatton, vol. 2, p. 384.

"No ceremonious pomp": Ibid., p. 408.

"Americans have no": *Reminiscences,* vol. 2, p. 288.

165 "Every man is": Kaplan, *Mr. Clemens and Mark Twain,* p. 341.

"I have settled": Irving, p. 444.

"bounding in": Hatton, vol. 2, p. 278.

"One thing alone": Dalby, *Bram Stoker: A Bibliography of First Editions,* p. 79.

"I am not": *Whitman,* p. 183.

166 "to many who": Ibid., p. 180.

"the cult of": Ellmann, p. 171.

"What the love": Kaplan, *Walt Whitman: A Life,* p. 46.

"morbid inferences": *Walt Whitman, The Correspondence,* Edwin Haviland Miller, ed. (New York: NYU Press, 1977), p. 72.

"a fine handsome": Ellmann, p. 168.

"frank and outspoken": Ibid., p. 170.

"I don't see": Ibid.

167 "of leonine appearance": *Reminiscences,* vol. 2, p. 92.

168 "Well, well; what": *Reminiscences,* vol. 2, p. 105.

"large-minded": *Reminiscences,* vol. 2, p. 100.

"The English theatrical": Horace Traubel, *With Walt Whitman in Camden* (July 16, 1888–October 31, 1888) (New York: D. Appleton and Co., 1908), p. 145.

"took a shine": *Whitman,* p. 179.

CHAPTER 9
*Mephistopheles*

173 "His eyes were": *Dracula,* p. 54.

"I write much": Austin Brereton to William Winter, n.d., Folger.

"We drank all": *Reminiscences,* vol. 1, p. 309.

174 "Henry's wine and": Irving, p. 447.

" 'I'm in a' ": Ibid., p. 448.

"poor strenuous Stoker": Ibid.

174  "I am chiefly": Ibid., p. 452.

175  "were at home": Lawrence, ed., *Collected Letters,* p. 786.

"Stoker, inflated with": Irving, p. 453.

"to put by": Percy Fitzgerald, *Sir Henry Irving* (London: Fisher Unwin, 1906), p. 287.

176  "divinely inspired": Irving, p. 453.

177  "no fool and": Martin-Harvey, p. 62.

"like cinders of ": *Reminiscences,* vol. 1, p. 56.

178  "Happily the end": Bram Stoker, "The Squaw," *Midnight Tales,* Peter Haining, ed. (London: Peter Owen, 1990), pp. 96–7.

179  "As the smoke": "The Dualitists," Ibid., p. 57.

"Count Dracula in": *Dracula Notes,* Rosenbach.

180  "It will bring": *Reminiscences,* vol. 1, p. 147.

"I am Dracula": *Dracula,* p. 26.

181  "seemed to grow": Bingham, p. 218.

"a sort of ": Joseph Harker, *Studio and Stage* (London: Nisbet, 1924), p. 121.

"to a mere bald": Michael R. Booth, *Victorian Spectacular Theatre, 1850–1910* (London: Routledge & Kegan Paul, 1981), p. 119.

"startling advance in": London *Times,* Dec. 21, 1885.

182  "Hatred, malignity": Booth, *Victorian Spectacular Theatre,* p. 126.

"For look where": "Much Ado About Nothing," Shakespeare, p. 148.

"Worst 'tear girl' ": Mrs. J. Comyns Carr, *Reminiscences* (London: Hutchinson, n.d.), p. 210.

184  "Miss Terry dressed?": Ibid., p. 209.

"fine face—leonine": *Reminiscences,* vol. 1, p. 147.

185  "The little chap": Ibid., p. 140.

186  " 'You see, my' ": Martin-Harvey, p. 337.

"absorbing interest": Bram Stoker, "Irving and Stage Lighting," *The Nineteenth Century & After* 70 (May 1911): p. 912.

187  "thought of it": Ibid.

"It's worthwhile to": Martin-Harvey, p. 314.

"To Beecham or": *London Illustrated News,* Aug. 24, 1889.

"I didn't know": *Lyceum,* p. 128.

188  "anticipated words by": *Reminiscences,* vol. 2, p. 11.

"quick and searching": Ibid., p. 103.

"no holocaust, for": Ibid., p. 104.

"He is a": New York *World,* Nov. 1, 1885.

"the shuddering lines": William Winter, *Shadows of the Stage* (London: Macmillan, 1892), p. 46.

189  "Florence has suffered": Bram Stoker to James McHenry, April 9, 1883, Department of Rare Books and Special Collections, University of Rochester Library.

"a three year": Ibid., Dec. 2, 1884.

"Washington died merrily": Ibid., Feb. 11, 1885.

"I think Florence": Ibid., Jan. 7, 1885.

"Since I pressed": Ibid., April 9, 1885.

190  "all sorts of": *Reminiscences,* vol. 2, p. 368.

"keen eye for": *Pall Mall Gazette,* Dec. 29, 1885.

"my little book": *Reminiscences,* vol. 2, p. 368.

"had in it": Ibid., p. 369.

"Good! Splendid! Keen!": James Whitcomb Riley to Bram Stoker, n.d., Leeds.

191  "is better for": Bram Stoker, *A Glimpse of America,* p. 18.

"hitch up alongside": *Dracula,* p. 80.

"Its reception into": Ibid., p. 313.

"I dare not": Ibid., p. 372.

192  "is like whispering": Ibid., p. 96.

CHAPTER 10
*The Bloody Play*

194  "would have been": *Dracula,* p. 40.

"I must watch": Ibid., p. 57.

"authentic document": Ibid., p. 486.

"Masses of seafog": Ibid., p. 103.

195  "whole forepart of": Dublin *Evening News,* April 17, 1887.

197  "discipline was so": *Memoirs,* p. 228.

"a full report": *Reminiscences,* vol. 2, p. 111.

"delivered this lecture": *The New York Times,* Nov. 26, 1887.

198  "It was a": *Reminiscences,* vol. 2, p. 106.

"a dear old": *New York Review of Books,* Jan. 28, 1993, p. 9.

"It would not": *Reminiscences,* vol. 2, p. 107.

"This was my": Ibid., p. 111.

"Abraham Lincoln": poster, Modern Manuscript Collection, Department of Special Collections, University Libraries of Notre Dame.

199  "Now that the": Bram Stoker, *A Glimpse of America,* p. 39.

"brought the rugged": *The Elocutionist,* n.d., Stratford.

"received by the": *Westminster and Lambeth Gazette,* Dec. 22, 1888.

"There is a": Bram Stoker's Lincoln lecture, holograph manuscript, p. 21, Modern Manuscript Collection, Department of Special Collections, University Libraries of Notre Dame.

200 "At such times": *Reminiscences,* vol. 2, p. 274.

"She was greatly": Ibid., p. 36.

"It was rather": Martin-Harvey, p. 64.

"at arm's-length": *Reminiscences,* vol. 1, p. 59.

"I have sometimes": Ibid., p. 364.

201 "Will you give": Oscar Wilde to Florence Stoker, June 1888, *More Letters of Oscar Wilde,* ed. Rupert Hart-Davis (New York: Vanguard, 1985), p. 73.

202 "too feminine, and": *Letters,* p. 194.

203 "much higher order": Joseph Harker, *Studio and Stage* (London: Nisbet, 1924), p. 113.

"education is as": *Irving,* p. 486.

204 "he had appropriated": Harker, *Studio and Stage,* p. 135.

"I judge it": *Memoirs,* p. 135.

205 "*woman*—a mistaken": Ellen Terry to William Winter, Oct. 29, 1895, Folger.

"Lady Macbeth seems": Manvell, *Ellen Terry,* p. 198.

"on a wet": Ibid., p. 201.

206 "hurried about—here": *The Pall Mall Budget,* May 2, 1889.

207 "I have no": Bingham, p. 237.

"suddenly the castle": *Reminiscences,* vol. 1, p. 23.

"The endless procession": Ibid., p. 24.

208 "It is generally": *Memoirs,* p. 141.

"A man of": Manvell, *Ellen Terry,* p. 194.

209 "brilliant white teeth": *Dracula,* p. 53.

"It will have": "Macbeth," Shakespeare, p. 1014.

"I would, while": Ibid., p. 1005.

"flung to the": *Dracula,* p. 271.

"Behold where stands": "Macbeth," Shakespeare, p. 1026.

"See! the snow": *Dracula,* p. 485.

## CHAPTER 11
### The Occult

211 "There are mysteries": *Dracula,* p. 265.

212 "I cannot help": *The Picture of Dorian Gray,* Wilde, p. 197.

"cool, white, flower-like": Ibid., p. 162.

213 "most wonderful pack": unidentified newspaper clipping, Stratford.

216 "I have no": Anne Clark Amor, *Mrs. Oscar Wilde* (London: Sidgwick & Jackson, 1983), p. 41.

"things rotten to": R. A. Gilbert, *The Golden Dawn: Twilight of the Magicians* (San Bernardino, Calif.: Borgo Press, 1988), p. 127.

217  "Since Oscar wrote": Ellmann, p. 320.

"Live! Live the": *The Picture of Dorian Gray,* Wilde, p. 164.

"It is the": Ellmann, p. 320.

"unmanly, sickening": *The Athenaeum,* June 27, 1891.

"all art is": *The Picture of Dorian Gray,* Wilde, p. 139.

218  "When I found": *Dracula,* p. 40.

"a wild desire": Ibid., p. 70.

"laughter was the": Kendrick, *The Thrill of Fear,* p. 153.

"The Bard": Hall Caine, *My Story* (London: Heinemann, 1908), p. 177.

219  "As he goes": *Reminiscences,* vol. 2, p. 119.

220  "To Bram Stoker": Hall Caine, *Capt'n Davy's Honeymoon* (London: Heinemann, 1893), dedication page.

"piled up one": *Dracula,* p. 85.

"Trees are trees": Cincinnati *Tribune,* Dec. 4, 1910.

221  "most dictatorial person": *Dracula,* p. 86.

222  "Dracula in the": William Wilkinson, *An Account of the Principalities of Wallachia and Moldavia* (London: Longmans, 1820), p. 19.

"Onwards it rushes": Bram Stoker, *Under the Sunset* (San Bernardino, Calif.: Borgo Press, 1940), p. 85.

"a brool over": *Dracula,* p. 99.

"The piers and": Whitby *Gazette,* Oct. 25, 1885.

223  "The day was": *Dracula,* p. 101.

225  "Every boat in": Ibid., p. 115.

"a most noble": Ibid., p. 85.

"grey day . . . all": *Dracula Notes,* Rosenbach.

226  "Today is a": *Dracula,* p. 98.

"nice healthy stalwart": Violet Hunt's diary, Aug. 8, 1890, Olin Library, Cornell University.

"Bram is a": Ibid.

"You are only": Violet Hunt to Bram Stoker, n.d., Leeds.

227  "Mamma to Noel": *Punch or the London Charivari,* Sept. 11, 1886.

228  "one of the": E. V. Lucas, "The Creator of Trilby," London *Times,* March 6, 1934.

"Oriental Israelite Hebrew Jew": Leoneé Ormond, *George du Maurier* (University of Pittsburgh Press, 1969), p. 454.

"he was not": Donna Perlmutter, "Made for Each Other," Los Angeles *Times,* January 2, 1991.

229  "Here I am": *Dracula,* p. 31.

230  "philosophical Home-Ruler": *Reminiscences,* vol. 2, p. 31.

"to read—and": Ibid., p. 29.

231 "What, in the": Bram Stoker, "Dramatic Criticism," *North American Review* (March 1894): 327.

"is not a": Ludlam, p. 90.

"You could not": *Today*, March 3, 1894.

232 "Irving may do": *Reminiscences*, vol. 1, p. 225.

"He had on": Ibid., p. 233.

"Don't let them": Ibid., p. 238.

"Goodbye, my faithful": *Dracula*, p. 65.


CHAPTER 12
*Cruden Bay*

233 "There seemed a": *Dracula*, p. 29.

234 "Second visit—delighted": registry, Kilmarnock Arms Hotel.

"terrific grandeur of": James Drummond, "Dracula's Castle," *The Scotsman*, June 26, 1976.

235 "I become intoxicated": Ibid.

"The requiem": Bram Stoker, *The Watter's Mou'*, p. 164.

"very place where": *Dracula*, p. 411.

"This story will": *The Athenaeum*, Feb. 23, 1895.

236 "I feel so": *Dracula*, p. 450.

237 "with a lancet": Ibid., p. 78.

"At least God's": Ibid., p. 72.

"if they two": Ibid., p. 225.

"the most convincing": Auerbach, *Woman and the Demon*, p. 22.

"old-fashioned inn": *Dracula*, p. 118.

"If Mr. Holmwood": Ibid.

238 "I sat next": *Reminiscences*, vol. 2, p. 166.

"as cold as": *Dracula*, p. 26.

"dark, and forceful": *Reminiscences*, vol. 2, p. 350.

"upper lip rose": Ibid., p. 359.

"a tall old": *Dracula*, p. 25.

239 "I wish you": *Reminiscences*, vol. 1, p. 247.

"New play enormous": Ibid., p. 249.

"a continuous stream": Sir Arthur Conan Doyle, *The Complete Sherlock Holmes* (New York: Doubleday, n.d.), vol. 1, p. 99.

240 "The style of": *The Speaker*, Aug. 27, 1892.

"master describes me": Florence Stoker to mother, July 21, 1891, Stoker.

"writer of verses": Douglas Sladen, *Twenty Years of My Life* (London: Constable, 1915), p. 237.

240  "Madame, I go": Hesketh Pearson, *Gilbert & Sullivan* (London: Hamish Hamilton, 1935), p. 274.

241  "Don't want to": Horace Wyndham, *The Nineteen Hundreds* (New York: Thomas Seltzer, 1923), p. 120.

"I would write": W. S. Gilbert to Florence Stoker, May 7, 1897, Gilbert and Sullivan Collection, Pierpont Morgan Library.

"I feel that": Ibid., Oct. 21, 1900.

"I was as": Ibid., Sept. 16, 1904.

242  "Do you know": Theatre Museum, unidentified newspaper clipping.

243  "You can count": Harry Furniss, "Henry Irving: An Artist's Sketch of an Actor," *The Strand Magazine* (Jan. 1906): 43.

"What Mr. Irving": Holroyd, *Bernard Shaw: The Pursuit of Power,* p. 348.

244  "Knighthood sits like": Irving, p. 578.

"I am very": *Reminiscences,* vol. 2, p. 240.

"me, with my": *Dracula,* p. 227.

"the centre of": Ellmann, p. 477.

"Open the windows": Ibid., p. 479.

"To think of": Coulson Kernahan, *In Good Company* (London: John Lane, 1957), p. 235.

245  "There was always": William Winter to Augustin Daly, April 7, 1895, Folger.

"childish love of": Irving, p. 579.

"Bram, my friend": Willie Wilde to Bram Stoker, July 16, 1895, Leeds.

247  "My dear Florence": Oscar Wilde to Florence Stoker, Feb. 21, 1893, *Letters,* p. 330.

"One of the": *The Athenaeum,* June 22, 1895.

## CHAPTER 13
### *Shaw's Dilemma*

251  "All men are": *Dracula,* p. 156.

"revive the rotting": Holroyd, *Bernard Shaw: The Search for Love,* vol. 1, p. 351.

252  "extraordinary insensibility to": Ibid., p. 358.

"up in a": Ibid.

253  "no lovers, only": Ibid., p. 368.

"a born actress": Ibid., p. 347.

"But if you": Ibid., p. 354.

254  "answering his helm": Irving, p. 600.

"I am sorry": Ibid., p. 604.

"I have never": Ibid.

"What I cared": Ibid., p. 606.

"I think he": *Memoirs,* p. 271.

254   "Your career has": Holroyd, *Shaw: Search*, p. 366.

     "I recognize that": Peters, *Bernard Shaw and the Actresses*, p. 266.

256   "in a nightmarish": *Noel Stoker Memoir*, Stoker.

     "Young man goes": *Dracula Notes*, March 8, 1890, Rosenbach.

     "Mina is sleeping": *Dracula*, p. 399.

     "She was so": Ibid., p. 475.

     "The sexual threat": Craft, " 'Kiss Me with Those Red Lips.' "

257   "a fragment": Christopher Frayling, *Vampyres*, p. 126.

258   " 'Tis now the": "Hamlet," Shakespeare, p. 1052.

     "I sympathize with": *Dracula*, p. 79.

     "Was this fair": "Othello," Shakespeare, p. 1144.

259   "Think dear, that": *Dracula*, p. 426.

260   "a composite picture": Florescu and McNally, *Dracula: Prince of Many Faces*, p. 9.

     "I have asked": *Dracula*, p. 309.

     "describe old dead": *Dracula Notes*, n.d., Rosenbach.

261   "There is throughout": *Dracula*, p. 6.

262   "however hard the": *Dracula Notes*, n.d., Rosenbach.

264   "an excellent roast": *Dracula*, p. 28.

265   "You yourself never": Ibid., p. 55.

     originally written: *Dracula* typescript manuscript, private collection. Quoted with permission.

     "And you, their": *Dracula*, p. 370.

     "As she spoke": *Dracula* typescript manuscript, private collection. Quoted with permission.

267   "But, on the": *Dracula*, p. 484.

268   "As we looked": *Dracula* typescript manuscript, private collection. Quoted with permission.

     "Your girls that": *Dracula*, p. 394.

## CHAPTER 14
### Dracula Debuts

270   "How did you": Irving's "dreadful" comment has become part of the Stoker myth. Stoker's son, Noel, told the story to Harry Ludlam, Stoker's first biographer.

     "simply would not": *Memoirs*, p. 119.

271   "to read, mark": G. A. Redford to Bram Stoker, May 9, 1897, Leeds.

272   "This series of": Richard Dalby, ed., *Dracula/Lair of the White Worm* (London: W. Foulsham, 1986), p. 11.

274   "a first cousin": *Punch*, June 14, 1897.

274   "an appreciative notice": Edgar Pemberton to Bram Stoker, Oct. 8, 1895,
      Leeds.

      "constructive art in": *The Athenaeum,* June 26, 1897, p. 835.

      "My dear, it": Charlotte Stoker to Bram Stoker, n.d., Stoker.

      "It is a": Bram Stoker to W. E. Gladstone, May 24, 1897, Department of
      Manuscripts, British Library.

275   "If I enjoy": H. M. Alden to Bram Stoker, Oct. 29, 1899, Leeds.

      "I have done": Mary Elizabeth Braddon to Bram Stoker, June 23, 1897, Leeds.

      "Your vampires robbed": Anthony Hope Hawkins to Bram Stoker, Jan. 27,
      1898, Leeds.

      "I think it": Arthur Conan Doyle to Bram Stoker, Aug. 20, 1897, Harry
      Ransom Humanities Research Center, the University of Texas at Austin.

      "As soon as": Philip Burne-Jones to Bram Stoker, June 16, 1897, Leeds.

276   "most lovely lady": *The Era,* Feb. 6, 1897.

      "have to be": Bram Stoker to Hall Caine, June 27, 1897, private collection.

277   "the writing wants": Hall Caine to Bram Stoker, Oct. 24, 1891, The Henry
      W. and Albert A. Berg Collection, Astor, Lenox, and Tilden Foundations,
      New York Public Library.

      "A slight sketch": J. W. Arrowsmith to Bram Stoker, Jan. 7, 1895, Leeds.

      "A pretty little": *The Era,* March 12, 1898.

278   "If there is": Irving, p. 632.

279   "had no part": *Reminiscences,* vol. 2, p. 335.

280   "Life lost part": Ibid., p. 338.

      "Ah, yes; Old": Ibid.

      "the old long": Ibid.

      "diary seems horribly": *Dracula,* p. 43.

281   "always thought to": Irving, p. 633.

      "that we never": *Memoirs,* p. 250.

      "Personally I have": George Bernard Shaw to Bram Stoker, draft reply,
      May 2, 1898, the Department of Manuscripts, British Library.

282   "ogre's den": Holroyd, *Bernard Shaw: The Pursuit of Power,* p. 25.

      "know how to": Walt Whitman, "Children of Adam," *Leaves of Grass* (New
      York: Modern Library, 1957), p. 86.

      "I am glad": Mark Twain to Bram Stoker, Feb. 13, 1894, The Mark Twain
      Project, Bancroft Library, University of California, Berkeley.

283   "Bram Stoker must": *Mark Twain's Correspondence with Henry Huttleston
      Rogers,* ed. Lewis Leary (Berkeley: University of California Press, 1969), p. 100.

      "tell Irving": Ibid., p. 114.

284   "Let me illustrate": *Dracula,* p. 249.

      "seen the great": Mark Twain, *Mysterious Stranger Manuscripts* (Berkeley:
      University of California Press, 1969), p. 668.

284 "about Commodore Vanderbilt": The Mark Twain Project, Unpublished Notebook 39, p. 41, Bancroft Library, University of California, Berkeley.

"a mangy cur": Mark Twain to Bram Stoker, Nov. 2, 1896, Henry W. and Albert A. Berg Collection, Astor, Lenox, and Tilden Foundations, New York Public Library.

285 "Tossing in that": *Reminiscences,* vol. 2, p. 289.

286 "And Bram Stoker": Detroit *Free Press,* Nov. 18, 1899.

288 "Known merely as": Detroit *Tribune,* Jan. 24, 1902.

"But who is": Ellen Terry to George Bernard Shaw, Feb. 18, 1898, *Ellen Terry and Bernard Shaw: A Correspondence,* ed. St. John, p. 219.

"I wonder what": *Irving,* p. 611.

"a humour and": Ibid.

### CHAPTER 15
*Farewells*

289 "I was a": Wilde, *De Profundis,* p. 514.

"My wallpaper and": Ellmann, p. 581.

" 'Euthanasia' is an": *Dracula,* p. 432.

291 "certain of one": Irving, p. 646.

"as a man": Martin-Harvey, p. 192.

"A fine subject": Irving, p. 649.

292 "Mention was made": Billy Rose Theatre Collection, New York Public Library, unidentified newspaper fragment.

"An Irishman's luck": Boston *Herald,* April 6, 1902.

293 "It represented the": Glasgow *Herald,* Nov. 8, 1902.

"spoke without a": Manchester *Sunday Chronicle,* Nov. 9, 1902.

294 "When first I": Bram Stoker, *The Mystery of the Sea* (New York: Doubleday, 1902), p. 7.

295 "I knew something": Ibid., p. 89.

"I am never": Ibid., p. 87.

"that the further": *Dracula,* p. 9.

296 "almost if not": Bram Stoker, *A Glimpse of America,* p. 24.

"In the case": *Sunday Special,* Aug. 10, 1902.

"distinctly fine": J. W. Brodie Innis to Bram Stoker, July 20, 1902, Leeds.

"I've done a": Ludlam, p. 123.

297 "tale of mystery": Aberdeen *Journal,* Nov. 30, 1903.

"story which begins": Boston *Herald,* March 5, 1904.

"It is not": J. W. Brodie Innis to Bram Stoker, Jan. 29, 1903, Leeds.

"enhance the author's": *The Literary World,* Sept. 1905.

298 "Like a miserly": *The Outlook,* Sept. 23, 1905.

298 "some beautiful grey": *Memoirs,* p. 261.

"What a wonderful": Irving, p. 658.

299 "seemed tired, tired": *Reminiscences,* vol. 2, p. 353.

300 "A kindly continent": Irving, p. 669.

"My counsel is": Ibid., p. 670.

301 "You have been": *Reminiscences,* vol. 2, p. 356.

302 "Muffle up your": Ibid., p. 357.

"It was all": Ibid., p. 359.

"It's summer done": Irving, p. 671.

303 "The request, the": Ibid., p. 672.

"up everything for": Letters to Bram Stoker, various dates, Leeds.

304 "We are filled": Thornley Stoker to Bram Stoker, Oct. 15, 1905, Leeds.

306 "lifting her little": Shaw, *Collected Letters (1926–1950),* ed. Dan H. Laurence (New York: Viking, 1988), p. 206.

"on the public": *Memoirs,* p. 191.

"No face there": Manvell, *Ellen Terry,* p. 257.

CHAPTER 16
*The Last Wave*

307 "We have been": *Dracula,* p. 403.

"It is, I": *Noel Stoker Memoir,* Stoker.

"a man cannot": *Whitman,* p. 182.

308 "Looking back I": *Reminiscences,* vol. 1, p. 34.

"built a monument": *The Sketch,* Oct. 24, 1906.

"an illuminating account": *The Bookman,* Dec. 1906.

"a fact, a": Brereton, *The Life of Henry Irving,* vol. 1, p. vii.

310 "Behave as if": Holroyd, *Bernard Shaw: The Pursuit of Power,* p. 31.

311 "the most famous": Ibid., p. 173.

"because you are": London *Daily Chronicle,* Jan. 15, 1908.

"If I were": Thomas Hardy to Bram Stoker, July 1, 1907, Miller Library, Colby College.

"a worn-out": Andrew Carnegie to Bram Stoker, Aug. 7, 1907, Leeds.

312 "This abomination": Los Angeles *Times,* Oct. 20, 1907.

"Prurient Novel is": Ibid.

"A close analysis": Bram Stoker, "The Censorship of Fiction," *The Nineteenth Century & After* 64 (Sept. 1908): 479–87.

"an ordinary official": Holroyd, *Shaw: Pursuit,* p. 225.

313 "a loftier distinction": Kaplan, *Mr. Clemens and Mark Twain,* p. 381.

"what a real": Ibid., p. 382.

313 "Fine, tell us": Henry W. Fisher, *Abroad With Mark Twain and Eugene Field* (New York: Nicholas L. Brown, 1922), p. 181.

"a drunken savage": Ibid., p. 152.

"the most advertised": Kaplan, *Mr. Clemens,* p. 382.

314 "was forced to": New York *Tribune,* April 23, 1891.

"The house was": *Municipal Gazette,* London, n.d., Stratford, and *Mark Twain Speaking,* ed. Paul Fatout (University of Iowa Press, 1976), p. 254.

"it looks to": *The Tatler,* Oct. 30, 1907.

"Stoke Poges and": *Punch,* March 15, 1911.

315 "not to take": Bram Stoker to Sir Thornley Stoker, Nov. 11, 1910, Stoker.

"I can now": Ibid., July 18, 1910.

"Not much for": Ibid., [Dec.] 1910.

"It is harder": Ibid., Jan. 11, 1911.

"the excellent skin": Oliver St. John Gogarty, *As I Was Going Down Sackville Street* (London: Rich & Cowan, 1937), p. 292.

316 "mahogany door": Ibid., p. 293.

"my dear lost": Michael Millgate, *Thomas Hardy* (New York: Random House, 1982), p. 464.

"At the beginning": Bram Stoker to A. Llewelyn Roberts, secretary, Feb. 25, 1911, Royal Literary Fund. Department of Manuscripts, British Library.

"This is not": Henry F. Dickens, Ibid., Feb. 24, 1911.

"I have enjoyed": W. S. Gilbert, Ibid., Feb. 25, 1911.

"This, I fancy": Bram Stoker to W. S. Gilbert, March 12, 1911, Leeds.

317 "Her woman's quick": Bram Stoker, *The Lady of the Shroud,* p. 161.

"our strong game": Bram Stoker, "The Lair of the White Worm," *Bram Stoker's Dracula Omnibus* (London: Orion, 1992), p. 389.

321 "locomotor ataxia generally": Dr. W. F. Bynum in letter to author, May 29, 1992.

"If Stoker had": Dr. R. B. Gibberd to author, telephone interview, May 12, 1992.

"the master of": London *Times,* April 22, 1912.

"a typical Irishman": *Irish Times,* April 22, 1912.

"had a genius": *Daily Telegraph,* April 22, 1912.

"Few 'intimates' of": Pittsburgh *Gazette,* May 5, 1912.

322 "I have spread": William Butler Yeats, "He Wishes for the Cloths of Heaven," *The Collected Poems* (New York: Macmillan, 1957), p. 70.

## EPILOGUE

323 "My revenge is": *Dracula,* p. 394.

"She may very": Martin Seymour-Smith, *Hardy* (New York: St. Martin's Press, 1994), p. 700.

323  "Aunt E wouldn't": Florence Stoker to Noel Stoker, June 26 and 29, 1933, Stoker.

325  "To Bram Stoker": Catalogue of the Library of the Late Bram Stoker, Esq., Sotheby, Wilkinson & Hodge, July 7, 1913, p. 7.

"that poor O.": Florence Stoker to Philippa Knott, March 14, 1923. Quoted with permission of Sir Rupert Hart-Davis.

"He keeps in": Ibid.

"I wanted him": Ibid., Jan. 30, 1937.

"The [Robert] Sherard book": Ibid.

"I have never": Ibid., n.d.

"Came home in": Ibid., Dec. 17, 1929, Trinity College Library, Dublin.

326  "a mistake to": Ibid., Jan. 31, 1921.

"frail and small": Vincent Price to author, telephone interview, Jan. 7, 1992.

"an ornament not": *Noel Stoker Memoir,* Stoker.

327  "I want to": Florence Stoker to G. Herbert Thring, Aug. 20, 1925, Society of Authors' Archives, the Department of Manuscripts, British Library.

"Your secretary omitted": Ibid., Feb. 20, 1925.

"I am quite": Ibid., May 12, 1925.

"I am glad": Ibid., July 20, 1925.

328  "Surely the German": Ibid., Oct. 14, 1925.

"are not worth much": Florence Stoker to G. Herbert Thring, April 9, 1936 (Noel quoted in letter).

"is considered my": Bram Stoker, "Dracula's Guest," preface by Florence Stoker, *Bram Stoker's Dracula Omnibus* (London: Orion, 1992), p. 430.

"I thought the": G. S. Street, March 27, 1924, Lord Chamberlain's Collection, the Department of Manuscripts, British Library.

329  "Dracula made my": Douglas Dawson and Somerset Alcombs, May 11, 1924, Ibid.

"So well did": undated newspaper fragments, Stratford.

"There is very": Ibid.

"whether such a": *The Era,* Feb. 16, 1927.

"I am Dracula": *Dracula,* Feb. 1, 1930, Lord Chamberlain's Collection, the Department of Manuscripts, British Library.

330  "avoids any of": Ibid.

"I shall remember": Stratford, unidentified newspaper clipping.

331  "to eradicate all": *The New Yorker,* June 29, 1992, p. 86.

"I'd never seen": *Actor-Managers,* p. 51.

# Selected Bibliography

## BOOKS

Archer, William. *The Theatrical World of 1893–1897.* 5 vols. London: Walter Scott, 1894–98.

———. Henry Irving, *Actor and Manager: A Critical Study.* London: Field & Tuer, n.d.

Auerbach, Nina. *Ellen Terry: Player in Her Time.* New York: Norton, 1987.

———. *Woman and the Demon: The Life of a Victorian Myth.* Cambridge: Harvard University Press, 1982.

Bingham, Madeleine. *Henry Irving: The Greatest Victorian Actor.* New York: Stein and Day, 1978.

Bloom, Clive, ed. *Nineteenth-Century Suspense: From Poe to Conan Doyle.* London: Macmillan Press, 1988. Chapters: Anne Cranny-Francis, "Sexual Politics and Political Repression in Bram Stoker's *Dracula,*" pp. 64–79; Philip Martin, "The Vampire in the Looking-Glass: Reflection and Projection in Bram Stoker's *Dracula,*" pp. 80–92.

Brereton, Austin. *The Life of Henry Irving.* 2 vols. London: Longmans, Green, 1908.

Carter, Margaret L., ed. *Dracula: The Vampire and the Critics.* Ann Arbor: UMI Research Press, 1988.

Craig, Edward Gordon. *Henry Irving.* New York: Longmans, 1939.

———. *Ellen Terry and Her Secret Self.* London: Sampson Low, 1931.

Cunningham, Gail. *The New Woman and the Victorian Novel.* New York: Barnes and Noble, 1978.

Dalby, Richard. *Bram Stoker: A Bibliography of First Editions.* London: Dracula Press, 1983.

Dijkstra, Bram. *Idols of Perversity: Fantasies of Feminine Evil in Fin-de-Siècle Culture.* New York: Oxford University Press, 1986.

Donaldson, Frances. *The Actor-Managers.* London: Weidenfeld & Nicolson, 1970.

Du Maurier, George. *Trilby: A Novel.* New York: Harper, 1899.

Ellmann, Richard. *Oscar Wilde.* New York: Alfred A. Knopf, 1988.

Farson, Daniel. *The Man Who Wrote Dracula: A Biography of Bram Stoker.* London: Michael Joseph, 1975.

Florescu, Radu R., and Raymond T. McNally. *Dracula: Prince of Many Faces.* New York: Little, Brown, 1989.

———. *The Essential Dracula.* New York: Mayflower Books, 1979.

———. *Dracula: A Biography of Vlad the Impaler.* New York: Hawthorn Books, 1973.

———. *In Search of Dracula.* Greenwich, Conn.: New York Graphic Society, 1972.

Frayling, Christopher. *Vampyres: Lord Byron to Count Dracula.* London: Faber and Faber, 1991.

Freud, Sigmund. "Totem and Taboo," *The Standard Edition of the Complete Psychological Works of Sigmund Freud,* ed. James Strachey. Vol. 13. London: Hogarth, 1955.

———. "The 'Uncanny.' " Ibid., Vol. 17.

Gilbert, Sandra M., and Susan Gubar. *The Madwoman in the Attic: The Woman Writer and the Nineteenth-Century Literary Imagination.* New Haven: Yale University Press, 1979.

Gittings, Robert. *Thomas Hardy's Later Years.* Boston: Little, Brown, 1978.

Haining, Peter, ed. *Shades of Dracula: The Uncollected Stories of Bram Stoker.* London: Kimber, 1982.

———. *The Midnight People.* New York: Popular Library, 1968.

Hart-Davis, Rupert, ed. *The Letters of Oscar Wilde.* New York: Harcourt, Brace & World, Inc., 1962.

Hatton, Joseph. *Henry Irving's Impressions of America.* London: Sampson Low, Marston, Searle, & Rivington, 1884.

Heilbrun, Carolyn G. *Toward a Recognition of Androgyny.* New York: Harper & Row, 1973.

Holroyd, Michael. *Bernard Shaw: The Pursuit of Power.* Vol. 2. London: Penguin, 1989.

———. *Bernard Shaw: The Search for Love.* Vol. 1. London: Chatto & Windus, 1988.

Irving, Laurence. *Henry Irving, The Actor and His World.* London: Faber and Faber, 1951.

Jones, Ernest. *On the Nightmare.* New York: Liveright, 1971.

Kaplan, Justin. *Walt Whitman: A Life.* New York: Simon & Schuster, 1980.

———. *Mr. Clemens and Mark Twain.* New York: Touchstone, 1966.

Kendrick, Walter. *The Thrill of Fear.* New York: Grove Weidenfeld, 1991.

Leatherdale, Clive. *The Origins of Dracula.* London: William Kimber, 1987.

———. *Dracula: The Novel and the Legend.* Wellingborough, Northamptonshire: The Aquarian Press, 1985.

Ludlam, Harry. *A Biography of Dracula: The Life Story of Bram Stoker.* London: Foulsham, 1962.

MacAndrew, Elizabeth. *The Gothic Tradition in Fiction.* New York: Columbia University Press, 1979.

McCormack, W. J. *Sheridan Le Fanu and Victorian Ireland.* Dublin: The Lilliput Press, 1991.

Manvell, Roger. *Ellen Terry.* London: Heinemann, 1968.

Marcus, Stephen. *The Other Victorians: A Study of Sexuality and Pornography in Mid-Nineteenth Century England.* New York: Basic Books, 1974.

Martin-Harvey, Sir John. *The Autobiography of Sir John Martin-Harvey.* London: Sampson Low, Marston, n.d.

Maturin, Charles Robert. *Melmoth the Wanderer.* Oxford: Oxford University Press, 1979.

Meisel, Martin. *Shaw and the Nineteenth Century Theatre.* Princeton: Princeton University Press, 1963.

Miyoshi, Masao. *The Divided Self: A Perspective on the Literature of the Victorians.* New York: New York University Press, 1969.

Osborne, Charles, ed. *The Bram Stoker Bedside Companion.* London: Quartet, 1974.

Peters, Margot. *House of Barrymore.* New York: Knopf, 1990.

———. *Mrs. Pat.* New York: Knopf, 1984.

———. *Bernard Shaw and the Actresses.* Garden City, N.Y.: Doubleday, 1980.

Pick, John. *The West End.* London: John Offord, 1983.

Polidori, John. *The Vampyre.* Tring, Herts.: Gubblecote Press, 1973.

Praz, Mario. *The Romantic Agony.* London: Oxford University Press, 1933.

Prideaux, Tom. *Love or Nothing: The Life and Times of Ellen Terry.* New York: Scribner's, 1975.

Roth, Phyllis A. *Bram Stoker.* Boston: Twayne Publishers, 1982.

Rowell, George. *The Victorian Theatre.* London: Oxford University Press, 1956.

Scott, Constance. *Old Days in Bohemian London.* London: Hutchinson, 1919.

Shaw, Bernard. *Collected Letters 1926–1950.* Dan H. Laurence, ed. New York: Viking, 1988.

Showalter, Elaine. *Sexual Anarchy: Gender and Culture at the Fin de Siècle.* New York: Viking, 1990.

Steen, Marguerite. *A Pride of Terrys: Family Saga.* London: Longmans, 1962.

Summers, Montague. *The Vampire: His Kith and Kin.* London: Routledge and Kegan Paul, 1928.

Symonds, John Addington, and Havelock Ellis. *Sexual Inversion.* London: Wilson and Macmillan, 1897.

Tennyson, Charles. *Alfred Tennyson.* London: Macmillan, 1950.

Terry, Ellen. *Ellen Terry's Memoirs.* Edith Craig and Christopher St. John, eds. London: Victor Gollancz, 1933.

Terry, Ellen, and Bernard Shaw. *Ellen Terry and Bernard Shaw: A Correspondence.* Christopher St. John, ed. New York: Putnam, 1932.

Traubel, Horace. *With Walt Whitman in Camden* (January 21 to April 7, 1889). Sculley Bradley, ed. Philadelphia: University of Pennsylvania Press, 1953.

Twitchell, James. *Dreadful Pleasures: An Anatomy of Modern Horror.* New York: Oxford University Press, 1985.

———. *The Living Dead: A Study of the Vampire in Romantic Literature.* Durham: Duke University Press, 1981.

Wilson, A. E. *The Lyceum.* London: Dennis Yates, 1952.

Winter, William. *Shadows of the Stage.* London: Macmillan, 1895.

Wolf, Leonard, ed. *The Essential Dracula.* New York: Penguin, 1993.

———. *The Annotated Dracula.* New York: Clarkson N. Potter, 1975.

Wolf, Leonard. *A Dream of Dracula: In Search of the Living Dead.* New York: Little, Brown, and Co., 1972.

Wyndham, Horace. *Nights in London.* London: The Bodley Head, 1925.

## ARTICLES

Bentley, C. F. "The Monster in the Bedroom." *Literature and Psychology* 22 (1972): 27–34.

Bierman, Joseph S. "The Genesis and Dating of *Dracula* from Bram Stoker's Working Notes." *Notes and Queries* 24 (1977): 39–41.

———. "Dracula: Prolonged Childhood Illness, and the Oral Triad." *American Imago* 29 (1972): 186–98.

Craft, Christopher. " 'Kiss Me with Those Red Lips': Gender and Inversion in Bram Stoker's *Dracula*." *Representations* 8 (1984): 107–33.

Dalby, Richard. "Bram Stoker." *Book and Magazine Collector* (London, Oct. 1991): 4–14.

Demetrakopoulos, Stephanie. "Feminism, Sex Roles Exchanges, and Other Subliminal Fantasies in Bram Stoker's *Dracula*." *Frontiers: A Journal of Women's Studies* 2 (1977): 104–13.

Fry, Carrol L. "Fictional Conventions and Sexuality in *Dracula*." *Victorian Newsletter* 42 (1972): 20–22.

Griffin, Gail B. " 'Your Girls That You All Love Are Mine': Dracula and the Victorian Male Sexual Imagination." *International Journal of Women's Studies* 5 (1980): 454–65.

Howes, Marjorie. "The Mediation of the Feminine: Bisexuality, Homoerotic Desire, and Self-Expression in Bram Stoker's *Dracula*." *Texas Studies in Literature and Language* 30 (spring 1988): 104–19.

Johnson, Alan. "Bent and Broken Necks: Signs of Design in Stoker's *Dracula*." *The Victorian Newsletter* 72 (1987): 133–9.

———. "Dual Life: The Status of Women in Stoker's *Dracula*." *Tennessee Studies in Literature* 27 (1984): 20–39.

MacGillivray, Royce. "*Dracula:* Bram Stoker's Spoiled Masterpiece." *Queen's Quarterly* 79 (1972): 518–27.

Pope, Rebecca A. "Writing and Biting in *Dracula.*" *Lit: Literature Interpretation Theory,* vol. 1 (March 1990): 199–216.

Richardson, Maurice. "The Psychoanalysis of Ghost Stories." *Twentieth Century* 166 (1959): 419–31.

Schaffer Talia. "A Wilde Desire Took Me: The Homoerotic History of *Dracula.*" *ELH* (summer 1993): 381–425.

Sedgwick, Eve Kosofsky. "The Character in the Veil: Imagery of the Surface in the Gothic Novel." *PMLA* 96 (1981): 255–70.

Senf, Carol A. "Polidori's *The Vampyre:* Combining the Gothic with Realism." *North Dakota Quarterly* 56 (1988): 179–208.

———. "*Dracula:* Stoker's Response to the New Woman." *Victorian Studies* 26 (1982): 33–49.

———. "*Dracula:* The Unseen Face in the Mirror." *Journal of Narrative Technique* 9 (1979): 160–70.

Stevenson, John Allen. "A Vampire in the Mirror: The Sexuality of *Dracula.*" *PMLA* 103 (1988): 139–49.

Weissman, Judith. "Women and Vampires: *Dracula* as a Victorian Novel." *Midwest Quarterly* 18 (1977): 392–405.

## BOOKS BY BRAM STOKER
### First Standard British Editions

*The Duties of Clerks of Petty Sessions in Ireland.* Dublin: John Falconer, 1879.

*Under the Sunset.* London: Sampson Low, Marston, Searle, and Rivington, 1881.

*A Glimpse of America.* London: Sampson Low, Marston & Co., 1886.

*The Snake's Pass.* London: Sampson Low, Marston, Searle & Rivington, 1890.

*The Watter's Mou'.* London: Constable, 1895.

*The Shoulder of Shasta.* London: Constable, 1895.

*Dracula.* London: Constable, 1897.

*Miss Betty.* London: Pearson, 1898.

*The Mystery of the Sea.* London: Heinemann, 1902.

*The Jewel of Seven Stars.* London: Heinemann, 1903.

*The Man.* London: Heinemann, 1905.

*Personal Reminiscences of Henry Irving,* 2 vols. London: Heinemann, 1906.

*Lady Athlyne.* London: Heinemann, 1908.

*Snowbound: The Record of a Theatrical Touring Party.* London: Collier, 1908.

*The Lady of the Shroud.* London: Heinemann, 1909.

*Famous Impostors.* London: Sidgwick & Jackson, 1910.

*The Lair of the White Worm.* London: Rider, 1911.

*Dracula's Guest—And Other Weird Stories.* London: Routledge, 1914.

# Index

British Library, 92, *93*
Brock, Thomas, 125*n*
Brodie-Innis, J. W., 213, 296, 297
Brown, Ford Madox, 153
Brown, Hannah Meredith, 115
Browne, James, 315, 319, 320–1
Browning, Robert, 130, 178
Browning, Tod, 330
Bryan, Alfred, *176*
Burdett-Coutts, Baroness Angela
  Georgina, 115–16, 117–18, 148
Burne-Jones, Edward, 178, 203
Burne-Jones, Philip, 275
Burnett, Frances Hodgson, 130
Burton, Sir Richard F., 25, 135, 238
Bynum, W. F., 321
Byron, George Gordon, Lord, 257

Caine, Hall, 126–7, 218–20, *219*, 244–5,
  276, 277, 308, 309, 322
"Calamus" (Whitman), 39, 166
*Captain Brassbound's Conversion* (Shaw),
  254, 309–10
*Capt'n Davy's Honeymoon* (Caine), 220
Carlyle, Thomas, 39, 128, 211
*Carmilla* (Le Fanu), 25, 132
Carnegie, Andrew, 311
Carr, Alice, 178, 184
Carr, Joe Comyns, 178, 278–9
Carrington, Charles, 312
Carte, Richard D'Oyly, 241
Castle of the King, *10*
Cavendish, Ava, 54
censorship, 198, 311–12; *Dracula* and, 271–2,
  328–30
Chadwick, George, 33
Charcot, Jean-Martin, 212
Charlemont, Lord, 18
"Children of Adam" (Whitman), 39, 44,
  282
cholera epidemic of 1832, 18–19, 22
"Chronicle of Young Satan, The" (Twain),
  284
Churchill, Winston, 311, 324–5
Cleopatra's Needle, 63
Clontarf, Ireland, 17, 18
clubs, theatrical and literary, 164
Cockburn, W. V., 140
Cody, Buffalo Bill, 187
Coleridge, Samuel Taylor, 188, 258
Collins, Wilkie, 122, 261
Collinson, Walter, 156, *156*, 163, 207–8, *208*,
  276–7, 302, 306

Congreve, William, 35
*Corsican Brothers, The* (Boucicault), 130,
  132–3
Coutts, Thomas, 115
Craft, Christopher, 256
Craig, Edith, 103, 270, *285*, *286*
Craig, Edward Gordon, 71, 74, 100, 103,
  125, 203, 308
Craven, Hawes, 118, 178, 202–3
Crawford, Oswald, 226
Crescent, The (Stoker residence in Clon-
  tarf), 17, 18
Critchett, Sir Anderson, 303
Crookit Lum (Stoker residence in Whin-
  nyfold), 294, *295*
Cruden Bay, Scotland, 204, 233–4, 235, 255,
  *255*, 276, 294
*Cup, The* (Tennyson), 135
Curzon, Lord, 313
*Cymbeline*, 54, 259

Daly, Augustin, 96, 245
Damala, Jacques, 238
*Dante* (Sardou), 291–2
deaf and dumb education, 27
Deane, Hamilton, 328
Dearg-due (Irish vampire), 64
Delmonico's restaurant, 158
*De Profundis* (Wilde), 289
*Devil's Mistress, The* (Brodie-Innis), 213
Dickens, Charles, 115, 122, 211
Dickens, Henry, 316
Dickens, Mrs. Henry, *133*
*Dictionary of National Biography*, xv
Diderot, Denis, 79
Dijkstra, Bram, xii
*Dmitry* (beached ship), 222, *224*
Dobbs, Noël, xiii
"Dolores" (Swinburne), 74*n*
Donaldson, Thomas, 197, 198
*Don Quixote* (Cervantes), 242–3, 244
doppelgänger myth, 132
Doré, Gustave, 92
Dormer, Daniel, 212
Douglas, Lord Alfred, 129–30
Dowden, Edward, 40, *41*, 44, 45, 82, 168
Doyle, Arthur Conan, 239–40, 275, 296,
  311, 319
*Dracula* (film), 272, 330
*Dracula* (Stoker), xv, 14, 78, 81, 161, 235,
  331; Americanisms in, 191; anti-Semitic
  elements, 228; autobiographical nature,
  5, 7, 9; blood transfusions, 19, 237;

# Photographic and Illustration Credits

### Prologue

Henry Irving: From *Reminiscences of Henry Irving* by Bram Stoker. London: Heinemann, 1906.

### Part 1

The Castle of the King: From *Under the Sunset* by Bram Stoker. London: Sampson Low, Marston, Searle, and Rivington, 1881.

### CHAPTER 1

Bram Stoker: Courtesy of Noël Dobbs.

Charlotte Stoker: Courtesy of Noël Dobbs.

### CHAPTER 2

Abraham Stoker: Courtesy of Ann Stoker.

Edward Dowden: From *With Walt Whitman in Camden* by Horace Traubel. Boston: Small Maynard & Company, 1906.

Walt Whitman: Courtesy of Duke University Library, Trent Collection.

### CHAPTER 3

*The Bells*: Courtesy of Leslie Shepard.

Theatre Announcements: Courtesy of the National Library of Ireland.

Dublin *Evening Mail*: Courtesy of the National Library of Ireland.

Oscar Wilde: Courtesy of the William Andrews Clark Memorial Library, University of California, Los Angeles.

Sir William Wilde: Courtesy of the William Andrews Clark Memorial Library, University of California, Los Angeles.

*The Shamrock*: Courtesy of the National Library of Ireland.

## CHAPTER 4

H. J. Loveday: Reproduced with permission from *Henry Irving* by Laurence Irving. London: Faber and Faber, 1951.

Watercolor: Courtesy of Ann Stoker.

Florence Anne Lemon Balcombe: Courtesy of the Harry Ransom Humanities Research Center Art Collection, the University of Texas at Austin.

Florence Balcombe: Courtesy of Ann Stoker.

## *Part 2*

The Lyceum Theatre: Courtesy of the author.

## CHAPTER 5

The Round Reading Room: Courtesy of the British Library.

The Lyceum: From *The Graphic,* May 21, 1881. Courtesy of the Theatre Museum, London.

David Garrick: From *A Century of Great Actors* by Cecil Ferard. London: Armstrong, Mills & Boon, 1912.

Edmund Kean: From *A Century of Great Actors* by Cecil Ferard. London: Armstrong, Mills & Boon, 1912.

Ellen Terry: From *Reminiscences of Henry Irving* by Bram Stoker. London: Heinemann, 1906.

## CHAPTER 6

Henry Irving: From a photograph by Lock & Whitfield, London.

Geneviève Ward: From *Both Sides of the Curtain* by Geneviève Ward. London: Cassell & Co, 1918.

Henry Irving: From *Henry Irving* by Laurence Irving. London: Faber and Faber, 1951.

Ellen Terry: Courtesy of the author.

## CHAPTER 7

The Beefsteak Room: From *The English Illustrated Magazine,* September 1890.

Lady Jane Wilde: Courtesy of the William Andrews Clark Memorial Library, University of California, Los Angeles.

William Ewart Gladstone: Courtesy of Clwyd Record Office, Wales.

Mrs. Henry Dickens and Stoker: Courtesy of Ann Stoker.

Alfred, Lord Tennyson: Courtesy of the Tennyson Research Centre, Lincoln.

Florence and Noel Stoker: Courtesy of Ann Stoker.

Sroker's Rescue: From *The Penny Illustrated,* November 4, 1882.

The Invisible Giant: From *Under the Sunset* by Bram Stoker. London: Sampson Low, Marston, Searle, and Rivington, 1881.

## CHAPTER 8

Bram Stoker: Courtesy of Ann Stoker.

William Charles Macready: From *A Century of Great Actors* by Cecil Ferard. London: Armstrong, Mills & Boon, 1912.

The Lyceum's American Tour: From *The Entr'Acte,* October 6, 1883.

Banquet at St. James's Hall: From *The Illustrated Sporting and Dramatic News,* July 14, 1883.

North River Ferry: Courtesy of the Ellen Terry Memorial Museum, Kent, the National Trust.

The Star Theatre: Courtesy of the Theatre Collection, Museum of the City of New York.

Bram Stoker and Ellen Terry: Courtesy of the Ellen Terry Memorial Museum, Kent, the National Trust.

Walt Whitman: Photograph by Napoleon Sarony. Courtesy of the Library of Congress.

## *Part 3*

Henry Irving: From *The Illustrated Sporting and Dramatic News,* January 16, 1886.

## CHAPTER 9

Bram Stoker: Courtesy of the Bram Stoker Collection, Shakespeare Centre Library, Stratford-upon-Avon.

Henry Irving: Courtesy of the Theatre Museum, London.

Irving with Ellen Terry: Courtesy of the author.

Statement from *Faust*: Courtesy of Leslie Shepard.

## CHAPTER 10

William S. Gilbert: Courtesy of the British Council.

Ellen Terry: Courtesy of the author.

Walter Collinson: Courtesy of John H. B. Irving.

## CHAPTER 11

*Moonshine*: From *Moonshine,* September 9, 1893.

The 1901 Constable Edition: Courtesy of Leslie Shepard.

Hall Caine: From *Capt'n Davy's Honeymoon* by Hall Caine. London: Heinemann, 1893.

Whitby Landmark: From *Dracula Discovered,* Caedmon of Whitby, 1981.

The *Dmitry*: Photograph by Frank Meadow Sutcliffe. Courtesy of the Sutcliffe Gallery, Whitby.

Whitby Abbey: Photograph by Frank Meadow Sutcliffe. Courtesy of the Sutcliffe Gallery, Whitby.

Bram, Florence, and Noel: From *Punch,* September 11, 1886.

### CHAPTER 12

Florence Stoker: From *The Gentlewoman,* February 6, 1897.

Sir Thornley Stoker: From *Illustrograph,* Midsummer 1895, Dublin.

Florence Stoker: From *Hollywood Gothic* by David J. Skal. New York: Norton, 1990. Courtesy of the Royal Academy of Art.

### Part 4

*Dracula* or *The Un-Dead*: Courtesy of the Bram Stoker Collection, Shakespeare Centre Library, Stratford-upon-Avon.

### CHAPTER 13

George Bernard Shaw: Reproduced with permission from *Bernard Shaw: The Search for Love* by Michael Holroyd. London: Chatto & Windus, 1988.

The Kilmarnock Arms Hotel: Courtesy of the North East Scotland Library Service.

Vlad Tepes: Reproduction of a woodcut in the Széchényi Collection of the Magyar Nemzeti Museum, Budapest.

*Dracula* Manuscript: Courtesy of the Rosenbach Museum & Library, Philadelphia.

*Dracula* Diary: Courtesy of the Rosenbach Museum & Library, Philadelphia.

Page from Chapter II: Courtesy of John McLaughlin.

Page from Chapter XXVII: Courtesy of John McLaughlin.

### CHAPTER 14

Fussie and Irving: From *Henry Irving* by Laurence Irving. London: Faber and Faber, 1951.

The Rider Edition: Courtesy of Richard Dalby.

Irving and Stoker: From *The Tatler,* October 9, 1901.

Mark Twain: Courtesy of the Mark Twain Collection, the Bancroft Library, University of California, Los Angeles.

Shipboard Entertainment: Courtesy of the Ellen Terry Memorial Museum.

Stoker: Courtesy of the Ellen Terry Memorial Museum.

A Philadelphia Newspaper: From *The North American,* Philadelphia, November 21, 1901.

## CHAPTER 15

Stoker and Irving: Courtesy of the Bram Stoker Collection, Shakespeare Centre Library, Stratford-upon-Avon.

The Crookit Lum: From *The Scots Magazine,* October 1977.

Henry Irving: From *Henry Irving* by Laurence Irving. London: Faber and Faber, 1951.

Program: Courtesy of Jeanne Youngson.

Stoker: Courtesy of the Bram Stoker Collection, Shakespeare Centre Library, Stratford-upon-Avon.

Bram Stoker (page 304): From *Henry Irving* by Laurence Irving. London: Faber and Faber, 1951.

(page 305): From *Reminiscences of Henry Irving* by Bram Stoker. London: Heinemann, 1906.

## CHAPTER 16

Promotion: Courtesy of the Bram Stoker Collection, Shakespeare Centre Library, Stratford-upon-Avon.

Mural Panel: Reproduced from *Illustrated Account of the Royal Exchange and the Pictures Therein* by Charles Welch, London, 1913.

Bram Stoker: From *The Bookman,* January 1911.

### Epilogue

The Auction: Courtesy of Leslie Shepard.

*A Note on the Type*

The text of this book was set in Bembo, a facsimile of a typeface cut by Francesco Griffo for Aldus Manutius, the celebrated Venetian printer, in 1495. The face was named for Pietro Cardinal Bembo, the author of the small treatise entitled *De Aetna* in which it first appeared. Through the research of Stanley Morison, it is now generally acknowledged that all old-style type designs up to the time of William Caslon can be traced to the Bembo cut.

The present-day version of Bembo was introduced by the Monotype Corporation of London in 1929. Sturdy, well-balanced, and finely proportioned, Bembo is a face of rare beauty and great legibility in all of its sizes.

*Composed by North Market Street Graphics,*
*Lancaster, Pennsylvania*
*Printed and bound by Quebecor Printing Martinsburg,*
*Martinsburg, West Virginia*
*Designed by Cassandra J. Pappas*